The Business of Letters

The Business of Letters

Authorial Economies in Antebellum America

Leon Jackson

STANFORD UNIVERSITY PRESS

STANFORD, CALIFORNIA

2008

Stanford University Press,
Stanford California
© 2008 by the Board of Trustees of the
Leland Stanford Junior University

Library of Congress Cataloging-in-Publication Data

Jackson, Leon.
    The business of letters : authorial economies in antebellum America /
Leon Jackson.
        p. cm.
    Includes bibliographical references and index.
    ISBN 978-0-8047-5705-8 (cloth : alk. paper)
    1. American literature—19th century—History and criticism.
2. Authorship—Economic aspects—United States—History—19th
century. 3. Authors and publishers—United States—History—19th
century. 4. Authorship—Social aspects—United States—History—19th
century. 5. Authors, American—19th century—Economic conditions.
6. Literature and society—United States—History—19th century. I. Title.

PS201.J33 2008
810.9'003—dc22   2007024051

Printed in the United States of America on
acid-free, archival-quality paper

Typeset at Stanford University Press in 10/12.5 Sabon

Acknowledgments

I have a gratifyingly large number of people and institutions to thank for assistance in the writing of this book: so many, in fact, that it is not possible to describe in detail for each and every case the sort of assistance that was rendered. Suffice it to say that behind every name there is a story, and usually a good one.

My first thanks must go to the institutions that gave me access to, and permission to quote from, the materials in their possession: American Antiquarian Society; Historical Society of Pennsylvania; Boston Public Library; Massachusetts Historical Society; Houghton Library, Harvard University; Schlesinger Library, Harvard University; Harvard Theater Collection; Harvard University Archives; Longfellow National Historical Site; Amherst College Library; Smith College Library; Mount Holyoke College Library; Philips Library, Essex Institute; Massachusetts Archives; Maine Historical Society; Vermont Historical Society; Library of Congress; Thomas Cooper Library, University of South Carolina; South Caroliniana Library, University of South Carolina; Wilson Library, University of North Carolina; North Carolina State Archives; Perkins Library, Duke University; John Hay Library, Brown University; Rhode Island Historical Society; Albert and Shirley Small Special Collections Library, University of Virginia; Connecticut Historical Society; Beinecke Library, Yale University; and the Ohio State University Library. I am also especially grateful to William Charvat's children, Ted Charvat, Judy Watkins, Catherine Charvat Fitch, and Jill Charvat, for their generosity in sharing their memories of their father, as well as some of his papers, with me. Although I have not always agreed with Charvat's theories, if I have seen further than him, it is as a dwarf standing on the shoulders of a giant.

I am grateful to the following friends and colleagues who read copies of my work-in-progress, shared their own work-in-progress or research notes, answered my endless questions, offered insights, and generally gave me hope: William Andrews, Susanna Ashton, Thomas Baker, Michael

Baenen, Sara Bader, Jennifer Baker, Ralph Bauer, Terry Belanger, Susan Branson, Tom Brown, Martin Brückner, Steven Bullock, Claudia Bushman, Lyndsay Campbell, Richard Candee, Ric Caric, Scott Casper, David Cowart, Cynthia Davis, Nina Dayton, Michael Durey, James English, Paul Erickson, Ann Fabian, Will Fassett, Ed Gieskes, Lawrence Glickman, Jonathan Glickstein, Teresa Goddu, Ezra Greenspan, Robert Gross, Paul Gutjahr, Chris Holcomb, Stephen Holmes, Richard John, Catherine Kaplan, Mary Kelley, Joel Kupperman, Bruce McConachie, Mary Kate McMaster, Michael Merrill, Stephen Mihm, Earl Mulderink III, Joel Myerson, James J. O'Donnell, Hershel Parker, Scott Peeples, Tara Powell, Stephen Rachman, David Rawson, Eliza Richards, David Shields, Robert Singerman, Geoff Smith, Mark Smith, Melissa Teed, Susan Vanderborg, Laura Walls, Joyce Warren, Howard Weinbrot, Bruce Weiner, James L. West III, Daniel E. Williams, Su Wolf, Paul Wright, Mary Saracino Zboray, and Ronald J. Zboray.

The writing of this book was made possible by the American Antiquarian Society and the National Endowment for the Humanities, which awarded me a year-long NEH-AAS residential fellowship in 2003–2004. Anyone who has visited the AAS knows that it is a researcher's heaven, and I am grateful to the staff there for their unparalleled kindness and support. I can honestly say that without them—every single one—this book would not have been written. I would especially like, however, to thank Caroline Sloat, Joanne Chaison, and Vince Golden for services above and beyond the call of duty. I also owe the largest debt of thanks to my fellow Fellows and to the visiting researchers who made my time there so illuminating and enjoyable: Meredith McGill, Molly McCarthy, Karen Kupperman, Mark Peterson, Ellie Herrington, Mike Jarvis, Martha McNamara, Martha Rojas, Nancy Isenberg, Hester Blum, Jeff Pasley, Beth Schweiger, Matt Clavin, Brian Lusky, Shelby Balik, Bernd Herzogenrath, Katarina Erhard, Scott Miltenberger, Jill Anderson, Carolyn Lawes, Robb Haberman, Rick Bell, David Hancock, Kyla Tompkins, and Melanie Hubbard.

Additional financial support was provided by the English Department and the College of Arts and Sciences of the University of South Carolina. I am grateful to my department chair, Steve Lynn, and to the Deans, past and present, of the College for this assistance.

I am grateful to Norris Pope and the editorial staff at Stanford University Press for their patience and assistance as I negotiated the publishing process. I would also like to give thanks to the two anonymous readers for the press—later revealed to me as Jeff Groves and Robert Gross—for their incredibly detailed and helpful feedback. Jeff's comments compelled me to articulate, and in some cases to change, the assumptions on which my project was based, while Bob has been a source of inspiration and encouragement for more years than I can count. They were ideal readers.

Melissa Homestead and Mike Everton have supported me for so long, and in so many ways, while I worked on this book, that they deserve their own paragraph. Over the years they read draft after draft of chapter after chapter, showed me their own work, shared their research findings, sent me endless encouraging e-mails, made me laugh when I was inclined to frown, and in general were the sort of colleagues one spends a career looking for. I am glad to have found them so soon.

My friends will not be in the slightest surprised that I also reserve a separate paragraph for my dogs, Bailey (1996–2005) and Buddy, who gave me the sort of round-the-clock encouragement, distraction, and joy that defies common sense. I wouldn't have finished this book without them.

My final thanks go to my parents, Janice and Harry Jackson, for their unstinting love over the years. In this impossible world, they are the best of all possible parents. My gratitude to them cannot be measured in words, but I dedicate every one to them nonetheless.

Contents

The Business of Letters

Introduction

The Business of *The Business of Letters*

⁓

There is no shortage of books or articles on authorship and economics in early national and antebellum America; indeed, when put together, they form a venerable tradition in American literary historiography. For the most part, such works have been concerned to explain when, and to a lesser degree how and why, authorship became a profession in America. Although it probably reached its highpoint in the career of William Charvat, who published seminal articles and books on the history of authorship in the 1940s and 1950s, this tradition actually stretches a century, from the beginning of the twentieth century to the beginning of the twenty-first. The works that constitute the authorship-and-economics tradition share a number of core presuppositions in common: that there is such a thing as professional authorship; that it developed out of, and reflected a rejection of, the world of amateur authorship; that it was an inevitable and irreversible process; that it was staged in the literary marketplace; that it crystallized in the middle of the nineteenth century; and that it can be measured objectively, through such indices as income, press runs, and publisher longevity, and less objectively through aesthetic practice and, especially, statements of authorial self-satisfaction. Whether scholars have applauded the growth of professional authorship and the development of the book trade, as Charvat so obviously did, or have resisted its more insidious implications, as scholars have more recently done, they have always shared these assumptions in common, which is precisely what makes their books part of this tradition.

This is not one of those books, however, and it does not belong to that tradition. *The Business of Letters* was written out of a conviction that the paradigm of professionalization studies was fundamentally flawed in conception, and that it has now outlasted any heuristic or collateral value it might once have had. Concepts such as 'professional' and 'amateur,' when applied to antebellum authors, as I explain at some length in the first chapter of this book, seem, when looked at carefully, to be both too ahistorical and too simplistic to be useful, while the ways in which the former are said to have transformed into the latter have come increasingly, as they have hardened into orthodoxy, to obscure more than they reveal.

In the chapters that follow, I have attempted to offer a new account of authorship and economics in the first half of the nineteenth century that offers a more historical and nuanced analysis than the professionalization model can provide. My account is predicated on three core arguments of my own that displace those advanced by practitioners of the professional paradigm. The first of these we might call taxonomic, because it argues that we need to cease speaking of authorial economics (in the singular) and start speaking of authorial economies (in the plural). Authorship in the antebellum period, I claim, was transacted through a multitude of distinct economies, each of which had its own rules and reciprocities, its own exchange rituals and ethical strictures, and even, sometimes, its own currencies. There is a world of difference, that is to say, between a work that was introduced into a patronage economy and one that was passed through a gift economy; between a work that was written under contract and one that was entered into a literary competition; between literature written to raise charity and literature offered as tribute. This book proposes to explain what such differences entailed and why they were significant.

My second argument is sociological (or perhaps anthropological) in nature, and it suggests that their diversity notwithstanding, the various authorial economies available to writers through the middle of the nineteenth century were characterized by what economic anthropologist Karl Polanyi calls embeddedness. By this, I mean that they served not simply to convey goods and money from one party to another, but also, and at the same time, functioned to create and sustain powerful social bonds. Borrowing, bartering, gifting, or selling a book an author had written created webs of connection that were no less important a part of a transaction than any money that might have changed hands. Indeed, status and social connection—which, following Pierre Bourdieu, I refer to as symbolic and social capital—were two of the more important currencies that were exchanged for works of literature during this period. And it is precisely because such 'currencies' cannot be quantified in ledgerlike terms that I have eschewed the imprints-and-income approach to authorial history that has been the mainstay of book history. Grasping the fundamental embeddedness of authorial activity in antebellum America is important for many reasons, not only because it helps us understand what was at stake in acts of authorial exchange, but also, and perhaps more pointedly, because it teaches us to appreciate that the cultural work of writing extends beyond what authors wrote to how they bought, sold, begged, borrowed, bartered, and gave away what they wrote.

My final argument is historical, and it proposes that the crucial transformation of nineteenth-century authorial activity was not the professionalization of writing, but, rather, its social disembedding. Over the course of the nineteenth century, that is to say, the economies through which authors worked became detached from the dense social worlds of which they were a part, and which they in fact helped to create. Exchange became less personal and less trusting, less flexible and less sustained. It became more characterized by the exclusive use of cash and contracts, and by various mediatory individuals and agencies who stood between an author and his or her readers. I also argue, in ways that I hope do not undermine my historical trajectory, that the disembedding of these various authorial economies was a complex and often incomplete process, no more inevitable than it was irreversible, and, for that reason, some of the traits we associate with embedded authorial economies persist to the very present.

Having just laid bare the largest operating assumptions of my book, it might also be prudent, at this juncture, to spell out some of the other suppositions, big and small, that undergird the project. I begin with the chronological parameters of the study. In essence, this is a study of the period from the 1820s through the 1850s, although it often creeps back to the later eighteenth century and occasionally into the later nineteenth. In one or two cases, most notably in the epilogue, I bring contemporary authorial practices—particularly those of twentieth-century academics—to the forefront. Such temporal fluidity is entirely in keeping with my argument that embedded economies had deep historical roots that were never wholly unearthed, but it also suggests a potential problem in terms of framing. Why, given the sprawling scale of the phenomena in which I am interested, do I start where I do? Why end where I end? "Really, universally," as Henry James so very aptly put it in 1907, "relations stop nowhere, and the exquisite problem of the artist is eternally but to draw, by a geometry of his own, the circle within which they shall happily *appear* to do so."[1] Just so. The geometry of my own narrative is, in part, simply a reflection of my scholarly training. I am a scholar of the antebellum period, so I have focused on the economies of authorship in the period I know best and in which I have the most sustained professional investment, but I am aware that the book might have been framed differently. I might have written about the seventeenth century (as Philip Round did) to establish the pedigree of my multiple economies, or I might have discussed the fin-de-siècle James himself (as Michael Anesko has very deftly done) in terms of his authorial and economic practice. There are some very real advantages, however, to staying focused on this forty-year period, since it shows with perhaps unique clarity both the erosion of embedded economies but also their great persistence. Dwelling, as I do, on the antebellum years doubtless emphasizes discontinuity and transformation, but not, I hope, at the expense of the *longue durée*. Had I taken a longer perspective in the book, the emphasis might have changed, but my argument, I suspect, would have stayed much the same, because the antebellum era does seem to be the epicenter of this transformation. And while I have always been reluctant to invoke historian Stuart Blumin's hilarious Blumin's Law—"it happened in my period"—in this case I think that "it" actually did.[2]

My title will also, I think, lead many people to expect a work of literary criticism, or at the very least a work of literary history, and to the extent that this is the case, there is bound to be some disappointment. Although the subject matter and chronological parameters within which I work are those familiar to literary historians, this is not, itself, a work of literary history. Rather, it is a history of literature, and, more specifically still, a social history of authorship. My goal, in undertaking this project, was to understand in as fine-grained a way as possible, a series of culturally inflected economic practices in which works of literature were entangled, and through which they passed. I have been considerably less concerned with the ways in which such practices were depicted *in* works of literature, and not at all in how they could be said to have been allegorized or homologized in such works. As such, I align myself with those who ask, in Leah Price's words, not "what book history can do for literary criticism" but, rather, what criticism "can do for book history."[3] There are, of course, some clear aesthetic conclusions to be drawn from my work but I have resisted very consciously and consistently making the ultimate pay-off of my argument a new set of textual interpretations. This isn't because I don't find such readings interesting or important, but simply because I set myself a different task: to tell the history of practices as practiced, not the history of the practices as represented. The book you now hold in your hands is already long, even without a literary critical dimension, and while it might have been richer for an additional interpretive layer, there is a decidedly practical economics that impinges on modern authors, just as it impinged on antebellum ones: very long books don't get bought or read, so they often don't get published either.

That does not mean, however, that my book is devoid of textual inter-pretation, even of scrupulous semiotic analysis; far from it, in fact. Every chapter features what I hope are sustained and nuanced interpretations. What sets my work apart is that my close readings are of exchange ritu-als and the rhetoric that surrounded them. These are "cultural texts," as Robert Scholes has called them, or, more precisely, they are scripted per-formances; but whether they are texts or performances, they are decid-edly cultural and eminently interpretable.[4] And while it might seem that my work is more indebted to a cultural historian like Robert Darnton, or his anthropologist colleague, Clifford Geertz, than to any literary critic, it is worth remembering that the anthropologists (and anthropological his-torians) took many of their interpretive methodologies from the literary critics in the first place; I'm just taking them back.[5]

Were I writing about any other commodity than literature, or work-ing in any department other than a literary one, it would probably not even be necessary to make apologies for my methodological or substan-tive choices. There is, after all, currently a vogue for so-called commodity histories—of cod, salt, coffee, tea, tobacco, and chocolate, among oth-ers—and while I share many scholars' discomfort with that genre's con-sumer triumphalism, my work does share with those texts a fascination with the mobility, the promiscuity, of goods and how they 'created' or 'built' or 'invented' various social phenomena.[6]

The question that then arises is, Why literature? If what I am interest-ed in exploring is not literature as a form of artistic expression but the various ways in which social bonds were created (and later not created) when literature qua commodity was circulated and exchanged, then isn't the commodity in question immaterial? Isn't what I have to say about the business of letters just as true of the business of baskets, or the busi-ness of broomsticks? In an important sense, the answer is yes. Grego-ry H. Nobles, for instance, has written illuminatingly about the tightly bound kin groups that produced brooms in antebellum New England, and how broom production also reinforced those kin networks before mass broom production associated with the Market Revolution eventu-ally eroded those bonds. Laurel Ulrich Thatcher, likewise, has discussed the way in which Native Americans in 1820s Vermont solidified their imperiled sense of collective identity by making and selling 'authentic' woodsplint baskets to white settlers.[7] Clearly, then, it would be true in one sense to say that what applies to literature just as readily applies to other objects of exchange. In a still more important sense, however, the opposite is also true. Brooms, after all, could not talk to their handlers, nor did they establish reciprocal relationships with them. When, on the other hand, author Samuel Kettell wrote a short story in 1837, entitled "Biography of a Broomstick" and narrated it from the broomstick's own point of view, he was able to simulate through his narrative voice a quasi-human bond with his readers. We may not like our brooms, but we like a man like Kettell, who in his preface promised "to do my best to make you merry," even if he was speaking through a kitchen implement. And this is the crucial point: words are powerfully affective and, perhaps, ineluctably social in a way that wood is not, because they can simulate the merriment—or distress—that we associate with human relationships.[8] The same point can be made with respect to antebellum baskets. While a recent volume on the subject promised readers *A Key into the Language of Woodsplint Baskets*, none of the baskets discussed spoke a language quite so clear, or created a bond quite so entangling, as the words on the newspapers that were often used to line them. The family that lined a Vermont basket with newspapers in 1821 probably purchased the basket from an itinerant Native American, a fleeting encounter, but the newspapers reflected a far denser entanglement. The family were subscribers with an ongoing economic and social commitment to their paper; they wrote their name on it; and they kept at least six months' worth of back issues in their household.[9] Brooms and baskets can convey meaning, but books and other written items talk. In purchasing or otherwise receiving them, readers enter into powerfully affective relationships not only with the implied author and characters, but also with those from whom they have received them. Indeed, they proved to be tenaciously social, even as the economies through which they passed began to disembed. Even as printing became one of the more heavily industrialized trades, that is, and its products part of the consumer revolution of the nineteenth century, written words, by their very communicative nature, resisted disembedding and commodification.[10] I cannot say with confidence that the affective freight of literature was unique—indeed, I conjecture that the difference with brooms and baskets was more likely a matter of degree than kind—but it suggests a complex developmental trajectory, both economic and cultural, that has not been explored with any intensity by historians of the Market Revolution. As such this book contributes to the study of literature in particular and of the Market Revolution in general, with the former nuancing and illuminating the latter.[11]

One final point of clarification remains, and that concerns the historical situatedness of my study. As Brook Thomas very sagely noted some years ago, the resurgence of interest in authorship and the marketplace in the 1980s coincided almost precisely with a severe retrenchment in the humanities that saw university—and university press—budgets slashed to ribbons. Even as it became increasingly less feasible for university presses to publish every likely manuscript, or for every library to buy them, the requirements for hiring, tenure, and promotion continued to creep ever higher, placing pressure on academics and academic aspirants and forcing them to consider the nexus of authorship, economics, and professional identity in very personal ways. The History of the Book, as a discipline, is a product of the current status of the book as commodity.[12] This has certainly been my own experience, and as such, the writing of this volume has entailed a dual learning process. As I researched the conditions of antebellum authorship, I also came to learn about the conditions of modern, academic authorship. I would not want to suggest that there are direct connections between the two—the formal, business economies seem especially different—but I do think that a consideration of embedded and multiple economies in the modern academy can help shed a little light on the nature of the antebellum phenomena with which this book is concerned. For that reason, I end my book somewhat unorthodoxly with a brief epilogue that considers William Charvat, the preeminent twentieth-century scholar of authorship, as an author himself, enmeshed in the multiple economies of the academic world. I hope this will help suggest some of the ways in which historical authorship can speak to our own condition.

In most other respects, the organization of the chapters follows a fairly conventional trajectory. The first chapter offers an introduction to my methodology and an overview of the various ways in which it engages with, and diverges from, current literary scholarship; it also, and incidentally, provides an overview of authorship in the late eighteenth and early to mid-nineteenth century. It is the most 'theoretical' and the only polemical chapter of the book. Chapter Two complements the first by offering an extended case study of North Carolina poet George Moses Horton, who flourished between the 1820s and the 1860s. Horton, an illiterate slave who composed verses spontaneously for students who wrote them down and paid him for them, is precisely the sort of author who escaped scrutiny under the old Charvatian paradigm of authorial professionalism, inasmuch as his informal (and illegal) oral poetry business left no quantifiable financial data; as such, he makes an excellent test case for my methodology. While Chapter Two discusses a number of authorial economies in tandem, chapters Three through Five each consider specific authorial economies, and they are organized, together with the second chapter, in such a way that the discussion moves from the most intimate and private of exchange practices to the most public. Thus Chapter Two focuses mostly on patronage and charity. Chapter Three explores the wide range of ways in which literature circulated through gift exchange in this period. The fourth chapter considers the way in which credit and debt relationships profoundly affected literary production and consumption. And Chapter Five examines the phenomenon of writing competitions in the early national and antebellum periods. My goal in arranging the chapters in this order is to establish the grounds of a larger argument that informal and embedded economies were not positioned in opposition to the world of business, but, rather, actually represented the ways in which business was done. The epilogue ties together the various arguments I have made by considering the relationship between the historical economies I study and the modern academic workplace, using the life of Charvat as an example of a modern practicing author.

The chapters I offer are designed to suggest the range and variety of authorial economies that were available in antebellum America, but they are not exhaustive, nor have I addressed every economy through which authors worked. One thinks, for example, of the 'gratuity economy' employed by newspaper carriers' in the hundreds of broadside new year's addresses they delivered to their patrons, an absolutely fascinating practice that bears striking resemblances to the modern practice of soliciting tips, in its use of both theatricality and euphemism to conduct transactions across clear social boundaries. One thinks also of the pervasive use of blackmail in antebellum America and the ways in which it inverted the protocols of the marketplace in demanding money in order not to write, and not to publish. I touch only glancingly on the subjects of charity and patronage, which really ought to have been given chapters to themselves, and I chose to excise, for reasons of space, a short chapter that considered the ways in which antebellum publishers engaged in a series of embedded economic practices in ways that paralleled those deployed by authors. In short, there is a great deal more to be said than I have been able to say here. My goal in writing *The Business of Letters* has not been to offer the last word on the subject but only the first few in what I hope will be an ongoing conversation.

CHAPTER ONE

From the Profession of Authorship to the Business of Letters

"Why is it," asked an author in the *American Monthly Magazine* in 1829, "that, prone as we are, as a nation, to improve upon all the new inventions which foreign talents have brought to light, we have none among us who have taken up the profession of authorship?" Other professions were overcrowded, hard to enter, and harder still to thrive within, this writer complained, but still no one set "himself down to write literature; it is never thought of by poor men as a means to get along in the world. The muses are courted as the pleasant companions of a leisure hour, not as the constant companions of life." The roots of the problem, according to this troubled writer—who lurked behind the pseudonym K.K.—lay not in those who courted, so much as in those who supported, or more precisely those who failed to support, the muses. No one wanted to buy American books. Once Americans started buying their own literature, authorship would inevitably become a popular—and paying—occupation. But while K.K. was indeed promoting "the profession of authorship," he or she was at pains not to be seen to be advocating the establishment of a native Grub Street supported by an indiscriminate reading public; his or her comments, rather, were "confined to the subjects of polite literature and belles-lettres," and by "the profession of authorship," K.K. meant writing for something *more* than the "mere means of profit." A professional author was not merely, or not even, one who lived from the products of his or her pen, so much as one who professed a certain, discriminating commitment to polite literature. Yet even the discriminating few were unwilling to risk becoming professional authors, according to K.K., because the reading public was so little likely to support their efforts. America's best authors were ready for professionalism, that is, but America, or at least the American reading public, was not.[1]

K.K.'s comments were absolutely typical of the elite thought of the late 1820s in their strident nationalism, their whiggishness, and their arbitrary definition of authorship as being, essentially, both belles-lettristic and above the concerns of mere profit-mongering. They tell us far more about the fantasies of the early republic's literary elite, however, than either the social realities of that literary elite or of the literary rank-and-file. Indeed, the very same month in which K.K.'s essay appeared in the *American Monthly Magazine*, its editor, Nathaniel P. Willis, bragged in private to Sarah Hale about how much he was paid for what he wrote ("five dollars for every article—often more"), refused to help her out, even though she was a fellow editor ("You could not afford, and I never would receive from you the price which my poetry brings me"), and justified such profit-mongering on precisely the grounds—economic professionalism—which were so deplored by K.K. ("as I wholly support myself by my pen I must needs look to these drossy considerations").[2] Willis's confession becomes still more ironic in light of the knowledge that even he did not, in fact, wholly support himself by his pen; as he confessed to a friend just a few months before writing to Hale, the publication costs of his magazine were being underwritten by his father in exchange for his promise to "renounce all journeys, horses, and amusements" for one year.[3]

Willis, opined fellow-editor John Neal in 1829, "preaches one thing and practices another, & that so often that everybody sees the man through the actor," yet separating preaching from practice remains a challenge when it comes to the subject of authorship.[4] Was a professional author one who was above the pursuit of profit, as K.K. suggested; one who actively pursued and actually made a profit, as Willis insinuated; or one who made some money but not quite a living, which for Willis was in fact the case? Our inability to answer this question with any degree of certainty means that while we can reject out of hand K.K.'s explanation for the tardy professionalization of authorship as at best reductive and rhetorical, and at worst as misleading, we are at an initial loss to find a clearer definition of, and explanation for, professional authorship. Unfortunately, approaches to the subject of literary professionalization in the nineteenth century have advanced little since those formulated in 1829.

THE PROFESSIONAL PARADIGM

A little more than a century later, literary scholar William Charvat returned to the problem that had vexed K.K. and, in a series of essays and lectures, followed by a posthumously published book that still defines the field of authorship studies, sought to explore the problem of American literary professionalization with the benefits of both historical hindsight and sociological insight.⁵ The aspirant to literary professionalism between the 1780s and the 1850s, according to Charvat, faced a daunting sequence of obstacles, both cultural and material in nature, which made professional authorship well nigh impossible. In the first place, he explained, the American literary field was dominated by an ethic of genteel amateurism that disavowed promotion, eschewed profits, and advocated anonymity; most writers, having internalized this ethos, believed that the pursuit of professional authorial status was a socially inappropriate aspiration and simply never entertained it. Among those Charvat placed in this category (although they violated his chronological parameters), were the poets Edward Taylor and Emily Dickinson. Those who were able to see through or beyond this restrictive worldview, however, were still hampered, because their conception of a respectable literary career centered on an anglophilic fantasy of being supported by wealthy patrons and benefactors who, according to Charvat, did not exist in America and never would. Those who either by force of vision or force of circumstance *still* sought to carve out a professional literary career in the open marketplace were nevertheless massively and consistently frustrated in their ambitions. Their written works were held back, for example, by the absence of copyright laws to protect them; by the undercapitalization of printers, who could not afford to produce them; by the provinciality of the publishers who were unwilling to pay for them or promote them; by the underdevelopment of the transportation infrastructure, which was unable to disseminate them; as well as by the timidity of the reading public, who—and here Charvat agreed with K.K.—were unable or unwilling, mostly, to buy and read them. Although several bold pioneers, such as Joel Barlow, Robert Treat Paine, Jr., Joseph Dennie, Susanna Rowson, and Charles Brockden Brown attempted to live by their pens, according to Charvat, each of them failed in turn, retreating into careers only peripherally related to literature, such as acting, newspaper and magazine editing, and teaching, or leaving literature altogether for careers in politics, diplomacy, and the law. "Professional authorship," noted Charvat poignantly, "obviously, was ready to begin, but the publishing world was not." All was not despair, however, for canny visionaries such as Washington Irving and James Fenimore Cooper established comfortable incomes based on their literary output in the 1820s, even if they were very much exceptions to the rule. Professionalism, Charvat claimed, emerged only gradually. In the 1840s and 1850s, the consolidation of the New York–Philadelphia publishing axis, the extension of railroads, the widespread use of stereotyping, and the development of aggressive book promotion, allowed authors such as Longfellow, Hawthorne, and Melville to flourish sporadically in the world of literary professionalism; with the advent of the 1890s, "security" truly became an "element in professional authorship"; but only as recently as 1910, according to Charvat, one hundred and thirty years after American authors' first attempts to establish professional status, was the struggle for literary security won. In 1910, finally, authors were able to acknowledge that the "business of literature . . . had come of age."[6]

Although Charvat never lived to complete his ambitious history of authorship in America, and, in the final decade of his life, publicly disavowed the sociological and business history approaches to the literary field that he had pioneered, many of his essays and chapter drafts were pieced together after his death by his Ohio State University colleague Matthew Bruccoli and published in 1968 as *The Profession of Authorship in America*. Charvat's careful archival scholarship retained a timely durability, and with the reemergence of historicist approaches to literature in the late 1980s, his theories about the tardy professionalization of authorship in America assumed a stature and authority they had never wholly enjoyed while he was alive.[7] Charvat is now seen as the "patriarch of history of the book studies," and as "a book historian before there was such a field," and practitioners in the field have showered his work with belated accolades. In 1996, for example, a conference was organized at Ohio State University to celebrate his work, the proceedings of which were subsequently published; his two major works have been reissued in paperback and are routinely assigned in undergraduate and graduate classes; his theories are called "indispensable," "seminal," and "a touchstone"; his "central points" are described as "indisputable"; and his works as a whole praised as "the points of entry into the field" and as "cornerstones for the study of the subject."[8] The clearest indication of the high esteem in which Charvat's ideas are held by the new generation of American literary historians is seen in the fact that the first and second volumes of the recently completed *Cambridge History of American Literature* base their treatments of authorship and economics first and last on Charvat's model of professionalization.[9]

We are living in Charvat's moment. Indeed, David Leverenz hardly exaggerates when he claims that Charvat's work is "as significant as Charles Feidelson's *Symbolism and American Literature* (1953)" for the study of American literature; rather, he somewhat understates the case, for whereas Feidelson always had his detractors and critics and is now considered utterly passé, Charvat's work, which hails from the same era, remains almost wholly unopposed.[10] It is true, of course, that recent scholars have argued that, for example, antebellum women, too, were centrally involved in the transition to literary professionalism, yet such arguments, while they add to the characters in Charvat's narrative or refine its chronological dimensions, leave his basic story intact and his central axioms unquestioned.[11] There is, as one scholar has put it, simply "no counter school to Charvatian practice."[12]

Unfortunately, our appreciation for Charvat's genuinely pioneering role in the study of American authorship and our willingness to defer to his status as an authority on the subject has blinded us to the fact that his—and thus our—whole approach to the phenomenon of professional authorship in America is conceptually flawed and in need of serious reconsideration. Although the bulk of my book, and, indeed, of this introduction, are given over to literary history rather than polemic, the assumptions on which it is predicated are sufficiently different from, and sufficiently opposed to, those established by Charvat and followed by almost everyone since, that it is important to explain why I feel that his work is no longer authoritative.

In the course of a characteristically positive review of the recent paperback edition of *The Profession of Authorship in America*, Brigitte Bailey notes shrewdly that Charvat's work is, "oddly enough, at once dated and quite current in its biographical and economic approaches to romantic authors."[13] While Charvat's use of economic and class-based language in his discussion of authorship does indeed seem "quite current" and resonates with the academy's interest in materialist and historicist approaches to literature, the explanatory matrix from which they emerged, I want to insist, derives not from any recognizable and appropriable tradition of Marxism, but rather from the extremely "dated" and eminently less adaptable tradition of Progressive historiography.[14] Pioneered by historians Charles Beard and Frederick Jackson Turner between the 1890s and 1920s and applied to literary history with dazzling effect by Vernon L. Parrington, the Progressive historians saw the American past in dualistic terms, as a struggle between the forces of aristocracy and democracy, slavish anglophilia and native integrity. Although sometimes pitched on ideological or aesthetic grounds, this struggle was always, the Progressives believed, economic in origin, and the first of the Progressive historian's tasks was to reveal the hard facts of economic greed that lay behind the sometimes disingenuous rhetoric advanced by the forces of aristocratic reaction. A second and equally important task was to champion those who represented the forces of popular democracy and who transcended the economic determinants of their time and place. Lastly, the Progressive scholar sought to show how, while the American past was studded with pioneers and visionaries born before their time, history inevitably caught up with and validated them.[15] Charvat's introduction to Progressivism probably came by way of Parrington, whose Pulitzer Prize–winning *Main Currents in American Thought* he cited and assigned to students in a pioneering American Studies course co-taught with business historian Thomas Cochran at New York University in the 1930s. Many of his uncollected essays and reviews from this period evince a strong Progressive/Parringtonian streak.[16] More to the point, however, and in ways that we have perhaps failed to note or consider seriously, the manichean drama and whiggish triumphalism inherent in Progressivist historiography is also built into the very foundations of Charvat's work on the professionalization of authorship and has the unavoidable tendency of limiting the research of those who build upon it.

We may begin by considering Charvat's foundational definition of professional authorship, on which his entire argument rests. "The terms of professional writing," Charvat writes, "are these: that it provides a living for the author, like any other job; that it is a main and prolonged, rather than intermittent or sporadic, resource for the writer; that it is produced with the hope of extended sale in the open market, like any article of commerce; and that it is written with reference to buyers' tastes and reading habits."[17] In the epilogue to this book, I will suggest that certain issues in Charvat's personal and academic life and experience rendered this particular formulation of professional authorship especially compelling. Here, however, it is sufficient to note his definition was informed, or at the very least confirmed, by the ideas of the sociologist Max Weber, whose influential collection of essays—*From Max Weber*—was published in English translation in 1946, when Charvat was a new professor at Ohio State University. Focusing primarily on the rise of politics as a vocation, Weber brought together the theological and economic meanings of the word "profession" in describing the professional politician as one who both "lived for" and "lived off" of political activity.[18] *Mutatis mutandis*, Charvat defines professional authorship in such terms, insisting that in order to be a professional author, one had to "live for" writing, to the exclusion of all other occupational activities, out of an ideological commitment to the aesthetic, and that one had to "live off" of it over an appreciable (but never explicitly defined) period of time. Thus neither Washington Irving nor Nathaniel Hawthorne could be considered a truly professional author, according to Charvat, "because of their years in government office and the long hiatuses in their productivity; Bryant and Poe because of their work as editors; Emerson because he was primarily a lecturer; and others for reasons similar to these." In fact, working his way through a list of canonical authors and measuring them by his standard for professionalism, Charvat was ultimately compelled to acknowledge that James Fenimore Cooper was the "*only* commercially successful writer of belles-lettres up to 1850."[19] The problem with Charvat's definition of the professional, of course, as with Weber's, lies in its abstract and anachronistic, if not downright ahistorical, nature. When professional authorship is defined in terms as restrictive as Charvat's, the literary history of the early national and antebellum periods will always seem like a narrative of repeated failure to attain professional status. One might legitimately question the validity of a study of the profession of authorship covering the period 1800–1870, that finds only *one* professional author in the first fifty of its seventy years of coverage. Such a story comported well, however, with the Progressive historians' meta-narrative of slow struggle for democratization, followed by decisive victories in every field. Progressive history was nothing if not dramatic.

The imposition of such an anachronistic standard of aspiration not only has the consequence of generating an inevitably whiggish, Progressive-style narrative, however, in which destiny (here professionalization) fulfills itself against all odds; it also blinds us to the complex reality of what actually *was* happening while destiny waited in the wings. Prying apart the religious ("living for") and economic ("living off") elements of Charvat's Weberian model of the professional serves as a useful opening gambit in understanding the nature of authorial economics in the late eighteenth and early nineteenth centuries. In the early national period, as it turns out, many individuals lived "off," or at least earned subsistence amounts from, their pens. In 1829, the same year that K.K. published his or her lament on the state of professional authorship in America, Philadelphia publishers Carey and Lea ran a widely reprinted article noting that as members of the book trade, they "were the first to offer and pay a regular compensation for articles in the Medical Journal;—they have allowed for lighter articles for their *Atlantic Souvenir*, sums with which the contributors have professed to be well satisfied:—in the course of the last year they disbursed to [American] authors and editors more than twenty thousand dollars; and in the present, they will have to exceed that amount, for the same purpose, by eight or ten thousand." In another open letter to the press, published four years later, the firm continued to hammer home the message that American authors could flourish economically, and, in fact, were flourishing. They pointed out, for example, that they had "paid *more* than thirty thousand dollars to [American] authors and editors within a year" and had American works in press that would yield their authors "little less than forty thousand . . . of which nearly thirty thousand will be for two works." It was America's publishers, they insisted, and not its authors, who were the great victims of the literary economy.[20] One of Carey and Lea's highest paid authors was, of course, James Fenimore Cooper, who received five thousand dollars for the copyright to *The Prairie* in 1826 and another five thousand for the copyright to *The Red Rover* a year later, but he was by no means the only author to earn appreciable amounts from his or her writings; physician and medical professor William P. Dewees received eight hundred and thirty-three dollars and thirty-three cents for the copyright to the second edition of his guide to midwifery, and over the course of twelve years earned no less than twenty-one thousand dollars from just four medical texts.[21]

Nor, indeed, were the lists of those who lived "off" writing limited to just a handful of significantly wealthy authors. In 1835, Alexis de Tocqueville observed that America was almost literally "infested with a tribe of writers who look upon letters as a mere trade," and calculated that for each of the nation's "few great authors" there were perhaps "thousands of idea-mongers."[22] James Hardie might well have been the sort of "idea monger" de Tocqueville had in mind. Between 1788 and 1826, he eked out a marginal existence in New York, New Jersey, and Philadelphia, by selling the products of his pen, and although he denounced the "unprincipled scribbler" who would write anything "for the sake of raising a few pence to purchase a dinner," Hardie unquestionably sang for his supper. His prodigious output included dozens of titles including Latin text books, global histories, biographical compendia, biblical anthologies, a guide to letter writing, a dictionary of "uncommon wonders," accounts of cholera epidemics he had witnessed, several Philadelphia city directories, an introduction to freemasonry, the report of a sensational murder trial, an exposé of the prison system, a census of buildings in Manhattan, and a history of New York City. Hardie also revised textbooks written by others, edited (and wrote most of the copy for) a short-lived periodical—the *New York Magazine*—worked as a proofreader and indexer for publisher Mathew Carey, among others, and operated a "Literary Office" in New York City that for a fee helped its clients "write petitions, memorials, letters, [and] advertisements" as well as "revise and prepare for the press . . . articles of a literary nature."[23] In the 1810s, Hardie worked closely with the New York bookseller Evert Duyckinck, Sr., who published several of his volumes, but when his sons, George and Evert, Jr., produced their immense and comprehensive *Cyclopaedia of American Literature* in 1855, Hardie was not included. His operation of a "Literary Office" notwithstanding, Hardie did not live "for" literature in any recognizably Romantic sense, and with the hegemonic establishment of a Romantic conception of authorship in 1850s, he was effectively written out of the history of American writing. Capacious though their sense of American literature was, the Duyckincks reflected a trend toward discounting purely commercial authors that has continued to the present and is typified by Charvat.[24] "The mass poet," noted Charvat with some dismissiveness, in his study of professional authorship, "writes primarily to exploit a market, and he is on that account excluded from this history." We have hardly paid attention to the economic activities of the "mass poets" and prose writers, let alone to authors such as Hardie, who were active in the early national and antebellum periods, even though, in some sense of the word, they were "professional" writers.[25]

Even while many authors lived "off" writing without living "for" it in any belles-lettristic or Romantic way, so, conversely, many individuals lived "for" writing, and even occasionally made money from the practice, but had few aspirations of living "off" of it in the sustained or exclusive sense of the term implied by Charvat. Discussing the three most prestigious poets in America in 1830, a reviewer reminded readers that William Cullen Bryant edited "a Jackson paper . . . [Fitz-Greene] Halleck reckons insurances, and [James] Hillhouse deals in hardware." These poets' multi-vocational profiles were absolutely typical for the era.[26] Authors in early national and antebellum America lived sometimes solely from the products of their pens, at other times solely from other forms of income, but most typically from a continuous combination of both, practicing what economic anthropologist Rhoda Halperin calls "multiple livelihood strategies."[27] Consider the example of the Newburyport, Massachusetts, poet Jonathan Plummer, who recalled in his 1796 memoirs that he had "had some practice as a physician, and earned something with my pen" but at other times "followed various kinds of business accounted less honorable," such as "Farming, repeating select passages from authors, selling halibut, sawing wood, selling books, ballads, and fruit in the streets, serving as a porter and post-boy, filling beds with straw, and wheeling them to the owners thereof, collecting rags, & c. & c." Plummer, who was considered an eccentric and marginal character, even in the freewheeling and socially fluid world of postrevolutionary Newburyport, nonetheless prospered economically if not socially from this blending of literary and manual labor and at his death in 1819 left an estate valued at fifteen hundred dollars. In his will, he stipulated that the proceeds from his estate should be used to underwrite the printing and free dissemination of six hundred copies of his memoirs, in which he described and defended his vocational experiments. Plummer, evidently, felt very little need to apologize for the way in which he made his daily bread.[28]

The shifting, composite occupational configurations available to those with serious literary pretensions are still more strikingly illustrated in the life of Connecticut poet James Gates Percival. Between 1810, when he matriculated from Yale, and his death a half century later, Percival combined his intense and prolific output as a poet with work as a farmer, a physician, a private tutor, an editor, a translator, a proof-reader for Noah Webster, a geologist, and a keeper of a botanical gardens. He also taught at West Point and worked in Boston as a military surgeon, trained as a lawyer, considered the ministry, applied for a Harvard professorship, and sought political and diplomatic appointments. Throughout these varied employments, Percival continued to write and sell volumes of poetry in order, as he explained, to "exalt my credit / Both in my purse & fame." Percival's friends bent over backwards to support and encourage his literary and non-literary career choices, finding him jobs, drumming up subscribers, reviewing his works, and granting him sinecures, and he more than coped economically. That Percival himself found every opportunity inadequate—turning down, for example, the chance to travel to Europe with a publisher's eight hundred dollar advance on a "new species of book—of *first impressions*"—was evidence solely of what one contemporary called his "fickleness."[29] His fickleness notwithstanding, Percival's endless experiments in combining authorship with other forms of income-generating work are evidence not of how difficult it was to be a paid writer in the 1820s, but of precisely *how* possible it was, and of how many such opportunities were available to a well-connected man such as he.

Does this mean, though, that Percival was either unable or unwilling to consider pursuing an exclusively literary career? The answer to both questions, as it turns out, is no. In 1822, Percival briefly eschewed all other occupations and "like a fool, concluded to try authorship as a profession." The experiment lasted only a matter of months. Percival's hasty retreat from the profession of authorship, however, had less to do with its lack of economic viability than with his overwhelming sense of insecurity and corresponding lack of emotional support while working exclusively at his writing desk. "With the exception of one or two young men," he wrote from New Haven, where he had attempted the profession of authorship, "I have not the slightest vestige of society. In fact, I have nothing here to excite me." Percival, who was as tortured a soul as can be found in the annals of American Literature—he attempted suicide repeatedly and managed to alienate all but the most dogged of his many friends—was neither poor nor persecuted as a "professional author," just lonely.[30]

So what sort of an author was Percival? Charvat's work is characteristically and constrictingly Progressive in its dualism, allowing only for two sorts of writers—"professionals" and "amateurs"—each of which he defined by reference to their specific configuration of income and occupation. Charvat's schema, that is, rests on what logicians call a 'fallacy of false dichotomy,' supposing that if one is not a professional, then, by definition, one must be an amateur, and vice versa.[31] Those, like Percival, who appeared to confound such categories, Charvat believed, were simply unsuccessful professionals. To dismiss such authors as having failed to achieve "professional" status, however, is to use crude and anachronistic tools that occlude the complex ways in which money and writing intersected in this period.

Indeed, the very idea that amateurism preceded and was slowly displaced by professionalism, or at least a professional ethos, is conceptually problematic. In point of fact, the modern concept of amateurism didn't precede professionalism so much as it emerged in tandem with it; amateurism, we might say, was 'invented' by exponents of professionalism as its necessary conceptual Other, inasmuch as it helped define what professionalism *was* by reference to what it was *not*. Such an idea is supported by the findings of occupational sociologist Robert A. Stebbins, who has pointed out that the very meaning of amateurism shifts along with meanings of professionalism; the two, that is, are mutually constitutive.[32] Although by the 1840s, the words amateur and professional were starting to take on the contrasting economic meanings we now ascribe to them, in the 1820s, the concepts signified quite distinctly from Charvat's twentieth-century usages; indeed, the two were, if not synonymous, then hardly dichotomous either. Take, for example, the meanings ascribed to them by Percival's sometime employer, Noah Webster, a figure who would surely fit Charvat's definition of a professional. Webster, a former schoolteacher and lawyer, was the author of the best-selling textbook of early national and antebellum America. Between 1783 and 1829, his *American Spelling Book* sold in excess of ten million copies, and he lived off the income for at least a dozen years while he worked on his pioneering dictionary project. An assiduous campaigner for copyright legislation, Webster secured protection for his speller and sold licenses for the right to print his work—sometimes by auction—to eager printers and publishers. He also conducted grueling promotional campaigns, criss-crossing the nation in person to address educators, legislators, and members of the book trade.

That Webster was propelled by ideological, if not downright idealistic, motives as well as by pecuniary desires is made evident by his consistent stream of political pronouncements, linking America's well-being to the caliber and nature of its education. Inasmuch as he lived both for and off of his writings, and lived successfully too, one would have to conclude that he was a professional author. Yet to ask whether Webster thought of himself in this way is to encounter a resounding negative. Indeed, to use a professional-amateur dichotomy at all is to invoke a conceptual distinction where, for Webster, none existed. In his pioneering *American Dictionary of the English Language* (1828), Webster defined an amateur as "A person attached to a particular pursuit, study or science, as to music or painting; one who has a taste for the arts" and a profession as "The business which one professes to understand and to follow for subsistence; calling; vocation; employment. . . . But the word is not applied to an occupation merely mechanical."[33] The almost complete lack of a clear distinction between these definitions suggests that the *idea* of professionalism, as Charvat understood it, hardly existed in the 1820s, even if we are able to identify an individual, such as Webster, who would seem, after the fact, to exemplify the concept. It is important to acknowledge that the concept of modern professionalism simply wasn't available to writers in this period. It would be difficult, otherwise to account for the case of William Joseph Snelling, "a talented, industrious young man," according to the *Massachusetts Journal*, "who . . . is most industriously exerting himself to obtain an honest livelihood," through the editorship of a journal, the title of which was *The Amateur* but that sometimes paid its contributors.[34] As late as the early 1850s, in fact, Nathaniel P. Willis could tell his sister, Sara (also known as Fanny Fern) with no sense of conceptual ambiguity that "The most 'broken reed,' I know of, to lean upon for a livelihood, is amateur literature."[35] That one would need to be discouraged from seeking a professional living through amateur authorship simply underscores the idea that these words signified quite differently in the antebellum period than they do now.

By the 1840s, it is true, some critics had started to make a distinction between professional and amateur authors. A writer in the *United States Magazine and Democratic Review*, for instance, divided writers into "two classes; authors by profession, and amateur writers: those who regard study and composition as the business of their lives, and those who look upon them merely as incidental occupations," and he or she went on to make what is now a familiar equation between the economic and evaluative resonances of these categories, suggesting that amateur authors were inferior (amateurish) and paid authors were experts at what they did (professional).[36] Yet even the announcement of such a conceptual distinction represented a minority perspective within the occupational taxonomies of the decade, as Willis's letter to his sister made clear, and the comprehensive polemic in which this writer engaged in denouncing the masses of amateur authors suggests that many refused to participate in this new occupational zero sum game. A. J. H. Duganne, likewise, invoking the category in something like its modern sense in 1851, felt compelled, nonetheless, to use sarcastic scare quotes around the word itself in noting that "Poetry has its 'amateurs.'"[37] New occupational categories were becoming available to writers, that is, and new visions of the relationship between authorship and money began to compete for legitimacy, but they existed side by side with other models for decades and, in fact, never wholly displaced them. Those who made a sustained and exclusive living from the production of literary texts, in fact, were a minority through the nineteenth century, and it is important to remind ourselves that they remain a minority to the present day. Indeed, a Columbia University survey conducted in 1979, determined that "half of American authors earned less than $5,000 [that year] from their writings." Only 5 percent of American writers in 1979 were full-time authors who lived from the products of their pens; the rest moved from part-time to full-time and back again as circumstances demanded.[38] While it is true, of course, that the number of authors who sought to earn an exclusive and sustained income from the production and sale of literary works in the marketplace undoubtedly increased between the 1780s and the 1850s, they remained, I believe, a minority, and it seems hard to justify viewing the history of either authorship or economics through the lens of such an unrepresentative aspiration.

Indeed, even if we were to assume that there was such a thing as authorial professionalism, could show that it was important, and went on to demonstrate that it became increasingly valued over the course of the nineteenth century—points that I am certainly not trying to make—we would err nonetheless in supposing that the wealth associated with professionalism or the want associated with amateurism always meant the same things, always emerged from the same set of circumstances, were always measured by the same standards, or were always directed toward the same set of goals. An article in a Baltimore magazine of 1839 supposed, somewhat facetiously, that there might be five thousand and thirty-two poets in America and broke down their career profiles in the following way: "Industriously engaged in useful occupations, 3; neglectful of their appropriate business, 3940; in alms-houses, 75; in states' prisons & c., 94; in debtors' prisons, 280; street mendicants, 49; ordinary loafers, 225; gentlemanly loafers, 115; uncertain, 251."[39] Clearly there are many forms of wealth here, and one is hard pressed to determine which group of poets are the wealthiest: the gentlemanly loafers, the industriously engaged, or the neglectful of their appropriate business. The varieties of impoverishment, likewise, suggest that one could be a poor poet in many different ways and for many different reasons. Indeed, the very fact that this tongue-in-cheek prosopography leaves a substantial category labeled "uncertain" suggests that the simple amateur-professional distinction is still less able to provide interpretive historical certitude.

The final argument that can be raised against the professional-amateur distinction, and the concept of amateur authorship in particular, is that it offers literary historians almost no interpretive leverage. To call an author amateur is not to initiate a conversation about cultural economics but to shut one down: to say that, in essence, there is nothing to say. The interpretive poverty of amateurism as a category is nowhere more strikingly seen than in the fact that while there has been a veritable flood of studies exploring this or that canonical American author " . . . and the marketplace," there has not been a single study of literary amateurism *qua* amateurism, the (non)economic regime that allegedly preceded it and that (again allegedly) held sway until the second quarter of the nineteenth century. We scarcely have any studies of literature's gentlemanly loafers, let alone its ordinary loafers, mendicants, and beggars, even though they bulked large in the annals of American authorship. The inability of literary historians interested in the economics of authorship to say much more about most cultural production prior to the 1850s other than that it was 'not professional' or 'not *yet* professional' seems to me to be a conceptual failure of simply immense proportions.[40]

As a preliminary move, I want to suggest that the economics of authorship in the early national and antebellum periods were so complex and tangled, and the concepts of amateur and professional as used by scholars today so crude and lacking in interpretive nuance, that work in this field would be best served by avoiding such terms altogether.[41] This is not to say that there weren't individuals who wrote in a context entirely innocent of any explicit economic activity, nor that there weren't others who both lived for and off of belles lettres in a Romantic/professional fashion, but to suggest rather that in their pure forms they were such uncharacteristic extremes that the sorting of all authors into either one or the other category does them, and literary history, a great interpretive injustice. If the ideals of professionalism and amateurism did not exist in the early nineteenth century as we understand those terms today and only emerged in the 1840s, then we need to develop a taxonomy of economic practices more relevant to the social ideals and realities of the period. Establishing such a taxonomy and using it to reexamine and revise the interrelations of authorship and money in this period are the two basic goals of my book. It is to the premises that undergird this new taxonomy that we must now turn.

TOWARD A THEORY OF MULTIPLE ECONOMIES

William Charvat's work, and the work of those who follow in his path, seems unhelpful, I have argued, not merely for the answers that it offers, but more for the questions that it asks, and still more for the questions that it is unable to ask. This book is categorically *not* about, nor does it pose questions in terms of, the "professionalization of authorship," a rubric that is at once ahistorical and self-fulfilling, and which forecloses more, and more interesting, avenues of inquiry than it opens. Rather, it is about "economies of authorship," or, to use a phrase with which my subjects would have been more comfortable, and at which they might have nodded their heads in recognition, "the business of letters."

In the chapters that follow, I have tried to ask new and frankly revisionary questions about the economics and economies of authorship in early national and antebellum America. Rather than noting that early national America was "not ready" for professional authorship and asking why, I have asked instead what it *was* ready for and what circumstances made *those* economic choices propitious. What ways of thinking about the relationship between money and writing were available to authors in this period? To whom were they available and on what terms? A second line of inquiry asks what patterns of transformation are apparent in the development of these authorial economies in the period under consideration. Over the course of the late eighteenth and nineteenth century, what, if anything changed, in the business of letters, what remained the same, and how might we account for this?

These new questions are inspired by, and in turn contribute to, new methods of analysis and new approaches to literary history. My work, obviously, is influenced by the now well-established field of the History of the Book and the study of print culture, which, in the words of Robert Darnton, considers the production, dissemination, and consumption of printed materials "as a whole, in all its variations over space and time and in all its relations with other systems, economic, social, political, and cultural, in the surrounding environment."[42] From among the outpouring of scholarship in this mode, the work of four scholars of American print culture and authorship in particular have been useful in helping me formulate my own considerations of the business of letters. At the most paradigmatic end of the spectrum, Richard Brodhead has argued convincingly that the study of authorship might be reconceived in terms of access to specific cultural resources, explaining that the distinct socioeconomic circumstances through which one comes to think of oneself as an author will determine how one understands what authorship means. For Brodhead, multiple cultures—and, implicitly, multiple economies—of letters coexist at any given moment in history. Ann Fabian and Robert Ferguson have provided compelling case studies of distinct cultures of letters at opposite ends of the socioeconomic spectrum that bear out Brodhead's particularistic vision of authorship, Ferguson by examining lawyer-authors of the nineteenth century and considering the ways in which the legal profession created and limited opportunities for creativity, Fabian by considering beggar-authors of the same period who turned to authorship less from aspiration than from desperation. The distance culturally, economically, and aesthetically between the lawyer-authors described by Ferguson and the (often) ex-convict authors described by Fabian indicate the possible range of economies of letters to be examined. Lawrence Buell, finally, has provided the most thorough and extensive prosopography of American authors yet undertaken, studying the careers and social backgrounds of 276 New England authors, rich *and* poor, who were active between the Revolution and the Civil War. His work lends a degree of empirical rigor and nuanced generalization to Brodhead, Fabian, and Ferguson's case studies, suggesting that, for instance, educational background and occupation really did have an impact on the material dimensions and trajectory of an individual's authorial career.[43]

That each of these scholars' works have been immensely useful to me will be obvious in the pages and chapters that follow, yet while I have drawn both inspiration and example from these and other works of scholarship based in the history of print culture, my own work is more fundamentally and methodologically indebted to what has been dubbed "the new economic criticism," a still emergent field of endeavor being forged by economists, anthropologists, sociologists, and literary historians, and which suggests that economics is as much shaped by culture and rhetoric as by the timeless and impersonal forces of a reified market.[44] Six premises in particular, all derived from the scholarship associated with the new economic criticism, inform my study. (1) Money exists in multiple forms at any given period in a culture's history; (2) even when confronted with a specific, uniform currency, individuals and institutions will tend to designate specific meanings to specific monies; (3) these monies are distinguished because they circulate within distinct economies with their own rules and operating protocols; (4) not only money, but other desirables such as knowledge, honor, prestige, and legitimacy can be interpreted to great advantage as forms of capital that are produced, circulated, and exchanged within their own economies; (5) these non-monetary forms of capital can, at certain times, and under certain conditions, be exchanged for other forms of capital, including the monetary; and (6) transactions within and between various economies are often misdescribed or misrecognized by the participants, or they are recognized and contested by the same.

A humorous sketch published in *Freedom's Journal* in 1828 provides a useful point of entry into the complex and contentious world of antebellum literary economics and an illustration of how these six premises can be applied. "A Susquehannah raftsman," the sketch ran,

subscribed to a work published by a Philadelphia bookseller, the terms being three dollars in boards. He was as dilatory about payment as country subscribers usually are, and was consequently called on by an agent. Expressing his readiness to pay, he took the collector to the river side, and pointing to a huge raft, "I was to pay in boards," said he, "so take the best you can find." The agent summoned him before the nearest magistrate, who after examining the conditions of publication, decided, with characteristic wisdom, that, whatever the word boards might mean in PHILADELPHIA, it signified plank every where else; and accordingly gave judgment for the defendant.[45]

One way of reading this sketch would be as an example of what Buell has called regional comic grotesque, inasmuch as it pits the urbane Philadelphian book agent first against the ignorant backcountry raftsman who can't tell book boards from lumber boards and then against the equally ignorant but intellectually obtuse magistrate who quibbles over the meaning of the word "boards" but misses the significance of the word "in."[46] More than even a statement of regional superiority, however, the sketch was a declaration of racial emancipation, for *Freedom's Journal*, the periodical in which it appeared, was the first periodical in America to be edited and owned by African-Americans. In inviting his readers to laugh at the antics of backcountry Pennsylvanians, editor John Russwurm—who had graduated from Bowdoin College and delivered the commencement address there—was suggesting that his genteel, book-owning African-American readers, who knew what a book "in boards" meant, were superior to both the provincial white raftsman and the magistrate, who did not.[47] But Russwurm, free-born son of a slave woman and a wealthy white planter, also knew that economic literacy as much as cultural literacy was at stake in this sketch. This was, after all, an age in which free but illiterate African-Americans were sometimes defrauded by being handed bank drafts and IOUs inscribed "*Payable to Nobody.*"[48] Yet even legitimate forms of payment could, in certain contexts, be valuable (and hence payable) to nobody. "Pay in Boards," that is, can and, indeed, must be read as an object lesson in discriminating (or failing to discriminate) between socially marked forms of payment and ownership claims.

The divergent understandings of the "conditions of publication" construed by each man in the *Freedom's Journal* sketch reflect what every savvy man and woman in the early national and antebellum periods knew, but which no contemporary American literary historian has more than noted in passing, namely that payment for written materials in the early nineteenth century took diverse and, to our eyes, unconventional forms. Hence my first premise: *America was a nation of multiple monies.* Well into the 1840s, families in rural areas paid for goods and services through a barter economy, exchanging agricultural produce for mass produced commodities like books and newspapers. An account book kept by a newspaper carrier in the 1790s reads much like the *Freedom Journal's* fictional sketch, noting that various subscribers had paid for their literary fare with, among other things, "190 ft of plank for Stable floors, Some Rotten," "Mink skins," "Mulberry Trees," and "By taking care of a Thief"; in 1822, likewise, playwright Mordecai Noah was paid "ten loads of wood" for the copyright to one of his plays; while as late as 1850, an exasperated newspaper editor could tell a delinquent subscriber: "You must pay up in cash or wood or Something."[49] In the South, not only planks and minks served as money, but also slaves, who, in the words of one historian, "could not only be bought (sometimes by the pound), sold, and rented in the market" but who also served as "collateral for commercial, speculative, and personal loans."[50] Even "conventional" money in this period was far more complex than literary historians have realized. Although no scholar of American literary professionalization has ever noted the fact, America lacked a national currency until 1863. British pounds, Spanish Dollars, Portuguese "Joes," and Continental Scrip circulated promiscuously in the period after the Revolution. Through the early nineteenth century, individual banks in every state issued their own notes, while hotels, churches, brothels, even libraries printed, or minted, and circulated their own private currencies. And while Southerners used slaves like money, abolitionists in the north also created their own currency, issuing coins with the figure of a supplicating slave stamped on one side and a monetary denominator on the other, pointedly suggesting the illegitimate relationship between each. All the while, banks boomed and busted, forged notes were rife, currencies became worthless overnight, and individuals with more wood or cheese than cash could still consider themselves wealthy.[51] Indeed, recent work by historians of eighteenth-century America on the ideal of 'competence,' or comfortable level of income, has called into question the very idea that individuals in this period were always inspired by the pursuit of excessive, cash-based wealth.[52] In such a complex, protean economic world—one where poets were sometimes paid in clothes, printers in rags, and novelists in copies of their own book, and where costs and standards of living were so diverse—confident assumptions about authorial income and literary economics based on cash accounts become hard to make. One goal of this book, therefore, is to historicize the concept of currency and ask what such a reconceptualization tells us about paid authorship in this period.[53]

The refusal of the Philadelphian subscription agent to accept the bargeman's offer of "three dollars in boards" underscores my second premise: that *individuals and institutions will tend to designate specific meanings to specific monies.* Three dollars in the form of boards was an acceptable and legitimate form of payment in the eyes of the raftsman, being equal to three dollars in cash required *for* a book in boards. The agent's refusal to accept the boards was an indication not that he was unable to recognize the value of the lumber, nor even that he could not have sold it in turn for three dollars in cash; his rejection, rather, indicated that payment in boards was not appropriate for the transaction, because three dollars worth of boards had a different social meaning than three dollars worth of paper money or specie. In her groundbreaking study of such acts of economic differentiation, which she calls 'earmarking,' economic sociologist Viviana Zelizer has observed that individuals and institutions often invest certain forms of money with specific social and moral meaning and designate or earmark them for certain specific uses. Earmarking, according to Zelizer, can be achieved by "restricting the uses of money, regulating modes of allocation, inventing rituals for its presentation, modifying its physical appearance, designating separate locations for particular monies, attaching special meanings to particular amounts, appointing proper users to handle specified monies, and earmarking appropriate sources of money for specified uses."[54] The earmarked nature of money becomes most visible when currency designated for use in one specific economy is appropriated for use in another. In 1797, for example, a young Bostonian named David Everett proudly confided to author Joseph Dennie that he had purchased a copy of the latter's book, *The Lay Preacher*, with money saved by forgoing haircuts. The significance of the purchase, for Everett, lay in the fact that he had deliberately adjusted the disposition and distribution of his earmarked monies (what he called a "trade with fashion"); the significance for literary historians today is that early national Americans actually made such dispositions in the first place, earmarking their personal funds into 'money for books' and 'money for haircuts.'[55] Yet while it was relatively easy for Everett to renegotiate his own budgetary categories, it was altogether harder to renegotiate the money of another. Often, the ability to earmark successfully indicated social power, especially when one moved outside the realm of personal funds; in the *Freedom's Journal* sketch, for example, the magistrate's legal authority enables him to earmark the raftsman's boards as legitimate payment for a book even though the subscription agent does not believe in their acceptability.

Authors in the early national and antebellum period encountered a broad range of monies and accepted payment in cash, credit, medals, and statuettes, along with clothes, kisses, and copyrights. One of the most common forms of authorial payment, in fact, was in copies of one's own book.[56] Even when standardized specie or paper money was used, however, authors could and did earmark different forms of payment to suggest each had a distinct moral resonance. Frederick Douglass, for example, made a sharp distinction between the "seven, or eight, or even nine dollars a week" he made as a slave in Baltimore and was forced to hand over to his master and his "first free dollar," earned as a fugitive in Massachusetts. "It was mine," he wrote. "I could spend it as I pleased. I could buy hams or herring with it, without asking any odds of anybody. That was a precious dollar to me."[57] A dollar, then, was not always just a dollar, nor even always worth a dollar; sometimes it was special and different and worth much more. Sometimes, too, it was worth less. Consider the experience of Douglass's fellow Baltimorean, Benjamin Lundy. In 1828, Lundy received a savage beating from slave trader Austin Woolfolk who was angry at having been described in Lundy's newspaper as a "monster in human shape." When Lundy sued Woolfolk, the judge found in his favor but awarded him only one dollar in damages, suggesting that while Woolfolk was technically at fault for the beating, Lundy's abolitionism was so offensive that only the most minimal and symbolic payment was due him. Where Douglass's dollar suggested liberation, then, Lundy's conjured up humiliation, although he managed to make it imply vindication.[58] What money means, how it is valued, even what it is worth, is always contingent upon circumstance. As anthropologists Maurice Bloch and Jonathan Parry put the matter: "Not only does money mean different things in different cultures, but . . . it may mean different things within the same culture."[59] Inasmuch as this book is concerned with the economics of authorship, I seek to examine the ways in which those in the literary field earmarked the monies they disbursed and received and assay the significance of such acts of earmarking.

The tendency to earmark or distinguish multiple monies is neither arbitrary nor capricious; rather, it reflects the fact that we engage in multiple economic practices, rather than in one monolithic economic activity centered on market exchange. Thus my third premise: *specific monies circulate within distinct economies and exchange practices with their own rules and operating protocols.* According to anthropologist John Davis, we "have available to us a range of different kinds of exchange—a repertoire of socially acceptable practices which are culturally, morally and even economically distinct." Davis's enumeration of the modern British repertoire of economic exchanges begins with "alms-giving, altruism, arbitrage, banking, barter, bribery, burglary," runs through "extortion, futures trading, giving, huckstering, insider dealing, insurance," and ends with "theft, tipping, trading, [and] wholesaling."[60] The distinctions are more than academic. Any given mode of exchange selected from the repertoire of economic practices available to an individual has its own rules and entails its own system of ethics. When the written word was exchanged in America in this period, it does not necessarily mean that it was simply being inserted into a profit-driven market. Historians of print culture, according to James Raven, are only slowly coming to realize "how often the financing, distribution, and consumption of print was not ordinarily open market—that all sorts of non-commercial interventions operated."[61] Books and other forms of printed material were sold, yes, as the Philadelphia publishers sold a book to the Susquehannah bargeman, but they were also stolen, given away, presented as gifts, and exchanged for favors. Authors wrote to raise charity, to receive charity, to compete for prizes, to pay ransoms, to raise bail, to leave legacies, and to please patrons.[62] They were supported by publishers, by subscribers, by institutions, even by public lottery.[63] And printed material was written for a salary, written for spending money, and written, sometimes, as a last resort: for survival. In every case, the association of writing and money presupposed an exchange, but the repertoire of exchanges and economies into which writing could be placed were immensely diverse and the rules of each quite specific. Thus when poet Fitz-Greene Halleck undertook to edit the poetry of Byron in 1832 for the princely sum of one thousand dollars, he was entering a commercial-based transaction, in which his services—and prestige—were exchanged for money determined by a market-driven price. When, by contrast, he gave a copy of his collection of poetry to fellow-author Catharine Maria Sedgwick in 1827, no money passed hands, for they were participating in a gift economy in which reciprocity was neither explicitly required, nor market value important. Sedgwick understood the rules of the gift economy explicitly as well as implicitly, for in presenting Halleck with a copy of *her* most recent book, *Hope Leslie*, a little later, she explained that it was "not in exchange as a return for the book Mr. H. was so good to send her." And when Halleck sent one hundred dollars to fellow-author Edgar Allan Poe, it was neither a gift nor a commercial transaction but rather a loan, and whereas Halleck expected nothing from Sedgwick, he expected repayment from Poe, even though, ultimately, he received nothing. Indeed, we may illuminate this particular transaction yet further by contrasting it with the "two-and-a-half dollar gold piece" that Halleck gave to the poverty-stricken McDonald Clarke, the 'Mad Poet' of New York, so he could continue to write, for while he expected repayment from Poe, he did not from Clarke, and while the money for Clarke resembled a gift, it was, in fact, a clear-cut case of literary charity, given out of pity rather than esteem. The wages Halleck received, the gifts he gave, the loans he disbursed, and the alms he bestowed were all forms of exchange, yet each operated within a distinct set of rules.[64]

But the meanings of money are defined not only by the people between whom it is exchanged, however, nor merely by the places in which such interactions take place, but also by the passage of time over which such transactions are staged. Economies, that is, entail a powerfully contingent temporal dimension. Typically invisible, temporal earmarking becomes especially striking when the timelines drawn around economic practices are at variance with what we consider common sense. Some antebellum sailors, to take an especially striking example, believed that it was unlucky to carry to sea money that had been earned on earlier voyages, so they would frantically spend what they had during their shore leave and, if necessary, throw the rest overboard before setting sail. Their acts of economic earmarking, in other words, were bounded by distinct units of time associated with particular voyages: a prudent practice, perhaps, given the predatory nature of shipboard life and the precarious safety conditions that sometimes cut short sailors' lives. The temporal dimension of earmarking practices, it should go without saying, was as much subject to contestation and change as the spatial. Thus Olaudah Equiano, who served as a shipboard slave in the 1750s and 1760s, secured his freedom precisely by violating the economy outlined above; by carrying his small stock of coin from voyage to voyage and making modest commercial ventures, he eventually accumulated enough money to purchase his manumission.[65] What one did with one's money was always important; *when* one did it, and for how long, turns out to be equally significant. Arcane though the practice of throwing money overboard may seem, it underscores the way in which time can define economic meaning and shape the contours of a specific economy. Each of the economic exchanges engaged in by Halleck, for example, had its own signature tempo. A commercial transaction like the commission to edit Byron might typically have entailed immediate payment; a loan such as that given to Poe presupposed return after a specified period of time; and the giving of a gift, such as that for Sedgwick, while discretely inviting reciprocation, quite explicitly avoided stipulating a time by which a counter-gift was expected. The passage of time could also transform one economic phenomenon into another. When Poe failed to pay back the money that had been loaned to him, for example, he essentially turned (with Halleck's collusion) a loan into a gift, although had Halleck chosen to take him to court, this 'gift' might have been redefined as theft. It was precisely to establish such an economic definition that the subscription agent in the *Freedom's Journal* sketch was dispatched from Philadelphia to the banks of the Susquehanna. It is no coincidence, under the circumstances, that when Equiano published his *Interesting Narrative* by subscription in 1789, he actually required subscribers to pay a portion in advance.[66] In an age in which readers routinely failed to pay for their literary subscriptions in a timely manner, and which more generally has been described as a "republic of debtors," the temporal element of any given economy became a crucial and controverted issue.[67]

   In attempting to bring order to the chaos of economic behavior in eighteenth-century America, Michael Merrill has developed a four-part typology which suggests the ways in which space and time both combined and in so doing defined what he calls the "rules of repayment." An exchange could be either indirect and delayed (Poe); direct and delayed (Sedgwick); direct and immediate (Plummer); or indirect and immediate, as when author J. H. Ingraham explained to Harper and Brothers in 1839 that if they promised to pay him for his manuscript within thirty days, his brother would advance him the money right away. The business of *The Business of Letters*, so to speak, is to analyze the diverse economies that were woven around the act of authorship and to understand how the rules of repayment entailed by each determined the way in which money and literature operated between the 1780s and the 1850s.[68]

   My attempt to excavate and reconstruct the authorial economies of early national and antebellum America is not limited to the realm of monetary transactions, however, but also considers the ways in which intangible commodities were circulated and exchanged by those in the literary field in ways parallel to, but ultimately distinct from, the ways in which monies were circulated and exchanged. Thus my fourth premise: *not only money, but other desirables such as knowledge, honor, prestige, and legitimacy can be interpreted to great advantage as forms of capital that are produced, circulated, and exchanged within their own economies.* In pursuing this broad and non-conventional understanding of commodities and economies, I am following the lead of social theorist Pierre Bourdieu and his American disciples, who find a traditional Marxist emphasis on the primacy of monetary capital and subsequent distinctions between a determining economic base and a determined cultural superstructure to be needlessly limiting.[69] For Bourdieu, life is not organized around a single, monetary economy whose mode of operation determines the nature of cultural life, but rather around a series of autonomous fields, some monetary and most not, each of which trades in a distinct currency or capital with its own values and rates of exchange. The pursuit of capital, according to Bourdieu, extends to "*all* the goods, material and symbolic, without distinction, that present themselves as *rare* and worthy of being sought after in a particular social formation."[70] Bourdieu identifies four specific forms of capital, in particular, which he claims are always in circulation. These are economic capital (in the form of money and other forms of material wealth), cultural capital (in the form of specialized knowledges, expertises, and tastes), social capital (in the form of connections and group memberships), and symbolic capital (in the form of prestige or legitimacy, and specifically the legitimacy that comes from effective mastery of these other forms of capital). Each capital according to Bourdieu, circulates within a discrete economy, with its own modes and modalities of practice.[71] Nineteenth-century biographies and biographical sketches help illustrate Bourdieu's theories, since they so often celebrated their subjects with succinct assessments of their capital assets. Thus an 1828 sketch of the poet Samuel Woodworth concluded with the observation that "Notwithstanding the want of pecuniary success which has frequently attended his different literary undertakings, he has invariably sustained the reputation of an honest man. . . . In manners, he is modest and unobtrusive; in conversation, shrewd and sensible; in public, a good and influential citizen; and, in private, the affectionate husband, the enlightened parent, and the faithful friend." Translation: Although Woodworth had little economic capital ("Pecuniary success") he could trade on his abundant cultural capital ("in conversation, shrewd and sensible"), social capital (as an "influential citizen"), and symbolic capital (with the "reputation of an honest man").[72]

The idea that commodities other than money functioned within discrete economies in the same way that money did within the world of commerce was, in fact, not lost on literary practitioners in the eighteenth and nineteenth centuries, many of whom were members of the business community as well as the community of letters, and who perceived the often-striking parallels between their avocational and vocational pursuits. Indeed, the metaphors used in the critical discourse of the early republic sometimes anticipate Bourdieu's concept of diverse capitals in an eerily prescient fashion. Three examples will suffice. The first comes from essayist and businessman William Tudor, who sought in 1821 to explain the weakness of American literature relative to that of England by adopting "the language of trade." In literature, he pointed out, "as in coarser branches of manufacture, it was almost in vain to enter into competition with England." The latter's "literary capital was great; her taste and learning long matured, and in everything of a finer texture." Still, he continued, America's "skill and capital, to continue this borrowed phraseology, have both been accumulating, and there are some branches where the wants of the country are now in great degree, and soon will be entirely, supplied at home."[73] The second example comes from an anonymous essay of 1791, discussing various levels and types of literacy (or what Bourdieu would call forms of cultural capital). Basic literacy, the author explained, was "like *small coin*, such as *silver pieces* and *pennies* . . . which enable a man to travel every where, and to be at home in all countries. They are alike current in market-places and stores." Eloquent rhetoric, by contrast, "may be compared to *bank-notes*, which are very valuable and easily transferred from place to place." Knowledge of Latin and Greek, however, was like valueless piles of "*old continental* money" and had "ruined all those persons who have amassed great quantities of them, to the exclusion of other more useful and necessary branches of education." Pedants, in essence, this essayist was arguing, were intellectually bankrupt, just as hoarders of Continental scrip were financially so.[74] Yet where the essayist of the 1790s placed great confidence in bank notes, three decades later lawyer-poet William Crafts regarded them as figures of intellectual inflation and axiological insubstantiality. In a newspaper essay of the early 1820s, Crafts shrewdly observed that "Reviews are the paper-money of literature—with this abatement in value, that they issue on the capital of others, and never on their own, with this common attribute, that they have no intrinsic value at all. . . . Like paper-money, they never give you the exact value of the article they represent; for reviewers are brokers in literature, and their trade is artifice. Like paper-money, they may cease to exist without the slightest diminution of specie capital.

Where they abound, they indicate the scarcity of precious metals—being artificial means of credit, borrowed of a friend, or bought of an usurer."[75] This was a singularly appropriate sentiment for the early 1820s, a period in which Americans were still reeling from the crash, in 1819, of the nation's banking system, which had printed notes far in excess of its reserves of specie. Such shifts in the specific use of money as metaphor suggests that it can serve as a useful index of cultural value.

The specific value of Bourdieu's study of the forms of capital lies not in the observation that intangible possessions function in much the same way as money, however, nor in his contention that each field in which capital circulates is functionally autonomous from each other, but rather in his assertion that capital is convertible.[76] Thus my fifth premise: *nonmonetary forms of capital can, at certain times, and under certain conditions, be exchanged for other forms of capital including the monetary.* Let us consider again the *Freedom's Journal* sketch, since its humor is predicated in large part on the apparent impenetrability of the economies in which these capitals circulate. The bargeman has very little economic capital but seeks to trade in what he has for cultural capital (a book), although in the process he shows precisely how completely devoid of cultural capital he is, inasmuch as he doesn't even understand what he is buying (a book in boards). In appealing to a judge for economic restitution, the subscription agent is relying on social capital (his access to courts of law), but unfortunately for him, while the judge possesses symbolic capital (judicial authority) in abundance and perhaps moderate economic resources, he is almost as devoid of cultural capital as the bargeman in whose favor he rules. The moral of the sketch *seems* to be that money cannot buy taste, connections cannot protect money, and authority is distinct from culture. The truth, however, is that *all* were interrelated and *all* were convertible under the right circumstances.

An obvious example of capital conversion, of course, would be the transformation of economic capital into cultural capital by purchasing books or paying for an education, or, *vice versa*, by selling one's cultural capital for money as an author or a professor. Thus Henry Wadsworth Longfellow's parents paid to have him educated at an exclusive academy in Portsmouth and then at Bowdoin College, cashing in their money for cultural capital, with the consequence that Longfellow, who was a gifted linguist, was in turn offered a series of academic posts—first at Bowdoin and then at Harvard—where he was able to reconvert that cultural capital, in the form of teaching and publications, back into money. Eventually, his prestige (or symbolic capital) itself accrued an economic value beyond or apart from his literary abilities. "Longfellow's worst poem," observed

Philip Pendleton Cooke in 1847, with clear-eyed resignation, "however a best chance effort of mine might excel it, would be vastly more valuable" to magazine editor George Graham, "than anything I could send him."[77] The act of conversion was not always reversible, however. "In general," writes David Swartz, "economic capital appears to convert more easily into cultural capital and social capital than vice versa," an observation borne out by the example of Edgar Allan Poe, who, while rich in cultural capital, lacked both economic and social capital and was unable, therefore, to convert his literary prowess into money except on the most unfavorable of terms.[78] Poe's relentless criticisms of Longfellow and others were in fact founded on exposing the, to him, fraudulent way in which mediocre authors traded on their social rather than cultural assets to secure economic rewards.

The real payoff of Bourdieu's approach, however, comes not from such relatively obvious illustrations of the idea that one can buy or sell cultural ability, so much as from the way in which de-emphasizing monetary accumulation helps us understand what, from a more 'common sense' point of view, would seem to be inept or unsuccessful interventions in the field of literary economics. Publisher Samuel Goodrich's decision to pay John Trumbull an almost unprecedented one thousand dollars for his *Poetical Works* (1820) and give him one hundred copies of the finished product in exchange for the copyright might be seen as the disaster Charvat described it as, inasmuch as most subscribers refused to accept the lavish volume once it was published and Goodrich lost all of his money.[79] According to Bourdieu, however, symbolic capital can be enhanced by "making a purchase at an exorbitant price," as a "point of honour." Although Goodrich, in his own words, "quietly pocketed" his loss, he soon thereafter began to think of himself as a patron of American literature, and so did others; spending too much, in this case, was money well spent.[80] By the same logic, Noah Webster's decision to give away hundreds of his books and donate a percentage of his sales to various charitable causes does not mean that he was uninterested in making money, since he manifestly was, so much as it indicates his interest in converting some of his abundant economic capital into symbolic capital. "The sum is small & the benefit will be great," he observed in 1790.[81] Such acts of capital conversion were manifold in the nineteenth century and exploring them in all their diversity is an important part of understanding the economics of authorship in this period.

So what kind of transaction was Webster involved in? Was he making a selfless charitable donation? Was he performing a strategic maneuver calculated to win the goodwill of the book buying public? Was he engaged in a combination of both? Or was this a third and completely distinct form of exchange? That the answer is initially unclear is a consequence of my sixth and final premise: *participants within literary economies are apt to misrecognize or misrepresent the nature of the transactions in which they are engaged.* We see inklings of this in our *Freedom's Journal* sketch, of course, in the obtuseness of all the participants involved, but better examples can be found elsewhere. Consider, for example, the case of Thomas Willis White, editor of the *Southern Literary Messenger.* Writing to one of his best and most frequent contributors, Lucian Minor, in 1838, White promised to "deposite [*sic*] to your credit in the Bank of Va. $40, *pin money*. No, I am free to say hard-earned money."[82] White's hesitation over the precise nature of the money he was giving ('pin money' versus 'hard-earned'), and the economy of which it was a part, is revealing. Traditionally, pin money referred to the allowance a husband gave his wife; according to one scholar, it was always "trivialized" and considered "a less fundamental kind of money than [a] husband's wages."[83] Hard-earned money, by contrast, was masculine and just recompense for honest toil. White's prevarication in denominating the money he was sending is perhaps understandable, for White was poor and Minor contributed extensively to his magazine, only rarely asking for payment, although in this case, he had done so, which caused White both a financial and a categorical headache. If he called his payment to Minor "pin money," White feminized and trivialized his contributor's efforts but was then justified in not paying him more often; if he called it "hard-earned," he valorized and maximized Minor's effort but was then compelled to admit, albeit tacitly, that his hard work did not always earn him the payment it deserved. Faced with this untenable choice, White equivocated and suggested that they were engaged in a domestic economy, or a commercial economy, or both, or perhaps neither. His lack of clarity was extraordinarily convenient, since White—as we shall see in Chapter Three—could not afford to pay Minor or his other contributors regularly, even if he, and they, had so desired.

Misrepresenting the nature of economic transactions was, in fact, often a means of saving face. Thus charity was often described as a gift, and gifts were sometimes called loans; tips were called payments, and payments were sometimes treated as gratuities or charity.[84] When historian William Hickling Prescott first offered fellow scholar Pascual de Gayangos payment in 1841 for the latter's truly substantial research and translation services, Gayangos proudly declined; only weeks later, however, after Gayangos had suffered an economic setback, he grudgingly consented to receive what Prescott called a loan and that Prescott in turn would refuse to have paid back. In strictly economic terms, Prescott had paid Gayangos; culturally speaking the two had improvised an economic narrative that occluded this payment.[85] My point is simply this: much as there was an economy of stories, so there were also stories about the economy. Individuals often fabricated accounts of what they thought they were up to, or what they wished they were up to, or what they wanted others to think they were up to, when they engaged in the business of letters. Read symptomatically, writings about the economics of writing can be extraordinarily revealing.[86]

Perhaps the greatest advantage to adopting these six premises, then, and those indebted to Bourdieu in particular, is that they offer a way out of the impasse encountered by Charvat in the 1950s. In explaining why he had moved away from the study of literary economics, Charvat pointed to the impossibility of making data like "sales of books and incomes of authors . . . reveal something about the ways in which writers and their writings function in a culture." The "economics of authorship," Charvat explained, was "wholly extrinsic" to most literary history and became "sterile" and "an end in itself."[87] Precisely because Bourdieu sees economic and cultural capital as interconvertible, and precisely because he implies that authors engage in stories about exchange as well as in the exchange of stories, however, his approach allows one to tell the histories of literature and economics in a synthetic and integrated manner.

The goal of my book, then, is to tell the story of authorial economics and the economies of authorship in the early national and antebellum periods in such a way as to do justice to the complex and manifold ways in which writing and payment were intertwined. As such, I am in broad agreement with scholar Regenia Gagnier, who has called on literary historians to move beyond traditional approaches of economists, with their "emphasis on price rather than value."[88] The *how* and the *why* of authorial economics, I believe, are as important as the *how much* and *why not more*, and perhaps more so, insofar as scholars have heretofore neglected to consider them.

ECONOMIES EMBEDDED AND DISEMBEDDED

Readers with an anthropological background who have followed my argument to this point will perhaps recognize in the positions I have staked out a recapitulation of the debate between the Formalists and the Substantivists that galvanized the field of economic anthropology in the 1960s. Since few others will be familiar with this storied controversy, I want very briefly to outline the basic ideas below. My reasons for veering into this ostensibly arcane debate are twofold. In the first place, it allows me to summarize my arguments to this point while placing them in a larger and far more suggestive frame of reference. Second, and more importantly, it adds to them a developmental, historicist edge and offers a theoretical vantage from which to create a new narrative about authorial economies to replace the old story of professionalization I have discussed above. With these two thoughts in mind, then, let us turn to the debate itself.

Very briefly, the Formalists argued that in all places and at all times, humans have behaved in the same way: seeking, in a nutshell, to maximize utility while minimizing expenditure. This economizing tendency, they contend, is predicated on an innate ability to use reason in order to make choices that promote self-interest. Their ideal-typical subject is sometimes called *Homo economicus*: man the maximizer. The desire to maximize economic self-interest, of course, seems abundantly true of business-oriented individuals in advanced capitalist societies, but, according to the formalists, it is equally true of people from other times and in other places too. The only difference, for the Formalists, is that in precapitalist societies, manifold impediments are thrown in the way of each individual's ability to maximize utility, and their activities are often buried under sedimented layers of obfuscatory cultural detritus. The job of the Formalist anthropologist, then, is to strip away these layers of cultural irrelevancy, and in so doing to reveal the rational economic behavior that lies beneath. This behavior can then be examined and interpreted through the rigorous application of math-based models of neoclassical economics.[89]

The parallels between Formalist economic anthropology and traditional scholarship on American literary professionalism should, I think, be reasonably clear, but they are perhaps worth spelling out. Throughout this chapter, I have been arguing, in essence, that William Charvat and those who follow in his footsteps, have pursued a basically Formalist agenda. Like the Formalists, Charvat and others suppose that all authors at all times have sought to maximize their utility through professionalization and competitive engagement in the literary market, or they have explained failures to behave in this way as a consequence of exogenous factors that have stood in the way of such behavior. (Recall Charvat's mantra: "Professional authorship . . . was ready to begin, but the publishing world was not.") Again, like Formalists, they have sought to use the tools of modern economics (albeit in a simplistic fashion) to assess the success of the authors they have studied: counting imprints, calculating incomes, and cataloging copyrights, as if only material achievement constituted success. Like Formalists, they have tended to disregard the cultural contexts of economic behavior itself as so much extraneous material to be stripped away. And, as a consequence, like Formalists, they have imposed their universalist assumptions concerning human behavior and human aspiration on literary history. A great deal of the criticism advanced in the first two sections of this chapter reflects my deep distrust of this vision of human nature and, hence, its version of human history. To be blunt, I do not believe that humans have striven always to maximize their personal utility, and I cannot endorse or write the sort of history that takes such an assumption as its basic frame of reference. As such, I find myself in broad agreement with those Substantivist economic anthropologists inspired by Karl Polanyi, who set out in the 1960s to challenge both Formalist theory and practice.

The Substantivists began with a concession, which was that, in some sense, classical economic theory might be useful for exploring modern market societies, but this was a small enough concession to make, for historically speaking, the Substantivists argued, most societies have not been organized around the market. Anything but, in fact. Indeed, the Substantivists insist that market exchange is only one of a variety of economic systems that have appeared and reappeared throughout history, and while they do not deny its ancient lineage, they claim that its social *dominance* is of very recent origin. Most economies, the Substantivists contend, are organized in ways quite distinct from, and in fact contrary to, those one would expect in a market economy, most especially in their relative lack of emphasis on individual gain and personal utility maximization. Outside of the market economy, the Substantivist argue, economic practices tend to be deeply "socially embedded": woven into the fabric of society and concerned with collective, rather than individual, well-being. Each economy has to be examined in all its rich specificity as one of a number, or repertoire, of possible practices. When neoclassical economic methodology is applied indiscriminately to the study of such societies, what results is at best an abstraction and at worst an anachronistic parody of history as lived. The Formalists, as Marshall Sahlins pointedly put it, "equipped the hunter with bourgeois impulses and paleolithic tools" and then "judge[d] his situation hopeless in advance." In considering stone age society, said Sahlins, what was called for was a stone age economics.[90]

Again, the parallels between Substantivist anthropology and my own position should be fairly obvious but are once more, perhaps, worth spelling out. In the first place, then, and like the Substantivists, I have argued that American history is defined not by one (market) economy but rather by multiple economies, each with its own currencies and conventions. Again, like the Substantivists, I have argued that the ubiquity and hegemony of the market—represented here by the will to professionalize—has been greatly overstated and in ways that minimize other economies of equal or greater significance. Like the Substantivists, I believe that when we seek to view economics through this lens of burgeoning professionalization, we greatly distort what was in reality taking place. (In fact, my criticism of Charvat and his school parallels precisely Sahlins' of the Formalists: that they have equipped authors with professional impulses and non-professional tools and then judged their situation hopeless in advance). And, finally, like the Substantivists, I have tried to offer a broad and nuanced taxonomy of economies that grows out of my historical evidence, rather than making reference to just one reified economic concept which then determines the evidence I find.

My resurrection of the Formalist-Substantivist debate would be indulgent, of course, if all it did was restate in an abstract and alien register what I have already argued at length in quite specific and concrete terms. In fact it does a great deal more. In the pages that follow, I shall argue that the Substantivist concept of embeddedness adds a crucial developmental dimension to my argument, setting the multiple economies I have described in motion and providing a theoretical basis from which to develop a historical narrative of the *transformation* of authorial economies more nuanced and compelling than the old story of professionalization.

As in the second section of this chapter, I want to set the stage for my narrative by advancing several premises that will implicitly—and at times explicitly—inform the argument of the book as a whole, although my elucidation of these points will be briefer. My premises are: (1) that substantial segments of economic life (including authorial activity) in the early republic were characterized by what the Substantivists call social embeddness; (2) embedded economic activity—*qua* economic activity—tends to be relatively invisible; (3) this invisibility is a consequence of the multiple social functions it serves, of which the merely economic is only one; (4) these social functions serve, typically, to create and sustain social bonds; and (5) over the course of the antebellum period, these economic activities became progressively disembedded from the social worlds of which they were a part and became, simply, economic activities.[91]

Lest the reader balk at this new list of premises, so many pages into the chapter, let me point out that they are closely related to those advanced in the second section. What, in essence, I am arguing is that in the early republic the circulation of economic capital was hard to separate from the circulation of social and symbolic capital, to the point, in fact, where it was sometimes difficult to see the economic capital at all; that sometimes economic capital was exchanged in order to generate social and symbolic capital; that the possession of social capital facilitated the flow of its economic cognate; and that over the course of the antebellum period, economic capital became more readily distinguishable from social and symbolic capitals and more typically a substitute for them. What is new here, in other words, is not the *kind* of points I am trying to make, but the sorts of tools with which I am trying to *make* them, for while Bourdieu's concepts lend themselves admirably to describing static systems, the Substantivists' tools are immeasurably better at capturing those systems in motion and showing how they change over time.[92]

My first four premises can all be illustrated together by considering more closely the meaning of the phrase embedded economy. In the most deeply embedded economies, according to the Substantivists, acts of production, exchange, and accumulation are not merely subordinated to social concerns but are, in fact, wholly submerged within them: indistinguishable, except heuristically, from the worlds of which they are a part. As philology suggests, the original meaning of the word economy was itself utterly socially embedded—the ancient Greek *Oikonomia* meant household management—and, indeed, housework remains one of the best examples of an economic practice that is still deeply socially embedded to this day. The constitutive activities of housekeeping—cooking, cleaning, shopping, and child-raising—are all, in any important sense, economic; they involve production, exchange, consumption, and labor. And of course, when chefs, custodians, purchasing agents, and nannies performs these tasks, we find it easy to put a value on their labor and pay them for it. When, by contrast, a 'homemaker' engages in these activities, they are so wholly embedded in the web of familial existence that it is hard to think of them as salaried activities, or even as economic activities; they become simply part of the act of homemaking. In such a context, the "economics" in "domestic economy" becomes invisible.[93] In wholly embedded economies, that is, there is no distinctly "economic" dimension that can be understood or perceived apart from the social contexts of which they are a part, nor is the economic element of the economy considered more important or determinative than the social: the two are mutually reinforcing. Indeed, there is some question as to whether one can speak, in this context, of "embedded economies," since even to name the economy as such is to grant it some kind of conceptual priority that it does not necessarily have. It is tempting, rather, to follow Marcel Mauss, who in writing about traditional gift-giving described such acts as "total social phenomena" in which "all kinds of institutions are given expression at one time." Such social totality is true of embedded economies more generally. A domestic economy, that is, is as much domestic as it is economic.[94]

Of course, not all deeply embedded economies are embedded within households, but all of them—by definition—are bound up in ongoing social relationships of one form or another. Both charity and gift-giving, for example, are economies in which the circulation of money is woven into the creation and maintenance of bonds, in the first case of pity and gratitude and in the latter of mutual esteem. In economies such as these, the self-interested pursuit of gain puts one at odds with the very bonds these economies create. Economic activity serves other and larger purposes in embedded societies than mere self-interest or even the basic provision of necessities. Because economics is never *the* point, or the *only* point, of an embedded transaction, the quantitative or monetary nature of the transaction is sometimes minimized or made invisible.

So much for the first four premises. Let us consider the fifth and last: that over the course of the nineteenth century, many embedded economies started to disembed. The concept of disembedding has caused some confusion among scholars who point out that since—to an extent neglected by economic theorists—all economic exchanges take place within a social context no matter how attenuated, all economies (at all times) can be said to be socially embedded. When embeddedness is defined as, simply, situatedness, such an argument can hardly be refuted, but as we have seen, embeddedness means far more, in the Polanyian sense, than being possessed of a context. All economies have contexts, but not all economies are subordinate to, or completely submerged in, those contexts, nor are they necessarily constitutive of them. When they are not, they can be said to be disembedded. By this definition, disembedding occurs when an economy starts to unravel itself from the social fabric into which it has been woven and operates in ways that are distinct from, and considered superior to, the social world more generally. When the business of life becomes, simply, a business, it has become disembedded, and when business defines life, that disembedding is complete. In such a situation, as Polanyi puts it, "Instead of economy being embedded in social relations, social relations are embedded in the economic system."[95]

Social historians influenced by Polanyi, and by Substantivist anthropology more generally, have argued that rural life in eighteenth-century America was characterized by precisely the sorts of embedded economies I have outlined above. In this world, exchanges were typically embedded in local and social relationships: with neighbors, kin, and coreligionists. Frequently conducted face-to-face, rural exchange relied less on cash than on barter and trade in produce and labor. Commodities were rarely paid for immediately but rather were exchanged through long-term, informal debt, a system of immense complexity, because individuals in the country were routinely and reciprocally indebted to one another. Indeed, reciprocity rather than competition defined this world. Accounts were only irregularly added up, debts were rarely called in, the value of what one owed was often negotiable, as was the means through which one repaid it, and the obligation to pay was itself based on affective rather than contractual ties.[96] At some point between the 1750s and the 1820s—and historians have argued vigorously about both timing and extent—this precapitalist world began to give way before the forces of the market. Socially embedded exchanges were replaced by impersonal transactions; barter by cash; custom by contract; long-term debts by immediate payment, or debt offset with interest; discretionary remuneration by legally enforced obligation; and reciprocity and communalism by individuality and the pursuit of profit.[97]

Although literary historians have by and large failed to engage with either the theories of Substantivist anthropology or the histories of eighteenth-century rural America, the scholarship emerging from these two fields can be applied quite directly to the subject of authorship and authorial economies.[98] Indeed, the key historical contentions of my book correlate directly to the Substantivist premises and the historical illustrations I have just outlined. In the chapters that follow, I shall argue that what previous literary historians have described, and hence dismissed, as amateur authorship—devoid of economic significance—conceals evidence of a vigorous world of exchange in which authors circulated their works through a variety of deeply embedded economies. The failure of scholars to discern and interpret the economic dimensions of 'amateur' authorship is a consequence of the relative invisibility of the economic elements in embedded economies. Because they were embedded, these economies served not simply to disseminate commodities but also to create and sustaining social bonds. For that reason, I believe that the major transformation in authorial economies over the course of the nineteenth century was not their professionalization but their social disembedding, although they disembedded slowly and in some instances very incompletely.

As the story of the Susquehannah raftsman and the book in boards illuminated antebellum America's many currencies and capitals, so another brief account of an economic transaction gone wrong helps provide a point of entry into the world of embedded and disembedded authorial economies. The transaction, or series of transactions in this case, took place between editor Willis Gaylord Clark and poet Sumner Lincoln Fairfield in the early 1830s, and appears to have taken the form of subscriptions Clark secured for Fairfield's new journal, the *North American Magazine*, although it is hard at this distance to be certain. What is certain, however, is that while the transaction began amiably enough, it ended in dispute after the *North American* published a savage review of Clark's new volume of poetry.[99] Writing to fellow editor Morton McMichael in 1834, Clark announced that Fairfield deserved nothing less than "a cauterizing." "As an ingrate," wrote Clark, "and as an abuser of those who have loaded him with favors, he stands preeminent. I have done him $40 worth of good,—and he has paid me by personality and ribaldry, as unprovoked as it has been contemptible."[100] It is not clear at this great distance in what the forty dollars' worth of good consisted, but what strikes one as remarkable in Clark's letter is the locution itself: *I have done him $40 worth of good*. Common sense tells us that the very essence of a successful favor lies in the fact that while it can entail the transfer of economically quantifiable goods and services, we do not dwell upon, or even mention, those economic quantities. What we stress, instead, is the goodwill from which such favors emerge, and the continuing goodwill of which they are a promise. To mention money is a breach of protocol. A favor is absolutely characteristic, in this respect, of an embedded economic transaction. Within embedded economies, things of economic value are routinely circulated and exchanged, but such exchanges perform more than merely economic functions; they also create and reinforce social ties. As Marshall Sahlins succinctly puts it of one of the most embedded of economies: "If friends make gifts, gifts make friends."[101] Moreover, and as the example of the gift or favor makes clear, the monetary value in such transactions is often embedded in the social to the point of invisibility. It is not that the cost of a favor is beside the point, since it is manifestly possible to be too extravagant or too niggardly in performing one, but simply that it is not the *only* point, nor even the most important one. This was an idea understood clearly by both Clark and Fairfield, who in the late 1820s and early 1830s exchanged letters (costing postage), manuscripts (costing time), and their respective publications (costing money) with some regularity without money ever being mentioned; they did one another favors because they were friends, and their friendship was cemented because of the favors they did. Their relationship, however, as we know, was less well-cemented than it might have been, and as it fell apart, the economic component became separated—or as Polanyi calls it disembedded—from the social. We can identify the moment of disembedding very clearly in Clark's reference to the monetary value of the good he has done Fairfield. What had once been seen as a personal favor in which the economic was occluded is now transformed into a commercial service with a distinct price tag: something one would do for even a stranger if paid the forty dollars. Indeed, the issue of recompense enters the equation quite explicitly, when Clark complains that for the forty dollars of good he has done, Fairfield has "paid" him with "personality and ribaldry." If friends make gifts and gifts make friends, then it is clear that Clark is (at least for a while) no longer Fairfield's friend, and what he has offered will no longer be considered as a gift. It has become, instead, a discrete and disembedded economic transaction for which he has been insultingly short-changed.[102]

The tendency for economic transactions to be both submerged within and constitutive of social relationships is characteristic not merely of favors but of embedded exchanges more generally. Indeed, it is the multiplicity of embedded economies through which authors were able to work and their immense pervasiveness in the late eighteenth and early nineteenth centuries that makes them such a powerful and inclusive frame through which to view authorship in this period. Gift-giving, charity, tipping, and the extension of credit and patronage, for example, are all forms of embedded economy in which even as money is circulated, social relationships are created and sustained, although in each case a different type of social bond is presupposed or brought into being by the transaction. We can get a sense of the range of ways in which literature circulated through just such embedded economies by turning once more at the repertoire of economic activities engaged in by Fitz-Greene Halleck. When Halleck gave a copy of his book to Catherine Maria Sedgwick in 1827, he was not simply giving her a book worth, say, two dollars; he was offering her a token of friendship that, coincidentally, had a two-dollar value. Likewise, in making Halleck a gift in return, she was not paying him back with a two-dollar book of her own but honoring the friendship. The social bonding performed by this exchange of gifts makes it hard to see the economic transaction taking place, but even though it is possible to interpret this as an exchange of two-dollar books, it would miss the point; it was a social as much as an economic gesture. If Halleck's gift to Sedgwick reflected a bond between equals, then his donation to McDonald Clarke expressed a less reciprocal bond: one based on pity from Halleck and gratitude from Clarke, although part of their connection was predicated on the fact that each was an author. The loan made to Poe also reflected a powerfully social relationship, for in early national and antebellum America, creditor-debtor relationships both replicated preexisting social bonds (one loaned to one's friends and family) and reinforced them powerfully (inasmuch as they generated a surfeit of trust and extended a relationship into the future). Although Halleck's loan was not specifically literary except insofar as his creditor was also an author, serial publications in early national and antebellum America—both newspapers and magazines—were typically purchased on credit, through means of a subscription system; as such they created ongoing bonds, and, when subscribers did not pay their dues, ongoing problems. Halleck's editing of the works of Byron seems the least embedded of these transactions inasmuch as he had very little connection, social or economic, with the publisher, George Dearborn.

There were, of course, degrees of embeddedness. While gift-giving and charity are typical of deep embedding, an important intermediate position might be called embeddedness through subordination. An economy could be said to be embedded in this way to the extent that it is subordinated to concerns other than those of self-interested profiteering. This form of embeddedness does not necessarily entail the absence of market practices but entails, rather, what sociologist Fred Block calls a relatively low degree of "marketness."[103] Such subordination was pervasive in the early republic. The activities of tavern owners, cartmen, auctioneers, victualers, hawkers, peddlers, doctors, and lawyers, for example, were all regulated by a variety of public statutes and licensing laws designed, according to William Novak, not merely to control quality and ensure safety but also to restrain competition. Indeed, the very institution we have come to associate most closely with rampant and impersonal competitiveness—the market—was itself embedded in, and subordinate to, communal standards associated with civic well-being, republican virtue, and individual restraint. As Helen Tangires has argued, public markets in early national and antebellum America were regulated by a variety of rules calculated to limit price gouging, exploitation, unfettered competition, and plain economic deceit. Operating on principles akin to the moral economy described by E. P. Thompson, these public markets, according to Tangires, sought to provision a community with the necessities of life, even while they provided a culturally and socially sustaining space for the community to meet. Within an embedded economy, in fact, the market was always a place as well as a process: it occupied both social and physical space.[104]

This subordinated form of market practice also had a pronounced impact on the dissemination of the printed word in antebellum America. Consider the activities of the American Tract Society. Through the 1830s and 1840s, according to David Nord, the ATS harnessed the most advanced techniques of the market and developed the most cutting-edge technologies of the printing trade to maximize their production of tracts and Bibles while at the same time minimizing overheads. The goal of all this activity was hardly to make profits, however, but—quite the opposite—to give texts away. Their stated goal was to put a Bible in the hands of every American, no matter what the cost. And when the Society did conjure up costs and sell its wares, they were priced differentially, based, according to Nord, on what "each individual buyer was able and willing to pay *all the way down to zero.*" Indeed, the managers of the ATS actually reversed the key dictum of the market revolution by creating demand *through* supply, rather than vice versa. This is a textbook example of embeddedness through subordination, inasmuch as the techniques and technologies of capitalism utilized by the ATS to produce and disseminate Bibles were embedded in, and thoroughly subordinate to, the values of an anti-materialist, if not anti-capitalist, evangelical culture.[105]

Nor was this subordinated form of market behavior limited to publishers alone. Authors, too, participated in what, at a superficial glance, seem like explicitly profit-driven market exchanges but that on closer inspection turn out to have harnessed utility-maximizing market means to relationship-maximizing social ends. No better example, in this respect, can be found than the Connecticut poet Lydia Sigourney. Immensely productive and wildly popular in her own day, she has been reviled by modern literary historians not only for her apparently saccharine Christian verse but also for her hypocritically ruthless pursuit of profit. Ann Douglas, for example, calls Sigourney one of those "prolific and careless souls" of the nineteenth century who was "as intent on acquisition as on art," while even a firm champion like Nina Baym concedes that her efforts were geared toward "reputation building and money-making."[106] Money making? Yes. Reputation building? Perhaps. Self-enrichment? No. As it turns out, Sigourney's hard bargains were always driven with a mind to benevolence. Writing to Theodore Dwight, Jr., in 1830, to propose publication of a collection of biographies for children, she noted that they would be useful for schools, but could not "disguise from [him] that one of my principal motives is to obtain something for the use of my parents, & to meet the interesting demands of religious charities which multiply around us." Again, in 1832, she explained to a publisher with whom she was making a tough bargain that "my means of charity are furnished by my poems."[107] The image of Sigourney pushing hard to make money to give away to others might strike us as incongruous, but it was entirely of a piece with the world of embedded economies and market exchanges with a low degree of marketness. Of course, Sigourney did not disavow the more traditional forms of embedded exchange; she was an inveterate giver of literary gifts and participated in a vibrant world of lettered so-ciability, which led her husband, Charles, to complain that (note the eco-nomic metaphor) "every puppy was welcome to [her] favour, if he would but pay the price of it in flattery, from Lickering and Hill, down to Sum-ner Pinckney [sic] Fairfield." Dramatic though the example of Sigourney is—in a three-month period she recorded writing 900 pages of text, 600 lines of poetry, exchanging 450 letters, and receiving or paying 860 social visits—she was, as we shall see, by no means unique in the way in which she blended both deeply embedded and strategically subordinated eco-nomic activities as an author.[108]

THE DISEMBEDDING OF THE ECONOMY

So what, then, happened to these embedded literary economies? Two answers suggest themselves. The first is: very little; the second: a great deal. Let us consider the second answer first. A powerful case can be made for the idea that over the course of the antebellum period, many of the economies through which literature had traditionally circulated started to unravel from the social fabric through which they were woven and of which, indeed, they were a constitutive element. Social relation-ships came to be replaced by commercialized and impersonal ones. The imperatives of the disembedded economy came to be enforced less by af-fect and reciprocity and more by contract and legal obligation. Modes of literary production became less personal and more mediated. The busi-ness of letters became less intimate and more fleeting. In short, it became a business plain and simple. According to Ronald J. Zboray and Mary Saracino Zboray, this transformation was rather suddenly and decisive-ly precipitated by the Civil War. The war, they explain, disrupted fami-lies and communities as men went off to battle, replacing proximity with distance, making the section or the nation rather than the family the new frame of reference, while authors became more instrumental and de-tached, writing propaganda for an anonymous reading public rather than local communities.[109] There is no question that the war had a profound impact on the production, dissemination, and consumption of the writ-ten word, but I would like to suggest that, in the case of authorial econo-mies, the transformation was under way decades before the firing on Fort Sumter. At least three areas reveal evidence of disembedding: the autho-rial process, the literary product of that process, and the social relations that gave rise to them.

We see evidence of this sort disembedding first in the tendency of some authors and publishers to frame literary production in solely economic or quantitative terms. As early as 1827, for example, Nathaniel P. Willis could brag to a friend that a newspaper he was sending contained "fifteen dollars of poetry" which he had written. In the early 1830s, likewise, editor Louis Godey could write to author Robert Montgomery Bird and ask him, with tongue only partly-in-cheek, to "hammer me out . . . one of your solid pieces about twenty-five dollars' worth of Literature." It was one thing to exult, as Catharine Maria Sedgwick had done, in 1837, over the fact that the *Democratic Review* was paying contributors "$5 a page!"; it was quite another to refer, as Willis did, to each of his poems, as a "five dollar inspiration."[110] While Sedgwick was clearly attracted to the pay scale, she did not, in her commentary, wholly subordinate her literary productivity to, let alone define it by, a set of economic parameters. Godey and Willis did. Their comments, off-hand as they were, seem to suggest that it was becoming possible for the first time to imagine the circulation and exchange of writing as no longer something that generated money coincidentally, as a by-product of more socially oriented activities but as, rather, a commercial process defined primarily by the money it could make.[111] Willis's newspaper, the *New-York Mirror*, even offered a vision in 1832 of a steam-driven writing machine that would produce "Waverly novels, ten shillings per hundred weight" and "Tragedies, seven pence half-penny per act." It was an apt symbol for an impersonal and depersonalizing means of literary production in which human connection played no part but in which cost and volume were paramount.[112]

If authors' relationships with their works were becoming more commodified and less embedded, so too were the works themselves. Consider the example of Willis's first literary employer, Samuel Griswold Goodrich. After a largely unsuccessful career as a publisher, Goodrich began in 1827 to write a popular series of children's books under the pseudonym Peter Parley. Flushed with success and perhaps overwhelmed by the demand for his texts, he became the first entrepreneur to create a literary franchise based on a fictional character, and by so doing, also created the first cadre of salaried ghostwriters. His efforts began in the early 1830s, when he started to hire assistants to research and write Peter Parley books for him. In 1836, for example, he offered Nathaniel Hawthorne one hundred dollars to produce a 'universal history' in the Parley house style, which appeared without authorial attribution in 1837 as *Peter Parley's Universal History on the Basis of Geography*. Upon receiving the manuscript, Goodrich wrote Hawthorne that he "liked it pretty well," and added "I shall make it do." The proprietorial tone in this comment was entirely fitting, for while Hawthorne and his sister Elizabeth had written the bulk of the manuscript, the book itself, and the Parley name, belonged to Goodrich. The *Universal History* went on to sell more than a million copies, but Hawthorne received no credit or acknowledgment and only his initial fee, if that.[113]

Precisely how thoroughly Goodrich treated the works of others as his own is revealed in his conflict with another of his ghostwriters, William Joseph Snelling. In 1830, Goodrich hired Snelling to "block out" some travel texts under the pseudonym Solomon Bell, another of his Parley-style personae. The first volume, *Tales of Travels West of the Mississippi*, appeared in 1830. When reviewers, recognizing the house style ("after the manner of Peter Parley," according to one), began to attribute the work specifically to Goodrich, Snelling was stung with pride and had friends publish a newspaper article revealing himself as the true author. Goodrich was also outraged, feeling that, having paid for the manuscript, the work was his no matter who had produced the words. Rather than publish any more of the Snelling manuscripts in his possession, he burned them. They were after all, and at least legally, his to do with as he pleased.[114] Goodrich, as Snelling later quipped, was merely a "putative father," but one who seemed willing to "claim all the babes that have been disavowed by their real parents."[115] Using such familial language revealed a concern for the idea of legitimate connection, for the conflict between Snelling and Goodrich reveals a nascent tension between the work of literature as an expressive and socially embedded act, typified by Snelling in the image of parenthood, and the work of literature as an alienated and fungible commodity, which in essence fostered texts to the highest bidder. As the Parley name became increasingly commodified, even Goodrich became unable to control its use. Other authors, recognizing its market value, began to write unauthorized Parley texts, and Goodrich spent much time denouncing and pursuing legal claims against these "spurious" Parleys.[116]

Many of the authors who worked for Goodrich came to detest him, as Snelling and Hawthorne did, but their relationships were, nonetheless, based upon personal acquaintance and, at least initially, feelings of goodwill. By the 1840s, however, even these kinds of connections were starting to unravel. The social ties that formed the ligaments of the literary world began, themselves, to commercialize. The example of Park Benjamin is instructive. Through the 1830s, Benjamin was a busy poet, publisher, editor, and man of letters, with a wide circle of literary friends for whom he routinely did favors. He read his friends' compositions, used his connections to secure them publication, and exchanged his works with them in turn. Benjamin knew both Snelling and Hawthorne, for example, and both of them appeared in his publication the *New England Magazine*.[117] In 1841, however, Benjamin broke new ground in establishing what is believed to be the first literary agency service in America. Placing advertisements in prominent magazines and newspapers, he announced that for a fee he would now read and critique any manuscripts sent to him, and that he would then submit them to publishing houses, an additional fee or percentage to be levied if the work was published. Payment was "invariably" required in advance.[118] Benjamin's agency clearly reflected a profound shift in authorial economics. Where Willis Gaylord Clark had once complained because he had been betrayed by a friend for whom he had done "$40 worth of good," Park Benjamin now advertised that for this sum (indeed, for a fraction of it), he would be anyone's friend. The kinds of activities out of which friendship had traditionally been created and through which they were typically manifest were now commodified and available to anyone with ten dollars and an unpublished manuscript to spare. America's "commodity frontier," to invoke Arlie Hochschild's felicitous phrase, was being pushed back, to embrace cultural territory previously considered more social than strictly economic.[119]

Clearly, then, we can see evidence that authorial economies were starting to disembed before the onset of the Civil War. And while the war certainly had a profound and qualitative impact on the nature of authorial experience, it did not, on the other hand, wholly eradicate the sort of embedded economies through which literature had traditionally circulated.[120] On the contrary, they are still with us today. Every love letter written, Christmas card inscribed and sent, every book gifted or loaned, every newspaper hawked by the homeless, and every newspaper delivery boy or girl's Christmas tip, suggests the ways in which the written or printed word still passes through economies embedded in the social or personal.[121] Both before the Civil War and since, goods and services have been transacted through a variety of economies, some social and some impersonal. The coexistence of socially embedded and commercially disembedded economies can be accounted for, according to Stephen Gudeman, by the fact that each meets distinct needs. What has altered is the relative significance and disposition of these two facets of the economy.[122]

Moreover, while a sense of community endures in even the most commercialized society, it is also clear that the foundations and dimensions of that sense of community have changed. In the early republic, the world of personal acquaintances was by far the most important context through which literature was produced, disseminated, and consumed. As face-to-face communities dissipated in the face of migration and urbanization, however, they were replaced by other forms of connectedness, less predicated on personal acquaintance. The increasing influence of sentiment and sympathy made it possible to feel connected to people at a distance and often those quite different from oneself. Indeed, in a controversial and much-debated essay, Thomas Haskell has argued that it was the very rise of capitalism, and especially the increasing reliance on contracts, that gave rise to a humanitarian sensibility able to appreciate the long-distance and wide-ranging consequences of actions on others one had not met.[123]

While other scholars have focused on large-scale socioeconomic and political changes, and especially on the sweeping rise of circumatlantic, hemispheric, and globalizing transformations of American literary culture, my own approach here is to focus on individual and microhistorical moments. My emphasis, that is to say, is not on national or transnational politics but on what ethnographer F. G. Bailey calls the "small politics" of daily social interaction and the constant negotiations these entail.[124] *The Business of Letters* does not offer literary criticism or even literary history so much as a history of literature as it was experienced by authors in the early national and antebellum periods. While the lines of transformation and continuity might not be as bold or as compelling as those offered in the narratives of traditional authorship studies, they will, I hope suggest in a more nuanced manner the experience of authorship.

CHAPTER TWO

The Black Bard and the Black Market

In this chapter I bring the theories and tools outlined in Chapter One to bear on the life and work of the slave author George Moses Horton and the various writers, both black and white, who came into contact with his works. Horton makes an ideal test case for my arguments in all sorts of ways. In the first place, he—as an African-American author—was almost by definition an invisible man, his economic activities both embedded deeply in the social worlds through which he passed and cloaked from prying eyes, so the methodologies I derive from Bourdieu, Zelizer, and Polanyi seem especially well suited to revealing what is not immediately apparent about his circumstances as an author. In the second, he participated in not just one economy but rather was drawn through many—patronal, charitable, and gift-oriented—so that tracing his experiences helps illuminate a broad swathe of literary life in early national America and supports the contention that authorial economics cannot be reduced to just one sphere of economic activity. A third advantage of studying Horton anew through the lens of authorial economics is that it allows us to rectify several well-entrenched but glaringly incorrect claims that have been made about circumstances surrounding his publication, and specifically the claim that he was defrauded of his literary income by either his master or the publishers of his work. Fourth, his experiences allow me to offer a novel and frankly counter-intuitive thesis, which is that the publication of his first collection of poetry, so far from being a breakthrough or an achievement, in essence marked a low point in his career as an author, although not so much because he was defrauded but, rather, because he became disembedded—or if you will—dislocated from his work. Finally, when we get the measure of Horton in this way, it also becomes clear that striking though his experiences as a poet were, they were by no means unique nor specific to his racial or regional identities. Many other authors in the North also worked through the same deeply embedded and equally "artisanal" means as Horton, suggesting the existence of a pervasive authorial economy that has heretofore been beyond our view. Yet Horton's practice *was* striking, even if it wasn't unique, and because his fate was so intimately tied to the lives of other authors whose career trajectories were strikingly different from his, he serves as an excellent subject for exploring the way in which multiple cultures and economies of letters could coexists at the same moment, even in the same place, in time, accessible to some on some terms, and others on different ones.

GEORGE MOSES HORTON AND THE BLACK MARKET

George Moses Horton was born in the late 1790s—the precise date in unclear—and grew up a slave on a farm in Chatham County, central North Carolina. His master, William Horton, was a tough driver who sometimes worked his slaves to exhaustion and encouraged them to drink when not working. William, according to Horton, cared little for the education of his family, and still less for that of his slaves, but Horton early "conceived an anxiety for books," and with the assistance of white school children and "old parts of spelling books," taught himself to read in the early 1810s.[1] Immersed in the New Testament and the Methodist hymns he read and heard sung, Horton began to compose hymns and devotional poems himself, which, he later recalled, "I retained in my mind, for I knew nothing about writing with a pen" (viii).[2]

Improvising on sacred and secular songs was common practice among slaves in the antebellum South, and Horton might never have drawn attention to himself but for the fact that in his late teens he became the property of William's son, James, who allowed him to travel by foot each Sunday to the University of North Carolina in Chapel Hill, eight or nine miles away, where he sold fruit.[3] Chapel Hill was thronged, at this time, with "negroes," who, according to one alumnus, "in different ways contributed to the amusement and comfort of students." Some offered food for sale and hunting dogs for hire; one allowed students to break boards over his head for a small fee; and several others performed imitations. One imitated "the crowing of cock," for example, another the sounds of a dog fight. Before buying his fruit, the students "pranked" Horton by requiring imitations from him, but rather than having him make the sounds of animals, they goaded him instead to imitate a man of eloquence, perhaps on account of his copious vocabulary. Horton's coerced orations opened him to ridicule, but the poems he recited did not, and the students soon "discovered a spark of genius" in the young slave (xiv).[4] In a period in which the rational and cultural capacities of African-Americans were still very much in question in many quarters, the authenticity and legitimacy of Horton's eloquence quickly became a focus of contention, but the issue was settled decisively, and very much in his favor, after he showed himself able to compose acrostics, extemporaneously and orally, on names given by his listeners.

The use of acrostics as an authenticating genre was a time hallowed practice. A widely disseminated story recounted that hymn writer Isaac Watts had produced one as a child in the 1680s to convince his mother that other poems she had found were written by him, and possibly Horton, devoted to the hymns of Wesley, was familiar with this account. It was, at any rate, either a stroke of brilliance on Horton's part, or a stroke of luck, to have to work with this form, for the acrostic was an ideally hybrid genre for the young slave: its mnemonic structure suited his primarily aural/oral cultural praxis, guiding him from line to line; its visual/nominal structure, in which the subject's name emerged from the text, suggested literary sophistication, graphological concern, and ludic prowess; and its popularity as a genteel, if juvenile, form of courtship poetry accrued him status as the exponent of a practical yet prestigious genre. For the next forty years, Horton would be known, if nothing else, for his acrostics.[5]

The following poem, an acrostic on Julia Shepard produced in the mid-1830s, gives one a good sense of Horton's skill in the genre and suggests something of the appeal his works had for the students:

> Joy like the morning breaks from one divine
> Unveiling streams which cannot fail to shine
> Long have I strove to magnify her name
> Imperial floating on the breeze of fame—
>
> Attracting beauty must delight afford
> Sought of the world and of the bards adord
> Her grace of form and heart alluring pow'rs
> Express her more than fair, the queen of flow'rs
>
> Pleasure fond nature's stream from beauty sprung
> And was the softest strain the Muses sung
> Reverting sorrows into speechless joys
> Dispelling fear which human peace destroys—
> Beauty.
> But Goddess thou the di'mond of the fair
> Willt from thy brow repel affection's prayer
> And smile to hear the unavailing sigh
> With tears disolving from thy supplicant's eye—

But light upon the beau to thee assignd
And leave all els with disregard behind
Then softly bind affection's sacred chain
Never thro life to be broke off again[6]

Modern readers will, necessarily, be arrested by Horton's striking and ironic allusion to chains, a point to which I will return shortly. For the moment, it is enough to note that as a result of acrostics such as this, Horton's "fame soon circulated like a stream throughout the college," and the students were so pleased with their discovery that they started to offer him money to write poems and love letters for them (xiv). These poems, according to Horton, were often "composed at the handle of the plough" and, since he could not write, were "dictated, whilst one of the gentlemen would serve as my amanuensis" (xiv). For his efforts, Horton received a fee ranging from twenty-five cents per poem, "which was unanimously established" among the students, to as much as "seventy-five cents, besides many decent and respectable suits of clothes" (xvi). According to Richard Benbury Creecy, who graduated from the University in 1835, Horton typically wrote—or at least sold—a dozen poems a week for money, which constituted a substantial income, while by the late 1830s he was producing—or, again, selling—as many twenty verses on a weekly basis.[7] Horton's income hardly matches up to the thousands earned by his canonized contemporaries Washington Irving and James Fenimore Cooper, but in Chapel Hill, where tuition at the University was thirty dollars per annum, and food and lodging for a year ran to ninety-five dollars, it was not inconsiderable.[8]

The economic differences between an author like Horton and those like Irving and Cooper extended not simply to how much money each made, of course, but also to how, precisely, they made it. While Irving and Cooper participated in what Raymond Williams has called a "market professional" mode of literary business, working with publishers, negotiating for royalties, and owning or trading copyrights, Horton's exchange of poems for cash or clothes corresponds, by contrast, to what Williams calls an "artisanal" mode of literary transaction, in which an author "offers his own work for direct sale" to purchasers, without the presence of intermediaries or institutions.[9] This followed in large part from *what* Horton wrote. An acrostic is a highly personalized genre in which the subject is quite literally inscribed into the verse; thus Horton only ever had one customer per poem, and the transaction, like the poem itself, was personalized and private. A more pressing reason for the personalized and unmediated nature of the exchange, however, lay in the fact that in selling his poems, Horton was breaking the law, since in

North Carolina a slave was not allowed to sell commodities without the express and specific permission of his or her master, which Horton did not have.[10] Horton's literary business thus offers a rare peek into what has been called the world of "informal," "hidden," or "shadow" economies—black markets—in which money is accumulated, expended, and exchanged in illegal, or at least unregulated, ways.[11] The fact that he was selling his poems to aspiring courtiers within a highly confined social environment also imbued his transactions with a sense of intimacy. This specific convergence of genre, exchange practice, legitimacy, and location, I want to argue, rendered Horton's authorial economy particularly fraught.

So what was Horton's economy? How might it best be characterized? To the extent that scholars have discussed this issue at all, the standard line has been that Horton was the first "professional" poet in the South, and indeed he identified himself as a professional in his 1845 memoir, although as I suggested in the first chapter of this book, the ways in which the word professional was used in the early nineteenth century were quite distinct from the restrictive economic meanings attached to them by scholars in the twentieth. Horton almost certainly meant that he "lived for" literature, and indeed, even though he was also able to an extent to "live off" of it, his authorial economy differed in qualitative as well as in quantitative ways from the practices we associate with canonical "professional" authorship.[12]

Horton's love poems, I want to argue, in fact stood at the intersection of two related but quite distinct economies. The first of these was a gift-exchange economy, the other an economy of patronage. Let's consider gift economics first. The giving of poems in courtship was just one facet of an elaborate system of reciprocation practices—social visiting, letter writing, child fostering, money lending—that was pervasive in the antebellum South and that helped both create and cement social relationships.[13] When the scion of a planter family gave a love poem to a single woman, that is to say, he participated not simply in a unilateral transaction but rather in a bilateral exchange, for the sense of obligation created by the bestowal of the gift encouraged the recipient to respond with, at the very least, an expression of gratitude, and, ideally, with a poem or protestation of her own. The obligations engendered by the bestowal of gifts were precisely the "chains" to which Horton's poem on Julia Shepard referred, and which the initial gifting of the poem was designed to forge. It was a common enough trope. Winifred Gales of Raleigh, North Carolina—whose husband would subsequently print and publish Horton's own verses—claimed that "letters" were "the links, in that tender chain which memory rests on our absent friends," and Sarah Fisher agreed, noting that every letter functioned to "brighten the chain of friendship." More usually, chains were associated—without any irony—with romantic attachment; revelers at an 1806 Independence Day celebration in Charleston, South Carolina, raised their cups to the toast: "The silken fetters of love—the only signs of American slavery." "Remember," wrote Virginian William Wirt to his fiancée a month before their marriage in 1802, "you are not the prisoner of an engagement. . . . There shall be no compulsion, no fetters but such as Love shall forge to bind you to the engagement." Nor was this imagery limited to Southerners alone. Young abolitionist William Lloyd Garrison, writing a love poem to Mary Cunningham, repeated the sentiment too, asking "Sweet MARY! Wilt thou be my bride? / To thee I bow—thy chains I'm wearing."[14] The giving of gifts created chains, because a gift simultaneously suggested a generous gratuity that was appealing while at the same time encouraging a reciprocal gesture which was ensnaring. These chains were silken or tender, because a gift relationship typically took place between people who were already (at least presumptive) equals. The gifting of poetry, in other words, was part of an embedded economy designed to create lasting affective bonds, and, in this case, to draw two people into the bonds of matrimony. Whatever else we might read into Horton's poem, then, with its pointed allusions to chains, what remains compellingly clear is that the author was fluent in the language of polite Southern courtship and its socioeconomic metaphors and able to ventriloquize the voice of the master class. And this was precisely what the students valued in his poetry.

Yet while Horton produced poems that were intended to be used as gifts, he, himself, did not participate in either a gift economy, or in a gift relationship, with his customers. Horton, rather, was engaged in a series of patronage relationships. My invocation of patronage here requires a degree of clarification, inasmuch as we tend not to see America as ever having sustained a patronal society. As William Charvat suggested in his unfinished history of authorship in America, insofar as there were no wealthy aristocrats in antebellum America, there could by definition be no literary patronage either, unless it was the slowly developing and metaphorical 'patronage of the people' that we associate with the marketplace. Whatever patronage there had been in Colonial America, Charvat he added, was, by the 1780s, "in a state of final and permanent collapse." Charvat is surely right within the context of his definition; the problem is that his definition is needlessly limited. Recent scholars of eighteenth-century English literary history, relying on sociological models and anthropological fieldwork on patron-client relationships, have suggested that patronage took more forms than merely aristocratic support, offered more rewards than purely economic recompense, and served more important functions than simply flattery. Indeed, Dustin Griffin has argued that we need to jettison our old model of groveling courtiers and haughty aristocrats and reconceptualize patronage as "a personal relationship between two parties unequal in status and resources, designed for mutual benefit of the two parties, and ultimately as a means of sociopolitical organization." By this definition, Horton's sale of poetry offers an almost textbook example of a literary client working for powerful patrons.[15]

Horton's engagement in a patronal literary economy, I believe, was both enabled and informed by the powerful and pervasive ideology of paternalism subscribed to by many white (and some African-American) Southerners. This ideology held that wealthy whites and their slaves were bound together not simply by one-sided forms of exploitation and subjugation but rather by reciprocal debts and obligations, rights and responsibilities, that were hallowed by tradition and usage. It was a planter's obligation, according to this worldview, to assume responsibility for his slaves and treat them as if they were family members (albeit of inferior rank), and it was the slaves' obligation to respond with obedience, docility, and gratitude. This paternalist ethos permeated every aspect of antebellum Southern society, but it was cemented by regularized and ritualized acts of generosity in which masters bestowed their largesse upon slaves. Stephen Nissenbaum has argued, for example, that in making generous gifts at Christmas, masters were not merely (or even) showing benevolence so much as they were performing a role as benefactor and in so doing reinforcing feelings of obligation and debt in their slaves.[16]

The same is true of the Chapel Hill students' relationship with Horton. Although his sale of poems to students might seem like an exchange on a level playing field, or even one where he, as a poet, held the superior position, his relationship with his customers was, I want to argue, shaped by the parameters and expectations of patronage relationships in general and of paternalist rituals in particular. Several pieces of evidence support this idea. First. there is the ritualized and regular nature of the purchases. According to Richard Benbury Creecy, who attended the University in the mid-1830s, students "usually invested a quarter a week," which suggests that their purchases were not based upon need but rather served as minor acts of patronage and *noblesse oblige.*[17] Second. students sometimes "paid" Horton for his poems with their cast-off clothes because, as he explained, "they would not suffer me to pass otherwise and write for them" (xvi). Again, the bestowal of fine used clothes on slaves was a typical paternalist ritual, and the students' language here, as reported by Horton, suggests that the clothes were not to raise Horton up so much as to make sure he did not drag his patrons down.[18] Third. these transactions—like those of paternalism more generally—created an enduring sense of ownership; the students at the University of North Carolina came to think of Horton proprietarily, as "our Poet." Indeed, their patronage of him like a slave owners' persisted for years and endured across generations, creating a sense of familial continuity; Horton served student Ruffin Thomson in the late 1850s just as he had his father William in the early 1820s. "George has no doubt forgotten me," wrote William in 1859. "I should like to see him very much."[19] Fourth. white observers themselves explicitly linked Horton to the British patronal tradition by comparing him to both Burns and to Dryden and by referring to his "mercenary muse."[20] And, finally, Horton seemed to accept such designations himself, engaging in such characteristic practices as acknowledging and thanking his gentlemen patrons by name (xv) and by referring to himself not as a slave but, repeatedly, as a "vassal," a word rich in connotations of a landed and paternalistic tradition.[21]

Horton's engagement in a patronage economy entailed both advantages and disadvantages. On the negative side of the ledger, his participation in a client-patron relationship wove him ever more tightly into a series of unequal and sometimes downright demeaning relationships. The notion that the students wished to keep Horton in a subordinate position is suggested by their habit of plying him with alcohol (xvi). (As Nissenbaum shows, the bestowal of alcohol on the lower orders was a common ritual of paternalism.) Serving as a literary client to patrons also led him to be infantilized. As late as 1843, when he was in forties, for example, a professor to whom Horton showed his poems, described him in print as "a negro boy." Finally, Horton's status as an inferior with pretensions also allowed his customers to play pranks on him just as they had when he first appeared in Chapel Hill bearing fruit. In one episode, for example, a student asked him to write a topical poem and then gave him the topic in Greek. The message seems clear: Horton might have some skill in rhyming, but he was never to forget that he was his customer's cultural inferior, able to approximate but never quite replicate their cultural capital.[22]

Yet if Horton's one-on-one engagements with patronizing white customers drew him into demeaning relationships, the intimacy, illegality, and unmediated nature of his mode of literary transaction also afforded him some distinct advantages. The key advantage Horton enjoyed was that of participating in an informal, cash-in-hand economy. Receiving payment in such a discrete and unregulated way gave Horton the freedom to define the meaning, and hence the uses, of the money he received.

In a nutshell, Horton was free from institutional earmarking; his money meant whatever he wanted it to mean. When Horton spent the money he received, he was doubtless doing so in local taverns and dry goods stores where the use of cash served as a disembedded and disembedding medium and, therefore, placed him on a level of parity with those with whom he did business. Ironically, then, Horton's engagement in a profoundly embedded and demeaning economy (patronage) provided him with the cash to assert his independence in a relatively disembedded and egalitarian economy (the commercial marketplace). While much of the money he earned, apparently, was spent on alcohol, of which he was extravagantly and debilitatingly fond, it was, if nothing else, spent of his own free choice: a gesture of defiance, too, since almost all slave economic activity, including the purchase of alcohol, required a written permit from the slave's owner.[23]

How did Horton's lot stack up against that of his contemporaries? The example of Sarah Fitzpatrick is instructive. Recalling her adolescence as a slave in Alabama, she explained that most "couldn't write in dem days an' ef a boy wanted to court a gal he had to git his Marster to write a letter fer him an den de gals Mistus had to read de letter to her an' write de boy back."[24] This was not Horton's situation; indeed, quite the opposite. For something close to a decade, Horton presented cultural capital, which he was not meant to have, to students, who were, in exchange for economic and symbolic capital, which he also was not meant to have, but which he accrued quietly and effectively through his poetic production. And while Horton was engaged in paternalist relations with those who were his social superiors, rather than in gift relationships with those who were his peers, he managed, through careful manipulation of the economy in which he was embedded, to eke out a modest degree of self-determination. He was, to invoke Francis Jennings's useful neologism, neither independent of, nor wholly dependent on, slavery, but, rather, showed himself to be "ambipendent." It was not a perfect situation, but it might well have been the best construction of an irreducibly imperfect one.[25]

"BID THE VASSAL RISE"

In 1826, Horton's literary economy was significantly complicated by the arrival in Chapel Hill of Nicholas Marcellus Hentz and his wife, Caroline Lee Whiting Hentz. Nicholas, who was the university's new professor of Modern Languages and Belles Lettres was a brilliant and erratic polymath. Born in France in 1797, he was a medical scholar, a painter of exquisite miniatures, and a gifted entomologist. After moving to America in 1816, he briefly attended Harvard, worked as a private tutor, taught French at George Bancroft's progressive Round Hill School, and published scientific papers and text books, together with an historical novel—*Tadeuskund, the Last King of the Lenape* (1825)—that evinced an uncharacteristically tolerant view of racial difference in America; when he was hired by the University of North Carolina, it was argued by one knowing commentator that his equal would "not be found by the Trustees in the whole Atlantic coast."[26] Yet it was not toward the prolific but socially awkward Nicholas, but rather to his wife Caroline, that Horton was drawn following the family's arrival in Chapel Hill. Beautiful, witty, and poised, Caroline quickly took Horton under her wing, and for the next five years, she coached him in poetry, correcting (what she took to be) his stylistic errors and committing to paper many of his verses.[27] Their bond seems to have become especially strong following the death of the Hentzs' young son, Marcellus, in July 1827, when Horton produced an elegy on the child, for which, he recalled, he received "much credit and a handsome reward" (xvii). And while Horton did not cease writing or selling acrostics, he also began to write both satirical and meditative verse. Her first year in Chapel Hill, Hentz endowed her protégé with appreciable quantities of cultural and economic capital.

Horton was in a sense fortunate in his adoption by Hentz, for while the students of Chapel Hill patronized Horton in order to rehearse for their roles as members of the South's planter elite, Hentz—a newcomer—patronized him in order to discover what her role in Southern society ought to be, which meant that her dealings with him were at once more tentative and flexible. Twenty-six when she arrived in Chapel Hill, Hentz had never before traveled beyond the borders of Massachusetts and was at first repelled by slaves as well as by slavery. In a letter written en route to Chapel Hill, she complained of the "swarm of greasy negroes" she saw "filling the houses and street" in Portsmouth, Virginia. "The houses," she continued, "look in general old and inelegant, interspersed everywhere with negro huts." Chapel Hill was more picturesque but significantly less elegant than even Portsmouth, and her sense of social disorientation was compounded by the cultural isolation of this tiny village. Horton provided not only distraction, but also orientation.[28]

Although Hentz is best known to scholars for her insistent defense of slavery in the 1850s, in novels such as *Marcus Warland* (1852) and *The Planter's Northern Bride* (1854), her opinions on racial servitude were significantly less conservative in the late 1820s. Hentz, in essence, believed that whatever moral and intellectual inferiority could be seen in African-Americans was a direct consequence *of* slavery and not a justification *for* it. Hentz, in other words, adopted a moderate environmentalist position on the question of race and liberty. Indeed, Horton's poetry struck her as powerful evidence in favor of such an argument, for while its stylistic weaknesses were a result of the disadvantages under which he, and indeed all slaves, labored, the fact that he could produce poetry at all spoke eloquently to the sense of potential within all slaves.[29]

This is not to say that Hentz believed Horton to be her equal. It is significant that when Horton presented her with his elegy on Marcellus—a genre that was almost always bestowed gratuitously on the mourner—she paid him for his effort. To turn what was, in essence, a gift into a commodity was an act clearly designed to put Horton, albeit gently, in his place by suggesting that it was inappropriate for her to be in his emotional debt. Hentz could bestow her largesse upon Horton, but he could not upon her. Shortly after the death of Marcellus, Hentz decided to secure Horton the ultimate gift: his freedom.[30]

In April 1828, Hentz sent a strident letter to her hometown newspaper in Massachusetts, the *Lancaster Gazette*, together with two of Horton's non-acrostic poems. The letter described Horton's efforts to read and argued that his love of poetry had "triumphed over the bonds of slavery, and the darkness and corruption which seem their inseparable attendants." Horton's triumph was only metaphorical, of course, and in some sense, his poetic sensitivity merely made his enslavement all the more galling. He was able to create his verse, she said, only "at night, when worn and wearied by the harassing and servile tasks of the day" and felt "deeply the degradation of the sable race to which he belongs." This was, then, a double tragedy: to be a slave, and to be fully cognizant of how debasing such enslavement was. As obviously as the secondary pain would seem to follow from the first, in making such a claim Hentz was promoting a moderately advanced view of African-Americans. Many defenders of slavery questioned whether slaves suffered to the same degree or in the same way as whites; Horton, according to Hentz, manifestly, *felt* his situation.[31] The poems she appended both thematized and dramatized his feelings. In "Liberty and Slavery," Horton contrasted his painful servitude with the freedom he desired, admitting that he "scorn[ed] to see the sad disgrace / In which enslaved I lie," while in "Slavery," he described his perpetually dashed hopes that he might one day become free, and expressed a desire for death, where the "wicked cease to trouble" and the "weary there can rest." But these were not passive or defeatist poems that addressed God in displacing salvation from the here and now to the hereafter. "Slavery," in particular, seemed to have been written quite explicitly for an out-of-state audience and was oriented very specifically toward soliciting money for manumission. "Come, melting Pity, from afar," implored Horton

> And break this vast, enormous bar
> Between a wretch and thee;
> Purchase a few short days of time,
> And bid a vassal rise sublime
> On wings of liberty.

Horton went further still, in fact, not only pleading as a "wretch" for his readers to purchase for him a "few short days of time," but suggesting that these same readers' tacit racism might perhaps be the very cause of his continuing wretchedness. In what are the boldest lines of the poem, Horton asked "Is it because my skin is black, / That thou should'st be so dull and slack, / And scorn to set me free?" Supposing the answer would be yes, Horton then sought to "hasten to the grave," leaning as far toward a suggestion of suicide as he could possibly go without a direct threat. The message of the poem, then, was clear; Horton's readers could either be responsible for his freedom, or they would be responsible for his death.[32]

The reaction to "Slavery" was both immediate and dramatic. Within four days of its April appearance in the *Lancaster Gazette*, it was reprinted in the popular women's magazine, *The Bower of Taste*, published in Boston; in May it appeared in the anti-slavery *Village Record, or Chester & Delaware Federalist* in Pennsylvania; by June, it was picked up by Benjamin Lundy's stridently abolitionist *Genius of Universal Emancipation* in Baltimore; and, finally, in July it was run in the African-American owned and edited weekly, *Freedom's Journal*, in New York.[33]

Hentz had not rested on her (or Horton's) laurels, however. In June she had sent another poem—"Poetry and Music"—to the *Lancaster Gazette*, offered the paper still more verses if they wanted them, and continued to work behind the scenes in Chapel Hill to promote Horton's story and to effect his release.[34] A significant breakthrough came in June, during the University of North Carolina's Commencement celebrations, when Horton's plight was brought to the attention of a member of the school's Committee of Visitation, "proverbial for his philanthropic feelings." An interview with the poet followed, and a month later a substantial essay on Horton appeared in the *Raleigh Register* of North Carolina, courtesy of the "philanthropic gentleman," together with another of Horton's poems: "Lines on the Evening and the Morning."[35] Over the course of the next few months, another five of Horton's poems were printed in the *Register* and several of these, together with the essay on Horton, were reprinted in newspapers and magazines from Tarborough, North Carolina, to Charlestown, Massachusetts.[36] Several of these reprintings were prefaced by tart comments on the injustice of slavery, and, indeed, two poems were written in response to Horton's "Lines on the Evening and the Morning." He had become a cause célèbre.[37]

Measured by modern standards of achievement, Horton's appearance in print would be considered an impressive accomplishment: valuable both as an endorsement of his print-worthiness and for its promise of publicity and attendant support. Within little more than three months, after all, Horton, abetted by unauthorized newspaper and magazine reproduction of his poems, had gone from being an obscure village troubadour, known only to the residents of Chapel Hill and environs, to being something of a national celebrity, heralded in publications across the union. When looked at more closely, however, it becomes apparent that the printing of Horton's verse was a decidedly mixed blessing. While it increased his visibility and helped dramatize the plight of those in slavery, it also had the consequence of interpellating him into new and increasingly less embedded economies than those through which had traditionally worked.[38]

The world into which Horton's words were drawn, to be more specific, was that of charity and charitable economics. It was a contentious field of endeavor. According to Susan M. Ryan, antebellum reformers were divided, in particular, over whether their benevolence should be driven by sentimental or anti-sentimental reactions to suffering and need. Sentimental charity was predicated on the idea that the observation of suffering created a bond of sympathy between victim and observer that was immediate, authentic, and unquestionable. Adherents of the sentimental model of charity tended to trust their feelings for the sufferer and therefore to trust the sufferer also; as a result, they typically sought to bestow largesse upon the victim directly, based on what he or she requested. Sentimental charity was, in other words, a very direct conversion of the symbolic capital of suffering for the economic capital of alms, the exchange being authorized by pity and guaranteed by conviction. Anti-sentimental models of charity, by contrast, were based upon reason and calculation rather than feeling. Reposing considerably less trust in the needy, its advocates tried to discriminate between the 'deserving' and the 'undeserving' poor. Placing considerably less confidence in the deserving poor and especially in their ability to use alms responsibly, they favored 'in kind' charity such as food, firewood, and clothing, rather than money. And favoring deliberative group action over individual initiative, they tended toward increasingly bureaucratized institutions. Theirs was a far more mediated and disembedded economy in which feeling and connection were replaced by calculation and utility.[39]

When Horton appealed, in his poem "Slavery," to "melting Pity, from afar" to "break this vast enormous bar / Between a wretch and thee," he was positioning himself, at least rhetorically, within the sentimental charitable tradition. In seeking the purchase of "a few short days of time," likewise, Horton was also stipulating precisely what he needed on his own terms, namely his freedom. His choice was hardly surprising given how much more intimate and socially framed sentimental charity seemed to be and how much more familiar it must have felt after years in a patronage economy.

Even at its best, charity of this kind was problematic, however, sustaining and reinforcing social inequality. The sorts of connection sentimental charity engendered were more virtual than actual; more imaginative—even imaginary—than substantial; and more rewarding for spectator rather than sufferer, donor rather than recipient. Horton's situation was still further exacerbated, because he was appealing, as he put it, "from afar." When suffering was embodied and embedded in the form of a wretch on one's doorstep it could prove readily fungible: any number of fugitive and former slaves managed to keep body and soul together quite literally by telling and selling their tales of woe from door-to-door. Horton's disembodied appeals, however, meant that while he received sympathy, there was less chance that he would actually receive money.[40]

Horton's position was made still more tenuous, because in time his works were relocated from a sentimental to an anti-sentimental economy of benevolence. The result was that his works were disembedded from their traditional economic frame of reference, leading, quite literally, to a series of dis-locations. These dislocations, as we shall see, ultimately deprived him of control over his words and the contexts in which they were lodged, disrupted the face-to-face and personal situations through which he had previously disseminated his texts, denied him any income from what he had written, and promoted uses of the money surrounding his work that were always beyond his control and rarely in his own or his best interests.

MANUMISSION CAMPAIGNS

Horton's shift from agent of sentimental charity to object of anti-sentimental charity and the concomitant loss of economic control it entailed is seen most dramatically in the overlapping series of campaigns that were initiated in 1828 to secure his freedom and that culminated in the 1829 publication of *The Hope of Liberty*. It is a tortured narrative, full of missteps and deviations, but one that led inexorably to the disembedding of Horton from his poetry. Horton's earliest glimmering of hope was in some respects the least mediated and therefore the most appealing. Central North Carolina was a hotbed of Quaker anti-slavery activity in the 1820s, and by 1826 their state Manumission Society numbered more than a thousand members in forty statewide branches. Horton initially held out what he called a "faint hope" that the Manumission Society would buy and free him, but for reasons that are not clear, the hope was never realized, and his poetic account of the affair speaks somewhat bitterly of "falsely promis'd" happiness that ultimately "gave way."[41] The second effort gained slightly more traction. In response to information from North Carolina that the Committee of Visitation member had written to Horton's owner, James Horton, and had hopes of buying him for a "fair price" in the Fall, *Freedom's Journal* began to solicit donations from its readers to help defray the costs of purchasing the poet, which were estimated to be in the region of four or five hundred dollars. Despite several pleas, however, it appears that *Freedom's Journal* was unable to raise the money.[42]

Just as hope seemed to be fading, however, North Carolina's governor, John Owen, interceded "like a dove" on Horton's behalf and extended his owner, James Horton, what the poet later called "an extraordinary proposition," which was "to pay $100 more than any person of sound judgment should say I was worth." This more than generous offer James Horton refused with a "frown of disdain."[43] Why did James Horton make such a cavalier decision? From a purely monetary point of view, of course, his rejection of Owen's offer makes no sense, especially since he was on record in August 1828 as saying he "might be induced to take a fair price" for his slave once the agricultural season was over.[44] Surely he would have been happy with a *more* than fair price? Although we will never be able to explain the transaction with certainty, it would appear that Horton was a victim of precisely the ethic of generosity that made his acrostics so popular around Chapel Hill. According to cultural historian Kenneth S. Greenberg, white Southerners responded to acts of generosity not only with gratitude but also with suspicion, since to be the recipient of a gift one was unable to return in some form or another placed one in a servile and demeaning position relative to one's benefactor. Indeed, it made one the object of charity. A gift created a debt, and a gentleman always repaid his debts; to be unable to repay a debt put one on the wrong side of the paternalist equation and made one little better than a slave. As Greenberg succinctly puts the matter: "Masters gave; slaves received."[45] A gift, then, was always a potential threat, since its receipt was a veiled challenge to reciprocate. A gift of poetry forged affectionate chains, as Horton put it, but chains were still, after all, chains. It was perfectly acceptable for a young man to give a gift to a single woman to initiate or sustain a courtship, of course, although the refusal of the gift or a failure to reciprocate in some form or another would normally have ended the relationship. It was equally as acceptable for a master to give a gift to a slave, since in so doing the master indicated his superiority over the slave, who could *not* reciprocate. It was even acceptable for one white Southerner to make a gesture of generosity to a presumptive social peer, so long as the recipient was in a position to reciprocate in a timely and dignified manner. What was not acceptable, however, was for one white man to make a gift to another in the knowledge that it could not be returned in the same manner or spirit. This was precisely the problem Horton ran into when he tried to make a gift of his elegy to Caroline Lee Hentz; in offering her something gratuitously, he was putting her in his debt, and, implicitly, suggesting his equality if not superiority to her. Her "handsome" payment for this poem effectively put him back in his place. And it was precisely Governor Owen's generosity that made James Horton so angry, then, for in offering Horton more than a fair price for his slave, Owen placed him in a position of presumptive inferiority, if not outright servitude. Because Horton was a relatively modest landowner, he would doubtless have felt vulnerable, if not utterly condescended to, when treated as an object of charity by the governor of the state, and the only way to retain his honor was to refuse the governor's gift. What Owen intended, perhaps, was a more than fair exchange within a market economy, but it was perceived by James Horton as an insulting attempt to put a price on his manhood and sense of mastery, so he refused the offer and refused it with "disdain." What this unfortunate episode underscores is that acts of exchange are protean and unstable, meaning one thing when viewed from one vantage point and something quite different when viewed from another. A purchase could, potentially, be seen as an affront, a loan, a gift, or as an act charity. George Moses Horton, who, as a slave, was by definition a victim of economics, had now become a victim of meta-economics. After October of 1828, there were no more poems published in the *Raleigh Register* and talk of Horton's emancipation fell silent.[46]

THE HOPE OF LIBERTY

Suddenly, in July 1829, after eight months of silence, and with apparently no fanfare, a small pamphlet was published in Raleigh under Horton's name, with the title *The Hope of Liberty*. The story of its appearance has been told many times and is extremely well known. That offered by Henry Louis Gates, Jr.—arguably the most prolific and influential scholar of African-American literature—is typical. Indeed, Gates has told the story several times. "George Moses Horton's master at North Carolina," he writes in his best-known account, "collected his slave's poems, published them as a book, and then falsely advertised widely in Northern black and antislavery newspapers that all proceeds from the book's sales would be used to purchase Horton's freedom!" In a slightly earlier version, he is still more damning, noting that "His master printed full-page advertisements in Northern newspapers soliciting subscriptions for a book of Horton's poems and promising to exchange the slave's freedom for a sufficient return on sales of the book." In a later version, he adds, further, that the preface to *The Hope of Liberty* prints "his master's name and address" above the preface's pathetic, closing stanza.[47]

Gates offers a dramatic story, to be sure; unfortunately, every single statement in every single version of his account is utterly incorrect. Horton's master had absolutely no hand in the collection, arrangement, editing, printing, publishing, advertising, or sale of *The Hope of Liberty*, nor does his name or address follow the Preface. Indeed, the volume was not advertised in any newspaper, North or South. (Full-page advertisements, in fact, did not appear in America until the mid-1850s.) Moreover, so far from being defrauded of the income associated with the volume, Horton had no claim to it in the first place. Indeed, he, too, had absolutely no hand in the publication of the volume, and there is some question as to whether he was even aware of its publication. Finally, as we shall see, the volume was not actually available for sale at all, by subscription or otherwise.[48]

Gates's account, to do him justice, is built (as I shall show) on earlier scholars' imputations of publishing malfeasance and seems, ultimately, to reflect a misunderstanding of the highly complex authorial economies in which Horton's work was snared by the late 1820s. The true story of *The Hope of Liberty*, it turns out, is at once more distressing and more mundane than any account that has been told until now, and in order to tell it, we need to begin by considering the life and charitable work of the man who did, in fact, publish it: Joseph Gales.

Born in England in 1761 and trained as a printer, Gales was early drawn into the vortex British radicalism. He was a founding member of the Sheffield Constitutional Society, whose views he promoted in his newspaper the *Sheffield Register*; a champion of the French Revolution; a proponent of universal male suffrage; a friend of Thomas Paine, whose *Rights of Man* he printed; and an ardent abolitionist. His activism perhaps reached high tide in 1794, when he organized an outdoor meeting of the "Friends of Justice, Liberty and Humanity" in Sheffield; in front of a crowd of 10,000 and sharing a stage with the West Indian creole, Henry Redhead Yorke, he launched a petition to the King to secure "the total and unconditional emancipation of the Negro slaves." Indicted for conspiracy immediately after, Gales fled England later that year and settled in America, working first in Philadelphia, and after 1799 in Raleigh, North Carolina, where for thirty years he printed and edited the *Raleigh Register*. Gales quickly established himself in his new home; he served repeatedly terms as Intendent of Police, Mayor, and State Printer, Director of the State Bank, Secretary of the Agricultural Society of North Carolina, the Wake Agricultural Society, and Bible Society. After visiting him in 1821, Unitarian minister Samuel Gilman told his wife that "His character is as solid as the hills, and altogether in short there is stampt on every one of his minute actions something, I do not know that it may be called *great*, but certainly uncommon and much to be desired."[49]

But while Gales had been vehemently opposed to slavery while in England, his position shifted once he became settled in the South and he slid toward a position of uncomfortable acquiescence. As his wife, Winifred, recalled in the 1830s, "The idea of purchasing slaves—of trading in the blood and sinews of our fellow-beings, was most revolting to our feelings. With Hazael, we were ready to exclaim 'Is thy servant a Dog, that he should do this thing?' And yet, apparently from necessity, during our residence at Raleigh, we were induced to purchase several, both as House Servants, and to aid us in conducting our Printing, Paper-making, and farming concerns." Gales himself invoked a similar argument, claiming that he could not justify "the practice as being right in itself . . . except on the broad plea of necessity." Indeed, Gales's attitude toward African-Americans was riven with tension. While he believed that slavery was a sin and very likely to lead to national disaster, once he settled in the South, he disavowed abolition; he was supportive of the polymathic black preacher Joseph Chavis, to whose multiracial school in Raleigh many of the white aristocracy sent their children, yet between 1799 and 1820 printed almost two hundred advertisements for runaway slaves, to say nothing of advertising slaves for sale and for exchange; he deplored slavery yet firmly declined to print in his paper an address that had been delivered by the North Carolina Manumission Society, for fear that African-Americans might read it. "I wish with you," he told them, "that an end could be put to Slavery but . . . it must be brought about by slow, but gradual means."[50]

The slow and gradual means Gales had in mind were those propounded by the American Colonization Society (ACS), of which he was a member. Founded in 1816, the ACS was devoted to the voluntary removal of free African-Americans to the African colony of Liberia; indeed, the organization sometimes went by the title the American Society for Colonizing Free People of Colour of the United States. Officially a conservative society opposed to both slavery *and* abolition, the ACS drew together under the colonization banner individuals with very distinct and sometimes clashing agendas and ideologies. For some, colonization was a means of removing a racially inferior and inherently corrupt group from the country; for others, likewise, it was a means of minimizing the possibility that free blacks and slaves would join together in rebellion. On the positive side of the ledger, however, some believed that colonization would see currently debased African-Americans blossom intellectually, socially, and economically and thereby open a means to Christianize Africa and promote stronger transatlantic ties of commerce. And, although it was not part of the organization's original brief, some members believed that the success of the colonization program would lead to progressive manumissions in America and the gradual erosion of the institution of slavery.[51] Gales was apparently of this opinion, and he became actively involved with the ACS almost as soon as an auxiliary was established in Raleigh, serving for many years as its secretary. Both institutionally and ideologically, the ACS exemplified the anti-sentimental strain of benevolence in nineteenth-century America; rather than granting African-Americans agency, it robbed them of it, making them objects of charity and the unwilling beneficiaries of gifts, the terms of which they could not negotiate. Colonizationist ideology and colonizationist institutions would profoundly shape the direction of Horton's first volume of poetry.

That Horton was known to the North Carolina auxiliaries of the American Colonization Society more generally is beyond doubt. Of the fifteen members of the Committee of Visitors who attended the University of North Carolina commencement in 1828, six were members of the society and two more would join the following year; they included the state auxiliary's president and vice president. College President Joseph Caldwell was also a member as were many of the professors of the school. Joseph Gales was, of course, a member. His son Weston was a member, and his son-in-law, William Seaton, was a national manager in Washington. Indeed, both the co-owner and the editor of Gales's political opponents on the *Raleigh Star* were members too. It is not clear if either Caroline Lee Hentz or her husband were members of the auxiliary, although several women were, but Hentz's early mentor and correspondent, Jared Sparks, was, and she and Nicholas were close friends with the Gales family, with whom they shared liberal Christian convictions. By late 1828, it is safe to say, Horton's writing had been drawn into the world of active colonizationists and colonizationist ideology.[52]

The North Carolina auxiliaries had a particular reason to be attracted to Horton, for as Dickson D. Bruce, Jr., has argued, the entire ACS philosophy was predicated on the idea of *voluntary* emigration to Liberia, and the organization actively sought out and promoted African-Americans who would speak on behalf of the cause. They also, as Bruce has shown, crafted texts with fictitious African-American voices through which to ventriloquize their message. In so doing, they simultaneously endowed African-American expression with immense authority while making it impossible for African-Americans to benefit from such authority, or the acts of authorship to which it gave rise, other than on the ACS's terms. Whether or not Horton himself wished to emigrate to Liberia—and this is a difficult question to answer, with evidence both pro and con—he was perceived as a potential ACS spokesperson, and it is clear that *The Hope of Liberty* was framed to make it seem as if this was the case.[53]

This framing began, of course, with the preface, or "Explanation" as it was called, to the Horton volume. Written in all likelihood by either Joseph Gales or his son Weston, it was a clearly colonizationist text. Briefly recapping Horton's life and talents, the author explained that many citizens, "some of whom are elevated in office and literary attainments"—a clear allusion to Governor Owen and President Caldwell—were now "interested in the promotion of his prospects." Their goal was to "obtain by subscription, a sum sufficient for his emancipation, upon the condition of his going in the vessel which shall first afterwards sail for Liberia." "It is upon these terms alone," the author advised, "that the efforts of those who befriend his views are intended to have a final effect." This, surely, was earmarked income. The ACS did not wish simply to free Horton, that is to say; they wished to be free *of* him. Horton's words, once again, were drawn out of any context he might have had in mind—disembed-ded—and placed far beyond his control.[54]

Precisely how far beyond his control Horton's words had moved by 1829 becomes distressingly clear when we consider the poems themselves. Although the "Explanation" claimed that the poems were printed "without correction, that the mind of the reader may be in no uncertainty as to the originality and genuineness of every part," a side-by-side comparison of Horton's newspaper verses and the versions printed in the *Hope of Liberty* reveals that someone—Joseph Gales, or perhaps Caroline Lee Hentz—had carefully but deliberately revised the former to minimize their abolitionist sentiment and instead suggest a colonizationist aesthetic. Consider Horton's most militant poem, "Liberty and Slavery." In the first stanza of the 1828 version, published in the *Lancaster Gazette*, Horton says that he is "Deprived of all created bliss, / Condemned to toil and pain," but in 1829 he is "Deprived of all created bliss, / Through hardship, toil, and pain." The erasure of Horton's having been *condemned* to slavery removes any human agency from his plight—hardship, toil, and pain are now, somewhat tautologically, what cause pain, toil, and hardship—and this grammatical sleight of hand also mutes his own condemnation. Again, in 1828, Horton seeks to "crush" the pain, but in 1829 only to "soothe" it. Lastly, and most strikingly, in 1829, Horton anticipated the admonition to "bid the vassal soar"—a phrase so inspiring it was used as the title of M. A. Richmond's scholarly study of the poet—but in 1828, Horton had actually written "bid the vassal roar," an imperative so different, so much more aggressive, and so unlikely to find the sanction of the ACS, that one can be fairly certain that its alteration was deliberate. It is true, of course, that Horton uses this image elsewhere, the phrase "bid a vassal soar sublime" appearing in a stanza appended to the "Explanation" that comes from Horton's other explicitly bitter poem on slavery, entitled "Slavery," but here, again, an alteration has been made, because in 1828, Horton had written "bid a vassal rise sublime." Again, the rebellious suggestions in roaring and rising have been muted in favor of the more passive image of soaring: a passivity consistent with the message of the ACS. Through the alteration of a word here and a phrase there, Horton had become the exemplary mouthpiece of the colonizationist movement and its charitable aims.[55]

In much the same way that the editing of Horton's poems placed them beyond his semantic control, so the economy through which they were disseminated placed them beyond his financial control. We need here, though, to be extremely careful in reconstructing precisely the economy through which the *Hope of Liberty* passed if we are to avoid the errone-

ous accusations of fraud and theft scholars have usually made. The crucial and slippery phrase that has thrown earlier scholars seems to be the
"Explanation's" claim that the volume would be used to "obtain by subscription, a sum sufficient for his emancipation." The word subscription
needs, in particular, to be placed in context.

Typically, a publisher turned to subscription in order to determine
how many copies of a book he or she could sell, especially if the book
was to be costly, since canvassing the market in this way minimized the
risk entailed in laying out large sums on production. Subscription forms
detailing the cost and content of the volume were circulated; often advertisements with the same information were placed in newspapers and
magazines; and when the requisite number of signatures had been collected from interested parties to offset the cost of production, the book
was printed and sent to subscribers, who in turn sent the publisher their
subscription fees. Any profits that accumulated once the production costs
had been met were typically divided between the publisher and author
and sometimes the subscription agent or agents.[56]

This, however, is *not* the way in which Horton's text was published.
To the extent that one can prove anything negatively, the evidence—or
more correctly the absence of evidence—for such an assertion is overwhelming. Between 2003 and 2007, I read every issue of every North
Carolina newspaper for the period July 1829 through December 1830
held by the American Antiquarian Society, as well as others in North Carolina archives, as well as every publication that had previously published
or referred to Horton; every African-American, abolitionist, colonizationist, and antislavery newspaper and magazine, and many hundreds
of other serials published within the same time-frame. I found no advertisements for, or references to, the 1829 edition of *Hope of Liberty*. After four years of diligent searching, I am fairly confident in asserting that
Horton's volume was *not* advertised. The absence of references to *Hope
of Liberty* is especially striking when one considers the variety of venues
in which Horton's fugitive verse had appeared less than a year earlier and
the rapidity with which the publication could have been promoted had
Gales and Son so chosen to make the text available. Consider: it was not
advertised in Gales's *Raleigh Register* even though he printed the pamphlet and advertised apparently every other text that he printed, nor in
his competitors' *Raleigh Star*, which had reprinted the *Register*'s essay
on Horton the previous year. It was not mentioned, advertised, or reviewed in the *Lancaster Gazette*, the *Genius of Universal Emancipation*,
the *Village Record*, the *Friend*, or the *Bunker-Hill Aurora*, all of which
had printed one or more essay or poem pertaining to Horton the previ-

ous year. There is no sight of Horton's work in *Rights of All* (the successor to *Freedom's Journal*) nor *The Amateur* (successor to *The Bower of
Taste*). Horton is not mentioned in the *National Intelligencer* of Washington, D.C., the nation's newspaper of record, even though it was edited
by Gales's son, Joseph, Jr., and his son-in-law, William Seaton, who was
the national manager of the ACS. Horton's text is likewise absent from
the ACS house journal, the *African Repository*, and, so far as it is possible to determine, from every other printed venue for the years 1829 and
1830.[57]

Why wasn't Horton's work advertised? Why wasn't it reviewed? And
in what sense can it be called a subscription publication? To understand
precisely what subscription meant in 1829, and how it related to Horton's appearance in print, it is useful to consult Noah Webster's *American Dictionary of the English Language*, which had been published just a
year earlier. Here, Webster offers as his third definition of the word subscription "The act of contributing to any undertaking."[58] It is this meaning that the author of the "Explanation" sought to invoke in using the
phrase "obtain by subscription, a sum sufficient for his emancipation."
The Hope of Liberty, that is to say, was not a commercial venture that
was sold by subscription; it was a gratuitous publication, introduced into
an economy of benevolence, in order to solicit contributions ("subscriptions") to a manumission fund. Its economy was a charitable one.

The crucial evidence for such a claim is not simply the use of the word
"subscription" but rather the date of the volume's "Explanation": 2 July
1829. Since at least the early 1820s, the American Colonization Society
had chosen 4 July—Independence Day—as a focal point for its fund-rais-
ing campaigns. The Society encouraged ministers to give colonization-
themed sermons on that day, or on the closest Sunday before or after,
with the expectation that members of the congregation would then give
donations to the Society. Some congregations even had a "Colonization
box" into which the contributions could be placed. Accordingly, the very
same day that Gales and Son penned the text of the "Explanation," they
placed an item in the *Raleigh Register* entitled "Colonization Society,"
asking that the clergymen of North Carolina bring "the claims of this Society to the view of their Congregations on Sunday next, or on the following Sunday, as the Society look to this source, principally . . . to aid
them in sending out a vessel or two this fall with colored free persons and
manumitted slaves to their settlement in Africa." With 4 July falling on
a Saturday in 1829, the ministers of North Carolina were perfectly positioned to develop their colonizationist sermons the following day, when
patriotic fervor would be at almost its highest.[59]

George Moses Horton's *Hope of Liberty*, I want to argue, was not advertised because it was not for sale; it was not reviewed, because relatively few people read it; and it was not mentioned more generally because it was largely an in-house venture. A flimsy pamphlet of twenty-two pages that could have been set up and printed in a matter of hours, *The Hope of Liberty* was produced no more than a day or two before it was gratuitously disseminated, on the 5th and on the 12th of July, to North Carolinian church-goers whose pastors were delivering colonizationist sermons.[60] There was no price on the volume, that is, nor any subscription form circulated, because it wasn't being sold; rather, it was being given away to readers in the hope that they would voluntarily make a "contribution" to Horton's manumission fund, a practice that is now called "front-end prospecting," and which we associate with the receipt of free adhesive address labels and greeting cards from charities and special interest groups. It was a strategy with which Gales was already familiar, for in launching the *Raleigh Register* in 1799, he had given away issues of the paper to create goodwill and create a base of subscribers. The idea was to invite a discretionary contribution that—thanks to the receipt of the volume—would have the feel of an obligatory transaction. It was a pragmatic strategy, situated somewhere between the sentimental and anti-sentimental models of charity. Once again, Horton's work was placed in a context of semi-coerced reciprocity, and once again it was a transaction in which he was not himself involved.[61]

That the venture was not intended to make money for Horton is abundantly clear from the "Explanation" itself, which explained that if the contributions "ultimately prove insufficient, they will be returned to subscribers."[62] Horton's volume, then, was not even a commodity as such, since it could be kept whether it was paid for or not; indeed, it could be kept even if the recipient was reimbursed. Nor was it introduced into a market economy; in fact, it is inconceivable that enough copies of this flimsy pamphlet could *ever* have be sold at market prices to raise the four or five hundred dollars James Horton was expecting for his slave. Horton's volume, rather, was intended to be a token of, and a spur to, benevolence, the expectation being that recipients of the pamphlet would be inspired to make truly substantial contributions toward Horton's manumission. *The Hope of Liberty*, that is, was predicated on the hope of charity.

The dissemination of Horton's volume was thus predicated upon an economy strikingly different from the artisanal economy through which he sold his acrostics. Patronizing though his poetry customers might have been, they paid him directly; the money associated with *The Hope of Liberty* was never intended to go to Horton but, rather, to his master, by way of the ACS. The payment that Horton received for selling his acrostics and love letters took the form of cash and its use was wholly undefined; the payment Horton did *not* receive for *The Hope of Liberty* was specifically earmarked for his manumission and colonization. Lastly, in selling his acrostics, Horton forged relationships with his customers; these relationships were often condescending, sometimes not, but they facilitated an ongoing source of income and goodwill. The publication of *The Hope of Liberty* was a wholly mediated, indeed impersonal, process through which third parties controlled his words, the contexts into which they were introduced, the nature of the economy of which they were a part, and the purposes to which any money associated with them would be applied.

As it turns out, the campaign to free Horton and send him to Liberia was a monumental failure. On 16 July, the *Raleigh Register* reported that "A collection was taken up in the Presbyterian Church of this City, on Sunday last, in aid of the funds of the Colonization Society," but that collection netted only eleven dollars and ninety-two cents on the day of the colonization sermon and an additional three dollars and eight cents were gathered in the following weeks. The Raleigh church's collection was consistent with the generally low contributions made to the ACS throughout North Carolina in the Fall and Winter of 1829, and how much, if any, of this money was earmarked for Horton is in any case questionable.[63] It cost approximately thirty dollars to send a free man to Liberia but ten times that to free him in the first place, which was almost as much as the total donations from North Carolina since July. The simple fact of the matter is that not enough money was raised to either free Horton or send him away.[64]

Part of the blame for the campaign's failure, I think, can be laid at the door of Joseph Gales. One of the most powerful, and certainly the best connected, print entrepreneur in North Carolina, Gales could easily have printed hundreds or even thousands of copies of Horton's pamphlet at very little cost. His experience in printing and selling almanacs and in freely disseminating Bibles through the Bible Society were perfect models for wholesale production, sale, and dissemination. He could have advertised them in his newspaper; he could have written about them in the ACS journal, the *African Repository*; and he could have relied on the newspaper exchange network of which he was a part to have spread news of Horton's accomplishments and of his needs across the nation in very little time. That he did not cannot be ascribed to inept or inappropriate planning; Gales, rather, simply wasn't interested in conducting that sort of campaign. His decision to disseminate Horton's pamphlet only locally and make it available through a charitable economy seems to have been in part a matter of prudence and in part a matter of practicality. As Governor Owen's experience with Horton's owner had made clear, *how* money was accumulated was as important as *how much*, and the terms on which it was offered were as significant as the reason for the offer itself. But more than this, Horton, I believe, simply wasn't considered that important. Over the course of the nineteenth century, North Carolina raised more money for, and sent more free African-Americans to, Liberia than any other state in the Union. Horton was only one man, and his gift for poetry did not elevate him above others, especially those with more practical skills.[65]

Several circumstantial factors also conspired to undermined the possible success of the campaign. One was timing. A Pennsylvania minister writing in 1829 explained to an ACS agent that "the season around the fourth of July calls for more than ordinary exertion in gathering in the harvest, & in consequence of the very general fatigue among my people our church, in that season, is not so well attended." Possibly, then, the agricultural calendar interfered with attempts to gain Horton's cause a hearing. Even if the churchgoers of North Carolina were not worn down by harvesting, they were bedeviled with apathy. Writing from Raleigh in August 1829 to send along the eleven dollars and ninety-two cents he had collected after his Independence Day sermon, Presbyterian minister Thomas P. Hunt told the ACS national secretary Ralph Gurley that the Society had "many nominal friends here" but that it was "difficult to get them to act." A third reason was more dramatic. Writing in September 1829, Hunt informed Gurley that he had been "just on the verge of recovering the Society, when an alarm was given that the slaves had become restive in this place, and had organized an insurrection, conceived and drilled by one of the most intelligent free blacks in this place." Although the rumors of insurrection seemed to be just that—mere rumors—whatever money might still have been collected for Horton at this point likely dried up. Nor, finally, could Horton look for assistance from the national organization, for in late 1829 the ACS found itself for the first time in debt from "the expeditions of the previous two years," which consequently "denied them the ability to aid in the removal of emigrants to an extent at all commensurate with their wishes or hopes."[66] Eventually, the campaign to free Horton ran out not only of money and motivation but also out of time. In early January 1830, the ACS brig *Liberia* left Norfolk, Virginia, with approximately one hundred and fifty free blacks on board, destination Monrovia. For better or worse, Horton was not among them. He had, quite literally, missed the boat.[67]

TAKING LIBERTIES

Visiting Raleigh in March 1830, the feisty travel writer Ann Royall recalled being shown a copy of *Hope of Liberty* by a young man working
in the office of the Secretary of State, and offered a brief account just a
few months later in her book, *Mrs. Royall's Southern Tour.*[68] It was the
first national news of Horton's volume, and it would be the last for seven
years. By the time Royall's book appeared, North Carolina was in a state
of lockdown after copies of an inflammatory pamphlet entitled *Walker's Appeal, in Four Articles, Together with a Preamble to the Colored
Citizens of the World* were discovered in various port towns around the
state. Its author was David Walker, who had served as a Massachusetts
agent for the *Freedom Journal's* aborted campaign to purchase Horton's
freedom in 1828. Walker's pamphlet was a frankly incendiary call for insurrection and contained the most sustained and bitter attack on colonization ever to see print. A series of frantic letters between various mag-
istrates and Governor Owen led to a statewide investigation, and in December 1830 the general assembly passed a bill making it illegal to teach
slaves either to read or write and levying harsh penalties for anyone circulating material "the evident tendency whereof would be to excite insurrection, conspiracy, or resistance in the slaves of free Negroes." While
Horton's pamphlet could hardly be considered insurrectionary by any
stretch of the imagination, the Walker scare—and his connection to the
manumission campaign—created a chilling environment for the poet.[69]

Shortly thereafter, Horton's support network began to fall apart. Nicholas and Caroline Lee Hentz left Chapel Hill for Kentucky in June 1831.
In August 1831, Nat Turner's slave uprising in Southampton County,
Virginia, led to widespread panic throughout the Carolinas and a backlash against African-Americans. At the University of North Carolina,
President Joseph Caldwell and a number of students petitioned the governor to be armed against possible slave insurrection. Joseph Gales, for
his part, published a number of inflammatory reports of slave conspira-
cies in Raleigh that turned out to be groundless. He himself left the state
in 1833. Turner's rebellion, together with Walker's earlier *Appeal*, essentially crushed all sympathy for literate or literary African-Americans in
North Carolina.[70] Horton would not appear in print in the South for another six years.

Yet Horton's work had a curious textual afterlife. In 1837, a new edition of *The Hope of Liberty* appeared in Philadelphia under the title *Poems by a Slave*, after abolitionist Joshua Coffin chanced across a stray

copy and passed it on to publishers Merrihew and Gunn. Where Gales and Son had undertaken a remarkably low-key dissemination campaign, Merrihew and Gunn adopted an aggressive stance, selling the work out of the American Anti-Slavery Society office at six cents per copy, fifty cents for a dozen, and three dollars and fifty cents for one hundred.[71] There was some drama to the publication, too, for as Lewis Gunn explained in his brief preface, it was not at all clear from the original text whether or not Horton had ever received his freedom. Because this preface has been so wholly and consistently misread, I offer it here in its entirety:

Of these poems, the present publisher has never seen or heard of but one copy, which was recently obtained by JOSHUA COFFIN, of this city, from a gentleman who met with it in Cincinnati a few years ago. The pamphlet is republished, without any alterations,—even verbal; except the insertion of the headline, "Poems by a slave," over the pages, and the omission of the title page, which ran as follows:

"The Hope of Liberty, containing a number of poetical pieces. By George M. Horton. Raleigh, printed by Gales & Son, 1829."

Observe 1st, That Gales, the printer of the pamphlet, is now one of the firm of Gales & Seaton, at Washington,—*no abolitionist.* 2nd, The publisher admits slavery to be "the lowest possible condition of human nature;" and that the slaves are not all happy, for George "felt deeply and sensitively." 3d, the man who could write such poems was kept for 32 years in "the lowest possible condition of human nature," and was to remain there if he would not consent to go to Liberia.

Whether the poems sold for sufficient to buy this man, so Dangerous to "Southern Institutions," and to export him, I have not been able to ascertain. Perhaps George is still a slave!

L.C.G.
Philadelphia, September, 1837[72]

Curious to find out whether Horton was, in fact, still in bondage, Coffin wrote to Joseph Gales, Jr., in Washington, D.C., whom he believed to have been the publisher. (Joseph, Jr. was the publisher's son but had lived in Washington since 1807, and had had no hand in the publication of Horton's work.) The response Coffin received and which he summarized in a letter to Merrihew and Gunn, the publishers considered so important that they had it printed on a slip of paper and tipped into all the remaining copies of the edition. In it, Coffin explained that he had written to Gales, Jr., "to ascertain the present condition of *George M. Horton.* He informs me that he is still the slave of James Horton. . . . It is understood by Mr. G. that he did not derive much pecuniary profit from the publication of his poems; and that since the death of his patron, the late Dr. Caldwell, President of the University, he has attended to other occupations."[73] Although the use of pronouns here renders the passage some-what oblique, what it appears to say is that Gales, Jr., believes that Hor-ton did not receive much money as a consequence of the publishing cam-paign. This is hardly surprising given that very little money was raised in the first place and none of it was meant to have been given to Horton anyhow but only used to secure his manumission and passage to Libe-ria.

Somehow or other, modern scholars have managed to read into Gunn's preface and Coffin's summary of Gales, Jr.'s letter a suggestion that Hor-ton had been defrauded of his rightful income. The first to make such a claim seems to have been critic Vernon Loggins. Writing in 1931, he claims that Gunn "hinted that the money realized from the sale of the original edition was kept by the North Carolina publisher, Weston R. Gales, for his own use" and that "Gales ignored the hint in his reply, and merely stated that the amount obtained from the sale of the book was not sufficient for the purpose for which it was intended."[74] Of course, no such hint was ever offered in Gunn's preface, Weston Gales was never written to by either Gunn or Coffin, and Joseph Gales, Jr., who did re-ceive a letter from Coffin appears to have made no allusion to accusa-tions of impropriety one way or the other, although we have only Cof-fin's summary to go by. Loggins's accusation nonetheless quickly caught on and was repeated by J. Saunders Redding in 1939: "It is not known who inspired the editor's hint in the preface . . . that Weston Gales had retained the money realized from the Raleigh printing, but an impartial judgment of Horton's later character makes one believe it was very likely Horton himself."[75] Again, one strains to understand such a construction, since it would require Gunn to have been in touch with Horton, while the preface makes it abundantly clear that Gunn knew nothing of Horton personally. Redding's supposition came, in turn, to be Blyden Jackson's certitude, and in a 1976 essay on Horton he refers to "the bitterness of his recriminations against the publishers of *The Hope of Liberty*, who he accused of diverting to their own use the money made from the book."[76] When Henry Louis Gates, Jr., claimed, a decade later, that Horton's own-er had arranged the publication of *The Hope of Liberty* and placed full-page advertisements in Northern newspapers, then, he was entirely in er-ror but was simply embellishing a misconstruction that had been in cir-culation for almost half a century.

In fact, whether he knew it or not, Loggins himself was not the first to create fictions about Horton. That honor goes to Caroline Lee Hentz herself, who in 1833 published her first novel, *Lovell's Folly*, in Cincinnati. Here, Hentz introduced a slave poet named George, based, according to her own footnote, on Horton. Hentz included several of his otherwise unprinted poems, altered only minor biographical details in her description, but, significantly, rewarded *her* George with "a freedom" which the slave on whom he was based had "little hope of enjoying." Hentz's prediction proved accurate. Although another volume of poetry appeared in 1845, Horton was to remain a slave until the Emancipation Proclamation was issued some three decades later.[77] In December 1866, some thirty-seven years after the first publication of *The Hope of Liberty*, George Moses Horton finally left America for Liberia.[78]

OTHER BARDS, OTHER MARKETS

Literature, writes Richard Brodhead, "has been differentially available throughout its history: available on some terms at some periods to some figures and groups of figures, but available on other terms—including not at all—to others." The terms on which literature, and specifically authorship, were available to George Moses Horton, as a North Carolinian slave in the 1820s, were defined by two starkly contrasting modes of exchange: the unregulated shadow economy of Chapel Hill, peopled by students, and the thoroughly regulated charitable economy of Raleigh, orchestrated by patrons like Joseph Gales and John Owen. These two modes, of course, or ones like them, were hardly unique to North Carolina. And at the same time, the world through which Horton moved in 1820s North Carolina was hardly the site of these two economies alone, but, rather, was the meeting point of many others, both material, symbolic, and cultural, of which Horton himself might perhaps have been aware. An investigation of the varying cultures and economies of letters in the 1820s can therefore be pursued along two distinct but intersecting axes. Consideration of the extent to which others participated in patronal, unregulated, and illicit authorial economies, on the one hand, helps illustrate the fact that Horton was by no means aberrant or unique in what he wrote or how he chose (or was compelled) to sell it. Consideration, on the other, of the opportunities afforded those like Hentz and Gales through their own "cultures of letters" and the economies they engendered are equally valuable, for they underscore the existence of multiple worlds of letters and illustrate Brodhead's contention that "writing arose in differently organized (if adjacent) literary social worlds, in differently structured cultural settings composed around writing and regulating its social life."[79] In a nutshell, an exploration of the first helps consolidate and recontextualize our insights into Horton, while an exploration of the last will outline the agenda for the remaining chapters of the book. A brief look at each, then, as a way of looking ahead.

In the first place, then, it is worth noting that Horton was by no means the only author to engage in a patronage economy in the early national or antebellum periods, although not all clients were seen, as he was, through the lens of paternalism. Innumerable authors sought the support of powerful patrons—often those connected to political parties—in order to gain payment, employment, or simply endorsement as authors. The best-known example, of course, is Nathaniel Hawthorne, who between 1839 and 1841 held the position of Measurer of Salt and Coal in the Boston Custom House, and between 1846 and 1849 served as a surveyor in the Salem Custom House. When Zachary Taylor (a Whig) was inaugurated as president in 1849, Hawthorne (a lifelong Democrat) was immediately ousted from his Salem job and replaced by a Whig appointee. In the ensuing controversy, some claimed Hawthorne had received his job only because of his political loyalties, others that it was given to him as a "compliment to letters and genius"; what everyone seemed to agree upon, however, was that his position had been bestowed as an act of patronage. Scores of authors—among them Washington Irving, James Kirke Paulding, George Bancroft, Robert Walsh, and Samuel Griswold Goodrich held government sinecures, while others, such as Edgar Allan Poe sought them without success.[80] Beyond the realm of politics, authors turned to dedications to curry favor with those in power, as when, for example, John Pendleton Kennedy dedicated his novel *Swallow Barn* (1832) to his political and literary mentor William Wirt, or George Lippard his *Herbert Tracy* (1844) to James Fenimore Cooper, from whom he sought favors. Even Caroline Lee Hentz practiced a little literary flattery herself, dedicating *Lovell's Folly* to Jared Sparks, whose friendship she had renewed and cultivated assiduously in the early 1830s in the hopes of securing her husband a new teaching job in the North.[81]

Perhaps the most striking and strikingly literal example of a patronage relationship, however, was that which developed between Timothy Dexter and Jonathan Plummer. Dexter was an eccentric and barely literate leather dresser who had speculated his way to an immense and unlikely fortune in the 1780s; by 1793, he was the fourth wealthiest man in Newburyport, Massachusetts, with property valued at almost forty-five thousand dollars. Desperate for distinction as well as wealth, he reinvented himself as 'Lord' Timothy Dexter, and adopted Plummer, an itinerant peddler and jack of all trades with a penchant for poetry, as his literary client. Almost as eccentric as Dexter, Plummer was nonetheless extraordinarily shrewd; seeing that Dexter was acting the role of the aristocrat, Plummer assumed the part of the humble courtier and began to publish poems and letters praising this "wise and wealthy citizen." By 1796, Plummer was serving as Dexter's "Poet Laureat," a role he played to the hilt.[82] The similarities with Horton are abundant. Just as Horton received not only money but also clothes as payment from his patrons, so Dexter not only paid his laureate with cash but also promised him a "suit of clothes to the tune of 20 dollars," which even became the subject of one of his poems. Again, in much the same way that Horton's various clients plied him with reading material, so Plummer recalled receiving a variety of books. And just as Horton, like any good client, thanked his benefactors in print and by name, so did Plummer. Although at least one of the poems penned to Dexter was printed in a Newburyport newspaper under the heading "humorous," it is clear that Plummer himself took their relationship seriously to the extent that it was an important source of income.[83]

Plummer's career parallels Horton's in other ways, moreover, since he not only served as faux-laureate to Dexter but also, like Horton, carried on a customized poetry business, offering "Love letters in prose and verse . . . on shortest notice." Like Horton, Plummer hawked his poems in person, often in the market square in Newburyport, where he was a common sight with his basket full of "Spectacles, Combs, Verses, Books, Fruit, Almanacs, & c."[84] Indeed, the example of Plummer helps to underscore that while George Moses Horton's engagement in an artisanal mode of production and his participation in an authorial shadow economy are examples of fascinating phenomena and almost wholly unexploited by American literary historians, they were by no means unique to Horton alone. Artisanal authorship, in fact, was especially common among early national and antebellum printers' apprentices, who, like slaves, did not receive payment for their regular labor and were thus compelled to work off the books with private clients to accumulate sources of cash.[85] As a printer's apprentice in the 1790s, for example, Samuel Woodworth developed a customized literary operation strikingly similar to that run by Horton. "I was . . . frequently employed," he recalled,

by timid or unlettered suitors, who had not sufficient confidence to venture a verbal declaration, to write their sonnets and love-letters, and to furnish them with acrostics on the names of their mistresses. As such services were always contracted for in confidence, and executed under a strict injunction of secresy, I considered them as "cash jobs," and often found them very convenient in recruiting an exhausted exchequer.[86]

The printer-poet Robert Stevenson Coffin also recalled writing verse to order and described mixed payments of money and clothes almost identical to those received by Horton, receiving on one occasion "a very handsome present, consisting of various articles of clothing, of which I was in great need, and ten dollars in money."[87] Yet the artisanal operations of Woodworth, Plummer, and Coffin pale in comparison with that of John Lofland, the "Milford Bard," who was active from the 1820s through the 1840s. An affable but helpless opium addict who had been expelled from medical school and was therefore unable to practice as a physician, Lofland advertised in Delaware newspapers that he would:

write for any person in Wilmington or the United States, on any subject connected with literature. Lectures and Orations on any subject, from $5 to $10, according to length; Sentimental Letters, $3; Inscriptions for Tombs, from $3 to $5; Medical Theses, $20; Pieces for Declamation, $3; Sentimental Tales, from $5 to $10; Essays, from $3 to $5; Addresses on presenting presents, $5; Advertisements from $1 to $5; Songs—Sentimental, Patriotic or Comic, $3; Acrostics, $1; Poetical Addresses to Ladies, New Year's Addresses, $5; and Poetry for Albums, & c., & c., 5 cents per line.

Lofland, in fact, did a roaring trade in catering to the needs of specific customers, confiding to his mother that in one week alone, in addition to penning a pamphlet, he also wrote "a number of other things, among which was a News Carriers' New Year Address—$10 for 200 lines; also a puff on Brother Maffitt, $2. Also a love letter, $3. [And] An Acrostic, $1."[88] Yet Lofland did not always thrive, and when he was otherwise unable to feed his addictions, according to John Hill Hewitt, he would "demean himself by going into low groggeries, and writing off a few stanzas on any subject the barkeeper might suggest, for a taste of the liquid fire." Other authors engaged in artisanal exchange even when they did not customize their wares; in the 1820s, William 'Pop' Emmons delivered a rousing speech from his beverage stand on Boston Common but also kept printed copies which he sold to his customers with their drinks.[89]

In all of these cases, then, we see examples of an entrenched tradition of artisanal, and often performative, authorship comparable to that engaged in by Horton. For Lofland, Plummer, Clarke, Coffin, Woodworth, and even Emmons, as for Horton, printedness, which for many was a token of authority, functioned instead as an unwelcome mediating institution, entailing economic overheads, and interposing the monitory presence of others, both institutional and individual; the freest authorial transactions, in every sense of the word, were those that disavowed printedness altogether in favor of the handwritten or even the spoken word, delivered directly to the paying customer.[90] Thus, Plummer kept body and soul together not only by flattering Lord Timothy Dexter, or by selling his poems directly to more common buyers in the Newburyport marketplace, but also by "reciting" for a fee, "selections of prose and poetry taken from his favourite authors."[91]

Such activities as these, while unmediated and unsupervised, were at the very least legitimate: examples, as it were, of what John Benson has called "penny capitalism."[92] Yet in much the same way as Horton's "artisan" mode of literary exchange was, at the same time, located on the wrong side of the legal divide, so other authors participated in creative activity that bordered on, or crossed over into, *de jure* criminality. Ironically, given the propensity of artisanal and otherwise marginal literary producers to eschew the printed word, the most habitual participants of the shadow literary economy were, again, apprentice printers. Denied a salary, and, sometimes, ruthlessly economically exploited by their masters, apprentices with literary inclinations took their revenge by participating in systematic acts of literary pilferage, typically by surreptitiously printing their own works for sale on their masters' presses, using their masters' ink and paper, but without their masters' knowledge or permission. Novelist and former printer's apprentice George Thompson, for example, recalled how, "prompted by gingerbread and ambition, and being moreover aided and abetted by another printer's devil, I, one Sunday morning, entered the printing office . . . and assisted by my companion, set up and worked off one hundred copies of a very diminutive periodical just six inches square. . . . This extensive newspaper we issued on three successive Sundays, circulating it among our juvenile friends at the moderate rate of one cent a copy."[93] While Thompson's memoirs are notoriously unreliable, no such questions of factual accuracy attach to the diary of Joel Munsell, who as a printer's apprentice in 1828 recorded that he and his companions were "engaged in printing some little thing for our amusement, & had to do it after our days work was over." It is likely that the 'little things' engaged in by apprentices or journeymen sometimes included pornography for sale through the shadow economy.[94] Of course, these activities were not illegal in the same way that Horton's were; the dimensions of shadow economic activity are neither historically fixed nor inherently constrained. Anything that takes place outside the bounds of a given society's sanctions can constitute shadow economic behavior.[95] Horton's illegitimacy lay in his selling without sanction, while Thompson and Munsell were guilty of taking without sanction, a form of literary pilferage. If we have failed to take cognizance of any shadow literary activities in antebellum America, it is in part a consequence of the fact that such activities were always conducted surreptitiously and left few recorded traces except when the perpetrators were caught. In part, too, it is a consequence of our obsession with professionalism, which precludes even looking for such activities.[96]

It will doubtless come as less of a surprise that many other authors in the nineteenth century either engaged with, or were drawn into, charitable economies. Yet even here instructive parallels with, and divergences from, the example of Horton can be adduced. Consider, for example, Helen DeKroyft who famously "became a bride, a widow, and *blind*, within a single month." Just as Horton relied on students to write down his poems, so DeKroyft—deprived of her sight—was compelled to turn to others to commit her thoughts to paper, relying on a series of amanuenses to pen her letters. Just as Horton found an early benefactor in Governor Caldwell, so DeKroyft was assisted by Senator Backus of Rochester, New York, who helped the indigent widow find temporary housing at the New York Institution for the Blind. Just as Horton's supporters believed that he had to be moved to a new location fitting his station (Liberia), so DeKroyft's benefactors likewise sought for her "a little cottage and a little plot." Just as for Horton this relocation was to be effected through the gathering and publication of his fugitive 'writings,' so it was for DeKroyft whose volume, *A Place in the Memory*, was published in 1849. And just as Horton's work was offered through, and framed within, a charitable economy that transcended the exigencies and axiologies of a market economy, so was DeKroyft's, with one reviewer writing that "those who purchase it, will not only obtain the full value of their money . . . but will do a substantial kindness to one worthy of their regard, and in need of their kindness."[97]

Yet here the similarities end. The campaign to disseminate Horton's volume and raise money for his manumission was, as we have seen, entirely the work of others; the result was that Horton was wholly disembedded from the economic transactions calculated to benefit him. Helen DeKroyft, by contrast, was intimately involved in the production and dissemination of her work, which she promoted before it was published by soliciting subscriptions in person. Indeed, not only did she collect the names of her subscribers, but she also requested that they "pay me in advance." Once the text was published, DeKroyft embarked on a series of promotional tours, traveling as far south as Charleston, South Carolina. Where the experience of participating—or more precisely of not participating—in a charitable economy had robbed Horton of control over his words, their contexts, or the money they elicited, it offered DeKroyft symbolic and economic capital in abundance.[98]

The moral to take away from such a comparison might simply be that we cannot assume solely from the presence (or absence) of a given economy that any specific configuration of subject positions or outcomes will emerge. Indeed, this is precisely why the remaining chapters of the book are organized around economies rather than around specific authors, canonical or otherwise. It is only by exploring the various configurations and permutations an authorial economy could take that we are able to understand the specific dimensions they assumed for any given individual. In the next chapter, we turn to the economy through which so many of Horton's poems were passed, but through in which he rarely participated himself: the economy of gift exchange.

CHAPTER THREE

Authorship and Gift Exchange

⁓

In late 1835, with a firm avowal of friendship and much flattery, Daniel Pierce Thompson sent a copy of his new novel, *May Martin, or The Money Diggers*, to newspaper editor and fellow-novelist John Neal. Thompson's present might at first have seemed like a gesture of genuine goodwill, and perhaps it was, but as the covering letter made clear, it was also propelled by somewhat less than benevolent motives. Confessing that his gift was "partly selfish," Thompson explained that he had made it for promotional reasons, "for we wish for a puff enough to blow it into such notice as may make sale of a few dozen copies which the bearer of this will deposit with your principal booksellers." This, then, was a gift with strings attached; its receipt in good faith was contingent upon something in return: in this case, a superlative review, or "puff." As such, it seemed somewhat more, and therefore also a good deal less, than a true gift.[1]

But what is a true gift? A common-sense, if somewhat long-winded, definition might be that it is a thing of value, bestowed freely and unilaterally upon another of equal social status, given from feelings of esteem and goodwill, and presented with no conscious expectation or explicit demand for repayment.[2] By these criteria, Thompson's gift fell short. *May Martin* was a thing of monetary value, to be sure, and it was given to Neal outside of an explicitly commercial context, but beyond that, there is little that conforms to the true gift paradigm. While Thompson addressed his letter to "Friend Neal," for example, the two were barely acquainted and certainly not friends. His present, moreover, was motivated less by esteem or goodwill toward Neal (although Thompson did admire him), than it was a manifestation of shrewd business instincts. And his expectation of repayment in the form of a solid review or puff was both conscious and explicit. Whatever else it was, then, Thompson's book would seem not to be a true gift, at least by the common-sense

definition, and so it is perhaps fitting that Neal appeared not to have responded with either a letter or a review.[3]

Perhaps better examples of the true literary gift can be found elsewhere. In 1843, for example, Emily Chubbuck—better known to the
world as Fanny Forrester—sent her friend and sometime mentor Urania Nott, a copy of her newest novel, *Allen Lucas: The Self-Made Man.*
" 'The Self-Made Man' made his appearance yesterday," she wrote, "and
I inclose you a copy. You must wink as you read, but I shall not trouble
myself about that; you have seen the like a time or two before, and would
not undertake to read with your eyes open. I should feel complimented
by some of the little newspaper puffs if I did not happen to know that
the writers of them could not have read the book. So if you see them, estimate them at their proper worth."[4] The contrast with Thompson's letter to Neal is striking. Where Thompson quite explicitly asks for a return
on his gift, Chubbuck does not; where Thompson places great stock in
puffs, Chubbuck discounts them entirely; where Thompson seems quite
proud of his work, Chubbuck is self-deprecating; where Thompson had
no connection to Neal, Chubbuck does, for Nott is her closest friend; and
where Thompson's letter is a studied piece, Chubbuck's is mostly chat-
ty. Even the titles of the books bestowed by Thompson and Chubbuck
seem appropriately and revealingly contrastive, for while Thompson's is
about money digging, Chubbuck's celebrates self-sufficiency. In a nutshell, Thompson's book seems to be a manipulative present, but Chubbuck's appears to be a true gift.

To the extent that they have considered authorial exchange practices
outside the commercialized marketplace, literary scholars have been especially strongly drawn to the sort of (true) gift bestowal made by Chubbuck. The theories of Lewis Hyde have been particularly influential in
pushing critical scrutiny in this direction, for he has argued that there is
an inextricable connection between literature and gift exchange. Works
of art, according to Hyde, are in a very fundamental sense gifts given *to*
the author: the products of that vital creative spirit which we sometimes
refer to as giftedness. That spirit can either be honored or debased: honored, when works are given away freely (or at least fairly), or debased
when they are treated as commodities and sold calculatingly to maximize
profit. (Thompson, according to this argument, debased his gift by treating his books as bargaining chips, while Chubbuck, by contrast, honored
hers by giving her works as tokens of esteem.) The choices authors make
in disposing of their works, according to Hyde, have profound consequences. Gifts are dynamic, free, embracing, and spiritually rich, while
commodities are static, costly, isolating, and spiritually impoverishing.

To treat one's gift *as* a gift is to create a generous and genuine community of the imagination, but to commodify it is not only to cut off art from its source but to cut off authors from readers.[5]

This is not a new idea of course. Antebellum author Lydia Sigourney had something very similar in mind when she wrote to James Hillhouse in 1837, soliciting gratuitous contributions for a literary annual she was editing. "The high authority of the injunction to 'covet earnestly the best gifts,'" she wrote, "induces me to venture on the liberty of soliciting from the author of 'Percy' and 'Hadad,' a short poem for an Annual, whose literary character I am anxious to elevate." Translation: God has given you a great literary gift, and you should honor this by making a gift of your work to my anthology. "I ought to mention," she added, as if to make the propriety of her request clearer, "that the Souvenir for whose benefit I make this application, is of a religious character."[6] Further translation: I shall honor your gift in turn by using it solely in a religious annual suitable for gift-giving. For Sigourney, as for Hyde, then, the gift is something whose value remains valuable only so long as it passes from hand to hand. Hyde, of course, is no Sigourney, and his concept of "anarchist property" is light years from her Protestant benevolist impulse, but both share a strong conviction that gifts and commodities are qualitatively distinct and that gifts are ethically and spiritually superior. Hyde's ideas in our time—like Sigourney's in hers—have proved to be immensely appealing to critics, who see in the idea of the true gift an antidote to everything they find crass and soulless about the marketplace, and scholars interested in oppositional authorial economics have often written as if such higher values can be found in the practice of literary gift-giving.[7]

Yet a closer look at the ideology of the true gift is warranted. Since the publication of Marcel Mauss's seminal essay on the subject in 1925, scholars working in the fields of anthropology, sociology, and cultural studies have come to believe that the common-sense definition of gift, or "true gift," giving will not stand up to either philosophical or historical scrutiny.[8] In the first place, they argue, and no matter how sincerely given, gifts are hardly unilateral. Recipients tend to respond with gratitude, thanks, and ultimately gifts of their own; indeed, even to recognize a gift *as* a gift, according to Jacques Derrida, is in some sense to have given something back to the donor. A gift given, in other words, is always part of an exchange.[9] Second, because gifts tend to be situated in exchange economies, they are somewhat less free than they might otherwise appear. To receive a present is to be drawn into a relationship freighted with expectations to reciprocate. Gifts both create and sustain bonds, that is, and in this respect, gift-giving is both an embedded and an embedding economy. Third, the sense of gratitude and indebtedness one intends to conjure up in bestowing a gift can, under some circumstances, be experienced as resentment and obligation, so that while a gift can be given out of goodwill and esteem, it can also be given to manipulate or be received with suspicion. Not all embedding, after all, is benevolent.[10] And lastly, while calculation and expectation of repayment are rarely explicit, or at least rarely as explicit as in the case of Thompson, they are always present in unstated or in only partially conscious fashion. These insights and others like them tend to fly in the face of work by Hyde, who chooses to ignore "gifts that leave an oppressive sense of obligation, gifts that manipulate or humiliate, gifts that establish and maintain hierarchies, and so forth and so on."[11] For Hyde, there is no such thing as a bad gift, only gifts given or received badly.

So does this mean that Lewis Hyde is wrong and that the anthropologists are right? That Thompson's gift was more honest than Chubbuck's? Not precisely. The "full truth of the gift," according to Pierre Bourdieu, lies neither in insisting on its generosity (as per Hyde) nor in exposing its duplicity (as per Mauss) but rather in accepting the validity and intertwinedness of each. As Thompson put it in his letter to Neal, a gift could be "partly selfish." Experientially, that is, gifts *feel* free; objectively, they are not; and each is, in a different but important sense, 'true.' Indeed, the very definition of the gift, according Bourdieu, boils down to the fact that it is an object that hides its economic nature yet relies upon it. The gift, that is, entails a tense dialectic of gratuity and calculation: it is generous yet interested, free but costly, and discrete yet entangling. What makes the contradictions within the gift tenable, according to Bourdieu, is the variety of objects that can become gifts and the interval of time that passes between their bestowal and reciprocation. An effective counter-gift, he argues, must always be *"deferred* and *different"* from the gift to which it responds. If the counter-gift is not different, it will seem like a swap or a loan, and if it is not deferred, it will seem like a repayment. The open-ended measure of time that passes between gifts and counter-gifts allows them to be experienced as free, even while when viewed after the fact they can be seen not to be.

The ever-present but never-mentioned element of calculation at the heart of gift exchanges also helps to explain their dynamic nature. As scholars have often noted, gift transactions differ from commodity transactions in the social entanglements they engender. An exchange of commodities for money leaves one free of entanglement, inasmuch as once paid for, the transaction ends in economic equilibrium and entails no loose ends or lingering obligations. An exchange of gift for gift, by contrast, creates a pattern of "alternating disequilibrium": A gives a gift to B, leaving B in debt; B returns a gift which, in order to be experienced as a gift, now creates a feeling of indebtedness in A, thereby initiating another cycle of prestation. It is this very disequilibrium, anthropologists argue, that turns the giving and receipt of gifts into so powerfully embedding an economy. It was a phenomenon that William Gilmore Simms found galling, noting to a friend that an editor "forgets all my free contributions of previous years . . . because I do not continue to give." Gifts may be given freely, that is, but one can never be free of them, or at least not without severing social bonds and saying what should never be said. "No one is really unaware of the logic of exchange," writes Bourdieu of gift-giving, "but no one fails to comply with the rule of the game which is to act as if one did not know the rule."[12]

We can get a clear sense of precisely how complex and potentially entangling the giving and receiving of gifts actually was by turning once again to Daniel Pierce Thompson, who seemed to make a habit of giving openly manipulative and socially inappropriate gifts, having apparently learned nothing from his transaction with John Neal. In 1839, for example, he wrote to the poet Henry Wadsworth Longfellow, explaining that he had "received, on its publication, a gratis copy" of Longfellow's *Outre Mer* from the author's sister Anne Longfellow Pierce, and that while he had "partially reciprocated" Pierce, he wished also to show his gratitude to Longfellow also by sending him a copy of his own newest work, *The Green Mountain Boys*. As in his dealings with Neal four years earlier, however, this gift was less straightforward than it initially seemed. Conceding that "gratitude, to be honest about it, is not my only motive in doing this," he went on to explain that he wished Longfellow to write a review of his novel, "for the next North American, or such other journal as you shall choose."[13]

Thompson's approach to Longfellow was a clever piece of social theater. Although they were distantly related—Thompson's cousin, George Washington Pierce, had married Longfellow's sister Ann in 1832—Thompson had never met Longfellow and had no direct claim on his goodwill. At a loss for any preexisting connection, Thompson invented one in the form of his own indebtedness to Longfellow for the copy of *Outre Mer*. It was a flimsy enough pretense, especially since the gift had not been from Longfellow himself but from his sister, and had been given four years earlier, in 1835. Its flimsiness is still further underscored when we know that Thompson had been plotting to give Longfellow a copy of his book as early as October 1838, before he had even finished writing it, and more than a year before it appeared in print. The claim of indebtedness was highly expedient, however, for it allowed Thompson to make good on the situation with a gift of his own, which he hoped would give momentum to the endless see-saw of reciprocal disequilibrium that characterized a healthy, ongoing gift relationship. By pretending to be in debt to Longfellow that is, he hoped that he would be able to draw Longfellow into a feeling of indebtedness to him and so reward him with the puff he so badly wanted.[14]

Longfellow's response helps illuminate the delicate dance of gratitude and obligation, silence and speech, that the giving of gifts entails. He began by thanking Thompson for his gift, noted that he had skimmed a few chapters, and admitted that he had not read much or closely. He then proceeded, politely but firmly, to decline reviewing Thompson's novel, explaining that once he had become an author he felt "exceedingly unwilling to play the part of critic." He admonished Thompson, in fact, and advised him to be less needy and less dependent on the approval of others. And he concluded by informing Thompson that he would have a copy of his own forthcoming volume, *Voices of the Night*, sent to him as soon as it was published.[15]

As an example of epistolary politeness, Longfellow's letter was unremarkable; as a model for negotiating the treacherous shoals of gift exchange, it was superb. Over and over, Longfellow managed to walk a fine line between the obligations of indebtedness and the desire to be free of those debts. Thus Longfellow claimed to have read enough of Thompson's novel to show the appropriate interest, but not so much as to be beholden to the author. He showed firmness in declining to review Thompson's work but kindness in suggesting that Thompson didn't really need reviews as much as he thought he did. And, his coup de grace, he responded to Thompson's "gift" with a "gift" of his own, the implication being that the accounts were now fairly balanced and no further claims could be made on his time or goodwill. Thompson's "gift," of course, had been an attempt to create a relationship based on alternating disequilibrium, albeit in a somewhat clumsy and manipulative way; Longfellow's "gift," by contrast, was a deft but equally manipulative attempt to terminate one by quite literally balancing the books. No words of reproach or rejection were ever voiced, but the success of the maneuver can perhaps be inferred from the fact that no puff was ever published, nor any further correspondence pursued. In a nutshell, this brief exchange of words, objects, and implications suggests the elaborate social push and pull of gift exchange. In 1840, Thompson made a final attempt to promote himself by writing a long and flattering review of his own novel and sending it, anonymously, to the *North American Review*, where it sits to this day in the file of rejected submissions. After this there was a long silence. No further correspondence appears to have taken place between Thompson and Longfellow for a dozen years. Through adept manipulation of gifts, Longfellow was free.[16]

My point is not to suggest that Longfellow objected to gifts, even manipulative ones, since he was himself a fairly dedicated literary gift-giver, sending copies of his works to many friends, including John Neal.[17] What I'd like to underscore, rather, is that while gifts facilitated the creation and maintenance of friendships, their bestowal did not guarantee those ends. We cannot simply assume that because a gift was offered, or even received, that it necessarily had an embedding effect. Gifts could be used to police the boundaries of a social circle as much as to render them porous. They were offered and received (or not), that is, within very specific and highly complex environments, so that the only way in which we can understand their transmission and receipt is by reconstructing the contexts through which they moved.

One of the goals of this chapter, then, is to examine a series of literary gift exchanges in both ritual and contextual detail to understand how and why gift exchanges did (or did not) work. I also want to suggest, however, that authorial gift exchange was a broader and more complex phenomenon than even the examples above might suggest. Our discussion thus far has centered on pairs of authors—Chubbuck and Nott, Longfellow and Thompson, Thompson and Neal—and it has emphasized their private transactions. Gift giving of this sort was undoubtedly an immensely pervasive phenomenon: far more pervasive than these few examples suggest. It included not only the presentation of books by authors to their friends, or to those with whom they sought to make friends, but also the giving of individual poems on sheets and written into albums, the sharing of diary entries, and the exchange of letters in familiar correspondence. Something of the scope of this phenomenon is suggested by the growing scholarship on coteries and literary networks in eighteenth-century America through which such gifts flowed. Indeed, it would not be an exaggeration to say that more words—written and printed—and more ideas—belles lettristic and utilitarian—circulated through gift exchange than through any other single economy in the late eighteenth century.[18]

Yet interesting and important though the dynamics of these transactions are, however, they offer only a partial view of the ways in which gifts and gift economies operated in late eighteenth- and nineteenth-century America. The act of authorial gift-giving was not confined to the private realm—the world of manuscripts, friendships, and coteries—but was woven into the very fabric of the commercialized world of letters. The functioning of newspapers and magazines and the well-being and prosperity of publishers depended to an important degree on the operation of far-flung and vibrant networks of gift exchange along with the reciprocity they generated. Gifts of newspapers and magazines facilitated national news reporting in an age before journalists were able to travel and gather news on behalf of a specific publication. Likewise, literary advertising and promotion were conducted by means of well-established gift exchanges that took the form of reciprocal puffs. No periodical publication could survive, or even sought to, outside the world of gifts and favors. Gift-giving was not distinct from business in other words; it was a way of *doing* business.

Because gift-giving was so pervasive a phenomenon, this chapter is necessarily long and somewhat complex in its organization, moving thematically (but not necessarily chronologically) from more private to more commercial acts of prestation. I start out by considering one of the paradigmatic acts of literary gift-giving: the poem or extract of prose written in an acquaintance's album to initiate or celebrate a friendship. I then turn to letter writing, arguing that familiar correspondence conforms closely to the gift paradigm we see in friendship albums. The discussion of letters also allows us to explore the role of money in gift practices, for while writing in an album did not entail fees, the sending of letters did. The question of who paid for letters in the nineteenth century offers a fascinating vantage point from which to explore the way in which money complicated gift-giving. From letters in the mail, I consider newspapers and magazines carried by the post office and the ways in which postal laws helped create a world of freely gifted publications among periodical proprietors and editors. Establishing the way in which newspaper editors and magazine proprietors made gifts of their works among one another helps explain, in turn, why it was that they might also wish to make other gifts among themselves. Drawing these three gift phenomena together, I reconsider the inner workings of the *Southern Literary Messenger*, the longest running periodical published south of the Mason-Dixon Line. Often derided by modern scholars as a poorly mismanaged operation that exemplified the worst aspects of amateurism, the *Messenger*, I will argue, made use of a resilient and far-flung network of friends and well-wishers who made gifts of their works to editor Thomas Willis White. So far from failing to achieve professional standards, as some scholars have argued, the magazine succeeded admirably by the standard it in fact set for itself, which was to create and sustain a world of literary gift exchange.

Gift giving is perhaps the most personal and hence the most deeply embedded (and embedding) of all economies, and therefore it has proved to be more stubbornly persistent and more notably residual than any other, but, nonetheless, over the course of the century it became less central while commercialism became more so; gift-giving became more isolated and cash transactions more pervasive; and the distinction between gifts and commodities more philosophically tenable and more conceptually rigid. Gifts do not disembed, otherwise they are no longer gifts, but the number of areas touched by gift exchange diminished until they had become simply the domain of ritual. This chapter closes, accordingly, by considering briefly the contraction of the gift in the literary world from something considered integral to business to something considered completely antithetical.

"TABLETS OF VANITY; ARCHIVES OF PRIDE AND FLATTERY": ALBUMS

In 1829, Edgar Allan Poe penned some verses in the album of Lucy Holmes of Baltimore that began:

> From childhood's hour I have not been
> As others were—I have not seen
> As others saw—I could not bring
> My passions from a common spring—
> From the same source I have not taken
> My sorrow—I could not awaken
> My heart to joy at the same tone—
> And all I lov'd—*I* lov'd alone—

Poe's anguished testimony to his isolation and uniqueness was perhaps sincerely meant, but socially and culturally speaking it was far wide of the mark. Indeed, in writing his lines in an acquaintance's album, Poe was in fact doing anything but being isolated and being anything but unique. The theme of his entry, for example, was at odds with circumstance, for albums were filled with melancholy sentiments and a mournful sense of loss not unlike Poe's. More to the point, the substance of Poe's poem was undercut by circumstance, for while it insisted on his intense social dislocation, the very purpose of album keeping was to create and sustain social bonds, and in belaboring his isolation in the process of writing in an album, he was in fact building, not burning, a bridge.[19]

By the late 1820s, the practice of keeping blank books or albums, in which friends and relations would indite verses, had become wildly popular in America, and we know that Poe had been writing in albums since at least 1827, a decade or so after they first started to appear in America. Album keeping, however, was a centuries' old tradition. Scholars have traced its origins to the mid-sixteenth century, when students in Germany started to collect inscriptions from their friends and professors. These *stammbücher*, as they were called, served as an ad hoc form of testimonial, vouchsafing the students as they traveled from school to school.[20] Over the course of the eighteenth century, the *stammbüch* merged with the more popular commonplace book to create the 'album amicorum,' or friendship album, and with the emergence of sentimental aesthetics and the advent of new printing technologies in the late eighteenth century, friendship albums become increasingly popular in Europe. By the time they came to America in the early nineteenth century, albums had diversified remarkably in style and content.[21] Gone were the interleaved texts of Renaissance Europe, replaced by specialized blank books, some of them plain, but others elaborately bound in tooled leather, filled with engraved plates, edged with gilt, and customized with the owner's name stamped on the cover in gold. Gone, too, was the aristocratic rigidity and intellectual posturing of the *stammbücher*. American albums typically contained a medley of original and 'selected' verse: witty jeux d'esprit, benedictions, acrostics, memorials, mourning poems, parting advice, promises to remember and pleas to be remembered, hymns, maxims, conundrums, and love lyrics. Albums could also contain exquisite calligraphy, pen and ink sketches, pressed flowers, leaves, braids of hair, daguerreotypes, newspaper clippings, and wax seals.[22] Indeed, commentators on (and in) albums noted the variety of materials they contained. Witness the following acrostic:

> A motley mess of dull, or witty,
> Lullaby, or song, or ditty,
> Beautiful, sublime, or neat,
> Unfit, or fit, to blot a sheet,
> Makes an Album, all complete.[23]

What tied the incredibly heterogeneous contents of the albums together and gave them a unity of purpose was not, I would argue, the poems themselves. Three other factors bulked far larger: the events that occasioned them, the intentions that motivated them, and, most importantly, the economy through which they were typically transmitted. When we consider these important contextual elements, the "motley mess" disappears and the logic of the albums becomes apparent.

The events that occasioned album verse tended to be what I call threshold events: moments when relationships were initiated, altered, or severed entirely. Such events included flirting, courtship, engagement, marriage, graduation from college, relocation, and the ultimate threshold event: death. The intention behind most album entries was to create relationships where they did not exist, sustain them where they did, or carry them over these thresholds when they seemed under threat. Album verse was able to achieve such objectives because it was circulated almost exclusively through gift economies which had the capacity to embed the participants in social relationships based upon generosity, reciprocity, and endless debt.[24] The poems found in albums seem, moreover, to correspond to three different types of gift, which I call courting gifts, parting gifts, and sustaining gifts. The distinctions are important, because each type of gift created a different sort of debt and presupposed a distinct form of reciprocity.

Let us consider first the courting gift. This was a poem that, as the name suggests, was designed to initiate a relationship, usually (but not always) of a romantic nature. A charming example can be found in the album owned by Elizabeth Turnbull, an instructor at a young ladies' academy in Baltimore. Entitled "The Batchelor's Wish," the poem took the form of an enumerated list:

> 1. Female companion to soften my cares,
> 2. Thousand a year to support my affairs;
> 3. Dogs and a gun, when to sport I incline,
> 4. Horses and chaise, to indulge me and mine;
> 5. Jolly companions, with whom to make merry,
> 6. Dishes each day; with six glasses of sherry;
> 7. Beds in my house, for my friends at their leisure;
> 8. Somethings or other, to add to their pleasure;
> 9. Pounds in my pocket, when cash I require.
>   These favors are all that on *earth* I desire,
>   And a passport to *heaven*, when from earth I retire
>   November 1825

Dominated by a stridently male and frankly bachelor set of desires—the guns, dogs, horses, sherry, and companions—the poem's homosocial fantasies are nonetheless bookended by the wish for a genteel female companion and for salvation: two requisites for a socially respectable man on the make. Moreover, the fact that salvation is not an earthly but heavenly desire, suggests that a female companion is the first and best thing he can hope for in this world. The enumerative structure of the poem, in which each number becomes the first word of the line both suggests the arithmetical orientation of the author (always an important trait in the world of merchants) and also a degree of playful literary sophistication that undercuts, somewhat, the obtrusive materialism of the piece.[25]

But more even than the explicit enumeration *in* the poem is the implicit calculation *of* it, for the very giving of the poem was an attempt to create a social bond where none had previously existed. As scholars of gift exchange have repeatedly pointed out, to bestow something of value upon another can create a sense of obligation that is only settled by reciprocation. Courting gifts, in particular, presuppose what Marshall Sahlins calls 'balanced reciprocity,' which he defines as bestowals which "stipulate returns of commensurate worth or utility within a finite and narrow period."[26] When our nameless suitor presented his poem to Miss Turnbull, he was doubtless hoping for something in return: a smile, some flirtation, an expression of gratitude, or perhaps a counter-poem. This received, a reciprocal but disequilibriated bond would be created on which subsequent exchanges could be based. Occasionally, the expectation of a counter-gift was quite explicit. On the eve of her departure from Painesville, Ohio, in 1843, Elisabeth B. Packard received a poem from hopeful suitor Henry Lease, who clearly wished for more than a verse in exchange for his own:

> Miss EBP I long to see
> This album filled with verses
> I will do my part with all my heart
> Give me, my love, before we part
> One tender kiss of dear delight;
> and all the friendship we have swore
> confirm in this our last good night
> and when in love and distant shores
> I wander, by the morn's pale light,
> In memory of our former loves
> I think on the [sic] and this *Good Night*[27]

According to Sahlins, "the pragmatic test of balanced reciprocity" is "an inability to tolerate one-way flows; the relations between people are disrupted by a failure to reciprocate within limited time and equivalence leeways." To decline to reciprocate a courtship poem, or to reciprocate it with sufficient expedition, was in essence to foreclose the relationship.[28] It is unclear if Elisabeth Packard's suitor received his sought-for kiss, but one can find suggestive evidence of unwanted gifts and thwarted courtships in albums in the form of poems razored from otherwise impeccably kept volumes, whole pages removed, and, sometimes, pairs of pages glued firmly closed. According to the logic of the gift I am claiming for this sort of verse, an unsought for love poem would be an embarrassment and a constant reminder of a gift unreciprocated: it was best removed from sight.[29] Clearly it is tendentious to read absence so forcefully, but fortunately, more definitive evidence of a courtship gone wrong can be found in the album of a young woman named Harriet from Elizabeth Town, New Jersey, where the reader finds the following remarkable exchange. It begins with a familiar line: "I remember, I remember," which is both the title and the opening phrase of Thomas Hood's well-known and popular poem of 1826. Hood's poem begins: "I remember, I remember, / The house where I was born." The poem in Harriet's album begins in imitation of Hood's but then swerves sharply into bitterness:

> I remember, I remember
> The girl I used to love
> And once I thought her oft pledged heart
> Would never from me rove
> It was a childish ignorance
> But now it gives no joy
> I know how great a fool I was
> E'en when I was a boy.

This sort of spleen is, in my experience, completely unexampled. It is a gift given to hurt; indeed, it seems hardly a gift at all, or perhaps only one in which the author would be repaid with the satisfaction of a reproach well targeted. Harriet, however, was determined to have the last word, and in pencil below the verse, she offered her own intertextual salvo: "Merit, without modesty," she wrote, "is insolence Addison."[30] The last word, of course, is the very antithesis of the ongoing conversations that constitute relationships. Courting gifts were given quite deliberately to open up, rather than to close down, the lines of communication; they were a form of narrative.[31]

Sara Willis—later known to the world as Fanny Fern—knew a great deal about the lines of romantic communication. Exceptionally pretty, with bright blue eyes and curly blonde hair, she was also, by her own confession, *"born a coquette."* It comes as little surprise, then, to find a number of courting poems in the album she kept while a student at the Hartford Female Seminary between 1828 and 1831. One poem, for example, begins: "Hail to the fair angelic girl / Whose blue eyes beam with love and brightness / And flaxen locks that sweetly curl / Upon a neck of snowy whiteness." Willis was besieged by admirers, and her album brims with courting verse of this sort, but what is striking is not the preponder-

ance of flirting poems but rather the abundance of parting poems. Loss
and neediness lurk in the shadows of Willis's otherwise sunny album and
are well captured in the unsigned entry that runs:

> When thou art far away
> From this loved spot—
> Will this our parting day
> E'er claim a thought?
> Or will remembering fade
> And dark oblivion shade
> The last request I made
> Forget-me-not[32]

Forget me not. This sentiment—situated somewhere between a command
and a plea—echoes throughout antebellum students' albums. "Though
oceans should between us roll," wrote one woman, "Though distance
should be our lot / Though we should meet no more / Dear friend forget me not." Another: "If I could have the choicest gifts / By asking them
of thee, / The first boon that I'd crave, my friend, / Would be *remember
me.*" "Forget me not Forget me never," demanded a third; "Remember
and forget me not," a fourth.[33]

The desire to be remembered was an indication of the fact that student life was as brief as it was intense. Women unrelated by blood came
quickly to think of themselves as not only friends but "sisters forever."
They found out all too soon, however, that this foreverness was an illusion.[34] Relationships formed at colleges and academies were tinged with
an almost inevitable sense of impending loss. College was terminated
by graduation, independence by marriage, and personal fulfillment by
motherhood. According to Anya Jabour, the dark tone found in women's
academy albums grew out of an intense but evanescent female world of
love and ritual and reflected an anxiety that graduation would disrupt so-
rority, marriage community, and motherhood health.[35] There is certainly
some merit to this argument, and we find in Sara Willis's album at least
one poem that stridently denounces marriage as the wrecker of sororal
connections. However, precisely the same anxious and yearning sentiments are found in albums owned by young men attending college and
academy. J. Cowen's album, kept while he attended a Quaker academy in
Providence, Rhode Island at the same time Willis attended the Hartford
Female Seminary, is replete with yearning poems entitled "The Evening
Sun," "Forget Not the Moment," "Hope," "The Forsaken," "Forget Me
Not," and "The Fall of the Leaf." Young men, too, experienced powerful emotional bonds and homosocial desires—addressed one another as
"loving brother"—and they too dreaded separation.[36] In fact few friend-

ships, male or female, survived graduation undiminished and most students knew that they wouldn't. Of the 162 students who attended the Hartford Female Seminary in the summer term of 1831, the year Sara Willis graduated, 128 came from beyond the immediate Hartford area. J. Cowen's Rhode Island classmates, likewise, hailed from locations as far flung as Baltimore, Maryland, and Wilmington, North Carolina. To graduate was, in all likelihood, to say goodbye to one's classmates forever. Little wonder then, that students worried that they would soon be forgotten.[37]

Of course, parting gifts were not limited to the occasion of graduation from college or academy, but were given whenever a bond was to be suspended or severed. When she was to be married in 1845, for example, Catharine Emerson's friends and family presented her with an album in which each had inscribed a verse or prose extract. Likewise, when Helen M. Everest was about to relocate to the South in the 1830s, her relatives and friends gave her an album filled with parting sentiments. One inscriber, meditating on Helen's final destination, counseled her in good abolitionist fashion to "Remember those in bonds as BOUND with them," but more generally album verse was concerned with social rather than economic fetters. "'Tis hard to part with those we love," wrote Helen's cousin, "To snap the fine wrought chain / That pure affection's hands have wove / Nor meet on earth again."[38]

It was precisely to avoid the chain of affection being completely broken that graduating students, family friends, and immediate relations wrote in albums. Their inscriptions were, of course, often concerned thematically with issues of fidelity, friendship, memory, loss, and connection, but as with courting gifts, the more important cultural work was performed at the economic rather than the semantic level, in the very act of gifting these inscriptions. Parting gifts, however, functioned quite differently than courting gifts. A courting gift was offered in expectation of balanced reciprocity: that is, for the gift of a poem, something of like value would be offered in return, and within a finite period of time. A gift given to one who was parting could not, however, be reciprocated, and that, I want to argue, was precisely the point. A gift received in earnest creates a claim, and a gift received in earnest and never reciprocated creates a claim that endures. This is an example of what Sahlins calls "negative reciprocity": the act of getting something for nothing. But while Sahlins associates negative reciprocity with impersonality and deceit, its operation here was intensely personal and quite guileless.[39] The gift given upon parting created a debt in its recipient that by definition said "I will never be able to repay you" and also, for that reason, "I will never forget you." It was, to continue the idea of relationship as conversation, an unfinished exchange and a refusal to accept closure.

Behind all such parting poems—and perhaps behind even the courtship poems too—lay a sense of youth as something fragile, finite, and brief, and of life itself as something fleeting and insubstantial, even illusory: what one album writer called a "vain world of tears." Growing out of the ascetic tradition of Christian unworldliness and fuelled by a powerful Protestant insistence on contemptus mundi, this view of life and death colored almost all albums if not every inscription within them.[40] Thus A. W. Maine indited the following pensive lines in the album of Weltha Ann Beckley in 1835:

> The sunshine quivers
> On your cheek glitring
> And gay and fair
> As yet your hands
> Are not too weak to shade you
> From its glare
> How soon twill fall unheeded
> On your Death-dewed glassy eye
> Why should I fear to tell you so
> I know that you must die[41]

Awareness of death and acknowledgment of its inevitability functioned on several levels in album verse. In the first place, it put the smaller acts of separation and loss, for example to marriage or graduation, into a larger theological frame of reference. A form of typologization in which the parting of friends merely foreshadowed the ultimate separation, this reduced the magnitude of separation. Second, and by way of contrast, it magnified such losses and served as a salutary reminder of the ultimate separation; as such it served as a form of religious discipline. "Cling Not to Earth," admonished a popular album verse.[42] And lastly, it served to make people cherish still more fondly the things they did enjoy in this world. Even though they reminded readers of the omnipotence and inescapability of death and the fragility of all matter, album verses were doggedly and even defiantly written to stave off death, to champion the undeniability of life.

Somewhere between courting gifts and parting gifts were those given in the context of an ongoing relationship. Designed neither to create bonds where none had existed nor to embalm those that were about to cease, these gifts—which I call sustaining gifts—served simply to buoy a relationship and reinforce it with non-specific gestures of goodwill. Verses of this sort were sometimes written in the wake of a death, to reassure the bereaved that he or she still had friends among the living; at other times, however, they were given simply because it seemed like a nice thing to do.[43] Thus Lydia Sigourney was moved to write a spontaneous poem in the album of her friend Elizabeth Dorr Tracy one evening in 1825 while both of them were knitting together. The poem—"Extempore on seeing Miss E. D. Tracy, Knitting a Cap, at the Montague Circle"—is certainly didactic, but the circumstances of its creation, which were both spontaneous and occasional in the extreme ("Norwich Tuesday evening, March 10th 1825"), suggest that it was given without calculation or planning, solely out of affection for her friend.[44] Sustaining gifts such as Sigourney's were predicated on a very different model of reciprocity than either courting or parting gifts. Where courting gifts were meant to be returned expeditiously and parting gifts were offered with an understanding that repayment was impossible, sustaining gifts were given to foster what Sahlins calls "generalized reciprocity." Generalized reciprocity creates a sense of obligation, to be sure, but repayment, as Sahlins explains, "is not stipulated by time, quantity, or quality: the expectation of reciprocity is diffuse."[45] Generalized reciprocity is powerful, in fact, precisely on account of its diffuse nature, for it creates the broadest sense of goodwill and expresses the most confident view of human trustworthiness. It is perhaps for this reason that poems written in this spirit seem so rare in albums; the truly thoughtless and loving gift was probably not one that required being written into so ritual-bound an object as an album. Most poems given out of general good feeling and based upon generalized reciprocity were either written on loose sheets or were included in letters. Indeed, as I shall argue below, letter writing itself can be seen as a form of reciprocal gift exchange.

There is something deeply appealing about album verse, based as it is on the idea of gratuity, dedicated as it is to the ideal of community, and propelled as it is by the force of reciprocity. Yet the logic of the gift, as I suggested in opening this chapter, was sometimes less benign than it initially appeared, and it was often attacked for its morally suspect nature. Albums themselves were derided as "Tablets of vanity; archives of pride and flattery."[46] When pundits attacked the practice of *soliciting* album verses, by contrast, they almost always disavowed moral in favor of economic language, as if by so doing they could reveal the calculating and coercive elements that lay beneath the veneer of gratuity. "The truth is," wrote one commentator, grasping for the best analogy, "our female friends are fast becoming merciless pirates, sailing on the ocean of society, and exacting tribute from every ill-starred vessel which may chance to cross their path. They are Highland chieftains, dwelling in mountain-fastnesses of social life, and venturing forth from time to time, to levy their black mail from the more peaceful inhabitants below. . . . They are Shylocks, stern and insatiate in their demands . . . exclaiming with the Jew, as they enforce their hard exactions."[47] Other commentators fell back, more decisively, on the image of album verse as a kind of tax: "To literary people," said one, "they are a great tax, and one which, in the present reforming times, ought to be repealed." "A friend at our elbow," commented another, "complains bitterly of the annoyance to which he is subjected in consequence of the perpetual and inconsiderate visitations of albums. He begs us to say, that it is a serious interruption to his studies and a tax upon his time." "He yields," the author continued, "implicitly to all the drafts upon the bank of his imagination, and pays them promptly, but, as he is in debt to the public for an indefinite number of poetic treasures, we cannot stand passively by, and see him impoverished and robbed by the eager thoughtlessness of his fair admirers."[48] Piracy, pillage, blackmail, usury, taxation: what each of these economic practices has in common is the idea of something taken, unfairly and by coercion, from someone else. Where gifts are given freely, album verse, according to these commentators, is extorted, or taken under duress. This does not make them *not* gifts; it simply emphasizes the coercive and social bond-creating tendencies implicit in any present.

To refuse to write in someone's album was to insult them, and several short stories from the 1830s and 1840s center on the trouble into which young men with no poetic talent fall when they are put on the spot and compelled to produce lines for albums.[49] Of course one could simply decline the invitation, but refusal was made doubly difficult because the entire practice of album writing was predicated on an elaborate social charade that disguised its coercive nature. Album solicitations were often initiated when a woman presented her album to the potential author, inviting him to admire the contents, sometimes requesting him to take the album home. On occasion, albums were even sent to a potential author by a third party. In such a way, the owners cloaked the request for a favor by making it seem as if the loan of the album was a favor of their own, so that the poem they sought then became a counter-gift. To receive a gift, even unwittingly, was to be caught in a web of expectations to respond. It was a conundrum to which editor Willis G. Clark gave much thought. To decline to write in albums, Clark explained, under the well-known pseudonym of Ollapod, was to court censure and even ostracism. "No one will know you," he said, "you will be cut by the lover of your bright-eyed cousin, and by herself. In fact, one might as well stipulate wantonly for a bad epitaph from a cutter of tomb-stones, as to attempt release from the scribblative obligation. There is no discharge in that war of the pen." The only response other than to say no—and risk censure—was to declare war oneself and offer a gift that was its own revenge. How often this happened in reality is unclear, but Ollapod offers a fictional account of what such a gift might look like. His story begins when he is given the album of a complete stranger—his sister's milliner—with a demand for verses. Not only is Ollapod sick of writing verses, he explains, not only does the milliner have no real claim on him, not only is she cross-eyed, and not only is she quite clearly his social inferior, but, to add insult to injury, her album is not really an album at all but an old account book, "ruled across in *blue*, and rectangularly, near the outer edge, in *red*, forming squares for the register of dollars and cents." This is a business text that has simply been pressed into service as an album by what Ollapod takes to be a social parvenu with pretensions to respectability. The use of the account book is, for Ollapod, the final straw, for it makes insulting clear what other albums at least have the courtesy to disguise beneath expensive paper and gilt edges, namely that the solicitation of courting verses is a profoundly calculating enterprise in which cultural capital is cashed in to produce both the social capital of connections and also the symbolic capital of prestige. Ollapod's revenge is not to ignore this crassness, but to amplify it, by using the very grid of the account book to help write his poem.

Thou canst not hope, oh! nymph divine,	
That I should ever court the	9
Or that when passion's glow is done,	
My heart can ever love but	1
When from Hope's flower exhales the dew,	
Then Love's false smile deserts us	2
Then Fancy's radiance 'gins to flee	
And life is robbed of all the	3
And Sorrow, sad, her tears must pour	
O'er cheeks where roses bloomed be	4–19
Yes! life's a scene all dim as Styx	
It's joys are dear at	3*f*6
Its raptures fly so quickly hence	
They're scarcely cheap at	18*d*
Oh! for the dreams that then survive!	
They're high at pennies	25
The breast no more is filled with heaven,	
When years it numbers	27
And yield's it up to Manhood's fate,	
About the age of	28

Finds the world cold, and dim, and dirty,
Ere the heart's annual count is   30
Alas! for all the joys that follow,
I would not give a *quarter-dollar!*   25–1.97 ½

This, charming *artiste*, is the sum
To which life's added items come.
If into farther sums I stride
I see the figures multiplied.
Subtract the profit ones from those
Whose *all* to loss untimely goes,
And in the aggregate you find
Enough to assure the thinking mind
That there's an overplus of evil
Enough to fright the very d___l!

Thus, my dear maid, I send to you
The balance of my metre due;
Please scrutinize the above amount,
And set it down to my account;
A wink to a horse is as good as a nod—
Your humble servant,   OLLAPOD.[50]

Ollapod's poem is a brilliant summary of the major topoi of album verse. In the first stanza, he adopts a typically modest and self-effacing stance, apologizing for his inability to write anything worthy for the milliner's album. In so doing, however, he also, if somewhat discretely, hints that his lack of poetic fancy has its roots in his lack of fancy for her. In the second stanza, he moves on to a still more common album topos: the tragic passage of time and the decay of fragile human life. Yet here again, his rehearsal is designed to deflate the milliner's attractions, for the progress of time he charts refers to the aging of the milliner herself, who, he says, might well have been attractive at eighteen, but—a decade later—at twenty-eight is not.[51] What makes the poem more insulting still is Ollapod's use of the account book structure itself, which serves to introduce a comic element into the verse, causing a slight visual, and hence metrical, pause at the end of alternate lines that undercuts whatever seriousness or sincerity the poem might otherwise have had. More importantly, it suggests an element of class revulsion on Ollapod's part. Repelled by what he takes to be the shameless calculation of the milliner's social climbing in seeking a poem from him, he seeks to put her in her place by speaking the only language he thinks she really understands: the language of the marketplace. Ollapod's rendering of accounts is devastating, suggesting that the milliner is a poor investment, well past her prime, and worth nothing to him. Finally, and again subverting a generic album technique, he concludes by totting up ("my metre due") and implies that he owes her nothing more. When read against "The Batchelor's Wish," Ollapod's poem even shows a gendered critique of the milliner, for while the former suggests that a man may turn numbers into words, the latter suggests that a woman may not turn words into numbers. There is always calculation in the giving and receiving of gifts, but that calculation should stay firmly under wraps.[52]

While extreme in its tone, Ollapod's recourse to economic language in dealing with an inappropriate gift situation was all too common. It is a gesture we will see over and over. The presence of economic and, especially, commercial tropes in social situations such as this is a clear indication that a gift relationship has gone awry.

"I WRITE TO YOU OUT OF MERE HUMANITY": LETTERS

In 1827, James Kirke Paulding sent a copy of his newest publication, a *Letter on the Use and Abuse of Incorporations*, to former President James Madison. The work was written, he explained, "to answer an immediate purpose here, during the Session of our Legislature," but he gave a copy to Madison for entirely different reasons. "My only object in sending it," he averred, "was that it might afford me a sort of excuse, to remind you of a person who once had the pleasure of being your guest, and of enjoying for a short period, the happiness of your fireside." "It was," he continued, "among the most happy periods of my life, and I often return to it with a feeling of gratefull pleasure I can hardly express. It would add to this pleasure if I could Know that I were not altogether forgotten by yourself & Mrs. Madison, and that you accept with Kindness this small testimony of my gratefull recollection." A modern reader might puzzle over the idea of Paulding seeking to express his feelings of nostalgia and friendship for Mr. and Mrs. Madison by sending them a polemical pamphlet on monopolies—one replete with lines such as "I scorn the cant of ribald ridicule, which either makes a sport of legislative corruption, or what is still more reprehensible, willfully labours to degrade the representatives of the people"—but the mystery resolves itself when we realize that in sending his package to the Madisons, Paulding was giving not one but, rather, two literary gifts. The first, of course, was the pamphlet; the second, on which I want to focus here, was the letter that covered it.[53]

There is a great deal to be said in favor of considering familiar correspondence through the lens of gift economics. Subjectively, the experience of receiving letters is akin to that of receiving other literary gifts. Letters are objects of slight monetary but great personal value: private and unique artifacts, crafted of words. They speak quite literally to our sense of self; they are given in friendship; received freely; and treasured as mementoes. Objectively, an exchange of letters raises many of the problems we see in other forms of gift exchange. Although apparently free, they cost time, effort, and, indeed, money. Although seemingly unilateral, they come burdened with expectations: that one will understand and reciprocate. And although sent in the spirit of friendship, they can be experienced as coercive and entangling. Then, too, because sending letters cost money in the form of postage fees—fees which were typically paid by the recipient rather than the sender—the pretence of gratuity surrounding the act of letter writing was significantly more complicated and significantly less stable than in the bestowal of album verses.[54]

As the practice of familiar correspondence burgeoned in the late eighteenth century, more and more people—women as well as men, children as well as adults, common folk as well as elites, and minorities as well as whites—learned firsthand to negotiate the challenges of gratuity and reciprocity that we have already seen played out in our discussion of friendship albums. What made the objective reality of correspondence so challenging was precisely the fact that it was bedeviled by the subjective ideal. Indeed, the very ideal of letter writing was something of an impossibility.

The notion of completely uninhibited and wholly reciprocal correspondence is captured perfectly in Fannie Elizabeth Foster's 1858 poem, "Answer to 'Write to Me'":

> Yes, I will write to thee often,—
> Would write to thee every day,
> Could it add to thy heart aught of gladness,
> Or chase any shadows away.
>
> Sometimes I will write by my casement,
> When the breath of the morning comes through,
> And Aeolus is touching his harp-strings,
> And sunbeams are drinking the dew.
>
> And sometimes at noontide will hasten
> Away from the din and the noise,—
> Sit me down by thy side, in my fancy,
> And tell thee my sorrows and joys.
>
> And where friendship's wavelets go softly,
> I oft in the eventide hie,

> To send thee sweet thoughts on the zephyrs,
> As they gently go murmuring by.
> And may I not think at each season—
> Perchance thou art writing to me?
> Or at least, that the breezes come laden
> With sweet benedictions from thee?[55]

What strikes one in reading this poem is the degree to which it presents correspondence as a decontextualized, even disembodied, activity. One cannot tell whether the speaker (or implied recipient) is male or female, whether the two are courting, a couple, relatives, or simply friends. One cannot ascertain their ages, the location of either, the degree of their intimacy, the extent of their geographical separation, the period in which they are supposed to be living, or the way in which they correspond. Indeed, it is on this last score that the poem is most wholly detached from reality, for while letter writing is a relentlessly material activity—involving pens, paper, ink, sand, sealing wax, writing tables, carriers, post offices, and carriers' fees—it is here rendered immaterial and, even, supernatural. Using the common romantic trope of the "correspondent breeze"— a figure that conjures up both Hebrew and classical notions of spiritual communion as well as ideas of sympathetic creative inspiration—Foster here more or less suggests that correspondence is sustained by the forces of nature. Letters, in her world, are transmitted on the "breath of the morning," by "zephyrs," with "the breezes." They bring nothing but happiness, reduce nothing but suffering, are written daily (indeed at every point in the day), and they are sent in the sound belief that they will be responded to "at each season" in a perfect cycle of reciprocity. A letter that comes so fully from the soul and that passes so effortlessly and naturally to the recipient cannot be seen as other than a gift.[56]

This image of correspondence is entirely consistent with the prescriptive literature on letter writing that burgeoned in the early national and antebellum periods, and which consistently dematerialized the act of letter writing.[57] Following the emphasis on correspondence as associated with breath, one manual advised writers to approach letters as "copies of conversation." Another built on this idea to suppress mention of the physical labor involved in writing. "Express yourself as you would if you were speaking to the person to whom you are writing," it counseled. "Do not begin a letter with 'I now take pen in hand,' & c." A third sought to abolish altogether the materiality of correspondence. "An epistolary correspondence between intimate and endeared connexions," it argued, "is a spiritual communion, in which minds alone seem to mingle, and, unembarrassed by the bodily presence, converse with a freedom, a fervour, and an eloquence rarely excited, and perhaps never more felicitously indulged, in personal intercourse."[58] What such maxims suggest is that the publicly promoted ideology of letter writing was wholly at odds with the material practicalities and economics of correspondence. As letter writers of the nineteenth century sat down to pen their missives, they worried less, I would argue, about wind and more about hot air, less about the metaphysics of communion and more about the economics of communication. Letter writing manuals, in this respect, were of little use. They had a great deal to say about gratitude in correspondence, but nothing about gratitude *for* correspondence; a vast amount about letters to secure outstanding debts but nothing about the debts created by letters themselves; much, in short, about business in letters and precisely nothing about the business *of* letters. An examination of twenty-two letter-writing manuals published between 1791 and 1859 revealed, in fact, an almost complete silence on the economies of epistolary reciprocity and postal ethics. Debate about those issues, however, was lively and persistent throughout the period, as a look at almost any sustained correspondence reveals.[59]

In initiating or sustaining a correspondence, letter writers had to ask and then answer at least three important questions that bore directly on the tension between the apparent gratuity of gifts and their actual entanglements: How quickly should one respond? How much should one write? And who should pay for the privilege? Such questions were important precisely because they recognized what letter-writing manuals did not, namely that correspondence is a form of exchange with economic rules of its own.

How Quickly Should One Respond? When author Emily Chubbuck opened a missive to a friend with the confession that she would "commence in a very letter-like manner, viz., by asking pardon for delays," she was hardly exaggerating how characteristic and very "letter-like" a gesture this was. Indeed, there is simply no comment so common in the annals of letter writing as the prefatory apology for not having written sooner.[60] Young Sarah Margaret Fuller, writing from Massachusetts to her demanding father, Timothy, who was congressman in Washington, became extraordinarily adept at such apologies: "I should have written you immediately," she begins one letter, but waited until uncle "mended my pen." "I should have written to you much sooner," she apologized some weeks later, "but I have been very busy." "I have not yet answered your letter," she told him later that year, "for I did not wish to until I had a decent pen." "I fear I have not very punctually kept my resolution of writing to you once in a week," she wrote in 1821. "Yet as I have not any thing very witty, very agreeable, or very entertaining to commit to paper, I do not think the omission is much to be regretted." "My dear father," she began one year later, "Yesterday I did not write to you as I went to church all day." "I was too busy to write to any being while I was at home," she admitted in 1824, "or you would have heard from me ere this."[61]

It might be argued, of course, that Fuller was young (the letters cited were written between her ninth and fourteenth years), or that her father was excessively demanding and almost forced her apologies before the fact (and he was indeed a strict parent), but apologies appear so often in letters, including those written by individuals we would consider mature, prompt, and prolific as to suggest that something other than character flaw was at stake, and indeed I will argue that this is precisely the case. Fuller's father, for example, was almost as full of excuses as his daughter. "I have deferred writing to you for some time," he confessed to her in one letter of 1820. "I have so many letters to write & so much other business to do, that I have found it quite difficult to keep my promise of writing a longer letter to you," he admitted in another of the same year. "[T]ho' I have not before written to you," he conceded some months after this, "it was not because you are not very much in my thoughts." "Is it in truth so long since my last letter?" he asked somewhat disingenuously in 1824; "I thought not." And noting in another letter that it would doubtless arrive late and disappoint his daughter, he advised her to "prepare yourself for great disappointments from correspondents—sometimes from forgetfulness, or negligence, or indifference, & not infrequently from the accidents at the P. Office. . . ."[62] Doubtless Fuller was correct in ascribing many epistolary delays to laziness and inept bureaucracy, but in a metaphysical sense, it might be said that no letter could be reciprocated quickly enough; letters were almost always and almost by definition *already late*.[63]

Letters seemed late, because they were instinctively measured by standards associated with oral communication. In a culture that equated friendliness with face-to-face interaction and the thrust and parry of oral exchange, letters were thus doomed inevitably to appear tardy. The appropriateness of this unreasonable standard of evaluation was simply reinforced by the typical description of a letter as conversation on paper. So long as the ideal of correspondence was modeled on conversation, the practice was fated to be compromised.[64] Of course, the very delay between letters bemoaned by correspondents could be seen as an advantage, inasmuch as it allowed epistles to be perceived as gifts in a way that the words of a conversation could not, and this too was noted by letter writers, but the delay between sending a letter and receiving a reply also allowed time for doubt, for anxiety, and for the worry that perhaps one's correspondent would not reciprocate feelings of esteem. It comes as no surprise, then, that Sarah Margaret Fuller, who was held to such an exacting epistolary schedule by her father should place such an interpretation on his own less-than-prompt responses. "I am sorry my dear sir you write to me so seldom," she wrote at the age of eleven, straining for a tone of adult disappointment. "Has your affection decreased? I fear it has; I have often pained you but I hope you still love me." The examples of the Fullers' correspondence suggests that letters almost always seemed late. They were inadequate because they could never approximate in reality the instantaneous and mystical nature with which they were burdened.[65]

Letter readers complained often about the tardiness of their correspondents, but because letters were depicted as gifts—given freely—such complaints were often couched in the language of sarcasm and rendered facetiously in order not to undermine the relationship correspondence consecrated. "Mem[o]," noted Robert Montgomery Bird in an 1832 letter to James Lawson, "I write to you out of mere humanity—Otherwise I am incensed at you neglecting my last letter, and am determined not to notice you for the future. Tell Mr. Legett, when you see him, I will write to him again in 1850."[66] Sometimes, likewise, writers challenged their correspondents to declare their affection. "Are you aware, my beloved sister," queried Caroline Howard in March 1819, "that your last letter bears the date of Dec. 9th? As *I* always believe the best of my friends, I will suppose *all* intervening communications lost, & that you are as attentive, as I know you to be affectionate."[67] Just as often, however, letter recipients dared their correspondents to announce their lack of interest. Thus when Emily Chubbuck complained to her sister Catherine that she had not heard from her, despite all her "trying and coaxing," she wondered whether Catherine "would be much obliged if I would follow your example." Such hostile probing, however, was simply a façade, and Chubbuck followed it with an equally mixed threat to continue writing herself, even "if it is only to plague you." Counter-intuitive as it may seem, it is in such partially hostile comments that we come close to the gift essence of the familiar letter, which, after all, exists solely in order to sustain a relationship. In the reciprocal logic of the correspondent, it is better to trade accusatory letters than none at all.

Writing to a Mrs. Porter in 1849, Lydia Sigourney—a prolific and prompt correspondent—noted that she had not heard from her in some time and could no longer remember who precisely owed a letter to whom, but, she added, "setting aside all the formalities of debt and credit, I am happy to take up my pen to address you."[68] Happy though Sigourney claimed to be, the presence of this economic metaphor more typically indicated the imminent breakdown of the epistolary gift relationship and the revelation of letters—more formally referred to as "favors"—as the stuff of a specifically economic arrangement. It was a trope that appeared again and again. Years before he became the polished writer who could squirm out of obligations laid at his door by Daniel Pierce Thompson, for example, Henry Wadsworth Longfellow used the account book trope to complain about the infrequency with which his family wrote to him. In an irate missive to his mother from 1823 he justified not having written to his family more often by reminding them that "none of you at home have written a single line." "I would not," he continued, "have you imagine that I, by any means, wish or intend to keep an exact account of 'Dr. and Cr.' . . . But the fact is, I do not hear from you as often as I wish."[69] While denying that he wished to enter letters in an account book with columns for Debtor and Creditor, Longfellow was nonetheless suggesting that even if correspondence had the appearance of a gift, it also carried the obligation of reciprocity, and he seemed to threaten the same kind of humiliation dished out by Willis Gaylord Clark to his unfortunate milliner album keeper: to expose the calculating balance of accounts on which gift economies are predicated. Only six years later, another of Longfellow's correspondents apologized for not having responded to his letters by confessing that she was "the worst hand in the world for debtor & credit accounts & may very often be largely in your debt," while fifteen years beyond that Parker Cleaveland sought to deflect Longfellow's ire with a still more elaborate rehearsal of the credit and debt conceit. "It sometimes happens," he began his letter, "that two merchants permit their mutual accounts to run on a long time without settlement, till they become perplexing, and so confused, that it is impossible to ascertain the exact balance. They then by *compromise* settle old accounts and begin *anew*. Our correspondence is in a similar state to this above supposed case. The balance, I know, is *greatly against me*—but how much I am unable to calculate." By declaring epistolary bankruptcy, Cleaveland hoped to throw himself on Longfellow's mercy and start anew, but the use of the trope nonetheless indicated a relationship in crisis.[70] Others used the account book analogy more flippantly, as did George Bailey Loring in 1839 when he told James Russell Lowell that he was "astonished and somewhat ashamed to find myself indebted to you to the am't of two long and *interesting* epistles." I will, he went on, "pay what I can now, towards discharging the debt." Eight years later, Lowell used the same figure of speech himself, telling Charles Briggs that he had no idea Briggs

owed him so many letters. "The balance of trade between me & my correspondents so seldom gets a tilt that way, that I was confirmed in my
impression that it was a generous delusion of yours by not receiving that
prompt payment for which I have always considered you remarkable."[71]
Whether used with humor or hostility, what the account book analogy
underscored was the uneasy acknowledgment of the fact that however
free letters seemed, they came burdened with obligations. Writers hated
to be called to account, but it was never far from their minds that accounts were being kept.

How Much Should One Write? Only slightly less worrying to letter
writers than a tardy epistle was a brief one. James Gates Percival, who
insisted over and over to James Lawrence Yvonnet that he was "no correspondent," "a very poor correspondent," "no letter writer," and "never
kept up a regular correspondence," felt constrained nonetheless to apologize for the brevity of what he did write. "Excuse me this short letter
for once," he wrote Yvonnet in 1823, "I am overhead in business right
now."[72] What brevity suggested, especially in the absence of an apology
such as that offered by Percival, was a failure to reciprocate in kind: a
cooling of ardor, or a lack of interest. Recipients not only read a letter's
lines, that is, and not only read between those lines; they also counted
them. "You write sneaking short letters," Mary Moody Emerson told her
nephew Waldo in 1822, as if in their very brevity there was something
deceitful and unworthy. Yet if Aunt Mary sniped at Waldo for writing
too little, then she was aware that she perhaps wrote too much herself.
Stricken with what she once called a "mania for the pen," Mary sent an
endless stream of complex and convoluted letters to her friends and relatives, only some of whom (such as nephew Waldo) were ever willing to
respond in kind. Waldo's brother, Charles, for example, seemed distinctly uncomfortable with the demands he felt his aunt's letters made upon
him and suggested as much in responding only with brief missives. Mary
countered with briefer letters of her own. "Tell Charles I continue to
write him," Mary wrote Waldo in 1831, "but his continued little letters
make me afraid to send so long a one." And to Charles himself, in an uncharacteristically brief note of the same month, she confessed "I dare not
write long to you least you should fear them & not continue these precious dots of paper."[73]

Mary's comment suggests that she understood, at least dimly, that a
healthy correspondence entailed constant modification of not only quality and intent but also quantity of content. To write a series of long letters
and to receive a series of short ones in response was to be told, as clearly
as it was possible to tell without words, that the correspondent wished

not to trade long letters. And while a really accomplished (or secure) let-ter writer could adjust to circumstances without comment, others felt the need to address their concerns explicitly. Writing to Louisa Gilman in 1813, for example, Caroline Howard explained her letter's brevity. "The *wide margin* will probably tell you that your long silence has a little abat-ed my confidence, but ten kind words from you will call forth every idea in my brain to wait upon you."[74] The metronomic ideal of reciprocity, in other words, in which gift was rewarded with counter-gift and counter-gift with further gifts, was in reality tempered by the realization that such ideals could not be sustained indefinitely or protected from the press of other obligations and exigencies.

Who should pay? Correspondence, in other words, entailed a form of epistolary haggling, and William Merrill Decker is surely right in argu-ing that "letters arise within private economies that call for personal ex-change 'in kind.'" To see correspondence as solely a form of barter, how-ever, obscures the fact that cash was a consideration, for whenever a pri-vate letter passed through the postal service, it cost money.[75] Between the passage of the Post Office Act of 1792 and its major revision in the Post Office Act of 1845, the cost of sending a letter by mail was determined by a complex calculation that factored the distance a letter had to travel by the number of sheets the letter contained. A 1798 postal manual, for example, outlined nine zones with fees ranging from six cents per sheet for distances of less than thirty miles up to twenty-five cents for distanc-es of more than four hundred and fifty; use of two sheets (or an enclo-sure) doubled the cost of postage, three sheets trebled it, and so on. Sub-sequent legislation reduced the number of zones to five but retained the range of fees.[76] Historians have conducted a lively debate as to whether the increase in the number of post offices and postal roads in the early republic promoted a general democratization of letter writing, or wheth-er the price of sending letters along these roads and to these post offices rendered it prohibitive for all but the wealthiest white men. While schol-ars dispute the types of evidence used and the conclusions to which they point, what is undeniable is that short of having a friend carry a letter pri-vately to its destination—a phenomenon that was not uncommon—let-ters cost an appreciable sum of money.[77]

Perhaps more significant than how much any given letter cost, howev-er, was the question of who would pay, for while the sender could exer-cise that option, he or she was not obligated to pay in advance, and it was far more common for the recipient to pay the postage on mail. Indeed, an elaborate but rarely stated etiquette surrounded the issue of payment for letters. What makes this etiquette fascinating is that it appears to invert the correlation we would suppose. Theoretically, when individuals sent a business letter, they prepaid the postage, while when they sent familiar letters they allowed the recipient to pay. The logic has been explained by the argument that familiar letter writers, who used the postal system far less often than businessmen and therefore had less cause to trust their missives would arrive, preferred not to pay for a letter that they were unsure would make it to its destination. Whether or not this is the case, it created a bizarre situation in which the recipient of impersonal business letters paid nothing while the recipients of personal and gift-like letters had to pay for the privilege of receiving tokens of esteem. Letter writers carefully policed the contents of their missives to determine whether they fell more nearly into one category or the other. When Robert Montgomery Bird sent a letter to James Lawson that began "Dear Lawson—(You dress salads so gloriously, I can't call you *sir* for my soul) . . ." it is abundantly clear from his informal tone that he had written a familiar letter and would expect Lawson to pay, but in a later letter—still extraordinarily witty but concerned with the duplicities of publishers—Bird concluded with a curt postscript: "As I consider this a business letter, I intend to pay the post." Of course, genre boundaries are permeable and subject to contestation. Finding his letter degenerating into gossip, Charles Fenno Hoffman concluded by promising his correspondent, Rufus Griswold, not to "say a word more lest you forget this is a business letter, although from a lack of change it will cost you a shilling."[78]

Just as often as they monitored the contents of their missives to determine whether or not they were business letters or friendly letters, however, correspondents also monitored the direction of their relationships to determine whether they were more business-like or friendly and used postage accordingly. Infuriated that his mother was not responding more promptly to his letters, James Gates Percival reacted waspishly by telling her "I will give you no further trouble than to read my letters, for I shall pay the postage of all I send." In insisting that he would prepay postage on letters to his mother, Percival was not showing her generosity so much as spite; the suggestion was that his mother was derelict in her obligations and would only show maternal concern when it did not entail financial sacrifices.[79] Yet if prepaying postage could be seen as a rebuke to the unfriendly, not paying postage could just as easily be criticized as a token presumptuous familiarity. When antislavery activist Benjamin Rodman of New Bedford sent a letter to a proslavery British consul, Edmund Molyneux, in Savannah, Georgia, in 1839, asking him for an account of his possibly nefarious role in a plan to defraud several slaves of their freedom, he not only received a terse denial in response but also a postscript, requesting that the next time he write he pay postage. Molyneux's retort made it clear that he wished for no intimacy with Rodman and would not pay in future to be insulted. The request for prepayment was a way of establishing boundaries. Very pointedly, Rodman sent twenty-five cents to the Savannah postmaster with a message hoping that Molyneux "will no longer consider me in his debt," and he then had both Molyneaux's letter and his own published in his local newspaper. It was an extraordinarily clever move on Rodman's part, for while his initial failure to prepay his letter might have been somewhat presumptuous, paying it in the way that Rodman did showed a quite literally calculating superciliousness. Rodman's payment of the postage fee, that is, was not a gift, inasmuch as gifts pass between equals, so much as it was charity, dispensed by economically the secure to their social inferiors. If Molyneux would not treat Rodman as his equal, then Rodman would treat Molyneux as his subordinate. Molyneux would now seem in Rodman's debt.[80]

Sometimes the refusal to prepay postage was unambiguously punitive, a fact that was not lost on Elihu Embree. An abolitionist editor in Tennessee, Embree had sent a copy of his newspaper, *The Emancipator*, to every governor in the nation. Infuriated at what they perceived to be an insult to their way of life, several Southern governors retaliated. The governor of Mississippi sent an unpaid letter to Embree explaining that he did not wish to subscribe and would not pay "even one cent" for the paper—a sentiment that cost Embree twenty-five times that amount—while the governor of North Carolina returned the paper to Embree deliberately unwrapped, so that it went at letter rate rather than the reduced rate for newspapers, and cost Embree a dollar rather than a cent and a half.[81] Yet even anti-slavery activists used the same strategy. Writing to an insistent Stephen Foster in 1829, William Lloyd Garrison confessed that even though he would be home in a few days, he was "determined to punish your pocket with a tax of 12½ cents before I leave, not only because you were promised 'a *long* letter,' but because you have been so urgent with your 'write! write!'"[82] What Garrison seems to be suggesting is that if Foster insisted on demanding letters, he must be willing to pay for the privilege. Emily Chubbuck was somewhat more considerate. Confessing that she was "not in the best possible humor for letter writing," she nonetheless promised her sister that she would do her best under the circumstances, "knowing that you will be obliged to pay the fee before you examine the contents."[83]

Even friendly correspondents were aware of the obligations that postal fees placed on participants in a letter exchange. Mary Moody Emerson sought to allay her nephew Charles's guilt on this score by assuring him she could afford to pay for his letters without trouble. "Never stop

a letter for postage sake," she told him at one point, and, when his letters seemed to taper off, she asked "'What will the *post Master* think'?
that I am becoming so poor that I have no bill?"[84] Some writers apparently were truly this poor. When Thomas Holley Chivers sent two letters to Edgar Allan Poe and then went a year without receiving a reply,
his automatic assumption was that because the letters had not been prepaid, Poe had not been able to afford to retrieve them from the post office.[85] Doubtless many people would have preferred not to have to pay
for their letters: a mock dictionary of 1837 defined "paid" as "A word
written on the outside of a letter that serves to render it acceptable to the
receiver." Yet according to the complex logic of epistolary etiquette, it
was inappropriate to expect a writer to give the gift of a letter and the gift
of postage at the same time. Years before he was confronted by Daniel
Pierce Thompson, John Neal learned this lesson the hard way. Writing to
Grenville Mellen in 1819, Neal issued a bald request: "'When you write,
please pay the post!' I am poor; and my correspondents are all better off
than I am." Neal's request might have been reasonable but it evidently
complicated his relationship with Mellen, making him so much the debt-
or to his friend that he quickly rescinded the order. Mere weeks later he
pled: "Pay no more postage. I can afford it both ways, and we must have
no more squeamishness."[86] If there was a potential for squeamishness in
writing letters, that potential, I have tried to suggest, was intimately tied
to the gift dimensions of epistolarity.

"DAMN YOU SEND ME A PAPER": EXCHANGE NETWORKS

Our discussion so far might perhaps lead the reader to suppose that
the Post Office was concerned primarily with the transmission of letters,
but a glance inside a postal sack at any time between the 1790s and the
1850s, would have revealed more newspapers than letters. The extent
to which the Post Office served—even existed—to transport newspapers
rather than letters is hard to overstate. Through the antebellum period,
they rarely made up less than 40 and sometimes amounted to as much as
60 percent of all items carried. And while they closely matched letters on
an item-by-item basis, they greatly overwhelmed them in terms of weight.
A government survey estimated that in 1832, newspapers constituted 95
percent of mail by weight. The presence of so many newspapers in the
mail was a consequence of the government's belief that the health of the
nation was dependent on its citizens' access to reliable and up-to-date
political information. To make sure that such information flowed free-

ly and widely, newspapers were transmitted to readers at only nominal costs: one cent per newspaper for distances of up to 100 miles and a cent and a half for distances greater than this. Fixed by the Post Office Act of 1792, these rates remained essentially unchanged through the antebellum period, with the result that while newspapers made up 95 percent of the postal weight in 1832, they generated only 15 percent of the Post Office's annual revenue. At such nominal costs, paid for in any case, by the recipient rather than the newspaper proprietor, it is hardly surprising that so many papers were transmitted by mail.[87]

Of course, the information in any given newspaper was only as reliable as the means through which it was gathered, and in an age before roving reporters and correspondents, news was collected largely on a local basis and shared by means of cooperative exchange of newspapers between editors, so that readers in Springfield, Massachusetts, could find out what was transpiring in, say, Springfield, Illinois. A great deal of an editor's day-to-day activity consisted of combing through the exchange papers with a pair of scissors and a paste pot, looking for interesting items to clip and paste onto sheets of paper to be given to the compositor. Hezekiah Niles, for example, estimated that he spent as much as three full days a week reading out-of-state publications for items of news to use in his *Weekly Register*.[88] Concerned to guarantee the quality of this news, the Post Office Act of 1792 permitted newspaper printers to send copies of their papers to other newspaper establishments free of charge. Newspaper editors thereby developed powerful and widely spread networks through which their ideas traveled and through which they received and communicated the ideas of others. When a youthful John Howard Payne began to publish his *Thespian Mirror* in 1805, a brief notice was published in the New York *Evening Post* and quickly passed through editor William Coleman's exchange network. "Paragraphs have been inserted in almost all the papers of the United States," Payne told his parents, "the *Political Register*, edited by Mayor Jackson, Philadelphia;—*Port Folio*, same place;—*Albany Centinel*;—*Federal Gazette*, Baltimore;—*Balance*, Hudson; Daily *Advertiser*, Philadelphia, etc., etc. . . . The purport of the whole is pretty much the same as M. Coleman's." Exchange networks certainly allowed news to travel quickly and often widely. Editor Charles Lummus liked to joke that he once ran a brief local story headlined "Huckleberries is Ripe" and promptly saw it reprinted across the nation.[89] So effective a technique was the exchange network that—Huckleberry errors aside—even magazine editors, who had to pay to use the post, exchanged their publications among themselves and with newspaper printers. By the early 1850s, *Godey's Ladies' Book* exchanged with

1,500 newspapers and *Graham's Magazine* with more than 2,100, even though the newspapers traveled through the mail without charge while *Godey's* and *Graham's* did not. Exchange networks meant that there was no such thing as a truly local or provincial publication in the antebellum period.[90]

At first blush, newspaper exchanges seem like a form of literary bartering—a swap of paper for paper—and certainly there is some truth to this. Hezekiah Niles, for example, required that editors of papers costing less than his send him the difference in cash as a condition of exchange, adding that he would willingly pay the difference himself when exchanging with papers that cost more. Niles was right, of course, in calling this an exchange "on reciprocal principles," but it was a "balanced" form of reciprocity, with the balance, moreover, being calculated in strictly economic terms.[91] More typically, editors disavowed such economic score-keeping, preferring, instead, to belabor the gratuity and goodwill on which their exchanges were based. The editor of the *African Repository*, for example, noted with satisfaction that many of the papers and magazines he received cost considerably more than his own and conjectured that they were sent "out of love to the cause in which we are engaged." Doubtless it was such love of principle that led the editor to continue sending his magazine to others "whose papers we do not receive in return," for what he was describing was a world of "generalized" reciprocity in which one did good without expectation of immediate or direct recompense. The editor of the *Reformer* went one step further in announcing that its paper was so inexpensive that he would insist on sending it to others "for a length of time" without any need for exchange. If editors wished to send their publications from time to time, the editor added, "we shall esteem it an especial favor." Discussion of exchange, in fact, was rich with the language of "favors," "courtesies," and "friends." It was, in other words, a language of gifts.[92]

Newspaper exchanges certainly resembled gift exchanges. An exchange relationship typically began when one newspaper sent a copy of its publication to another using the printer's privilege to transmit papers without charge. Because only newspapers and not letters enjoyed this privilege, the editor would write on the margin "exchange," "please to exchange," or "Do me the favour to exchange." When the *Boston Cultivator* started publication in 1839, it promptly received forty-eight different papers from editors "who solicit an exchange, without a single request on our part."[93] These initial papers were a form of courting gift, akin, functionally, to the flirtatious poems written in albums and designed to create bonds. If the recipient found the paper useful or enjoyed reading it, or (sometimes) if the editor was a friend or a political ally, he would send a paper in return and an exchange relationship would be initiated. Editors often heralded publicly the initiation of a new exchange. "We have received a number of THE LOWEL CASKET A LITERARY JOURNAL," wrote James O'Halloran of the *Burlington Sentinel* in 1837. "It is finely executed & is full of entertaining matter. We accept the exchange with pleasure." The *Sentinel* in fact accepted many exchanges with pleasure. A single issue published in July of that year included items from the *New Yorker, Genesee Balance, New Hampshire Telegraph, Saturday Courier, Fall River Patriot, New Orleans Bulletin,* and the *Albany Argus,* together with an account of the meeting of the Burlington Democrats, and several unattributed pieces concerning Texas that could not have been gleaned directly. Only one item in the paper has the byline 'For the Burlington Sentinel.'[94]

The benefits of making gifts of papers extended far beyond the mere gathering of news; it was a means of creating and sustaining relationships. "Copy largely from the editorial departments of your brethren," advised William Joseph Snelling in his facetious "Hints to Editors of Newspapers." "It will please them because it looks as if you respected their opinions, and they will reciprocate the compliment. They will take your part if you get yourself into trouble, and speak of you as a worthy citizen and a man of sound judgement."[95] Exchange networks, as Snelling perceptively noted, had a tendency to generate alliances and networks of like-minded editors; some have seen them, indeed, as crucial to the formation and success of political parties in the early republic.[96] Sometimes, it is true, political opponents would exchange papers or magazines, out of a mutual need to know their enemies. Gamaliel Bailey, editor of the abolitionist *National Era,* noted with some satisfaction that its exchange list for the South was "very extensive." Exchanging papers, for Bailey, as with the exchange of gifts among traditional groups more generally, was a means through which truces could be established. It was not that Southern editors cared for the *National Era,* nor it for them, but it was expedient to remain in contact, and Bailey hoped, too, that by keeping the lines of communication open, his message might in time become more palatable.[97] More generally, though, newspaper exchanges were a means of policing networks, keeping out opponents while drawing allies closer together. A Democratic editor sought to test the limits of goodwill with self-deprecating humor, sending a single issue of his paper to a Whig publication with the following message on the margin: "We are whole *swine,* but we wish to see how you whigs can lie—will you exchange?" The reply: "No, you bristly brute." At other times, refusal to exchange papers reflected less an ideological antipathy than an overburdened exchange list, or, perhaps, aesthetic snobbery. When Charles Lummus (of Huckleberry fame) sent a copy of his *Lynn Weekly Mirror* to Joseph T. Buckingham of the *New England Galaxy* with the word "exchange" written hopefully across the masthead, he received it back some days later with the second "e" of *Weekly* scratched out and an "a" in its place. To decline the gift of an initial paper was not simply to refuse an exchange but to refuse a relationship.[98]

Gifts are tricky things, and, as Willis Gaylord Clark noted in discussing proffered albums, they were hard to escape. To decline giving them was awkward and to decline receiving them more awkward still. A gift refused was, in important ways, a slap in the face and as the consummately antisocial act was hard to endure with good grace. The experiences of William Rodgers are a case in point. In 1824, Rodgers sent a copy of his paper, the *Nautical Intelligencer*, to Samuel Atkinson of the Philadelphia *Saturday Evening Post* with the customary request to exchange. Pleading an overextended exchange list, Atkinson sent a copy of the *Post* in return with a marginal note declining to enter into an exchange relationship. Rather than accept the refusal, however, Rodgers sent Atkinson another copy of the *Intelligencer* with a note to the effect that he would decline all further copies of the *Post* and throw any more he received into the ocean. Atkinson then replied with a copy of *his* paper with a doggerel rhyme deriding the *Intelligencer* written on the margin, to which the *Intelligencer* responded, and so on.[99] Nothing about this scenario makes obvious sense. The *Intelligencer*, which wished to receive the *Post* ended up refusing all copies; the *Post*, which had declined to send its paper issued forth a steady stream. More to the point, the confrontation between the papers seems far from the world of reciprocity we associate with gifts. In fact, the encounter corresponds quite closely to the logic of the gift, and readers with a knowledge of anthropological literature might recognize in the structure of the dispute a variation on the Northwest American ceremony known as the Potlatch. In a Potlatch, leaders of various tribes vied with one another to give away the most or the most valuable of their possessions; it was, in the words of Marcel Mauss, a "war of wealth," one in which the combatants sought to shed material capital and by so doing accumulate symbolic capital.[100] This was precisely what the editors of the *Intelligencer* and the *Post* sought to do, since each felt scorned by the other. When the editor of the *Post* sent the second, third, and fourth copy of his paper, he was not expressing esteem but contempt, not generosity but hostility. His aim was to show that he was at once rich in newspapers and perfectly indifferent to the editor of the *Intelligencer* and his needs. When the editor of the *Intelligencer* sent copies of his paper back to Atkinson, he was showing his contempt in turn but seeking also to indicate that he wished to owe nothing to Atkinson. He would throw his papers into the sea before he would go into his debt. The mutual unwillingness of the editors to engage in reciprocal relations culminated, ironically, in their reciprocal relatedness. They were as entangled by the exchange of gifts as friends or lovers, but they neither liked nor loved one another. Although the confrontation ended with the refusal of the *Post* to bandy any further words—or newspapers—with the *Intelligencer*, it is hard to tell who came off the victor. Doubtless, each believed the other to be the loser of the affair.

Since a willingness to receive and exchange gifts (in the form of papers) was the baseline for connectedness, it should come as little surprise that most editors monitored their exchange lists carefully, using them as a bellwether for the state of their editorial relationships more generally. When one publication was dropped from another's list—an all too common event as lists burgeoned and more interesting or useful papers came to notice—the editor of the paper dropped inevitably felt a sting that was as much personal as professional. The editor of the *Ariel*, for example, expressed deep hurt at the "unceremonious" way in which his magazine was dropped from the exchange list of the *Bower of Taste*, when that magazine absorbed another with which the *Ariel* had exchanged. "A little courtesy in such cases, is all we contend for—if a wish to decline had been expressed, we should say nothing—but as it is, we must say it was rather ungenteel."[101] Still more touchy was the editor of the *Lynn News*. When three months passed without the customary arrival of the popular Boston *Olive Branch*, he announced that he believed his paper's "turning out to be derogatory to our character; and it shall go hard with the Olive Branch, as far as oysters are concerned, if it does not at once clear us from the imputation it has bought upon us by its heartless proscription."[102] Such feelings of insult and corresponding threats of reprisal make no sense except in terms of the logic of the gift, according to which a gift bestowed is an open hand, a gift refused a hand closed, and a gift returned is an attack on one's character. It comes as little surprise, then, that when austerity measures compelled John Neal to trim the exchange list of his *Yankee* magazine, dropped editor John Greenleaf Whittier assumed the move had stemmed from a "want of kind feeling" on Neal's part rather than anything else. Sensitive though Whittier was, he was simply following the logic of the gift.[103]

Gifts create bonds, but bonds bind, and not everyone wishes to be tied to another in a relationship based on a potentially endless cycle of mutual indebtedness. This, at least, was probably the feeling of one recipient of the *Burlington Sentinel*. After apparently sending several copies of the *Sentinel* to an unresponsive fellow editor, James O'Halloran was reduced to invective, scribbling across the masthead of his publication: "Damn you send me a paper."[104] Like Daniel Pierce Thompson, like Ollapod's milliner, and like the hapless Mary Moody Emerson, O'Halloran failed to understand that a gift given did not entail a foolproof sense of obligation in the recipient. Although he seemed to be participating in a world of gift exchange, O'Halloran was edging toward a world of binding contract.

"HAMMYDIDDLE IN PLENTY BUT NO PAY": THE 'SOUTHERN LITERARY MESSENGER'

By exploring the role of gifts economics in the exchange of albums, letters, and newspapers, I have tried to make it clear that prestation was a broadly based phenomenon through which reams of written and printed material circulated in early national and antebellum America. In organizing my discussion so that it moves from more intimate to more utilitarian manifestations of gift exchange, I have, in addition, tried to suggest that gift-giving was not only a private activity but a public one; not merely an 'amateur' pastime but one engaged in by men and women of business. To these observations, a third and very important one can now be added, which is that for some literary entrepreneurs, gift exchange was not even an adjunct to literary business but was the means by which business itself was conducted, providing both motive and modus operandi.

In no case is this more true than in the world of magazines and newspapers, where the cooperation of many parties was required and where collaboration (and hence goodwill) for sustained periods of time was not only desirable but downright necessary. Magazines, that is to say, required immense amounts of social capital. And we can be yet more specific here. According to sociologist Robert D. Putnam, social capital can manifest itself in two ways: as bonding capital and bridging capital. Bonding capital tends to circulate among and constitute tightly woven groups; bridging capital, by contrast, tends to reflect connections forged between disparate individuals and communities.[105] Each sort supported the well-being of periodical publications. It has long been known, for example, that periodicals in the antebellum period were sometimes sustained by literary clubs and societies, those consummate manifestations of bonded capital. *The Portico* in Baltimore, for instance, drew most of its material and moral support from the members of the local Delphian

Society, the *Western Monthly Magazine* in Cincinnati from the Semi-Colon Club, the *Monthly Anthology* in Boston from the Anthology Society, the *Monthly Magazine* in New York from the Friendly Club, and the *Round Table* from a club of Hartford litterateurs orbiting around Samuel Goodrich.[106] It is increasingly becoming clear, too, that even when periodicals were not sustained by the existence of formal organizations, they were buoyed by informal networks of friends and friends of friends, a social formation typical of bridged capital. Joseph Dennie's *Farmer's Weekly Museum*, published in the implausibly far-flung location of Walpole, New Hampshire, managed to establish a remarkable stable of writers and gain two thousand subscribers across the nation by dint of Dennie's ability to harness the energies of his collegiate network of friends who contributed material and drummed up supporters out of loyalty to their former classmate and who led him to be accepted in more distant communities.[107]

Little enough attention has been paid to the way in which social capital—by that name or any other—facilitated the production of periodicals and magazines; absolutely none has been give to the extent to which any of this social capital was generated and sustained through sometimes elaborate networks of gift-giving. More than any other literary genre or institution, the serial publication was a beneficiary of systematic and shrewd gift-exchange practices that generated the connections that constitute social capital and thereby buttressed the business of magazines.

If we have failed to appreciate the degree to which early national and antebellum magazines relied upon gift economics, it is primarily because such activities have been obscured by scholars' relentless emphasis on the amateurism of such publications. It is an image that was effectively and influentially codified more than fifty years ago by Frank Luther Mott, in his Pulitzer Prize-winning *History of American Magazines*. Anticipating the arguments of his close-contemporary William Charvat, Mott explained that while most periodical proprietors in this period "had some anticipation of financial reward," few in fact realized their ambitions. Eighteenth- and early nineteenth-century periodicals were, in his memorably pithy opinion, characterized by "short lives and small circulations." More to the point, periodical proprietors rarely paid their contributors, paid them little when they did, and often paid tardily. Indeed, even after the 1840s, when a handful of magazine editors like George Graham and Louis Godey began to pay selected celebrity contributors very well, "adequate payment to contributors" remained the exception rather than the rule. The relentless focus of modern scholars on what antebellum periodicals lacked, rather than what they had, what they failed to achieve rather than what they managed, and what they ought to have been rather than what they were, has tended to consign them to the interpretive black hole of "amateurism," which, as I suggested in Chapter One, means that little can be said of them other than they were not, or not yet, wholly professional. This narrative, or one very much like it, has, in fact, been endorsed by almost all scholars of early national and antebellum periodicals. Speaking of the former, for example, Michael Gilmore describes their contributors as "amateurs, for no one who wrote for the magazines made a living at it," while on the subject of the latter, Michael Davitt Bell explains that "neither editors nor authors could expect much remuneration for their efforts," adding that for promoters of periodicals in general, "failure remained the norm."[108] Even Ellery Sedgwick, who claims that the antebellum periodical, more than any other genre, "made professionalism possible," points out that "very few" authors could make it to "the very top of the pay scale" and argues that most periodical editors of the time remained mired in amateurism.[109]

Thomas Willis White would seem to fit this profile almost perfectly. The proprietor and sometime editor of the *Southern Literary Messenger*, which he founded in Richmond, Virginia, in 1834 and steered until his death in 1843, White seemed constantly on the brink of financial collapse. His printers sometimes went on strike; he often suffered from shortages of paper; he could not afford a full-time editor; he paid his contributors only rarely; and when he did pay them, he almost always paid late. A printer by trade, modest by nature, and indeed almost embarrassingly self-deprecating, White regularly admitted to his correspondents that he was "a wretched economist," "no critic," "thickheaded," "a simpleton," and "a numskull."[110] And as if this was not enough to damn him in the eyes of posterity, White also had the singular misfortune to put a young Edgar Allan Poe on his payroll for about fifteen months. Poe repaid White's patience and generosity by deriding the *Messenger* and, after White's death in 1843, claiming that under his own stewardship the *Messenger*'s subscription base had been increased by 600 percent, an assertion that has only recently and definitively been proven false.[111] Criticized by Poe and routinely condemned out of his own mouth, White has thus offered to magazine historians a textbook, indeed, almost a caricaturish, example of the editor-as-amateur. The assessment of literary critic Robert D. Jacobs is typical in this respect. Damning White with faint praise as a "courageous little printer," Jacobs argues that he was doomed from the start as a magazine proprietor, because he failed to "secure regular contributions from competent professional writers." Instead, he relied on what Jacobs calls "lady scribblers" and "amateur authors" who "showed neither professional standards nor consistent production."[112]

In the pages that follow, I want to argue that so far from being an amateur buffoon, White was in fact a shrewd, tenacious, and effective manipulator of gift exchanges, which he pressed into the service of his magazine. By using gifts to make and keep friends, accumulate favors, dispense rewards, and create goodwill, White managed to keep the *Messenger* alive in the teeth of all adversity. The extent to which he succeeded is attested to by the facts. The *Southern Literary Messenger* was the longest-running magazine published in the antebellum South, surviving from 1834 to 1864, and with thirty years to its credit, it lasted not only longer than any other Southern magazine but also for longer than most Northern magazines too. Its subscriptions, we now know, rose slowly, but steadily and consistently, throughout White's years at the helm, even though these included the Panic of 1837 and its aftermath. And its roster of authors was incredibly prestigious, including such luminaries as Lydia Sigourney, James Kirke Paulding, Sarah Hale, former President James Madison, and others. Finally, and in mitigation of his image as a bumbler, it is worth noting that while White often had to scramble for money, he always found it; while he had to hustle for contributors, he always got them; and while he wheedled for puffs, exchanges, favors, and review copies, they were always forthcoming. That White did as well as he did—and under the circumstances he succeeded admirably—can be explained almost wholly by reference to his adroit participation in a world of gifts and gift exchange.

White's supporters formed three concentric circles. The innermost group was comprised of those who served as de facto editors and substantial contributors to the magazine. Among them were James Ewell Heath, Edwin Vernon Sparhawk, Lucian Minor, and Nathaniel Beverley Tucker. All of them were members of the Virginia elite, many of them had trained as lawyers, and they tended to shared a proslavery and states' rights ideology. These were men to whom White turned on a regular basis, writing them sometimes two or three times a week. They were his friends in need and in deed.[113] The secondary circle consisted of less regular contributors: authors who lived outside of Virginia whom White had not met, or with whom he had less intense relationships. Unlike the inner circle, they did not necessarily share White's political or regional affiliation, and some of them, in fact, were quite stridently opposed to slavery. Their relationship with White was typically defined by literary rather than ideological affinity. The outermost circle of White's universe was

made up of printers, publishers, editors, and periodical proprietors located around the nation. Some of them White knew personally, for he had
worked as an apprentice and journeyman not only in Virginia but also
in Washington, Philadelphia, and Boston, while others were simply those
whom he knew by reputation. Linked more by business than esteem and
united more by expedience than admiration, White reached out to such
men in order to establish a network with whom he could exchange publications, through whom he could solicit subscriptions, and from whom
he could ask for puffs. Many editors of the 1830s had a support structure
similar to that enjoyed by White but, typically, such networks existed pri-
or to the establishment of their magazines; indeed, it was often the existence of such groups that spurred the founding of the publications. Because White was neither the intellectual nor the social peer of those who
supported his magazine, however, and because he did not enjoy the support of a powerful coterie as he launched the *Messenger*, he used gifts to
connect to (and in some sense create) each group, with the ultimate goal
of drawing members of the outer circles closer to the center of his literary
universe.

Typical of those in White's inner circle was Nathaniel Beverley Tucker. Son of a distinguished Virginian jurist and novelist, Tucker came to
White's attention shortly after he was appointed professor of law at the
College of William and Mary in 1834. In November of that year, White
reached out to Tucker with an initial gift, sending him the first two issues of the *Messenger* and expressing his "anxious desire that you will
contribute some day to enrich and adorn its columns." It was a fairly in-
nocuous present, modest in cost, and with little coercive freight. Tucker
quickly obliged, offering an essay that appeared in the December issue. A
vociferous and prolific intellectual, he saw in White's magazine the perfect means through which to promote his political agenda.[114] White, for
his part, saw in Tucker a new friend and, following his first contribution,
a potential savior. A flood of letters to Tucker followed, and within weeks
White's gifts became more extravagant and more openly manipulative. In
January 1835, he informed Tucker that he had subscribed to a new edition of Washington's letters "on purpose to present it to you." The "return I wish to ask at your hand," he explained, "is that you will notice
the volumes as they are received by you." Only four days later yet another thick volume—this time George Bancroft's *History*—arrived. It is
"for your Library," explained White, generously. "This is the disposition
I wish you to make of every work you may review for my Messenger."[115]
These were frankly coercive gifts. By belaboring the expense he had gone
to in procuring them, and by offering them to him without charge, White

made it hard for Tucker to refuse them and impossible to accept them without writing reviews in return.

The preemptive and manipulative gift was White's signature strategy, and he used it often and with great success, perpetually pushing at the boundaries of decorum. Overstepping the boundary was another of White's signatures. In March 1835, for example, he sent Tucker's wife a seventy-nine-piece set of china. "I send it as a token of my affectionate regard," he wrote, "and beg that in the same spirit it be received by your lady and yourself." While we do not have Tucker's response, it is clear that the gift made him uncomfortable, inasmuch as it both presumed a greater degree of intimacy than their brief relationship warranted and created an unseemly feeling of indebtedness. In response to Tucker's apparent embarrassment, White sought to minimize the value of the gift and to reassure his contributor that it reflected a generalized and not a balanced sense of reciprocity. The plates "were not sent as rewards," he insisted, "but were offered in simplicity of feeling. . . . It is a golden maxim with me, 'to do unto others, as I would be done by.' I endeavor to keep this maxim continually before my mind,—and to conform to it as near as possible."[116] Tucker relented, and over the years of their relationship, published dozens of essays, reviews, and filler items for White, while also taking time to vet submissions, correct proof, and work on tables of content and indices. White continued to make Tucker gifts, but they were less extravagant than the china and less obviously coercive. That Tucker was sincerely interested in supporting the *Messenger* is beyond question; the degree to which he did so, however, was dictated by White's endless stream of gifts.[117]

White's relations with other members of his inner circle were no less based on the preemptive bestowal of gifts. To Lucian Minor, for example, he gave finely bound volumes of the *Messenger* "as a kind of remembrance," free offprints and books issued from his press. Sometimes, his gifts were less tangible. "I wish to God," he wrote in 1835, "I had $2000. It should be yours to make a year's tour throughout Europe."[118] Finally, White belabored his goodwill in his salutations and subscriptions, addressing Minor as "My Friend" and describing himself as "Your Constant Friend," "Your devoted friend," "Your Real Friend," and "Your true friend." By showering Minor with warm wishes and polite gifts, White was able to create a relationship in which favors passed in both directions. Minor, in fact, turned out to be one of White's most stalwart supporters, writing essays and reviews, reading proof, vetting submissions, collecting subscriptions, and preparing indices. He almost never asked for money and on several occasions flatly refused to receive it when offered. Minor was almost endlessly accommodating, yet even here, White offered gifts that were frankly manipulative as, for example, when he sent Minor a packet of paper, a bottle of ink, and several quills. "Thus equipped," he wrote somewhat piously, "I hope you will go to battle for me in good earnest."[119]

Tucker, Minor, and other members of the *Messenger*'s inner circle were, by and large, happy to put up with White's sometimes ham-fisted social engineering, and between them, they produced hundreds of pages for the *Messenger*. Yet there were limits to what even the most accommodating author could produce, and the magazine sometimes suffered for lack of material. Responding to a litany of complaints from White, Joseph Hopkinson explained what he believed to be the *Messenger*'s fatal flaw. "I have long been satisfied by repeated examples," he wrote, "that a journal such as yours, cannot be sustained for a long period by gratuitous contributions of original matter—the friends of the publisher or of the enterprize, will for a time furnish their aid with spirit and punctuality—But at length they grow weary, or are 'not in the vein'—or are drawn off to new objects."[120]

Hopkinson was absolutely right in supposing that the *Messenger*'s inner circle was susceptible to what might be called contributor fatigue, and, doubtless, he was right, too, in tracing the failure of many magazines to this source. Philip Pendleton Cooke recalled in 1839 that in the magazine's early years he was "guilty" of "systematic contribution" because "the 'madness of scribbling' . . . itched and tickled at my fingersends," but that in time the "fever with which I was afflicted has given way to a chill."[121] White's strategy was not to presume too much on the goodwill of his contributor friends, but, rather, to search constantly for new friends on whose goodwill he could rely. In the first instance, White simply used the friends he had in order to make new friends. On repeated occasions, for example, he asked Tucker to approach his colleagues at William and Mary for support, and, indeed, many of them did become contributors in turn, although typically they remained in secondary orbit around the magazine. Or, again, he sought to tap into the network of New York man of letters James Lawson by offering to puff any of their works in the *Messenger*, explaining that "I like to serve my friends, and my friends friends also."[122] Just as often, however, White simply reached out to relative or complete strangers, and with his incredible faith in the power of gifts, sought to make new friends who would contribute to his periodical for free.

White's transactions with Barber Badger, editor of the *New York*

Weekly Messenger, exemplify the way in which he was able to generate substantial support from an apparently slight acquaintance. Writing
to Badger in May 1836, White reminded him that they had met twenty
years earlier while journeymen printers in Boston and on this slight and
distant connection, he took it upon himself to send five issues of his magazine, explaining that he would like Badger to read them carefully and
then print a review of them in the *Weekly Messenger*. White's connection
to Badger was glancing enough, but then again so was his request, being
little more than an extended version of the sort of puffing that went on
routinely in the process of exchanging papers and magazines. But White
didn't stop here. "If hereafter," he continued, "you can devote a little
time to rendering my periodical more interesting, I hope you will do so
in an essay for its pages—in remuneration for which I offer you the enclosed remuneration." It is impossible to tell at this distance in what the
remuneration consisted, but the awkward redundancy of White's phras-
ing is nonetheless immensely revealing. While polite convention understood gifts to be given freely, White quite literally saw them as preemptive
remuneration. When he sent a finely bound volume, a set of offprints, or
even a sum of money, he was very often trying to pay for services he was
not sure were even available. In Badger's case, the tactic seemed to work
at least to a degree, since a review of the *Southern Literary Messenger* appeared in the *Weekly Messenger* within days. White, presumptuously, but
typically, offered to send the next month's issue in sheets to ensure a still
faster turn around in what he hoped would be a "detailed review."[123]

But White gained considerably more from this transaction than simply
a puff or two, for Badger passed White's letters on to the *Weekly Messenger*'s proprietor, William Scott, to whom White immediately made a gift
and from whom he immediately started to solicit favors. Writing to Scott
in August 1836, White explained that he had already started sending him
exchange copies of his magazine but would also list him on the cover
of the publication as a "paying subscriber" and would also send him a
bound copy of the magazine's first volume, "For all of which," he added magnanimously, "I positively refuse to receive once cent in money."
Such trifles were merely his way of saying thank you for puffing his magazine, contacting other New York editors, and finding perhaps "100 paying subscribers." And as if this was not enough, White also hoped Scott
would "add to the variety of my columns." Scott, in turn, served as an
agent through whom White was able to seek additional authors. In courting these tertiary contributors, White relied not on their goodwill to him
but to Scott, using his friend as a proxy. In November 1836, for example,

he had Scott deliver ten issues of the *Southern Literary Messenger* to a Miss Medina and instructed him to "urge her, *as from yourself*, to send me something for the Messenger." Miss Medina promptly obliged.[124]

Edgar Allan Poe came into White's orbit in similar fashion, being introduced to White by another contributor, John Pendleton Kennedy, whom he had been courting. In addition to sending his stories and reviews to the *Messenger*, Poe also wrote several puffs in Baltimore newspapers, to which he clearly had access. "I must insist on your not sending me any remuneration for services of this nature," he told White. "They are a pleasure to me & no trouble whatsoever."[125]

In such a way, seeking gifts from friends, using gifts to make them, and reaching out through them to find yet more, White was able to develop a remarkably far reaching network of secondary and tertiary contributors, always seeking through deliberate and sometimes clumsy acts of generosity to draw those on the farther reaches of his world closer to the center of his literary universe. He succeeded admirably. While in 1836, he had felt of a want of contributors, by 1839 he was complaining that he had too many, telling Charles Campbell that he was "literally overrun with copy."[126]

Overwhelmingly, the submissions that came flooding into the *Messenger* office were free. To James Lawson, he explained that if a tertiary friend wished to submit something for the *Messenger*, he should "know before hand that he need expect no other reward for his labor than my poor thanks."[127] This is not to say that White never offered his contributors money, because he often did, and sometimes he even paid his authors. Yet even here his actions make far more sense when viewed through the logic of gift exchange than viewed through the lens of contractual obligation. White's scheme of payment is perhaps the hardest aspect of his editorial practice to understand, because as modern scholars we are so habituated to thinking of monetary transactions and gift exchanges as antithetical. For White, however, money could be used as a gift in much the same way as less fungible items such as copies of the *Messenger*.

When dealing with his closest friends, White very sincerely offered them money for their writings, and he expected them just as sincerely to decline, which they often did. The purpose of such transactions was to allow each man to appear generous, White by making an initial offer and his contributor by refusing it. White invariably concluded such exchanges by noting that his gratitude left him speechless, an appropriate response inasmuch as an effective gift exchange was not meant to be subject to scrutiny. Thus James Lawson was often offered money, for example, but he chose to decline on several occasions. "You are so generous as to make me a present of the Poetry," responded White in one letter. "Be it so. I will accept it, because I know you are sincere. The gift is precious to me, and I value it more than I know how to tell you of." Likewise, he found himself at a loss for words in response to Minor's more generous gift. "It is useless for me to say what I felt on reading your letter," he told his friend. "Regret at your declining to receive compensation hereafter for what you may do for me, is too unmeaning a word to convey to you what I should like to say."[128] There was, in fact, a certain, socially scripted reticence on the part of those who gave gifts as well as from White as their recipient. Identifying a long list of contributors to Beverley Tucker, who was making an index for the *Messenger* (his own gift), White noted that with a few exceptions, "no one would accept of cash for their articles,—and it was with some delicacy that they even accepted of volumes of my work for their compliments."[129]

Dissolving the contractual bond between work undertaken and payment received allowed White to treat submissions as gifts to him. It meant, too, that when he did have money and when he gave it to his contributors, this also was to be understood as a gift, this time to them. And again, when he did pay and took time to deliver money, the forbearance he received was in turn yet another gift to him. One might dun an employer for pay but never a friend for a gift. So while Lawson sometimes made a present of his poetry to White, White sometimes made a present of 'payment' to Lawson with the tacit understanding that such sums were more discretionary than contracted for in nature. As we saw in Chapter One, White occasionally stumbled in making these gifts, describing a sum given to Lucian Minor in 1838 as both "pin money" and "hard-earned." By 1841, he had greatly honed his rhetoric. "Presuming, like myself" he told Rufus Griswold in that year, "a little change would not come amiss to you at any time, let me get the favor of you to receive from Mr. Field Four Dollars." Never an especially subtle man, this was really one of White's better puns, using "change" to refer both to the modest amount of money he was offering and also to the rare but welcome change of circumstances that allowed it.[130]

To one other category of authors White extended payment, and this was to those whom he felt *needed* cash, or at least needed it more than he did. To some, in other words, White offered charity. Typically, the recipients of White's charitable payments were women, although the argument can plausibly be made that the payments he made to Edgar Allan Poe after he had fired him from the editorial position at the *Messenger* were made as much from pity as anything else. Responding to Charles Campbell's 1840 complaint that he had not been paid, White explained that he had not paid him "because I believed you did not stand in need of . . . money" and "because I did not know whether you were in earnest or not, when you mentioned the subject." Recompensing him at the rate of a dollar and a half a page, White insisted that his motives were good and that "I have never withheld remuneration from any one who I knew needed it."[131]

That there was a logic to White's payment practices is, I think, beyond dispute, but it was difficult for even his contemporaries to get the measure of it, because the crucial variables in the payment equation were subjective rather than objective, social rather than economic, and veiled rather than obtrusive. When White offered money, it was less a contractual obligation than an attempt to determine the nature of his relationship with that person and determine whether or not they were close enough to forgo payment. The less one liked White, the more likely one was to be paid by him; the more he liked one, the less likely he would be explain his intentions. With those who were genuinely fond of White, this was not a problem, but for those who were agnostic or antipathetic, it was potentially a recipe for disaster, with clarification being offered only in the wake of misunderstanding.

James Russell Lowell's relations with White typify the confusions that could be engendered by the sort of economy on which the *Messenger* was predicated. In early 1840, he had sent White two poems, which appeared in the March issue of the magazine. Evidently expecting some sort of remuneration, he sent a follow-up letter to White and received in return one that contained, in his memorable phrase, "hammydiddle in plenty but no pay." Four days later, payment of a sort did arrive in the form of several free issues of the magazine and a note that he was now listed as a paid subscriber for the year. Mollified, for the moment, and amused by the fact that White believed him to be a Harvard professor, he sent more poetry and even went so far as to tell his friend George Bailey Loring, somewhat jokingly, that all their friends should subscribe to the magazine. Loring promptly submitted some material of his own for which he too received two free issues of the *Messenger* together with a copy of a play White had recently published.[132] To this point, and with the exception of Lowell's initial discomfort, everything was developing in much the way White had come to expect: an author had made him a gift of some work; he had made a gift of his magazine; more contributions had arrived from that author; and he had met yet another author through this one. What White failed to understand was that his gifts notwithstanding, Lowell expected, eventually, to be paid, and to be paid fully, while what Lowell failed to understand was that White couldn't possibly imagine paying

Lowell, since Lowell was, after all, now his friend and not his employee. Their divergent views on the situation became evident very soon thereafter. In April, Lowell received two more issues of the *Messenger* with an "amusing" letter, which he promptly copied into one addressed to Loring, noting that White had subscribed this letter "Your friend" while "in his first letter it was 'respectfully yrs.'" White's letter was "written with *blue* ink, & *should* have been written with *green*," noted Lowell, by which he meant that White must be naïve indeed if he thought that a handful of poems and a few business letters made them friends. It did not.[133] Lowell continued to send poems to White, confident that in time he would receive full payment but being perhaps a little more emphatic in his hints to this effect. By June, his patience was running thin. To Loring he described a letter he had received from White ("two pages") in which the editor told him that "when he gets three thousand paying subscribers he will pay me—writes to come to Richmond & stay at his house, flammydiddles me & c." Lowell fired off a letter to Richmond noting that by the time White had that many subscribers he probably *would* be a professor.[134] By August, Lowell had reached the end of his tether. "I don't think I shall write any more for him," he told Loring. "Tis a bad habit to get into, for a poor man, this writing for nothing." And Lowell was as good as his word; after August he never again published in the *Messenger*. Less than two years later, Lowell was being offered twenty dollars a poem, and within four he was commanding some of the highest pay for poetry offered by magazine editors, one even going so far as to complain that Lowell seemed to treat all editors as "bargain-driving, sharpers."[135]

It would be tempting to see this episode as a conflict between the professional Lowell and the amateur White—between New England dollars and Richmond Hammydiddle—and indeed that argument has been made.[136] To see the ethos (and economy) of the one as displacing that of the other, however, is to miss the point. Lowell was, in fact, one of the most generous and patient authors of the antebellum period, and he participated in the period's literary gift economy as readily and as enthusiastically as anyone. Even as he washed his hands of the impecunious White, for example, he sent a series of poems to Emerson to be published in *The Dial* without ever asking for payment, explaining that "As far as a man loves anything so far it is his, and if you like the Sonnet well enough, you have as much right to it as I."[137] In negotiating with his friend Charles Briggs over the terms on which he would contribute to the latter's new magazine, *The Broadway Journal* in 1845, he again hedged on the question of payment for an essay, confiding: "I am so little in the habit of measuring what I do by dollars and cents that nothing is harder for me than to set a value on my wares. . . . . I had a thousand times rather give it to you (as it would be my natural impulse to do) than think you had paid me more for it than you can easily afford." And he went on to explain himself in terms that closely approximate Sahlin's maxim on gift-giving and friendship: "I wish you to treat me as a friend. I do not speak in a worldly sense, meaning that you should do the best for me you can, but that you should call on me to do the best for you that I can."[138] Agreeing to write regularly for the antislavery *Pennsylvania Freeman*, he declared that he was "unwilling to take anything" in payment, and it was only with the greatest reluctance that he accepted pay for his contributions to the *National Anti-Slavery Standard*, doing so, he explained, because his abolitionist sentiments had already curtailed what he called "the most profitable sources of my literary emoluments."[139] Perhaps the clearest evidence of Lowell's penchant for literary generosity, however, is seen in the inscriptions he placed in copies of a prose volume he gave to friends in the 1840s: "with the author's love," "with author's respects," "with author's affectionate respects," "with author's sincere regards," "with author's regards & thanks," and so on.[140] Lowell delighted in making literary gifts to his friends; quite simply, White was not his friend.

White, however, had plenty of friends—including George Bailey Loring, who continued to contribute after Lowell had withdrawn in high dudgeon—and, perhaps more importantly, he was able to continue making and keeping them through his enthusiastic if somewhat less than virtuosic bestowal of gifts. While Lowell floundered in his first effort as a magazine editor, offering hammydiddle aplenty and sinking after three issues, White kept his periodical afloat for ten years, until his death in January 1843.[141]

White, of course, was by no means the only magazine proprietor to use gifts manipulatively to leverage contributions from random authors, but few were as adept. At almost the same time as she was being courted by the *Southern Literary Messenger*, Lydia Sigourney received several free issues of a magazine entitled *The Zodiack*, whose editor, E. Perry, clearly wished for contributions in return. Sigourney obliged, sending "the only unpublished poem" she then had, but made it clear that she did not want to engage in a further act of reciprocal disequilibrium by insisting that the editor send her no more copies. The *Messenger*, however, remained her "favourite magazine." It is not immediately clear why White succeeded where Perry did not, but that White was a master of gift manipulation is beyond question.[142]

Perhaps the best indication of how successful White was at using gifts to support his magazine is that following his death, the magazine went into a period of sharp decline. Briefly run by men in Richmond and Washington, the interim editors scrambled to find a replacement editor, before finally selling the magazine to Benjamin Blake Minor. A distant relative of Lucian Minor, Benjamin initially claimed and then quickly squandered the goodwill White had spent a decade cultivating. Contributors didn't object to gifting their works to the *Messenger*, but they looked askance at receiving no gifts in return and bridled at being asked to pay for copies of the magazine. Philip Pendleton Cooke, who had contributed prolifically to the *Messenger* under White's proprietorship, spoke for many when he wrote, in 1844, that if Minor "means to ask me to write for the Messenger for nothing and in addition to this, to pay him $5 per ano for the work—he is stupid and a little mean." Minor lost approximately 600 subscribers a year for the three years he was at the helm, and stability was only regained when John R. Thompson purchased the magazine in 1847 and returned to White's tried and true method of dispensing flattery and smoothing ruffled feathers with free copies of the publication.[143]

THE FREEING OF THE GIFT

Gifts make friends: by their very definition they cannot disembed. Yet three signal changes did, however, impact gifts over the course of the nineteenth century. In the first place, certain significant gift rituals became commercialized and, in the process, were transformed from production to consumption-defined exchanges. While readers have always consumed the literary gifts they received, that is to say, for a significant period of time, those who gave those gifts wrote what others consumed; after the mid-nineteenth century, this was less likely to be the case, and giver as well as the recipient were bound up in acts of consumption rather than production *and* consumption. The example of albums is instructive here. By mid-century, the practice of making inscriptions in friendship albums was giving way to a newer vogue for autograph collecting. Longfellow received hundreds of requests for his autograph, for example, while N. P. Willis felt so overwhelmed that he had a form letter printed up, which he simply signed and mailed out to autograph hunters. While autograph hunters, like those who owned friendship albums, believed, in the words of one scholar, that they experienced "an almost mystical encounter with their subjects" through these inscriptions, the individuals from whom they solicited autographs were—and remained—strangers.

If an autograph written, or pasted into, an album was a gift, then it was hardly one that created or sustained more than a virtual, or an imaginary, relationship.

The practice of inscribing texts in friendship albums, themselves, did of course persist, but it became a routinized practice. A Princeton student writing in the early 1870s, for example, noted that "Autograph writing in this college has almost developed into a science." Album inscription, moreover, also became increasingly restricted to graduation time—a ritual that persists to this day in the signing of high school year books—so that inscriptions ceased to function as a courting or sustaining gifts and simply embalmed relationships that were over.[144]

Friendship albums, finally, were increasingly displaced by gift books and annuals: lavish, mass-produced texts designed for the Christmas and New Years' season. While the annuals and gift books were often produced by the same firms that made friendship albums and physically resembled them in form, right down to gift-themed titles such as the *Forget-Me-Not* and the *Token*, they came already filled with content. The last vestige of the traditional albums in the gift books was the fill-in-the-blanks presentation page, which created an aura of the personal around these impersonal commodities. These were gifts, to be sure, but the focus of the gift-based bond had shifted, decisively and permanently, from authorial production to readerly consumption. Producing literary gifts became big business.[145]

The second transformation in gift exchange was that even as literary gifts were becoming a burgeoning business, literary businesses were freeing themselves of their own gift-related practices. Consider the example of newspaper exchanges. Exchanging newspapers (and to a lesser degree magazines) was, first and foremost, a means for gathering and collating distant news, but it also had the effect, I have argued, of creating and sustaining bonds of amity and reciprocal obligation. Those bonds were considerably weakened when, in the 1840s, the first news-brokering agencies began to appear. Designed, initially, to share the expenses of receiving foreign news by means of the new technology of telegraphy, news agencies such as the New York Associated Press began slowly to replace gratuitous newspaper exchanges with fee-based reporting services. By the 1860s, other firms were syndicating the news and selling partially printed sheets to newspapers, which they could then customize to their own design. The rise of news agencies and syndicates, which by the 1870 also encompassed syndicated fiction, had the consequence of turning former networks of editors and contributors into paying customers and clients; as an 1856 Associated Press rule sheet bluntly put the matter: "Parties failing to pay an AP bill beyond one week after presentation will have their news report cut off . . . but will be responsible for the expense of the cut-off report as if it were delivered."[146] As news exchange was replaced by news purchase, much of the intimacy within the newspaper and periodical trade was lost.

The third and final transformation in the practice of gift exchanges came about as a consequence of the first and second. As gifts became more commercialized, and as commerce became less invested in its own traditional gift exchange practices, gift exchanges themselves started to be viewed in a wholly new way: as pure, as free, and as distinct from the soiling practices of the market. The ideology of the free gift legitimized the ruthless and disembedded world of commercial economics, that is to say, by holding out the promise that there remained one sphere of exchange that was wholly free of calculation or obligation, even though, as we have seen in this chapter, business and gift exchange had traditionally been mutually constitutive. This is not to say that gifts ceased to be economic—in the broadest sense of the term—only that they ceased to be perceived as economic. We see a good example of this in the rise of Christmas as a festival that became increasingly commercialized, even as it proclaimed ever more loudly that it was the one time of year in which generosity, sincerity, and gratuity reigned supreme. It is no coincidence that it was Christmas-season gifts books and literary annuals that came to displace the year-round friendship album as the literary gift genre of choice. "The interested exchange," writes Jonathan Parry, at the end of his own survey of the subject, "and the disinterested gift thus emerged as two sides of the same coin."[147] It is a coin that has circulated widely and whose currency remains high. Indeed, it is precisely because gifts are now no longer seen as 'economic' that it has been necessary to argue the case at such great length and through so many detailed examples in this chapter.

CHAPTER FOUR

Toward a History of Literary Debt

By 1829, James Hervey Pierrepont needed to settle some old debts. He was in arrears for four volumes of his local paper, the *Times and Dover Enquirer*; he owed twenty-five dollars to Nathaniel Marsh for books he had purchased in 1827; and he had yet to pay medical suppliers Bartlett and Brewster eight dollars and seventy cents owed them from a transaction dating back to 1825. In writing to request payment—a practice known as dunning—Bartlett and Brewster explained that they had actually dissolved their partnership two years earlier and needed now to close their books. The debts that Pierrepont had accumulated by 1829 were hardly the consequence of an isolated period of economic mismanagement or misfortune, however; rather, they were part of a life-long pattern of financial dereliction. A decade earlier, he had received an irate letter from book seller James F. Shores, which noted that Pierrepont had left several books unpaid for for more than a year "& the interest since that time has taken away my profits." If, said Shores, "you can conveniently hand me the amt, or a part of it *tomorrow*, (as I have a large sum to make up) it would greatly oblige." Pierrepont did not oblige, but then again, he rarely did. He had once taken a newspaper for *seven* years before paying for a single issue. And while he occasionally paid for a newspaper up front, this was a rare occurrence. More typical was his transaction with Brown and Shuttuck of Boston who wrote him in October 1833 to remind him of an unpaid bill for books and to request that he pay "the money for it before many days." Pierrepont, predictably, took three months.[1]

Pierrepont's unwillingness to pay for his literary wares on time was a consequence of neither impoverishment nor disreputability; a Harvard-educated physician, he was a pillar of his Portsmouth, New Hampshire, community. In 1823, he was assessed for tax on $1,468 of property, which placed him in the second wealthiest decile in Portsmouth for that year, while by 1829, he was living in a house worth $3,000 and owned $2,700 of shares in various local banks. There is no question that Pierrepont was comfortably well-off if not staggeringly affluent. He also enjoyed prominent positions of trust. He was President of the Portsmouth Medical Society, the Portsmouth Temperance Society, and the Portsmouth chapter of the American Colonization Society, an honorary member of the Massachusetts Medical Society, and the recipient of an honorary degree from Dartmouth. Indeed, he was sufficiently well regarded in the literary world to be a proprietor of the Portsmouth Athenaeum, to which he donated many of the books for which he so tardily paid. An ambitious and moderately successful man, Pierrepont purchased hundreds of dollars of books every year, even squandering money he had set aside for clothes, yet he rarely paid for what he purchased in anything like a timely manner.[2]

Pierrepont was, perhaps, exceptional in the number of books, magazines, and newspapers that he purchased; the tardiness with which he paid for them, however, was absolutely typical of the period. Consider the following examples. James Kirke Paulding failed to pay for his newspaper for two years, Captain J. W. Kent of Newburyport for three years, J. H. Winslow of Portsmouth, New Hampshire, for four years, William Palmer (location unknown) for eight years, and Hervey Moore of Newport, Rhode Island, for twelve years. Nor were these cases aberrations within any given publication's subscription list. Whole communities of readers defaulted on their payments. According to a subscription agent's ledger for the New Haven *Religious Intelligencer*, for example, thirty-two people in Berkshire County, Massachusetts, subscribed to the *Religious Intelligencer* in 1829, and only twelve of them paid on time; out of twenty-four additional subscriptions taken in January 1830 only three had paid by May 1831. Neither wealth, age, race, profession, nor location characterized this failure to pay. Put simply, Americans across the board were habitually derelict in settling their literary debts.[3]

Of course readers did not default on newspapers and magazines alone. Naturalist John James Audubon had a terrible time trying to get his subscribers to pay for their lavishly illustrated copies of *The Birds of America*. Insofar as each subscription cost many hundreds of dollars, this was a grievous amount for Audubon to forgo, and he relentlessly pursued subscribers—including Daniel Webster—to get his due. In Chapter One, as we saw, a fictional sketch described an agent being dispatched to the banks of the Susquehannah to dun a subscriber for a book costing "two dollars in boards." The subscriber, the sketch author notes, was "dilatory about payment as country subscribers usually are."[4] Yet it was newspapers and magazines rather than books (expensive or otherwise) that were most singularly afflicted. Serial publications seemed almost to encourage tardy payment, inasmuch as they relied on a subscribe-now, pay-later system, and, still more, because the subscribers in whom trust was reposed were spread over so wide a geographical area. The consequences were dramatic. A single Pierrepont in such a system was an inconvenience; a hundred were a disaster; and a typical publication could be burdened with thousands. The annals of newspaper and periodical history are littered with the wrecks of publications forced into failure by persistent subscriber dereliction.

The figures, in fact, speak for themselves. When the *Western Monthly Review* went under in 1830, for example, editor Timothy Flint calculated that his subscribers owed him in the region of three thousand dollars; less than a year and a half after the launching of the Rochester, New York, *Craftsman*, in the late 1820s, the editor estimated that he was owed five thousand dollars in unpaid subscriptions; and William Duane, who assumed ownership of the Philadelphia *Aurora* in the 1798, discovered the paper was owed between fifteen and twenty thousand dollars in outstanding debts. "Mark this plain observation of experience," wrote Duane to a correspondent a few years later, "*Newspaper debts are the worst of all others!*"[5]

Publications like the *Craftsman* and the *Aurora* were political papers, of course, so it might be expected that their balances would shift with the vicissitudes of ideological commitment and electoral turmoil, yet precisely the same pattern of wide-scale dereliction and cumulative debt impacted the most idealistic, as well as the most worldly, of publications. Consider the *Liberator*. Launched in January 1831 by pioneering abolitionist William Lloyd Garrison, it had a frankly non-commercial agenda. In his maiden editorial, Garrison announced that he and his partner were determined to "print the paper as long as they can subsist upon bread and water, or their hands find employment." His readers, too, were equally as idealistic, and the community that coalesced around the publication was as intense as it was vigorous and committed. Yet even here, subscribers were slow to pay for their paper. As early as 1835, in fact, Garrison's paper was $2,500 in debt, and it remained in debt for the next thirty years. "I admit that we have not been methodical or sharp in keeping our accounts," he confided to a friend in 1835, "but we suffer much more from the negligence of our subscribers than from our own." He hardly exaggerated. An audit conducted in the late 1830s, and recorded in a ledger entitled "Black List," contained the names of literally hundreds of subscribers who were at least fifteen months behind in paying for the paper.

Those named included not only the obscure or the non-committal but also such worthies as literary entrepreneur Samuel Griswold Goodrich (who owed $8.80), together with organizations like the Chester Crossroad, Ohio, Antislavery Society ($5.00), the Plymouth, New Hampshire Female Antislavery Society ($6.00), and the West Chester, Pennsylvania Female Anti-Slavery Society (.50¢). Beside the entry for the Salem Anti-Slavery Reading Room ($3.90), an auditor had written, simply, "good for nothing." That the *Liberator* lasted for as long as it did was thanks largely to substantial donations made by philanthropist reformers such as James Forten, rather than to rank and file subscribers or abolitionist stalwarts. When Garrison noted in his valedictory editorial for the *Liberator* that he "began the publication of the *Liberator* without a subscriber" and that he was ending it "without a farthing as the pecuniary result of the patronage extended to it during thirty-five years of unremitted labors," he was unquestionably making a virtue of a necessity. Abolitionist reformers, that is to say, were no more likely to pay their subscriptions on time than the crassest political mavericks.[6] Even the *Dial*, the house journal of the Transcendentalists, had to prod its readers from time to time to get them to pay their dues, while its philosophical cousin, the *Western Messenger*, foundered in debt and survived only with bailouts from the American Unitarian Association.[7] Rich and poor, worldly and idealistic, urban and rural: readers paid little and for that little they paid slowly.

This chapter begins, therefore, by seeking to resolve one of the great mysteries of antebellum media history by explaining why Americans were so slow to pay for the newspapers, magazines, and books to which they subscribed. It is a challenge worth addressing not only in terms of business or media history, however, although it is certainly worthy on that score, but because it addresses quite specifically the subject of *authorial* economics. Although we tend to think of newspapers as sub-literary, and magazines as corporate, or perhaps authorless, genres, the men and women who edited them without a question thought of themselves as authors. An editor was a man (or woman) of letters. Then too, and to the extent that it affected cash flow, a magazine or newspaper's subscription woes impinged also on the economic life of those who were paid contributors. Finally, an examination of subscription debt and the problems it caused brings back into focus a heretofore neglected literary genre—the newspaper dun—that clearly and wittily illuminates the intertwinedness of literature, economics, and social life. Perhaps more than any other genre, in fact, the dun helps illustrate the ways in which authorial economies of the early republic were socially embedded and how they disembedded over the course of the nineteenth century.

ACCOUNTING FOR SUBSCRIBER DERELICTION

The explanation of subscriber dereliction I will offer in this chapter is not the first. Three other theories have been offered, which we might call, respectively, the moral flaw, the psychological dysfunction, and the moral economy models. All three, I believe, fail to resolve the mystery of subscriber dereliction satisfactorily, but an examination of each will help bring into focus the tangled knot of issues that needs to be unpicked.

The moral flaw argument is the oldest and proceeds from the idea that Americans' failure to pay for their reading material was at bottom a form of ethical dereliction. An argument more tacit than developed, we tend to find it most often in early to mid-twentieth-century scholarly discussions of newspaper and magazine subscribers, where it manifests itself in the form of a tone of disapproval. According to Milton W. Hamilton, for example, "the rural subscriber had little excuse for failure to pay the paper." Biographer Don C. Seitz called the newspaper reader "the most unreliable of debtors," being both "careless about paying and indifferent to the distress caused by his delinquency." More recently, Jeffrey Pasley has referred to such individuals as "deadbeats."[8] The problem with the moral flaw argument is twofold. In the first place, scholars have been unable to say why antebellum America was afflicted with such a pervasive immorality. More practically, given this plague of dereliction, they cannot explain why any editor possessed of sanity would ever presume to begin a publication, knowing what scoundrels the American reading public were.

A more ambitious interpretation has been offered by journalism historian Thomas C. Leonard. His language, to be sure, owes much to the moral flaw school. Antebellum readers, he says, were "deadbeats" who routinely "stiffed" newspaper proprietors with their "cavalier disregard" of payment schedules. Generous discounts, pro-rated payment plans, and pleas for charity all fell on deaf ears and left readers "unmoved." To account for the situation, however, Leonard turns not to models of ethics but to psychiatrist Eric Berne's theory of transactional analysis, which explains that people often enter into and sustain dysfunctional relationships because these enable them to receive covert but personally gratifying "strokes" or emotional rewards. Refusing to pay for what one takes, according to Berne, offers a sort of catch-me-if-you-can *frisson*, and the more powerful the creditor, the more intense the experience. Subscribers thus refused to pay for papers as a way of thumbing their noses at authority in the form of cash-strapped printer-editors. Editors, by Leonard's account, were especially prone to this sort of treatment, because they represented a generalized authority figure. The editors, for their part, were equally complicit in this relationship. Their failure to dun aggressively or cut off derelict subscribers, according to Leonard, allowed them to indulge their "stubbornness and pride": pride in extensive circulation figures that gave them "bragging" rights and stubbornness in refusing to accept that most would not pay. Refusing to accept reality, they mired themselves in "self-deception" and "swaggering defiance," sending out newspapers for which they knew they would never receive money. The editor-reader relationship, Leonard concludes, in language that draws directly on Berne's therapeutic context, was "a bad marriage" that endured because each party got something, albeit covert and unwholesome, from the union.[9]

Leonard's arguments are problematic to say the least. That some subscribers were flagrantly and shamelessly dishonest would, as I suggested above, be hard to deny; a newspaper agent's account book from the first decade of the nineteenth century notes, for example, that S. Farwell of Groton, Massachusetts, left town owing twenty-four dollars for his subscription to the *New England Palladium*. Others stood their ground and quite explicitly refused to pay for their fare, as did one outraged proslavery subscriber to Elijah Lovejoy's Alton, Illinois (and decidedly anti-slavery) *Observer*, who wrote "I never will pay for it . . . and the only wish I have on the subject is, that you, your press, and your agent, were all in hell." Only slightly less mendacious was the Unitarian minister who returned a bill to the *National Anti-Slavery Standard* unpaid, spluttering "First, I doubt if I owe you so much (seven dollars). Second, if I do, I owe it not, for you have no right to let such arrearages accumulate at such a rate. You ought to forfeit them by your own negligence."[10] There were any number of individuals who sought, for one reason or another, to squirm out of paying for what they read, that is to say, but to suppose that every reader subscribed to a newspaper to punish an arrogant printer stretches credulity; indeed, the very range and diversity of derelict subscribers seems to rule out hostility-to-authority as an explanation. To presuppose that the same character flaw afflicted not only farmers but also former presidents, not only Baptists but Mormons, not only evangelicals but socialist reformers, and not only the poor but the comfortably well-off, is to posit something little short of a mass psychology of deviance for which there is no supporting evidence. Then, too, the idea that printers were uniquely or especially held out for punishment will not withstand scrutiny, since Americans fairly regularly failed to pay butchers, tailors, doctors, and farmers. Pierrepont, we will recall, paid as slowly for his medical supplies as for his newspapers, and we know that his patients were as tardy in paying him as he was in remunerating publishers.[11] On the other hand, we can also reject the idea that American editors were as much masochists as their readers were sadists. If being an editor was as unrelievedly mortifying and as economically unfeasible as Leonard suggests, then it becomes a challenge to explain why anyone would choose to start a newspaper or magazine in the first place. Obstinacy may explain why editors dug in their heels when in trouble but not why anyone would ever wish to become an editor knowing what trouble it would inevitably cause. That newspapers and magazines failed in the nineteenth century is undeniable, but clearly editors believed that they were going to get something other than "bragging" rights or martyrdom for their pains. Leonard's argument, in other words, fails because it relies on the existence of a mass psychological dysfunction that not only lacks credible evidence but that is so extreme as to be at odds with common sense.[12]

Many of the shortcomings in Leonard's argument would seem to be addressed by Charles G. Steffen, who offers a more ideologically inflected explanation of reader debt, based on E. P. Thompson's notion of the moral economy. Thompson, we will recall, developed the concept of the moral economy to account for the prevalence of food riots in eighteenth-century Britain, explaining that so far from being the chaotic and reckless frays depicted by contemporary observers, they were principled actions in which the hungry expressed their conviction that they had an inalienable right to the necessities of life at a price that was fair, including, when necessary, at no charge at all. Building on this idea, Steffen argues that newspaper readers regarded the news in the early national period in much the same way that peasants regarded bread in the eighteenth century: as a necessity for which they were only willing to pay a nominal fee, if that.

Steffen's argument has, at first blush, more to commend it than Leonard's, because it can account for subscriber dereliction in several differing constituencies in a fairly nuanced way. For those of a republican inclination, for example, an informed citizenry was vital for social stability, while for advocates of liberal commercialism, news was essential for the smooth-running of the market. Readers therefore staked their claim to their papers on ideological grounds. Readers, says Steffen, "felt strongly that they were entitled to the news." Thus non-payment was less a knee-jerk form of deviance than a "strategy" in readers' "struggle against the proprietary claims of editors": one in which readers were "determined to lay their hands on newspapers by fair means or foul." Like Leonard,

Steffen also sees editors as complicit in the world of newspaper debt, but he replaces Leonard's account of covert emotional rewards with an explanation based more on economic compensation. The larger one's circulation figures, he explains, the more advertisers one could attract, and it was here—in advertising revenues—that the rewards of newspaper proprietorship were to be reaped. To cancel papers to derelict subscribers would be to reduce one's circulation and thus to lose advertising. Editors therefore made a rational calculation, accepting a moderate loss in one area to make a larger gain in another. The same argument he claims, was, mutatis mutandis, true of political papers, where substantial circulation could lead to political patronage and a smaller circulation would lead to its evaporation. Thus editors offered up weak duns but largely let the system be.[13]

Steffen's explanation has the virtues of being rooted in historical context and exhibiting some flexibility. Unfortunately, however, it stands up to scrutiny no better than Leonard's. Four points in particular render his argument untenable. First, while it is true that news was sometimes seen as a necessity for both the economic and political well-being of the nation, readers were as likely to default in paying for novels, natural histories, fashion magazines, and other printed genres as they were for newspapers, and it would be hard to extend a moral economy claim to these sorts of works. Second, it is not entirely clear that there was a significant correlation between circulation figures and the number of advertisers or rates charged for advertising, and the only data Steffen provides comes from a British rather than an American paper. A modest number of newspapers were designed primarily as advertising sheets, and it is true that contemporary American newspaper editors sometimes made large claims for them, as did Alden Spooner in 1817, when he said that it was "a fact that *advertisers* rather than *subscribers* are the life and soul of a newspaper," yet the evidence from account books suggests that income from advertising was, in reality, markedly less significant than income from subscriptions. An 1830 account book for the *American Advocate* of Hallowell, Maine, reveals that subscriptions accounted for 66.8 percent of its possible revenue, advertising only 11.6 percent. A study of payments received by the St. Clairsville, Ohio *Gazette* between 1841 and 1847 reveals, likewise, that revenue from advertising amounted to no more than 19.8 percent of the paper's income and dipped to as little as 4.2 percent.[14] Third, even a cursory examination of newspaper account books and receipts makes it clear that advertisers themselves were as derelict in paying for their insertions as readers were for their subscriptions. In 1830, the *American Advocate* managed to collect 68 percent of the total subscription revenues it was owed for that year but only 29 percent of the money it was owed in advertising. A Wisconsin firm, typical in this respect, advertised in a local paper for four years and two months before paying a penny. Even if more money was to be made from advertisements, in other words, which is questionable, it was no more certain to arrive in a timely manner than were the readers' subscription dues, and its tardy arrival cannot be explained by reference to a moral economy.[15] Finally, publishers of periodicals that had neither advertisements nor relied upon political or religious patronage tended to continue sending their wares to derelict subscribers, leaving one to wonder what *they* might have gained from the exercise. Neatly though Steffen's theory seems to account for all the loose ends left by Leonard's, it is no more plausible, in the final instance, than his psychological model.

Distinct as the moral flaw, psychological deviance, and moral economy arguments are, the weakness they share in common is an assumption that debt is a self-evidently meaningful phenomenon and that one has therefore to look elsewhere to explain its incidence. In so doing, they overlook the fact that debt, itself, is a socially complex and historically contingent construct, the meanings of which have varied widely across time.[16] To presuppose that a lapse in time between purchasing an item and paying for it reflects moral failure, say, or political protest, is to project values and assumptions onto early national debt that were not necessarily relevant to those involved. In developing the argument of this chapter, by way of contrast, I operate on the assumption that the best way of understanding literary debt in the early republic is to explore what those in the early republic had to say about debt itself. We need to look, in other words, to the economic culture of the early national period and understand its ethics of credit and indebtedness, or what one might call, following the folklorists, debt ways.[17] It is in these debt ways, I believe, rather than in arguments about moral economy or mass psychology, that we will find an explanation for the behavior of individuals like Pierrepont and a plausible account of why they believed that their conduct was above, if not completely beyond, reproach. An analysis of early national debt ways will also explain why newspaper and periodical proprietors were themselves so willing to tolerate subscriber dereliction. Fortunately, there is an extensive body of scholarship that explores the phenomenon of early national debt ways, especially as it manifested itself in rural America following the Revolution, and my discussion is indebted profoundly to this corpus of work.

In this chapter, I look first at traditional and especially rural debt ways as a crucial frame of reference for interpreting the behavior of those who subscribed to newspapers and magazines, even among those who did not live in the country. Debt, it turns out, was both widespread and widely socially accepted. Exploring how Americans came to find themselves in debt and what they thought of credit and debt relations in general will put us in a position to understand not only why subscribers paid so slowly for their papers but why editors and printers were willing to tolerate such tardiness. Conditions in early national America, I shall argue, generated a culture predicated on what sociologists call "thick trust," a culture in which debt functioned to draw people into ever tighter social relationships. Of course, there is a big difference between being in debt and declining, under any circumstances, to pay for what one has purchased, and so printers did sometimes dun their customers. The dun is a wholly neglected genre worthy of serious consideration, and in a separate section, I examine the literary strategies printers and editors used to encourage their subscribers to pay what they owed and explain why such pleas seem so half-hearted or ineffectual to modern scholars. In the 1820s and 1830s, the nature of literary credit changed dramatically and all of a sudden printers and editors started to dun more aggressively and to resort to legal tactics to secure payment. The transformation of literary credit relationships, I argue, was a direct consequence of transformations in the organization of the paper-making trade. Changes in technology and capitalization led to consequences that ramified throughout the literary world. By the 1840s, many newspapers and magazines, especially in the major cities, were no longer willing to work with traditional debt ways and required payment for their papers up front. This was, I conclude, not simply a shift in literary economy but a herald of a significantly more atomized and commercialized society in which there were more strangers than neighbors.

RURAL ECONOMICS AND TRADITIONAL DEBT WAYS

Although he lived in a thriving coastal city, John Hervey Pierrepont (1768–1839) was raised in the countryside by his grandfather, and it was here, I would argue, that he inculcated the rudiments of his economic behavior. Men such as Pierrepont's grandfather—a "plain, industrious farmer"—were sometimes celebrated in the antebellum period as paragons of virtuous and sturdy self-sufficiency, but modern historians have made it clear that while those who lived in the country valued economic independence they were not literally self-sufficient but, in fact, participated in dense networks of cooperation and exchange, many of which were based upon mutual indebtedness.[18] This was in the first instance a matter of practicality. No rural family, no matter how capable, could raise a barn on its own, gather crops without help, make repairs without the skills of others, or acquire every tool they required without being willing to trade. Country folk, rather, turned to their neighbors and found a degree of independence in a concomitant degree of interdependence. Residents of farms and small villages loaned their equipment, their time, their expertise, and their goodwill to their fellows and received the same in turn. They also traded their produce, livestock, and their skills with one another. They even offered collaborative emotional support. Women of a community, for example, came together when one of their number was going to give birth; men and women alike took turns sitting through the night with the community's sick and dying. Quite literally, then, as well as more figuratively, rural Americans were sustained from cradle to grave, by bonds of mutuality and cooperation.[19]

It is important, of course, not to romanticize rural life. As recent historians have pointed out, it could be contentious and claustrophobic, poisoned by rumor and riven by feud, and the tendency of communities to band together for mutual support revealed its less pleasant side in a distrust of outsiders or strangers. The wandering poor, for example, were "warned out" of towns unwilling to support them, forcing them to return to their place of birth for assistance. Yet even warning out presupposed community; it was the product of a world, according to Gordon Wood, in which "everyone was supposed to belong somewhere." That sense of belonging was tied intimately to networks of trade. To trade mutually, that is, was to belong, and to belong was to be willing to trade mutually; indeed, the act of lending and borrowing was sometimes referred to as "neighboring."[20]

Rural exchange could take a number of different forms. The simplest is captured in an entry in farmer Tobias Walker's journal from 1852 which reads: "A.M. [I] Helped Jesse Taylor slaughter a cow at our barn; P.M. He helped me build a board fence." The close temporal proximity of Walker and Taylor's activities ("[I] Helped . . . He helped") makes it easy to see how one repaid the other in a tit-for-tat form of reciprocity. Often, however, reciprocity was less clearly immediate and less obviously balanced. Rural exchange reflected the rhythms and vicissitudes of agricultural life; payment could be delayed by days, weeks, months, or years and might only be made when a fence *needed* to be repaired, or when a crop was *ready* for harvest. Individuals tended to pay what they could, when they could, and in ways they could; sometimes this meant that payments were made slowly or intermittently, and sometimes it came about that payments were in excess of amounts owed. Rather than reflecting a tit-for-tat model of immediate and balanced exchange, in other words, rural transactions more often resembled a see-saw model of alternating credit and debt; indeed, it was quite possible to be simultaneously a creditor and a debtor depending on the rate at which the mechanisms of reciprocity moved.[21] The debt ways of rural folk, moreover, were characterized by what sociologist Alvin Gouldner has called 'heteromorphic' as opposed than 'homeomorphic' reciprocity, by which he means that "the things exchanged may be concretely different but should be equal in *value*, as defined by the actors in the situation." It was not necessary, in other words, to repay a neighbor who had helped one slaughter a cow by helping (homeomorphically) to slaughter the neighbor's cow, if both parties could agree that helping to board a fence was (heteromorphically) of equal value.[22]

The experiences of Delaware farmer John Ball typify the challenges of rural exchange practices in all of their heteromorphic and temporal complexity. At some point in the late 1790s—and the vagueness of the date is significant—Ball loaned his neighbor, Andrew Giffen, several hundred dollars. Giffen repaid the debt slowly, over many years, and also heteromorphically, providing Ball with "divers sums of money," "divers Articles of property," and much "work and labour." These repayments, he recalled, included "a Beef Cow, Half a Stack of Hay, 13 bushels and a half of corn, 600 pounds weight of Hay, 3 bushels wheat, a Cart Saddle, a Barrel of Cyder, 2 days work drawing logs, 3 yards linen, 2 items of Cash—1 dollar and 10 dollars." Together, in fact, they more than repaid the loan and actually put Ball in debt to Giffen. Yet even as Giffen was repaying Ball, Ball continued to trade with Giffen, paying for the cider by helping in Giffen's orchard, offering him cloth in exchange for a heifer, and crediting the log drawing for work he had performed for Giffen "treading out wheat." With the see-saw model of reciprocity, it was unclear at any given point who was in debt to whom, and in fact Giffen and Ball's accounts were not finally balanced until after Ball died in 1804.[23]

Rural Americans were able to accept the complexities and vagueness of their economic relations, because they trusted one another. Trust, in fact, was not simply a condition for economic exchange, it was one of the items traded in the course of an economic exchange—a currency that could appreciate or depreciate in value, and which could be traded, or at least be traded upon, at various different rates of exchange.[24] Indeed, trustworthiness is simply another name for what Bourdieu calls symbolic capital, or prestige: that form of capital that comes from the effective use of other forms of capital.

Depending on the circumstances, those engaged in commercial transactions could draw on several different forms of trust that ran along a spectrum from what sociologists call "thick" to "thin." Thin trust is the sort of trust we repose in strangers, and it is predicated on a belief that those whom we do not know will behave in the sorts of socially acceptable ways we would expect from those whom we do. Thick trust, by contrast, is the confidence we have in those we already know, based upon a conviction that they will continue to behave as they have in the past. As trust moves from thick to thin, its basis shifts from acquaintance, to reputation, to extrapolation, and, finally, to postulation. That is to say, in its transition from thick to thin, trust is based on increasingly abstract and fungible forms of knowledge. The sort of exchange engaged in by Giffen and Ball was categorically predicated on the thickest kind of trust. Villagers trusted their neighbors, because they knew them personally and because the economic exchanges in which they participated were embedded in ongoing social relations. Ball did not have to balance his accounts with Giffen, because he trusted that over the long haul Giffen would deal with him honestly. Giffen was not concerned if Ball owed him a little, or he owed a little to Ball, because he trusted that over the long haul both their needs would be met. Under such circumstances, the period of time that elapsed between one act of exchange and its reciprocation were, if not irrelevant, then certainly less important than the nature of the relationship the two parties enjoyed. Their exchanges, in other words, were deeply embedded, the exchange of goods and services serving to create and cement social ties.[25]

The embedded nature of rural exchange and the thick trust to which it gave rise are further revealed by the account books kept by rural Americans, which followed a very old-fashioned, single entry format. Double-entry bookkeeping, which was far more sophisticated, had actually been developed as early as the fourteenth century as a way of abstracting and calculating running profits, and it was sometimes forcefully advocated by agricultural reformers, but rural Americans continued to use single-entry accounts into the nineteenth century, with a page for each person with whom they did business. Their preference was deeply tied to their social world. Figures in double-entry account books, as Mary Poovey points out, had no concrete referents, while those in single-entry books referred to actual personal relationships and specific material transactions; indeed, some rural account books doubled as diaries and some diaries became de facto account books.[26] The emphasis on ongoing, trust-based personal relations was also reflected in the fact that books were not balanced at regular intervals but, more typically, when it was mutually convenient, or, perhaps, when a book became full. Sometimes, indeed, as in the case of Giffen and Ball, book accounts were only balanced upon the death of one party. The pervasive use of crops, cloth, and labor suggests that the value of one's credits and debts was subject to ongoing heteromorphic negotiation. Indeed, even in legal terms, book debts, as they were called, reflected a negotiable and only weakly binding authority, being tacit rather than explicit promises to pay. Book debts could not bear interest, they were not negotiable (meaning that the debt could not be sold to a third party), nor did they entail payment within a stipulated time. Weak though their math might have been, they served the needs of rural Americans admirably and reflected their extension of thick trust to one another.[27]

The disadvantage of thick trust was that it permitted only a limited range of transactions. It was not possible to trade solely with one's friends and neighbors, or to rely solely upon personal knowledge of another's conduct. It was often necessary to trade with strangers or those at a distance, and in such cases Americans extended one another thin, or at least thinner, trust. As their extension of trust altered from thick to thin, so did their approach to credit, debt, and exchange. When dealing with neighbors, as we have seen, credit was typically extended informally, through either implied or oral agreement, or through the use of book accounts. It was underwritten by a profoundly embodied form of symbolic capital, based upon personal acquaintance. When dealing with strangers, by contrast, they drew up contracts, required payment in cash, stipulated precise schedules for settlement, charged interest for loans, and levied penalties for deferred payments. It was not that they did not trust their trading partners, so much as the means by which that trust was underwritten were based on more abstract qualities that needed additional buttressing. Their methods of debt forgiveness and debt collection also reflected these trust choices. When a stranger defaulted on a payment, it was not uncommon to pursue legal proceedings in order to collect. Alternatively, one could sell the debt to a third party at a discount and have them collect on it in full, a practice made possible because written credit instruments were, in legal terms, assignable. Recourse to legal action and assignable credit instruments was vital to the economy, because it kept money in circulation, and allowed creditors to pay their own debts, but it also reflected a world in which exchange was only very weakly embedded. To sue a trading partner was to create ill will, while to sell the debt to a third party was to wrench a transaction from its original context and turn it into a fungible currency, indeed a commodity. Such actions were anathema in the world of thick trust. To demand payment—immediately and in full—from a neighbor in a peremptory fashion was not only considered bad manners, inasmuch as one had to see that person constantly, but it was also bad business, insofar as one might well find oneself in debt to this person in the future. Quite simply, one didn't dun one's neighbors. As a contemporary adage put it: "If you wish to make friends, trust and never demand your pay; if enemies, demand it."[28]

The positions outlined above, it must be stressed, represent extremes. Not all long distance or strictly commercial transactions were conducted heartlessly and with an exclusive emphasis on the timely bottom line, nor did everyone engaged in traditional, rural exchange decline to dun their lackadaisical customers. Typically, merchants and traders sought a happy medium between the sort of relentless dunning that made enemies and the sort of passive acquiescence that cost (and lost) fortunes. A model dunning letter printed in a *The New Universal Letter-Writer* in 1800 captures almost perfectly the balanced ideal for which merchants and others strove. "Sir," writes the imaginary tradesman to his customer:

> A very unexpected demand has been made on me for money, which I was in hopes of keeping longer in my trade, [and this] obliges me to apply for your assistance of the balance of the account between us, or as much as you can spare. When I have an opportunity to inform you of the nature of this demand, and the necessity of my discharging it, you will readily excuse the freedom I now take with you; and as it is an affair of such consequence to my family, I know the friendship you bear me will induce you to serve me effectually.[29]

Although the description of this letter ("From a Tradesman to a Correspondent") and the place of publication (Philadelphia) suggest a world of urban commercialism, we can see many features in this letter which we would otherwise associate with traditional debt. In the first place, the relationship between the tradesman and his customer is framed in social rather than business terms; the two are "friends" as much as, if not more than, they are economic actors. In the second place, and precisely because of this friendship, the tradesman is extremely apologetic in tone, explaining that he is only dunning his customer because he himself has been dunned. Had he not received a "very unexpected demand," that is to say, he would not himself inflict so unexpected a demand on his customer. Third, and even though he is himself the subject of a demand for payment, he is not in turn demanding, asking only for as much as his customer can afford, and even this he frames diffidently, as "assistance" and service, rather than as repayment or obligation. Finally, in making even the modest request that he does, he stakes his claim not on the grounds of contractual relations or abstract accounting but in terms of sympathy, explaining that his family will suffer if he is unable to meet his own payments. Since this is a model letter in a letter-writing manual rather than an actual epistle in a concrete context, it should come as little surprise that the customer is not only able to pay his debt but to pay it immediately and in full. All too often, in reality, and as we saw in the case of James Hervey Pierrepont, debts were paid slowly, they were paid partially, they were paid heteromorphically, and they were paid in irregularly delivered installments.

Having elucidated the dimensions of both rural and commercial debt ways and their corresponding reliance on thick and thin trust, we are now in a position to entertain an interpretation of subscriber dereliction quite different from those offered above. In the simplest terms, I want to argue, Americans paid for their literary materials slowly, because they paid for almost everything slowly. It was a sign of neither moral turpitude nor psychological dysfunction but, rather, of the widely diffused and deeply entrenched rural ethic of debt that pervaded early national America. Such an argument, at the very least, has demographics on its side, for in 1800 only 3 percent of Americans were city dwellers, while as late as 1860, only one in six could claim a city as their home. Yet even geographical pleading might be dispensed with, for Gary Kulik has argued that much of what historians consider to be characteristic of rural economic values was in fact simply a rural manifestation of a far more pervasive republican ethos that pervaded town as well as country, factory as well as farm, and rich as much as poor, and we certainly see an interpenetration of rural values in the urban letter offered in the *New Universal Letter-Writer.* Whether settlers brought these values into the countryside, however, or rural immigrants brought them into the cities, or both, they were certainly widely diffused in early national America.[30]

Such a contention might certainly explain why readers paid for their literary wares so tardily, but the point I wish to make is broader than this. What I would like to argue, in fact, is that so far from being the passive victims of this cluster of economic practices, American printers, publishers, booksellers, newspaper editors, and periodical proprietors were often active and willing participants and shared the same values. We know this, in the first instance, because they said so often. An item that ran repeatedly in newspapers in the 1820s and beyond, sometimes under the title "What We Call Duties," captures perfectly the editors' acceptance of the logic and rhythms of the rural economy and also recapitulates the model dunning letter we considered above. It reads, in part:

Duties—Every man ought to pay his debts—if he can.
Every man ought to help his neighbor—if he can.

Every young man and women ought to get married—if they can.
Every representative in Congress and the Legislature, ought to inform
                                                                   their
Constituents what they are doing—if they can.
. . . . .
Every man should please his wife—if he can.
Every wife should please her husband—if she can.
. . . . .
Every body should take the paper—if they can.
And, *additionally*, every subscriber should pay for his paper—if he can.
And, *finally*, every reader may add to the above—if he can.[31]

The construction of the piece, tempering categorical imperatives with circumstantial mitigation while inviting both collaboration and improvisation captures almost perfectly the ethical world view that gave rise to rural debt ways. One did *what* one could, *when* one could, including settling one's newspaper and magazine debts. Other editors were less expansive but no less emphatic in embracing such sentiments. The *New-York Mirror*, for example, claimed to deplore aggressive dunning, observing that there was "a certain courtesy between an editor and his readers, which renders the subscription price a *debt of honour*." Elihu Phinney of the *Otsego Herald* concurred, reminding his readers in 1808 that in fourteen years he had "never urged payment in a single instance, even by a gentle call, in the [pages of the] Herald," while James Hall assured jittery readers of the *Western Monthly Magazine* that he would never "authorize any suit against a subscriber."[32]

More than simply proclaiming such sentiments, however, newspaper and magazine editors also practiced them. Many editors, for example, participated in the heteromorphic barter economy with its rural rhythms and cycles of payment. Thus Isaiah Thomas of the *Massachusetts Spy* placed an announcement in his paper in May 1780 noting that "Those persons who take this paper, and engaged to pay me in Rye, Indian-Corn, Butter, Cheese, Sheep's Wool, & c. are requested to make payment, as I am in want of these articles." In 1809, the *Salem Register*, required town-dwellers to pay in cash but allowed those "in the country to pay in wood and provisions." As late as 1847, a Missouri editor could, with only passing sarcasm, place an announcement, reading: "WANTED, at this office, corn, wood, and MONEY. Don't all bring money thro' mistake!"[33] Subscribers rarely did. The account books of the *Rhode Island Republican* reveal that readers used a variety of currencies and followed a number of tempos for payment. Thus Eben P. Sherman of Newport paid regularly and with cash, Hezekiah Kimball paid in cash but irregularly, and his fellow townsman, Henry Coggeshall, settled his bill with four dollars worth of cabbages. Some readers, moreover, mixed both forms of payment and temporal rhythms. Thomas Peckham, for example, paid his bill at different times with some cash, a note drawn upon a third party, sixteen and a half bushels of potatoes, and a copy of the Court Record. An account book for the *Vermont Gazette* indicates, likewise, that Charles Dyer paid for his subscription with "one sheep," "cash," and "2 Bushel wheat." And while such details were often listed, the editor of the *Republican* also noted simply that a subscriber had made "sundry payts." at "sundry times."[34] All the newspaper and periodical subscription books consulted in research for this chapter were of the single-entry variety, reflecting a concern with ongoing transactions and relationships rather than the abstract calculation of profit and loss. Thus they reflected the sort of circumstantial factors ("if he can") mitigating prompt payment typical of rural economic practice more generally. Calvin Spaulding, for example, noted when a subscriber to the *American Advocate* was "poor," "rather poor," had "gone poor," or had "no property." And, finally, newspaper account books reflected the very traditional practice of collecting debts post-mortem when an estate was liquidated.[35]

While the system of paying *if* one could, *when* one could, and with *what* one could reflected the rural ethic of readers, it was not a one-sided affair; the tenets of rural mutualism required that readers, too, extend forbearance. The more picturesque side of this was depicted by the *Boston Morning Post* when it described the work rhythm of the typical rural editor: "If they have a large amount of job work on hand they let the paper go for a fortnight, if the editor's cow gets lost in the woods he leaves his paper and hunts her up, and his subscribers don't grumble a word at his independence." Such a scheme, the *Post* added, "works better there than it would here—for even in this goodly city, an omission like that and for such a reason, would cost an editor half his subscription list."[36] Yet there were more serious sides to the arrangement. Printers and editors were debtors as well as creditors, and they expected the same patience from those to whom they owed money as that which they showed to those who owed it to them. Nor was the *Post* quite correct in supposing that this was wholly a rural phenomenon. While it is true that city editors did not stop the presses to go chasing their cows, they did work within the same sorts of systems of reciprocal indebtedness and reciprocal forbearance. New York City editor Horace Greeley noted, and at least for a while endorsed, the existence of just such an ethos, pronouncing: "You cannot ask favors, and then churlishly refuse to grant any,—borrow, and then frown upon whoever asks you to lend,—seek indorsements, but decline to give any."[37] Frequently, publishers were in debt to their authors. Thus, Isaac Pray presumed on the goodwill of contributor John Greenleaf Whittier, asking him for a short story and promising to "try & pay you when money gets plentier," while John L. O'Sullivan confessed to the same poet that as he had been "rather loose in accounts I really do not know how we stand," meaning, in essence, that Whittier was *his* creditor. Henry William Herbert made this point clear, explaining to a friend that he sent his manuscripts "on credit to a publisher in the far west."[38] And, of course, as we saw in Chapter Three, Thomas Willis White made a veritable career out of purchasing contributions to the *Southern Literary Messenger* on credit, even if most of those credit purchases did turn, over time, into gifts. Above all else, members of the business community whether in the country or city required a certain degree of goodwill in order to maintain their customers and their clients.

Consider again the example of James Hervey Pierrepont. While it is true that he occasionally received a hostile dun, the duns he received from his literary creditors more typically followed the polite model promoted by the *New Universal Letter-Writer*. This is made abundantly clear by the ubiquity with which booksellers and publishers requested payment at his convenience rather than according to a contractually determined schedule. Indeed, invocations of convenience are ubiquitous in this sort of correspondence. Thus while James F. Shores had complained in 1819 about the year Pierrepont had taken to pay for his books, the two were still doing business close to a decade later, with Shores writing tactfully: "If perfectly convenient, the amount of the above bill will be acceptable about this time." Corresponding with him in 1832, Munroe and Brown turned an imperative into an interrogative, in writing: "We inclose your Bill. Will it be convenient to transmit the balance by next mail, if you find it correct?" Again, Carter and Hendee in 1830: "We hope you will not put yourself to any inconvenience respecting the balance of your a/c, as we are willing to wait until it is perfectly convenient for you to pay it." Or, to offer just one more example, Cummings and Hilliard in 1835: "The payment you will make convenient to yourself, as we are at present some what in your debt." As the letter from Cummings and Hilliard makes clear, the monies that passed between them and Pierrepont, *for* whom as well as *to* whom they sold books, tended to a see-saw rather than a tit-for-tat model of reciprocity, but above and beyond their tangled credit relations, the courtesy and forbearance of booksellers and publishers suggests that they also enjoyed an ongoing relationship with him. They did not dun Pierrepont, that is, because he was a valuable customer, and while he took his time to pay, he typically paid in the end.[39]

The booksellers also followed the model of the *New Universal Letter-Writer* in tending to send out duns only when they were themselves in debt to suppliers with whom (presumably) they were in contractual and interest-bearing relationships. "I rarely dun my customers," publisher William Wells, Jr. told Pierrepont in 1816, after he *had* just dunned him, "& shd not have written my last, but that I have a large sum to pay at the end of this month." "Be assured, my dear Sir," Wells added, "I shall always be happy to attend to any commands with which you may favour me."[40] In attending to Pierrepont's orders in spite of his tardiness in paying, Wells was both honoring the tempo of traditional debt ways and, at the same time, ensuring that the two of them would remain on good terms and continue to do business.

Wells, in fact, had little viable alternative. Pursuing claims through the courts was not only expensive and time consuming, but it also led to the sort of hostility that destroyed social, and hence, commercial relationships. When Wells and his partner, Robert Lilly, tried to collect outstanding debts accrued by one of their agents, Thomas Jordan, for example, the results were messy in the extreme. Following months of escalating tension concerning their accounts, Lilly had Jordan arrested in May 1822 for failure to pay a debt of $2,800. This was, Jordan claimed, seventy dollars more than his entire account with Wells and Lilly, and, indeed, he claimed that so far from being in debt to them, they were actually in debt to him. The following day, therefore, Jordan responded by issuing a writ against Wells and Lilly. Deputy Sheriff John S. Williams recorded that he "made a diligent search for the goods and Estate of the within named Robert Lilly to attach . . . but I could not find any within my precinct. I therefore arrested his Body and he gave Bail, and at the same time I attached a stick of wood as the property of the within named William Wells." Three days later, Wells and Lilly issued *another* writ against Jordan, and again Sheriff Williams went to work and "attached one Bay coloured horse—one chaise and harness—as the property of the within named Thomas Jordan." Both parties were now at their wits' end, and rather than continuing to arrest one another for mutual debt they elected to take the case to court, with Jordan planning to "exhibit such confused accts of theirs . . . as will astonish any Jury." When the trial began, months later, the accounts between Wells and Lilly and Jordan, indeed, were so impenetrably complex that the judge had to have outside auditors go through their papers not once but twice, at a cost of thirty-three dollars, before the jury ultimately found in favor of Wells and Lilly. Jordan was required to pay his debts and also court costs of $ 64.81.[41] Perhaps more damaging than the costs, however, was the impact the struggle had on Jordan's standing in the business community. Business credit in early national America, unlike the credit extended to individual and local customers, tended to be most readily available to those whose social reputations were untarnished, while, conversely, public knowledge of one's unwillingness to pay business debts effectively undermined access to future credit. In letters to a trading partner, Jordan complained bitterly that following his first arrest, the sheriff had tried to "take hold of my arm to parade me thro' the most public streets" on the way to jail, while in the second he noted that Wells and Lilly had had the sheriff attach his horse and chaise "in the Street," rather than elsewhere, "for the purpose of exposing me and injuring my Credit if possible." In an age in which merchants' ideals of manhood and respectability were based on business prowess, moreover, financial difficulties—which contemporaries aptly referred to as "embarrassments"—were quite literally a form of dis-crediting: an attack on one's credit-worthiness.[42]

Although their cases are not exactly symmetrical, the ways in which William Wells interacted with James Hervey Pierrepont and Thomas Jordan suggest both the advantages and disadvantages associated with rural and commercial debt ways. In not requiring Pierrepont to settle his bills immediately and fully, Wells solidified their relationship but sometimes found that it compromised his ability to pay bills of his own. In dealing peremptorily with Jordan, Wells secured full payment, but only at the cost of terminating their business relationship, losing in the process the connections Jordan had secured, and creating suspicion among third parties. (According to Jordan, Wells and Lilly were "disliked in both town & country.") Thus Wells found himself confronting a dilemma summed up perfectly by a New Hampshire contemporary: "To dun is irksome—to be dunned is provoking—not to dun who can live?"[43]

THE WORLD OF THE LITERARY DUN

The question of whom to trust, in what way, and under what circumstances, was a difficult one for all merchants, as the example of Wells shows, but those problems took on a special and possibly unique complexity when it came to selling newspapers and magazines. In an ideal world, editors would extend informal credit only to those whom they knew personally, relying instead upon advance cash payment or, at the very least, contractual obligations, when dealing with strangers. This was what merchants, as we have seen above, tended to do, relying on one payment ethic for local trade and another for trade at a distance. And, to be sure, some periodical proprietors tried to do exactly this. The *Literary Mirror*, for example, cost two dollars a year and required "subscribers at a distance" to pay one dollar in advance.[44] The problem with this type of arrangement was that the product being sold tended to undermine the very distinctions on which local versus long-distance ethics were predicated. As explicitly communicative media, printed materials tended to eradicate perceptions of distance by drawing readers and authors into intense emotional relationships. Few authors of repute in the antebellum period failed to receive letters from strangers who, nonetheless, claimed friendship. "Altho' a stranger to you," one reader told Longfellow, "I address you in this familiar manner, for it seems as tho' you were an old friend." Wrote another reader to Lydia Sigourney: "Although I have not had the honor of knowing you personally, yet when we much admire the writings of an individual, though that person be a stranger, it seems to be, that it is natural, that we should feel toward him something of the confidence of an acquaintance." A stranger, likewise, confessed to John Greenleaf Whittier: "I have long known you, for though your face I have never seen, I have been warmed by your poetry." Even the normally unsentimental editor, Lewis Gaylord Clark, admitted to John Pendleton Kennedy that "though not personally acquainted with yourself, your writings, with which I am 'very intimate,' have caused me to regard you as in some sort a *familiar.*"[45]

If this sort of fictive intimacy was characteristic of the relationship between readers and poets, then it was even more so of the relationship between readers and those who edited newspapers and periodicals. Editors, after all, spoke directly to their readers through their columns; readers corresponded with editors by means of letters; and subscribers communicated with one another by means of advertisements and cards. This intimacy was underscored still more by the very seriality of serials, the very periodicity of periodicals, which appeared week after week, month after month, and year after year in an ongoing and potentially endless manner. Far flung though readers might be from the editors of magazines or newspapers, they *felt* close.[46] Some editors sought quite deliberately to conjure up an illusion of intimacy with their readers. Nathaniel P. Willis was one of the first to create the image of the editor-as-friend, inviting his readers into his cozy sanctuary in monthly editorials, where they met his dogs, admired his furnishings, listened to his gossip, and "agreed to be friends." Even those who did not aspire to such domestic intimacy found themselves cheek by jowl with subscribers. Writing a letter to George Graham, an editor considerably less ostentatious than Willis, one reader admitted that "I do not feel that I am addressing an entire stranger, since I have for a long time been accustomed to commune with you through the medium of your high toned and most valuable Magazine." Antebellum editors, in fact, received not only friendly letters from their readers, but also unsolicited gifts, invitations to weddings, and sometimes even marriage proposals.[47] Even the more austere and utilitarian newspapers that eschewed editorializing in favor of commercial or political news created in their readers a sense of participation in a public sphere, and most featured letters or articles addressed familiarly to "Mr. Printer." Writing to cancel his subscription to the definitively stuffy *National Intelligencer* in 1823, Fred Nelson confessed that he felt "as if about to part from an old friend."[48]

Periodicals and newspapers, in other words, created the aura and projected the values of thick trust into social realms more appropriately associated with thin trust. They were strangers who claimed to be, or who, alternatively, were claimed as, neighbors. Having created this aura of intimacy, or having had it placed upon them, editors naturally found it difficult to deny those readers a modicum of economic trust and forbearance, or to insist upon prompt payment as they would with a stranger. The dilemma was summed up almost perfectly in an anguished editorial in the *Salem Register* in 1808. "The printer is in a very difficult and disagreeable situation," he wrote. "He trusts everybody,—who he knows not—his money is scattered everywhere—he hardly knows where to look for it. His paper, his ink, his presses and his types, his labour and his living, all must be punctually paid for."[49] And there was the rub. How, after all, did one dun a man whom one trusted, whom one had invited into one's private study, with whom one had shared gossip? How did one treat as a stranger a member of one's community, albeit a community based on shared feelings rather than shared geography? The answer was that one did it with great tact, a tact made all the more imperative for the public way in which newspaper and magazine duns were offered. At the same time, how did one trust a man one didn't know? How did one collect money when one didn't know where it was? And how did one pay one's own debts when one could not collect money from others? The answer was that one pursued one's creditors with great vigor and determination. It was, of course, difficult, if not downright impossible, to do both. The editor of a serial or newspaper was effectively caught, in other words, between competing necessities: on the one hand to honor and sustain a sense of community and the thick trust it presupposed, and on the other to ensure the sort of cash flow necessary for trade at a distance. These tensions are clearly evident in the literary techniques employed by dunners.[50]

In dunning their customers, printers tended to use three strategies: appeals to sympathy, claims to justice, and an emphasis on materiality. We can see all three of them at play in a poem entitled "Pay the Printer." In the first stanza, the printer calls attention to his straitened circumstances. The underlying message was that the printer was an individual much like the reader.

> When the cold storm howls round the door,
> And you by the light of taper,
> Sit cosily by the evening fire,
> Enjoying the last paper,
> Just think of him whose work thus helps
> To wear away the winter,
> And put this query to yourself—
> Have I paid the Printer?

Sympathy, of course, was not the only grounds on which a printer could appeal to his subscribers, and in the second stanza, the author stakes his claim on a labor theory of value and concomitant claim to economic justice:

> From east and west, from north and south,
> From lands beyond the water,
> He weekly brings you lots of news,
> From every nook and quarter;
> No slave on earth toils more than he,
> Through summer's heat and winter;
> How can you for a moment, then,
> Neglect to pay the printer?

The third and final stanza suggests, in fact, that of all trades, printers were singularly victimized when it came to derelict customers:

> Your other bills you promptly pay,
> Wherever you do go, sir;
> The butcher for his meat is paid,
> For sundries is the grocer;
> The tailor and the shoemaker,
> The hatter and the vinter,
> All get their pay, then why neglect
> To settle with the Printer?[51]

While I have suggested that, in fact, members of all trades suffered from the tardiness with which customers paid for their goods, there is, nonetheless, some grounds for the claim that printers found it especially hard to claim their due with authority. The problem lay in the fact that newspapers and magazines were not only physically flimsy but also tended to have more intellectual than material heft. Because the relationship with an editor seemed more virtual than actual, and because a text was as much a product of imagination as fact, readers apparently came to feel as if the editors themselves were intangible, their needs imaginary. "Editors and publishers cannot live on air," explained the *Western Monthly Magazine*.[52] It was a common lament, and printers' duns often proceeded by trumping images of intangibility with ones of irreducible materiality:

> Out of wood, and clothing scant,
> Dry goods due for, hats in want,
> Children fretful, wife complaining,
> Credit difficult sustaining,
> Notes to manage, discounts rare,
> Debt enough, can't live on air:
> Though I would by no means *dun* ye,
> Think ye—do I not want money?[53]

Or again, in a dun from 1816:

> Says Thomas, indeed, we did none of us think
> That printers could feel, or could want meat or drink.
> Or like other people, would cloathing require
> Or wood for the warming themselves by the fire.
> And if none of these wants any trouble could cause,
> They might live as bears do—by sucking their paws.[54]

Over and over, printers framed their demands for repayment in the language of material necessities: food, clothing, and warmth. Here, if anywhere, is where we see arguments based on a moral economy being deployed, for printers believed that they had an irreducible and inalienable claim to sustenance. Food imagery appears in many duns. "The man who takes no papers," quipped one, "Or taking, pays not when they're read, / Would sell his corn to buy a horn, / And live on borrowed bread." And again: "Pay up subscribers who have read, / For printers dearly earn their bread." A Pennsylvania printer played upon the conventions of pay in country produce by announcing that he wanted "grain, pork, tallow, *candles*, whiskey, *linen*, *beesewax*, *wool*, and anything else he can eat." The editors of the Brookfield, Massachusetts, *Political Repository* simply noted—with perhaps more optimism than the circumstances warranted—that "we retain the old-fashioned custom of eating yet."[55]

Sometimes, too, printers sought to emphasize the materiality of the very text and the effort that went into producing it. The most ingenious example was a magic square that appeared in several newspapers in 1829. An almost solid block of text, akin to a concrete poem, the square repeated the phrase "pay the printer" in such a way that it could be read backwards, forwards, from left to right and back again. Not only did the square contain what one editor called "two thousand hints," but through its very iconic density it underscored the idea that printing was a skill that created something solid and valuable.[56] The very fact that each printer who repeated the triangle had to set the type from scratch made the feat that more impressive. Whether or not it actually moved any subscribers to pay their dues, it certainly underscored that printers lived in a world of things and not merely of ideas.

In an 1836 dun, the editor of the Montpelier *State Journal* called upon subscribers to pay their debts and noted that money from rural subscribers could be sent to town with state delegates who would be visiting the capital for legislative session. "It is not often that we give 'the grand hailing sign of distress,' " he noted, "but the present call is no joke."[57] Although printers' impoverishment was indeed no joke, they often resorted to jokes precisely to make their point. Consider this single-sentence dun from the *Western Carolinian*. "The printer of an Eastern paper says, that many of his patrons would make good wheel horses, they *hold back* so well."[58] Twenty-two nasty words. Expanded and translated, this sentence suggests that derelict subscribers are as ploddingly obstinate with their money as farm animals are with their burdens and, moreover, that while slowness is a virtue in a wheel horse, it is categorically a vice in subscribers. To say precisely this, however, would have been to antagonize customers and lose their goodwill. Far less offensive duns had, quite literally, led to gun fights and death; the point of an effective dun was not to provoke ill will but, rather, to collect payment without terminating an ongoing social relationship.[59] Jokes were especially useful in this respect, for as Freud argues, jokes "make possible the satisfaction of an instinct (whether lustful or hostile) in the face of an obstacle that stands in its way. They circumvent this obstacle and in that way draw pleasure from a source which the obstacle had made inaccessible." Jokes, in other words, allow one to communicate a potentially hostile observation in an indirect manner. Jokes, Freud goes on to explain, circumvent social sanction through such techniques as condensation of meaning and displacement of message.[60] We certainly see evidence of such 'joke work,' as Freud calls it, in the *Carolinian's* brief dun. Two techniques appear: the first is a form of bonding, the second a form of distancing. In the first place, then, the dun does not actually *say* that subscribers are animals; rather, it makes an analogy. The analogy, moreover, is presented through a clever pun that allows any reader, no matter what their state of indebtedness, to enjoy the ingenuity of the condensation in which "hold back" can connote both equine restraint and readerly tight-fistedness. The reaction provoked by the cleverness of the pun draws its readers together in a momentary community of laughter. Any possibility that offense will be taken by the analogy is yet further muted by the fact that it is offered second hand, from the mouth of an "Eastern editor," a typical piece of regional othering. Yet even as the joke helps bond, it also separates, dividing readers into those who laugh at the derelict subscribers and those who *are* the derelict subscribers. To take offense at the joke is to concede one's dereliction and the aptness of the analogy; the reader, then, is subtly pressured to shift identities from the laughed at to the laugher, a move effected by paying one's dues. A dun such as this enables derelict subscribers to feel included in a community even while evoking in them a sense of discomfort at not playing their proper community function by paying for what they enjoy.

Sometimes the humor was more ominous still. Rural payments, we will recall, were often only settled upon the death of a debtor, when his or her estate was liquidated to satisfy creditors. Several editors turned this tradition to humorous (and hostile) use. "Many subscribers to newspapers and periodicals," noted the *Western Monthly Magazine* tartly, "have died in the publishers' debt; and, what is worse, many are living in the same state of delinquency." The implication was perfectly clear, if less than pleasant; if an editor had to wait until a subscriber died to collect his due, then he would soon start to wish for the subscriber's death. A still more explicit version of the same joke was offered in 1849:

> A subscriber for years being sad in arrears,
> Still neglecting his bills for to pay,
> To the editor said—"Unless I am dead,
> I shall pay you on Christmas day,"
> The time flew by and the debtor was shy,
> But the editor thought what he said;
> In his paper next week, the truth he did speak,
> And announced that his subscriber was *dead!*[61]

Occasionally, a dun turned downright nasty. The Ann Arbor *Wolvereen* perhaps went furthest in this direction in offering up a frank malediction: "A man that would cheat the printer, would steel [sic] a meeting house and rob a graveyard. If he had a soul, ten thousand of its size would have no more room in a mosquito's eye, than a bull frog has in the Pacific Ocean. He ought to be winked at by blind people and kicked to death across lots by cripples."[62] A dun such as this was highly unlikely to glean positive results, however. It was one thing to joke about the death of a subscriber, and entirely another to wish a subscriber's death in so open a fashion. The hostility in this passage is so naked that it hardly leaves room for contrition or reaggregation on the part of the defaulting subscriber.

When all other literary means had been exhausted, a newspaper or magazine editor who worked in the traditional vein would sometimes print the names of derelict subscribers together with the amounts they owed and the period for which they had owed them. The blacklist was the ultimate sanction, because it suggested not that such individuals were unable to pay their dues, but rather that they were unwilling. Those who were blacklisted were advertised as untrustworthy. A blacklist was a community judgment, an attempt to shame subscribers before their peers. This, at least, was the argument implied by the editors of the *Knicker-bocker* in 1841. "We have heretofore appealed to the sense of justice of the *Delinquent Subscribers* to this magazine," they announced, and would do so one last time. If dues were not then promptly received "*the name of the subscriber will appear in a List of Delinquents, in a conspicuous page of the work.*" True to their word, they printed a list of derelict subscribers on the inside front cover of the magazine two months later.[63] It might perhaps seem strange for a magazine published in New York City and with more than five thousand subscribers scattered across the nation to attempt a gesture as futile as naming specific names, but there was a certain logical consistency to the act. If a false sense of neighborliness led to subscriber dereliction in the first place, then it made sense to appeal to this same sense of imagined community in levying a sanction. A blacklist would not secure repayment but it at least created the possibility that others would pause before extending them credit. Blacklisting one Lewis Fowler of Poughkeepsie, the *Port Folio* crowed: "This *fowler* may think to *make game* of Editors, but he shall find himself mistaken. After the fraud he has practiced on us, who will trust him?"[64] The irony, of course, is that in appealing to this fictive community, newspaper and magazine editors were merely reinforcing the conditions that created such tardy payment in the first place.

The futility of blacklisting subscribers is underscored by the experience of the *Ladies' Companion*, a New York based magazine active between 1839 and 1844. At least initially, the *Companion* collected dues in haphazard fashion, dunning only when a volume was complete or a ledger full. In May 1839, for example, the editors announced that they were transferring the names of subscribers into a new account book and that this was therefore a good time for those in debt to the magazine to settle their bills. Payment at this time, they noted, should be a "point of duty" that would save the magazine "much unnecessary expense and trouble." With as many as 17,500 subscribers scattered across the nation, it was unlikely that many would oblige. And so in December of that year, the *Companion* adopted a radically different tack, publishing on its front cover the names of 52 derelict subscribers. A stern editorial in that month also noted that "Whoever receives the *first number* of a new year, *is liable for the whole year's subscription.*" Lists with new names continued in almost every issue for the next sixth months. It would not appear that the black lists were especially effective, since three years later, as the magazine began to founder, the editors had returned to less hostile pleas to their readers. "We do earnestly appeal to their feelings in this particular," wrote the editors, "and hope that they will be convinced of the correctness of these remarks, and at once ease their own consciences by remitting their arrearages."[65] The magazine moved, in other words, from appeals to justice, to attempts to shame, and finally to appeals guilt in order to secure repayment.

A similar shaming strategy was mentioned in a column in the *Southern Rose*, where editor Caroline Gilman noted ominously that a British magazine was now sending issues to derelict subscribers with a special, brightly colored wrapper "as a distinction and warning." In an age in which magazines were collected personally from the Post Office and in which whatever arrived at the Post Office was public knowledge within the community, the colored wrapper would tell the subscriber's neighbors more clearly than a closely printed blacklist that he or she was in default.[66] Yet Gilman herself preferred to rely on a more wholesome sense of community—of knowing and being known—to create a world of reliable subscribers. As the wife of a prominent and well-traveled Charleston minister, Gilman could rely on personal recognition and reputation to garner trust. Writing to Harriet Fay in the early 1830s, she recalled: "I took an excursion on the Rail Road lately. At the first & last stopping places persons recognizing Mr. G came forward to subscribe. I also made an excursion up the Cooper. There were a great many planters on board the Boat. They greeted & thanked me for what I was doing in the most respectful terms."[67] Yet dense though the webs of Gilman's own social network may have been, the railroad and the steamboat on which she met her friends served to disseminate her works ever further and to unknown—and indeed to unknowable—individuals. Even within her own adopted city of Charleston, whose free white population diminished over the course of the 1830s, there were enough people to make it impossible for Gilman to truly know even all of her local subscribers.[68]

How was it possible to do business with those one had not met, to trust those whom one did not know? In 1841, Lewis Tappan came up with a novel answer. A failed businessman who had also served a stint as the editor of a daily newspaper—*The Journal of Commerce*—Tappan established what is believed to be the first nationwide credit reporting agency. Relying on a far-flung network of correspondents in innumerable villages, towns, and cities across the union (679 informants worked for him within five years, more than 2,000 after ten), Tappan began to compile an immense archive of reports on the business habits, trustworthiness, and credibility of the nation's men of business, which he sold to other businessmen considering doing business with them. A year's subscription to the service—presumably payable in advance—cost from $50 to $300, depending on the income of the client. Tappan's Mercantile Agency attempted, that is to say, to commodify and disseminate the sort of information on which thick trust was based to those who would otherwise only be able to rely on the thinnest and most abstract kinds of confidence. It was, as one scholar has so aptly put it, less an attempt to depersonalize than "to *repersonalize* as well as rationalize business." Tappan's informants and agents functioned as intermediaries between strangers, creating virtual (and also highly asymmetrical) bonds of intimacy.[69]

While several publishers became subject to the Agency's investigations, few publishers could ever have afforded to have used its services themselves to determine the trustworthiness of its potential subscribers; that just wasn't practical.[70] Yet many publishers of magazines and newspapers took a leaf out of Tappan's book in establishing their own networks of agents to not only solicit subscriptions but also to collect them. Gilman, for example, developed a network of subscription agents and periodical depositories throughout Charleston based on the city's well-established ward system. Rather than presenting herself to strangers as a stranger, or to strangers as a friend (a fiction that only went so far), she invited her subscribers to present themselves to agents who actually lived in their neighborhoods and who might well have been literal neighbors.[71] The use of subscription agents was clearly intended not merely as a practical means of backing up trust by collecting money at a distance, but also as a way of establishing actual (as opposed to virtual or fictive) relationships that would facilitate such collections. Gender conventions also played into the establishment of trust. Writing to John Neal in 1838, Park Benjamin asked him to "recommend any first rate business person, faithful and capable, who, will take the agency of the paper in Portland? I should think some woman of substance might be obtainable in that quarter." Benjamin's preference for a woman agent seems at first glance to be out of step with the age's concern with separate spheres and the idea that a "woman of substance" should avoid the world of business, but this was precisely the point; in having a woman serve as an agent, Benjamin hoped to rely on moral suasion, friendship, and trust to ensure his cash flow rather than relying on legal exertion. So did Gilman, who used at least one "collector lady"—a Mrs. Pringle—to handle subscription payments.[72]

Yet neither Benjamin nor Gilman's use of agents enabled them to circumvent the paradox of being a literary subscriber: if one knew, or felt one knew, the proprietor of a publication (or her agent) then the relationship could be considered social and the ethic of stringent and timely payment was less than appropriate, while if one did not know, or was not known by, the proprietor, it was hard, if not impossible, to enforce a timely payment, no matter how appropriate it might be. Then, too, the use of agents sometimes resulted not in an increase of trust but simply a whole new community of business intermediaries whom it was impossible to trust. They could be, as Hezekiah Niles put it "dishonest & frequently negligent." Thus editor Sarah Griffin confided to John Neal that "We have *never had* an agent who did not pocket all ^or most^ the money he collected," while Amelia Bloomer related a similar story to Lydia Sigourney, confessing that after founding a temperance magazine with some friends, they had been defrauded by their subscription agent. "At first he done well for us," she explained, "making good returns, but after a little time absconded taking money to a considerable amount belonging to us."[73]

If it was hard for publishers to trust agents they hardly knew, then it was just as hard, at times, for subscribers to trust them either. Increasingly often, the person who appeared at the door to collect a subscriber's money was only pretending to be an agent. "Nathaniel Sleeper," announced the *Ladies' Companion* in 1841, in what was to become a generic complaint, "has been representing *himself* as an agent in the States of Massachusetts, Vermont and New-Hampshire. The said *Sleeper* is unknown to us—consequently, he is an *imposter*."[74] The key word here is not the italicized "himself" but rather the less emphasized "representing," for the conundrum raised by the use of subscription agents was how to offer anything other than a representation of intimacy, knowledge, or trust, in the absence of an ongoing, embodied relationship. Even Gilman had to rely on strangers as agents as her magazine made inroads into the North, and while none of them appeared to defraud her, the trust she extended them was of the thinnest kind.[75]

It was as her own magazine struggled that Gilman first pointedly alluded to the shaming strategies used by British publications. It was the first stage on a road few were willing to travel. When Gilman's printer, James S. Burges, ceased his connection with the *Southern Rose*, he traveled several stages further, printing a notice on the wrapper of the magazine that moved from cajolery and complaint to a scarcely veiled threat of legal action. "Many who have *patronized* the work for years," he wrote, "have not contributed one cent toward its support; and many have paid their *first year's* Subscription—but no more. The publisher has not received in the last two years sufficient to pay the actual cost of printing, without including the necessary compensation to the Editor. He has therefore concluded to give delinquents *one more* call, to give them an opportunity of paying, and at the end of the Volume placing all outstanding debts in the proper hands for final settlement."[76] The destination toward which such a notice pointed—the Court of Common Pleas—suggested that the end of an era was close at hand. The point at which a magazine was compelled either to threaten suit, or actually to pursue legal action, it would be impossible to sustain the sort of goodwill necessary to get readers to subscribe in the first place. In order not to end up making legal threats, it would seem, it was necessary to not even begin traveling down the road at whose end such actions awaited. This, in a nutshell, was the conundrum of subscription in the antebellum period.[77]

THE DISCREDITING OF THE AMERICAN READER

In 1850, Harper and Brothers in New York began to publish a periodical entitled *Harper's New Monthly Magazine*. It was an almost immediate success. With an initial press run of 7,500 copies per issue, it was, by the end of its first year, printing 50,000. By 1855, it was selling 140,000 copies per issue, and within a decade, it was selling 200,000. *Harper's* very quickly established itself as the most popular and remunerative periodical of the century.[78] Many competitors struggled to explain the magazine's achievement. A writer in the July 1852 *American Whig Review*—it would go out of the business the same year—pointed out, with some bitterness, that Harper and Brothers had its own printing press and bindery, its own well-established network of agents, and a prestigious stable of authors. Most of all, this writer complained, *Harper's* raided the contents of British literary magazines for much of its copy, which meant that it could enjoy high prestige material at no cost, thanks to the lack of international copyright legislation between the two countries.[79]

A typical issue of the magazine—from April 1855—suggests the ways in which it was able to combine both English and American contributions to create a blend of the exotic and the familiar that was immensely appealing. The contents ranged from the homely (an essay on dogs) to the morbid (an essay on the catacombs of Rome and another on 'vampyres') and featured several serialized novels, including one by Thackeray (*The Newcombes*), and a short story by Herman Melville ("The Paradise of Bachelors and the Tartarus of Maids"). Several pieces on travel (central America and Europe) were offset by the cozy domesticity of the "Editor's Easy Chair," co-written by Ik Marvel and George William Curtis. This issue's "Easy Chair" touched on Valentine's Day, lecturing, and railroads: the very subjects—the commercialization of leisure, the democratization of knowledge, and the development of new technologies of dissemination and communication—that created the conditions which fueled the success of such magazines.[80]

The range of materials *Harper's* included and the resources at its disposal were, indeed, significant factors in accounting for the magazine's success, as were the larger contextual factors touched upon in the "Easy Chair" pieces. Perhaps the most important factor of all in accounting for the magazine's success was, however, dismissed by the *American Whig* critic as a symptom of that success rather than its cause. According to the writer:

There is not a village, there is scarcely a township in the land into which your work has not penetrated. . . . It is hawked on every street of our larger cities. It lies upon the counter of every news-room. It is dispensed by thousands from wholesale book-houses.[81]

In a nutshell, that is to say, Harper and Brothers solved the problem of selling by subscription simply by not selling by subscription, or at least not exclusively so. The magazine could be purchased by the issue, at a cost of twenty-five cents, as well as by the year, and it was available not only directly from the publisher but, as this sketch suggests, through a host of intermediaries, including periodical depots, book stores, and street vendors, all of whom received cash in hand at the time of purchase. In cutting through the gordian knot of trust and credit on which subscription was based, *Harper's* effectively solved the problem of the typically inverse ratio between circulation and income that dogged most magazines and newspapers. The magazine received money for every copy sold.

Much of the credit for the magazine's strategies can be attributed to Harper and Brothers, for they were indeed shrewd and astute business-men, but the decision to minimize subscription publishing was not one they made themselves, so much as it was one that was forced upon them by circumstance. Of all the items in the April 1855 issue of *Harper's*, the one that comes closest to explaining the conditions behind the strat-egy of the magazine is Herman Melville's obscure and meandering sto-ry, "The Paradise of Bachelors and the Tartarus of Maids." One of his so-called diptychs—paired narratives that contrasted nations and social classes—the Tartarus portion of the story describes the narrator's visit to a Massachusetts paper mill. Hidden in a deep ravine, and resembling "some great whited sephulcre," the mill is a daunting place.[82] The work-ers are all women, "blank-looking girls, with blank, white folders in their blank hands, all blankly folding blank paper" (328). No human voices are heard, only the "low, steady, overruling hum" of the paper machines, which the narrator describes as "iron animals" (328). A young operative who takes the narrator on a tour of the mill ignores the women's suffer-ing but boasts of the plant's new paper-making machine that "cost us twelve thousand dollars only last autumn" (331) and of the cotton rags—raw material for paper—which have been gathered not only locally but from "far over sea—Leghorn and London" (330). The narrator leaves the mill chilled to the bone not only by the freezing weather, but also by the cold and harsh working conditions he has witnessed.

Melville's account of the paper mill—which was based on an actual visit he made to a mill in Dalton, Massachusetts—is, as Judith A. McGaw has astutely pointed out, actually a veiled critique of the state's textile mills, and many of the details in the story reflect that target, but Melville was nonetheless absolutely accurate in pointing to both the immense cost of the machinery used in the paper mills and to the fact that the raw ma-terials were collected from a wide geographical region.[83] These reflected a dramatic revolution in the way paper was made and financed and which directly disrupted the credit economy on which all newspaper and maga-zine producers had traditionally operated.

Until the 1820s, most paper mills were very much part of the same trust-and-barter economy that pervaded all aspects of rural American life. Just as readers purchased their newspapers from printers with crops and services, so printers paid for their paper with both books and rags. Ebenezer and George Merriam, who ran a publishing company in Brook-field, Massachusetts, were typical in this respect. They sold their books on credit and in exchange for country produce and services, and they purchased their raw supplies in much the same fashion. Their paper bill, which constituted between from 33 to 45 percent of their production costs, was paid for primarily in printed goods and credit, with only 20 percent of the bill being paid for with cash. When the Merriams' customers were unable to pay for their newspapers, books, and magazines, the Merriams were unable to pay for their paper, and the paper makers were not paid. In the world of reciprocal and circular indebtedness something eventually had to give, and what gave was the paper business. Following the great financial Panic of 1819, papermakers began to feel unprecedentedly vulnerable before the vicissitudes of the market, and by the mid-1820s, according to Jack Larkin, the largest paper suppliers were "opting out of the commodity exchange network still so pervasive in rural economic life." All of a sudden, the Merriams were forced to pay for their paper almost wholly in cash, a commodity in desperately short supply.[84] Others felt the same pressure. James Hall of the *Western Monthly Review* explained that the flattering evasiveness of traditional duns were now beside the point, for he had to "deal with paper makers, printers and binders, men of stern faces, laconic speech, and inflexible gravity, who understand not softenings and circumlocutions, and who hold compliments, in lieu of reality, in abhorrence. They are, moreover, bigoted observers of set days, and certain ceremonies of restitution for the past, and pledges for the future."[85] The stern faces, set days, and ceremonies of restitution were all a result of the high degree of capitalization that began to be necessary to operating a paper mill in the 1820s. New technologies that were extremely expensive to purchase but extremely efficient in producing vast quantities of paper cheaply began to tempt paper makers. Paper mills needed cash to pay for this technology and, since local rag supplies would not adequately fill their new machines, they also needed cash to purchase rags from abroad. Melville's story hardly exaggerates the hemispheric scope of an operation nestled in the Berkshire hills: by 1832, 22 percent of the rags used in the mill he would visit were purchased from Europe. In 1855, the year Melville's story was published, a batch of paper was made from the wrappings of disinterred Egyptian mummies. In such a far-flung, transnational world of commerce—the bill for the mummy wrappings, for example, was said to be $25,000—a promise of turnips and assistance in raising a barn the following year were laughably irrelevant.[86]

When paper makers started to demand cash for their product, it created an immense domino effect that cascaded through the literary world: printers started to dun publishers, publishers started to dun readers, and readers started to dun one another. Increasingly, newspaper and magazine publishers found this system untenable, and so they turned away from an economy based on credit. It was here, in the world of paper making, that the roots of *Harper's* challenge lay, and their success lay in how effectively they circumvented the trust economy with which it was so incompatible and replaced it with a cash economy.

In lieu of a trust-based system of sales, magazine and newspaper publishers had, in essence, two options. The first was to disavow subscriptions in favor of the sale of individual issues on a cash-in-hand basis. Such a strategy was first pursued by the publishers of one and two penny daily newspapers that started to appear in New York in the early 1830s. The new dailies did not dispense altogether with either subscriptions or home delivery, but they started to sell their penny papers to armies of young boys at two-thirds of a penny, after which the boys could either deliver them to subscribers they had themselves drummed up or sell them on the streets to passersby. Others were sold to vendors with news stands, or to wholesalers who ran periodical depots. Either way, the responsibility for collection now fell on the newsboys and other vendors rather than the newspaper proprietor. Since all transactions were made in cash, and long-term relationships based on annual subscription were replaced by fleeting encounters with strangers, both trust and the risks it entailed were removed. By the 1840s, street sales had become common not only in the major cities of the East but even in smaller towns such as Milwaukee, and by 1860s it had become for many publications the dominant mode of sale. According to one pundit, writing in 1866, "The subscription business of many of our leading journals is almost nominal."[87]

The second strategy designed to circumvent subscription problems was known as the 'cash system.' This developed because, while street selling was useful for newspaper proprietors in densely populated areas, it was much less efficient for publishers of magazines, whose readers were spread widely and for those newspapers that addressed national rather than local issues. Quite simply, the cash system required that all newspaper subscriptions be paid for by cash in advance. In the absence of full payment, no newspapers or magazines would be sent. Introduced first in the late 1830s, it was attempted repeatedly through the 1840s. In 1841, for example, the editor of the *Arkansas Gazette* announced that from that point onward he would send "no paper to a new subscriber, without receiving a subscription price *in advance*." He would not, in other words, treat new subscribers as friends he had yet to meet. His decision was manifestly an attempt to disembed newspaper subscription from the web of sociability and trust in which it had been ensnared for so long. He adopted a similar strategy with current subscribers. Rather than blacklisting and publishing the names of derelict readers, the editor announced that those who had not paid would simply find their names "struck from the subscription list." The editor was perhaps aware that in pursuing such a policy, he was flying in the face of long-standing standards of communal trust, and he called on other newspaper editors to back him up and establish a consistent front based on a new, and disembedded, form of literary economic behavior. A week later, he reported exultantly that another local editor had "also adopted the cash system" and repeated his call for its general adoption.[88]

Reporting on attempts to promote such methods in 1839, a Massachusetts paper noted that "a number of the Western papers are adopting the cash system in their business" and that they were introducing it "about as fast as they can and not frighten people."[89] And there (again) was the rub, for readers who were used to regarding selling and sociability as intertwined, indeed inextricable, activities, found the idea that newspaper and periodical proprietors might not trust (and by extension know) them thoroughly unnerving. Many publishers tried to soften the blow. When Horace Greeley's *New Yorker* shifted to the cash system in 1840, for example, it appeased subscribers by reducing the price of the magazine. The *Arkansas Gazette* also sought to smooth ruffled feathers, by explaining that they would print advertisements prior to payment if they came from "regular *punctual* customers" or if guarantee of payment was "assumed by some person of known responsibility." In so doing, they in essence, brought trust back in to the system through the back door.[90] Indeed, editors bent so far backward to accommodate themselves and their subscribers to the system that the whole concept became for some a scarcely veiled heteromorphic joke. "A country Editor," quipped one pundit in 1840, "tells his subscribers that he has been compelled to the cash system, but will continue to accept *potatoes* at *par*."[91] This is a good example of what cultural critic Raymond Williams would call an emergent economic system being woven into—or perhaps strangled by—a residual one. The cash system, in fact, proved so abrasive to sensibilities nurtured on communal values that as late as 1917, Phil Bing, a professor of journalism and author of a handbook for editors of rural newspapers, felt compelled to justify the practice with some defensiveness, before moving on to explain how best to dun derelict subscribers. Slowly but surely, however, the cash system became the norm.[92]

From the very outset, *Harper's New Monthly Magazine* used both of these strategies. An advertisement published in 1850 explained that the periodical could be purchased by the issue, or through an annual subscription "when payment is made to them in advance." It was also sold directly to customers and through "Booksellers and Periodical Agents."

The advertisement encouraged individuals to club together and buy the publication at a discount. And it offered free "Specimen Numbers" to agents, while most publishers charged a fee, which encouraged more individuals to become middlemen. By using both cash subscriptions and sales of individual numbers and channeling them through its unprecedented network of contacts, it was able to create a stable periodical empire that would not be matched or beaten in the nineteenth century. Such success came at a cost, though, for while *Harper's* without a doubt projected a familiar, if not intimate, aura, the way in which it—and other magazines and newspapers that adopted street sales and the cash system—was sold led to the slow but inexorable disembedding of the act of periodical reading.[93]

Street sales, for example, bore all the hallmarks of disembedded transactions: nothing was available for free, and nothing was offered on credit or in trust. Writing in 1849, George Foster noted that when they had first appeared in the 1830s, newsboys would often 'cry' the headlines for the passing crowds, but that when they discovered that many were relying on such summaries rather than buying the paper itself, they clammed up, offering only the most tantalizing hints. If you wanted the news, Foster explained, you had to "fork over your pennies . . . and read it honestly, and with a clear conscience."[94] The news stand exchange was still more characteristically disembedded: transitory, anonymous, even silent. As an account of a New York news stand from the 1860s put it: "There is no conversation between buyer and seller. The money is laid down, the journal is taken up, and the change given, without a word."[95] Even the newsboy himself was seen as rootless and placeless. He was, according to an 1840 account, "a creation of the hour, he owns no ancestry." Where subscriber and distant proprietor regarded one another with trust—perhaps because they *were* distant—the newsboy was a figure of ill favor with a well-earned reputation for pickpocketing, even if—and again perhaps because—he was so physically proximate to his customers.[96] A street purchase, then, was a fleeting encounter between strangers, defined solely by a one-time exchange of cash for a product that was neither based upon, nor constitutive of, an ongoing relationship, or of significant trust. As *New York Herald* editor James Gordon Bennett put it in 1837, his paper was "subservient to none of its readers—known to none of its readers—and entirely ignorant of who are its readers and who are not."[97]

The cash system, likewise, engendered a desocialized and increasingly disembedded system of purchase. Leading the way were the so-called story papers: brash and cheap publications, taking the form of outsized newspapers but combining just a little news and editorializing with hefty serialized novels and novellas. One of the most popular, *The Flag of Our Union*, stated its unwillingness to extend trust to its subscribers in the bluntest terms:

We cannot help but laugh in our sleeve to see many of the weekly papers constantly dunning their subscribers to "pay up," and ever croaking at "delinquents." We have no trouble of this kind but are ever on the best of terms with our subscribers. Our terms are strictly *pay in advance*; we take the name, and the money together; and the President of the United States would not get the Flag, if he sent his name, unless the pay was enclosed also. When the time expires for which the subscriber pays, the paper is *immediately* stopped; and in our enormous list, the largest in the world with one exception, *there is not one unpaid subscription.*[98]

The system apparently worked, for founding editor, Frederick Gleason, recalled that within two years of its establishment in 1846, *The Flag* was selling 40,000 copies per issue and within ten years "nearly 100,000," from which he derived "an income of $25,000."[99]

Other story papers echoed *The Flag*'s brash hostility to trust-based subscription schemes. One of them, the *True Flag*, went so far as to revise the old newspaper chestnut, "What We Call Duties," for the new era. The traditional version, we will recall, began "Every man ought to pay his debts—if he can / Every man ought to help his neighbor—if he can" and concluded "Every body should take the paper—if they can / And . . . every subscriber should pay for his paper—if he can." The *True Flag*'s version still began the same way: "Every man ought to pay his debts—if he can. Every man ought to help his neighbor," but its conclusion was strikingly different: "Every one should take a newspaper," it ran, "and PAY FOR IT—any how."[100] The concluding "any how" was doubly emphatic, suggesting both 'no matter what' and 'by any means necessary.' By mid-century, indeed, the idea of payment in advance had percolated far enough into popular culture, that it had quite literally become child's play. Witness the *Dew Chalice*, a handwritten newspaper circulated by students at a young ladies' academy in Natick, Massachusetts, in 1854. Even though this was the sort of publication that more or less by definition both thrived upon and created dense bonds of trust and amity and whose terms of subscription were the categorically non-monetary "Open ears, sealed lips, attentive minds & understanding hearts," it nonetheless aped commercial paper when its adolescent authors insisted on "Pay always in advance."[101]

Herman Melville never wrote a story about subscription and credit, or about *Harper's New Monthly Magazine*, but they were subjects about which he almost certainly thought a great deal. Harper and Brothers were Melville's primary American publishers, and between 1847 and

1852, they issued seven of his novels. When *Harper's New Monthly* debuted in June 1850, Melville started to buy the individual issues, month by month, and in September 1851, he began to subscribe, keeping his subscription active for eight years. The magazine published an anticipatory chapter from *Moby-Dick*, and after Melville's career as a novelist foundered, it also published seven of his short stories.[102] But Harper and Brothers were not only Melville's publishers; for many years they also served as his bankers, advancing or loaning him sums of money against sales of his future publications. Unfortunately, Melville's expenses far outstripped his income, a situation compounded by the fact that the Harpers charged Melville interest on their advances. By August 1848, Melville was in debt to the firm to the tune of $256.03; by August of 1849, he owed $1,332.29; and when, in April 1851, he wrote seeking an advance on *Moby-Dick*, Harper's politely but firmly declined, noting that "there is a balance due us of nearly seven hundred dollars."[103]

There is no question that Melville—who was seriously in debt to others—felt betrayed by the lack of trust shown in him by the publishing firm with which he had done so much business over so many years. Although Melville came to a new arrangement with the company, according to which he could contribute to *Harper's New Monthly Magazine* and be paid, even though he owed them money on his book account, he remained bitter concerning his debts. In his first magazine piece, entitled "Cock-A-Doodle-Doo!" (December 1853), the narrator beats and humiliates a "lantern-jawed rascal, who seems to run on a railroad track . . . and duns me even on Sunday, all the way to church and back."[104] His next contribution was "The Paradise of Bachelors and the Tartarus of Maids," which so astutely described the relentless industrialization of the paper trade and the cold-heartedness it engendered.

It was not until 1855, however, that Melville began work on a novel that would fully anatomize the issues of trust, credit, and credibility. This novel, published in 1857, was *The Confidence-Man: His Masquerade.* A complex and episodic work that scholars find it hard even to summarize without controversy, *The Confidence-Man* describes the journey of a steamboat down the Mississippi. As the boat pursues its course, picking up and dropping off passengers, a variety of confidence men—or possibly one confidence man in a variety of guises—seek to scam the people they meet. Some show themselves to be all too trusting, parting with their money, their goodwill, and their sympathy to a complete stranger. Others show an appalling lack of trust, refusing to entertain the possibility that the stranger is bona fide, even when it would seem clear that he warrants charity. Although they were not terms with which he would have been familiar, Melville's novel offers a stunning analysis of a world in which thick trust has given way to thin: a world in which the harder it becomes to ever "know" others, the more one feels the urge to do so. The passengers on Melville's boat seem to be caught, like so many Americans in this period, between the Scylla of traditional confidence in those with whom one did business, and the Charybdis of modern distrust, according to which anyone might be a confidence man. In one of the most striking scenes of the novel, the ship's barber, who operates, like the penny paper vendors, on a cash-only basis with a shingle that reads 'No Trust,' is not only encouraged by the confidence man to take down the sign but is then scammed into giving him a free haircut.

Did Melville's experiences in the increasingly distrustful literary marketplace influenced the plot of the novel? There is certainly some evidence to suggest that they had. Some believe, for example, that one of the confidence men aboard the ship was a poorly disguised portrait of *New-York Tribune* editor, Horace Greeley, a pioneer in the 'cash system' of newspaper sales. Likewise, the novel begins with a group of pickpockets working a crowd that is entranced by a book peddler selling sensational crime pamphlets concerning "the lives of Meason, the bandit of Ohio, Murrel, the pirate of the Mississippi, and the brothers Harpe, the Thugs of the Green River country, in Kentucky." While there really was a gang of criminals known as the Harpe Brothers, it is hard not to see this as Melville-the-inveterate-punster's sly dig at the Harper Brothers, who refused to show any confidence in the author when he begged them for an advance on his work.[105]

By the middle of the century, the split between those who reposed confidence in their readers and those who did not had become not only a matter of country dwellers versus city dwellers but also of South against North. And so it was, in October 1860, as the nation teetered on the brink of a Civil War over slavery, that the editor of the *Charleston Mercury* drew an explicit parallel between sectional identity and subscription ideology. "The New York *Tribune*, the chief organ of our Northern aggressors," wrote the *Mercury*:

has a subscription list verging on three hundred thousand subscribers—and all *paying* subscribers—for the paper is sent to no one who does not pay *in advance*, and it is stopped, with the exhaustion of pre-payment. The Editor boasts that he receives a peck [sic] full of letters every morning, containing the money for subscriptions; and his success, is the success of all kindred presses at the North. How is it with the Southern presses, faithful to the rights and institutions of the South? Take the CHARLESTON MERCURY, which, for thirty-five years, has been a prominent press in the South—what has been the fate of its Editors? The *first* ruined—

the *second* barely earned a narrow subsistence—the *third* injured, but sold out in time—the *fourth* died a ruined man. The *fifth* is our humble selves, of whom we will say nothing. What paper at the North has brought to the public understanding, more ability, eloquence or fidelity, than the CHARLESTON MERCURY (we speak not of ourselves)? . . . Yet how meagre has been the patronage conferred upon it, compared with its Northern contemporaries. How many tens of thousands of dollars due to it, have been lost, uncollectible and unpaid! How many tens of thousands of dollars are now due to it—and chiefly by the very men—the planters—the slaveholders of the South—whose property and institutions—whose liberties and lives, it has labored to protect![106]

By the time the war was over, so was the era of literary credit, and with it the world of sociability on which it was based and which it did so much to foster.

'THE NEW YORKER' AND THE RETURN
OF LITERARY CREDIT

Throughout this chapter, I have argued that newspaper and periodical purchase on credit were a product of a rural economic world whose debt ways were both predicated upon and at the same time reinforced a 'thick' form of trust. Over the course of the antebellum period, but especially following the technological and economic transformation of the paper making industry in the 1820s, the practice of extending literary credit was placed under increasing pressure, although the very communicative nature of the printed word operated as a counter-force, inasmuch as it conjured up an aura of connectedness and intimacy at odds with the untrusting nature of a pay-and-go economy. Through the 1830s and 1840s, I argue, first penny newspapers and then literary magazines began to experiment with forms of cash payment designed to obviate the need for credit; thus Horace Greeley's magazine, *The New Yorker*, began with a typical buy now and pay later form of subscription and by 1839 began to insist on payment in advance. By the 1850s, story papers such as *The Flag of Our Nation* and periodicals such as *Harper's New Monthly Magazine* (as well as Greeley's newer venture, *The New York Tribune*) were thriving on such schemes; and by the 1860s, pay-and-go purchases had become the norm. Such techniques, I argue, finally, had the consequence of disembedding the act of magazine and newspaper purchasing from the world of literary amity and intimacy.

Yet history is not always so simple as this linear narrative would imply, and as I suggested in my first chapter, economies do not only disembed; sometimes they reembed too. Just as Horace Greeley's *New Yorker* (and later *Tribune*) suggest the trajectory of disembedding, so a twenti-eth-century magazine, also, coincidentally, called *The New Yorker*, offers a striking counter-example. Founded in 1925 by Harold Ross, the maga-zine struck, almost from the first, what one critic has called a decidedly "antimodern" pose.[107] Hundreds of thousands of copies were given away free to servicemen and -women during the Second World War, because while the magazine was very much interested in profit, it kept its econom-ic and its cultural agendas separate. There was, likewise, a strict separa-tion of editorial and advertising operations at *The New Yorker*—indeed, they occupied separate floors of the same building and were discouraged from socializing. Writers were almost never offered contracts. They sim-ply wrote and, in time, were paid. Just as Herman Melville went deep in the hole to Harper and Brothers, so writers often found themselves in debt to the magazine. In a 1976 memo to staff, longtime editor William Shawn evoked language that recalled the thick trust of tradition, telling his employees to "believe one another, and . . . trust another, almost reck-lessly."[108] Not only did the magazine's writers trust the magazine, so did its readers, who evoked their connection in a language of familiarity that spoke more to the antebellum period than the American Century. Writ-ing to *The New Yorker* in 1956, Mary Stewart began: "Since we have been subscribing since 1926 or '27, I feel that I can address you as a close friend."[109] Indeed, so in key with antebellum rhythms did the magazine seem to be, that in 1985 it actually introduced a "bill me later" option for subscribers rather than requiring that they pay in advance.[110] In 2004, I subscribed to *The New Yorker* using the "bill me later" option, and, purely for research purposes, delayed my payment for approximately five weeks. On the sixth week, I received a dunning letter. In its entirety, it reads as follows:

Dear Leon Jackson:
   We understand how easy it is to overlook a small invoice.
   But the fact is, the above invoice remains unpaid. And although we know you intend to pay it, I'm sure you can understand that we can't keep sending you our magazine on faith.
   So please use the enclosed envelope to return this duplicate Invoice with your remittance. Do it today!
   That way, we can both be sure that The New Yorker will continue to illumi-nate your world each week.

Sincerely,
Peter Webb
Circulation Department

P.S. Already mailed in your payment? Sorry—our letters must have crossed in the mail. Just disregard this notice.[111]

This, surely, was a voice from the 1820s or 1830s that claimed me as its friend; that was willing to extend me at least a little literary credit "on faith"; that minimized my expense (a "little invoice") as opposed to its own; and that gave me the benefit of the doubt, although couching my own excuses in a rhetoric of veiled cajolery and passive aggression.[112] Under the circumstances, I chose not to find out whether *The New Yorker*'s collection policies were as forgiving as those of the antebellum period, and the check went into the mail the same day.

CHAPTER FIVE

Literary Competitions and the Culture of Emulation

On 15 December 1829, Edwin Forrest appeared before a packed house at New York's Park Theatre for the premiere of John Augustus Stone's new play, *Metamora; or, The Last of the Wampanoags*, a highly romanticized and bloodcurdling account of King Philip's War. Forrest was, by consensus, the most compelling and compellingly popular actor in America—handsome, muscular, and decidedly populist—and his role as the eponymous hero of Stone's drama had been widely anticipated in the local press, not least because the play had won first place in his much-touted competition for a tragedy, "of which the hero, or principal character, shall be an aboriginal of this country." The audience were not disappointed in their expectations, and during the performance Forrest received what one reporter called "the most unequivocal proofs of approbation" from the "delighted spectators."[1] Although set in the 1670s, *Metamora*'s concern with the fate of the nation's indigenous population was extraordinarily topical, since a week before the premiere, President Andrew Jackson had placed the removal of Georgia's Native Americans at the center of his first Address to Congress. Audiences, quite rightly, took the play to be a scarcely veiled commentary on the politics of Removal, and the protagonist's dying prediction that "the curse of Metamora stays with the white man!" thrilled and appalled them by turn.[2] Yet *Metamora* outlived its initial context, just as it outlasted its opening season, and for the next three decades it was Forrest's most popular and lucrative role, earning him lavish praise and a plentiful income.[3] As Forrest's competition winner, Stone received $500 and half a night's box office takings, but even this substantial sum was massively dwarfed by Forrest's profits. Twelve nights in St. Louis bought in $2,157, for example, while single evenings in Mobile and New York netted $656 and $828.50, respectively. Over the course of his approximately 200 performances as Metamora, Forrest must have earned over one hundred thousand dollars.[4]

Critics have come to pay attention to *Metamora* recently for its powerful engagement with the racial politics of antebellum America, just as they have come to dwell on Forrest for his highly publicized role in the cultural politics of the same era, yet no critic has examined, or even given more than passing mention to, the specific economic context that gave rise to the production of the play in the first place, namely, the literary competition.[5] Writing competitions were, in fact, integral to Forrest's cultural praxis in the 1820s and 1830s; over the course of his career he organized no less than nine of them, with prizes ranging from five hundred to one thousand dollars, and he read close to two hundred submissions in the process. In a very real sense, Forrest's competitions may be credited—or blamed—for the outpouring of nationalistic melodrama in the mid-nineteenth century, and, indeed, one antebellum critic, William Cox, made exactly this point. "It appears," he commented somewhat sourly, "that at any time authors can be forced into existence as easily as mushrooms; and it is really curious to observe, as soon as a five hundred dollar premium is offered, what a flood of inspiration deluges the whole land!"[6]

Yet interesting and controversial as Forrest's personal engagement with competitions is, the phenomenon of the literary competition is more interesting still, if only for its ubiquity, and for this Forrest can take little credit. Between the 1780s—a quarter century before Forrest's birth—and the 1850s, literary competitions flourished in America, dealing out tens of thousands of dollars to successful entrants, helping neophyte authors establish themselves, cementing the reputations of important writers, and creating a more or less permanent class of competition judges. Competitions were organized by institutions as diverse as magazines, newspapers, playhouses, publishing companies, churches, gift books, tract societies, and wealthy individuals (including not only Forrest but also P. T. Barnum), and they offered premiums for genres as different as poems, plays, prologues, essays, articles, analyses, disputations, dissertations, tracts, treatises, short stories, novels, and even conundrums. Some were utterly trifling affairs, such as (to pick an example at random) that run in 1826 by the *Rural Repository*—"a neat little paper, published in Hudson, in the octavo form"—offering a ten dollar prize for the "best original tale, or essay" of between two and four pages in length.[7] Yet not all competitions were obscure, as the attention given to Forrest's events makes clear, nor were the entrants. Susan Warner, Edgar Allan Poe, Nathaniel P. Willis, Henry Wadsworth Longfellow, Lydia Sigourney, Sarah Hale, William

Cullen Bryant, John Greenleaf Whittier, Sarah Helen Whitman, and Harriet Beecher Stowe were all competition winners. Champions of the concept included John Adams, James Madison, Benjamin Rush, and Benjamin Franklin. The appeal of competitions, in other words, was immense, and if we expand the frame of reference to include the literary competitions organized by schools, academies, and colleges in the early national and antebellum periods, then it would be fair to say that almost every American author with a diploma or degree participated in this economic and cultural mode of exchange to a greater or lesser degree. Nor, indeed, was the competitive impulse limited to literary productions alone. There were prize competitions organized to encourage animal breeding, agricultural innovation, scientific development, and domestic production. There were prize jellies and jams, prize fights, prize races, and prizes for binding books and setting type. Early national, and, especially, antebellum America were dominated by a culture of competitions; indeed, it would be fair to say that the organization and dissemination of prizes is the largest antebellum cultural and economic phenomenon about which we know almost nothing.[8]

What lay behind the immense vogue for literary—and other—competitions in antebellum America? Was it simply, as William Cox suggested, a form of authorial opportunism? a sublimated, or displaced, form of market behavior? It is tempting to read such mercenary motives back into these competitions, if for no other reason than that the language used seems, at first blush, to suggest as much. In announcing his first playwriting competition, for example, Forrest argued that the "dearth of writers" producing native drama seemed to be more a consequence of the "want of proper incentive, than of any deficiency of the requisite talents" in the literary field. The invocation of "proper incentive" here appears to refer to a monetary incentive, especially since Forrest went on to announce a premium of $500 for the best entry.

There was, in fact, more than a grain of truth to Cox's analysis, and as the decades passed, it became still more true. What makes the competitions so interesting, however, is not how like a market economy they seemed, but how much their original formulators tried to ensure both that they were and, at the same time, that they were not akin to market practices. Consider, first, the differences. In the early nineteenth century, literary competitions were—in prescriptive theory, at least—so far divorced from economic speculation that in 1826, the American Tract Society could advertise without any sense of irony a fifty dollar premium for the best essay received on the topic of the "*Ruinous Consequences of Gambling.*"[9] While entering a literary competition was, in some very literal sense, a gamble, that is, it was categorically not understood to be a gamble for money. There was no sense of irony, either, in the 1829 competition that offered a gold medal worth one hundred dollars, or a "piece of plate" of equivalent value, for the best essay on "the inadequacy of the wages given to poor females for their labour."[10] Prize money could be received for writing *about* wages, that is, but it was not, itself, meant to be a wage-like form of income. The money was meant, as it turns out, to serve as a goad, or spur, to compete, but it was not meant to be the reason *why* one competed. One competed simply because competitiveness was held to bring out the absolute best in individuals, in cultures, and in societies. It was *this* underlying conviction that spurred the explosion of competitions in the early national and antebellum eras.

Yet while this ideal was meant to be non-monetary, and divorced from the market, it was an idea that grew directly from world of money and markets in the first place. The idea of perfect and unfettered economic competition had been adumbrated, of course, by Adam Smith in the 1770s, and by a host of thinkers before him, but competition within the economic marketplace, no matter how pleasing in theory, was bedeviled by greed, avarice, and dishonesty in practice.[11] The appeal of literary competitions lay in the fact that they were artificially created spheres of conflict and competition that imitated the market both in philosophy and structure, but in which every element of the contest was engineered to avoid the calamities of capitalism. Using money that was not 'really' money; relying on judges who affected an 'invisible hand' of impersonality but who were carefully chosen; and offering anonymity that worked only in one direction, literary competitions mimicked the operations of the marketplace, yet sought to transcend its imperfections. Literary competitions thus stand apart from the other authorial economies studied in this book, because they not only disembedded earlier and more decisively than any other authorial mode, but because the very disembeddedness they revealed was deliberately engineered and highly valued.

In this chapter, I examine in some detail the ways in which promoters and champions of writing competitions sought to create perfect, and perfectly circumscribed, arenas of cultural and economic conflict and at the same time show how in reality every element of the literary competition came under sustained and repeated assault by those who wished either to vaunt one aspect of the phenomenon at the expense of another, or who sought to undermine the endeavor altogether. I begin my discussion with an analysis of emulation and approbation, the key concepts in the eighteenth-century lexicon of competitive motivations, and consider how a fascination with these ideas fuelled the move to organize literary competitions. The life and work of Charles Sprague, the Banker Poet, are examined as typical of the competition system at its best. I then consider the way in which the shift from using medals and trophies to awarding cash altered the range of meanings that could be ascribed to competition prizes by entrants. The competition schemes of Edwin Forrest and other dramatists of the 1830s and 1840s illustrate this tendency. I move on to examine Edgar Allan Poe's heretofore neglected experience with competitions, arguing that by the 1830s, the emulative ideal that had propelled the earliest public competitions was now being displaced by a new understanding of competitiveness that combined both elements of the ruthless market and the world of charity. The chapter ends with a consideration of the competitions organized by story newspapers of the 1840s, which saw the absorption of the traditional, restricted competition into the broader competitive marketplace. Ultimately, the attempt to create a realm of artificial competition was no match for the competitive force of the market itself, and winning competitions, which had been a token of cultural superiority, became a token of having 'sold out.'

THE CULTURE OF EMULATION

Let us start out by considering an imaginary competition of the early national period, one based on the ideas and ideals of the institution rather than the messy reality. A fine example can be found in the correspondence of former President John Adams and his friend, the noted physician, Benjamin Rush. In 1812 Rush sent Adams a copy of his most recent book, *Medical Inquiries and Observations upon the Diseases of the Mind*, a work so original that, he told Adams, he expected "no quarter from my learned brethren." "You apprehend 'Attacks,'" replied Adams, with a hint of relish;

I say, the more the better. I should like the sport so well that, if I could afford the expense, I would advertise a reward of a gold medal to the man of science who should write the best essay upon the question whether the writings of Dr. Franklin or Dr. Rush do the greatest honor to America or the greatest good to mankind. I have no doubt but such a point mooted would produce a salutary controversy. You would not have been so industrious nor so useful if you had not been persecuted. These afflictions are but for a moment, and they work out greater glory.[12]

Adams here provides fine and flattering description of an ideal-typical competition, but, more valuably still, in describing the paradox of the salutary controversy, the staged attack, the glorious affliction, he provides a key to understand the two concepts that lay behind all competitions of this era: emulation and approbation.

While emulation today means simply imitation, or perhaps respectful imitation, in the early national period it connoted a complex psychology of ambition that was more than imitative and quite often less than respectful. "Emulation," according to Adams himself, whose *Discourses on Davila* (1790–1791) was one of the more extended discussions of the subject, was "imitation and something more—a desire not only to equal or resemble, but to excel."[13] To strive to improve upon, or surpass, the achievements of others, then, was to *emulate* them, and the basic impulse to do so was referred to as the *spirit of emulation*. In other words, emulation was a form of intense competitiveness. It was a deep-seated impulse according to Adams; indeed, next "to self-preservation" it was "the great spring of human action" (360). Yet where self-preservation was clearly inner-directed, emulation was directed outward; it suggested not simply, nor even, the desire to do one's *own* best, but rather to surpass the best of another. Emulation was always transitive, and in this respect, it resembles closely Harold Bloom's concept of the anxiety of influence, according to which "there are *no* texts, but only relations between texts."[14]

Readily provoked, emulation typically begat further emulation; the knowledge that someone was trying to be better than one was inspired one to be better than *them*, thus creating a chain reaction of aspiration and counter-aspiration, achievement and counter-achievement. Emulation thus was held to engender great efforts. According to Adams, "the most heroic actions in war, the sublimest virtues in peace, and the most useful industry in agriculture, arts, manufactures, and commerce" were all a consequence of this proliferating emulative desire to surpass the achievements of others (324). And one saw evidence of this competitive striving everywhere, he claimed: not only between scientists and scholars like Franklin and Rush, but "between families and all the connections by consanguinity and affinity; between trades, faculties, and professions; between congregations, parishes, and churches; between schools, colleges, and universities; between districts, villages, cities, provinces, and nations" (347). In his imaginary competition, therefore, Adams's entrants would be moved by the spirit of emulation to write the "best essay" on the relative merits of Franklin and Rush, just as, Adams implied, Rush and Franklin had themselves emulated one another in seeking to be the best scientist.

Obscure as it seems today, it would be hard to overstate the ubiquity, authority, and influence of emulation as an explanatory concept and a moral imperative in the Western imagination. Apparent as early as the eighth century B.C., when it was discussed in Hesiod's *Works and Days*, emulation emerged as a formal rhetorical category by the mid-sixteenth century and was given a strong boost with the translation of Longinus's treatise on the sublime in the mid-seventeenth. It is evident in the rhetoricians of classical antiquity, in medieval schools, Renaissance courts, Jesuit seminaries, and the secular institutions of the Philosophes.[15]

Americans of the later eighteenth century, such as Adams, were especially predisposed to favor emulation. In the first place, its emphasis on "imitation and something more" helped them mediate between a late neoclassical reverence for the past and a newly emergent Romantic emphasis on originality. Second, and insofar as it balanced imitation and innovation in this way, it suited their newly postcolonial status by allowing them to retain the forms and trappings of English culture while seeking to go beyond them. As such, it enabled them to negotiate what one literary historian has called the "resistance-deference syndrome" that bedevils postcolonial societies. Third, and lastly, it balanced republican and liberal conceptions of the self, the former so dedicated to the subordination of the individual to traditional virtue and the latter to self-promoting activity.[16] Precarious a concept as it was, emulation allowed Americans to have their cake and eat it, and they placed a high explanatory premium upon it, as Adams's *Discourses on Davila* makes abundantly clear.

Yet powerful and primal as the spirit of emulation was, it was predicated, according to Adams, upon a still more primal urge: the urge for approbation. This was the "desire to be observed, considered, esteemed, praised, beloved, and admired" (311). All people wanted to be thought of as special in the eyes of others, Adams averred; indeed, the *"passion for distinction"* was "as real a want of nature as hunger" (311, 313). People strove to do their best, in others words, because being better than others assured them of approval; it fed their hunger for admiration. If this "ardent desire of the *congratulations* of others" (319) propelled emulation, then, conversely, it followed that in the absence of others to judge and approve, very little ever got done. Adams made this point in explicitly literary terms by asking "If *Crusoe*, on his island, had the library of *Alexandria*, and a certainty that he should never again see the face of man, would he ever open a volume?" "Perhaps he might," he answered grudgingly "but it is very probable he would read but little. A sense of duty; a love of truth; a desire to alleviate the anxieties of ignorance, may, no doubt, have an influence on some minds. But the universal object and idol of men of letters is *reputation*" (318). Competitiveness, then, was fuelled by approbativeness.

A pervasive but informal competitive culture predicated on emulation and approbation operated in eighteenth-century America, long before formal literary competitions were ever established, and it fuelled a variety of impromptu literary jousts and competitions. As David Shields has shown, for example, the dynamic interplay of approbation and emulation could generate forms of sociable pleasure through participation in literary games like Crambo. A pastime that can be traced back to at least the fourteenth century but that enjoyed an especial popularity in the seventeenth and eighteenth centuries, Crambo was played with three or more participants. In the most common version of the game, the first participant would compose a line a poetry and each person in turn was then required to compose two subsequent lines: one to complete the preceding couplet and another begin a new one. Those who failed to come up with a succeeding line, offered a poor line, or lost the thread of the narrative were excluded from the group until just two players squared off in a poetic duel.[17] In a very literal sense, Crambo was a pure manifestation of emulative psychology and aesthetics: Adams's "imitation and something more—a desire not only to equal or resemble, but to excel." The first participant in the game of Crambo offered a line of poetry which the second imitated (phonetically), in creating a couplet, but improved upon, or excelled (in terms of wit). His or her second line (the third in the game) threw down the gauntlet for the next player, challenging them in turn to not only resemble but surpass. The collaborative nature of the game introduced the interconnectedness and indebtedness of the participants as well as their agonistic relationship, so that in playing Crambo, the act of emulation was less a diachronic sparring with the past than a synchronic, indeed a face-to-face, contest in the present. As such, Crambo was a typically embedded and embedding form of authorial exchange, in which competition ensured a social bondedness even as it pitted players against one another.

Crambo was a popular pastime for members of New York's Sketch Club, a convivial group of artists, authors, and men of affairs who gathered fortnightly between 1829 and 1869. At one notable meeting, held in February 1830, poets William Cullen Bryant, John Inman, and Robert C. Sands squared off in a modified stanzaic Crambo duel on the subject of "the sublime," which was recorded by Inman, the Club Secretary. The poem ran to sixteen stanzas but the first four developed in this way:

> Sands
> Ye everlasting hills that tower sublime
> Grand as eternity and old as time
> The greatest object to be seen in nature—

Sec
Your glories in my soul are deeply graven
Since that blest day when first in old New Haven
I learned your qualities and nomenclature
Bryant
Ye piles of granite, basalt & grey wacke
That bear the umbrageous forests on your back
And carry clouds and tempests on your forehead.
Sands
Gypsum & slate, asbestos, pudding stone,
Whoever fall your flinty ribs upon
Are very likely to come off with soreheads[18]

For all the apparent frippery of the exchange, the competitive dynamics of this Crambo were actually quite complex. Sands, the instigator, began with a fairly conventional invocation to the sublime, only to see his attempted elevation undercut by Inman's absurd forced rhyme of nature and nomenclature; this was imitation, indeed, at least phonetically, and 'improvement' through ridicule: a move quite literally from the sublime to the ridiculous. Rather than rising (or perhaps sinking) to Inman's challenge, Bryant sought to outdo Sands's initial sublimity, a strategy he might well have felt compelled to adopt as the nation's sublime poet of record. In an extraordinary coup de grace, however, Sands got the better of both Bryant and Inman. His use of bathos proved him a better comic poet than Inman, and in using this comedy he was also able to sabotage Bryant's pretensions. Indeed, Sands's second stanza was powerfully emulative, for not only did it best Bryant phonetically with its ludicrous rhyme of soreheads for forehead, but in invoking the "flinty ribs" of the mountains, it also good-humoredly troped Bryant's best-known poem, "Thanatopsis" (1817) with its "hills / Rock-ribb'd, and ancient as the sun." Sands bested Bryant in the present, in other words, by twitting his earlier poetic achievement.[19] Sometimes the combination of synchronic and diachronic forms of emulation was more explicit still, as when Inman, Sands, and Bryant played a game of Crambo in which they competed with one another in producing a paraphrase of British poet James Thompson's *The Seasons* (1727). So pleased were they with "this tremendous effort of poetic talent," according to the Club minutes, that they decamped immediately to eat their "host's excellent oysters, & wine of the vintage of /97 with extraordinary zest." Such accounts and others underscore Shields's contention that Crambo was the signature game of the age of sociability: the friendly, acceptable face of emulation. Competitiveness here, was associated not with anonymity or hostility but with amity and personal interaction.[20]

A slightly less friendly but nonetheless related phenomenon took the form of the agonistic literary graffiti or Pasquinades that littered the walls of America's colleges in the eighteenth century. Robert Treat Paine, Jr. (whose father and namesake was a noted Crambo player himself) recalled that his introduction to competitive aesthetics began as a student in the 1790s when he saw "several abusive satirical verses" about himself written on the wall of a Harvard building. Although no poet, Paine, deeply immersed in Harvard's collegiate culture of honor, responded to these Pasquinades with vigor, and ever after described this as the spur that led him to authorship. Three years later, Paine entered (and won) his first formal competition. Bryant likewise cut his teeth in poetic jousts with his academy classmates, before moving on to Crambo and, eventually, formal competitions. Hostile though the writing of Pasquinades could be, it remained a socially embedding practice, although the relationships it created were asymmetrical and demeaning in nature.[21]

Even in the early national era, by which time *formal* competitions of the sort Bryant and Paine had entered were commonplace, an informal ethic of emulation persisted, informing individual literary efforts. Consider the example of James Fenimore Cooper. According to his daughter Susan, his first novel, *Precaution* (1820), was a product of emulative thinking, written in reaction to his disgust at the English novel he had been reading to his wife. He had thrown the book aside, she remembered, with the exclamation: "I can write you a better book than that, myself!" "Playfully challenged" by his wife to deliver on the claim, Cooper began to write a tale "in the style of the rejected volume." As he proceeded, he found himself "amused and interested" by the project, and was subsequently inspired to complete and publish it by the idea of "taking his friends by surprise in this way." The resulting text was a faux-English novel of manners and as such reflected perfectly the emulative model: the product of a challenge to best another in competition, it both imitated the "style of the rejected volume" yet sought to make it a "better book," and its completion was spurred by the anticipation of his wife and friends' approval. Yet here, again, emulation remained an embedded act, situated within the familial practice of domestic writing.[22]

Although one finds references to informal emulative games such as Crambo as late as the 1840s, the formal contests that followed differed in important ways.[23] What distinguishes Crambo, as well as the jousting of the Harvard students and the activities of authors like Cooper, from the literary competitions of the nineteenth century is the absence of formal organization, appointed judges, and specific prizes. Indeed, there were no prizes at all in Crambo but the prize of staying the course and eventually besting one's opponent. Then, too, and unlike more formal competitions, the participants also served as judges, thereby keeping the evaluative and aesthetic roles socially intermingled: Crambo was definitively embedded. Like the verbal jousting of the Harvard students, games of Crambo were a product of what Shaftsbury called the 'Sensus Communis': something shared but interiorized and intangible.[24]

Yet emulation and tangibility were woven ever more tightly over the course of the eighteenth century. Although the desire for approbation was as diffuse as it was ubiquitous, John Adams argued that individuals found a ready focus for their needs in visible, and especially material, tokens of esteem. Ribbons, rings, scepters, trophies, and titles were all sought with avidity as indicators of superiority over others and prized for the respect they engendered. Why else, Adams asked, were people obsessed by "marks and signs? A ribbon? a garter? a star? a golden key? a marshal's staff? or a white hickory stick?" Such things were signs of distinction and hence almost instinctively coveted (319). While observations such as these eventually earned Adams the reputation of a closet monarchist with a penchant for the trappings of Old World ornamentalism, his interest in the accoutrements of distinction was fuelled less by a specific anglophilia, I would argue, than by a more general conviction that emulation and approbation were powerful, even dangerous, forces that functioned best when controlled with tangible, graduated rewards.

Indeed, eighteenth-century thinkers in general feared the spirit of emulation and the desire for approbation just as much as they admired them. Bernard Bailyn's now classic definition of the eighteenth-century view of power, with its "endlessly propulsive tendency to expand itself beyond legitimate boundaries" captures perfectly the anxieties eighteenth-century thinkers also held concerning the push of emulation and the pull of approbation. While each inspired great effort, they also encouraged ruthlessness, hostility, envy, and, in those who did not succeed, a hopeless loss of motivation. Emulation, indeed, has been well described as a "slippery virtue that always hovered on the brink of a vice."[25] This was certainly Adams's opinion. Yet pundits of this period did not back away from such passions; rather, and as Albert O. Hirschman has brilliantly illustrated, they sought to harness them and play off one against the other. The earliest arguments in favor of capitalist market relations, for example, were based on the idea that the lust for personal wealth served to counteract the lust for personal power. The overwhelming dilemma of how to cope with the dynamism of the lust for political power, likewise, was solved— at least theoretically—by the notion of institutional checks and balances, a phrase in fact coined by Adams, outlined in *The Federalist*, and enshrined in the Constitution.[26] Adams believed that similar solutions could be applied to other arenas, including the realm of cultural achievement, and again using the language of constitutionalism, he proposed the establishment of a comparable system based on "the checks of emulation and the balances of rivalry" (356). That system was the formal competition.

A literary competition, in other words, was nothing more nor less than an exercise in social engineering comparable to that of the Constitution or the Smithian, capitalist market: an exercise in which one passion—here the urge for approbation—was used to propel and counteract another—here the urge to excel—the whole process catalyzed by the use of an award or premium and restrained by the institutional trappings of rules, judges, and competitive decorum. In a very real sense, then, there was a utopian dimension to the idea of literary contests, based upon the idea that a well organized event would create a space for perfect competition and, consequently, for intellectual perfection. Fuelled by the Enlightenment's faith in progressive improvement, the ideologues and organizers of competitive events believed that they were a crucial but unstable engine for social melioration. The intense strain such a system was seen to hold in check was manifest in Adams's somewhat oxymoronic language, with its references to "salutary controversy" and its coupling of "affliction" with "glory."

Viewed in such terms, it becomes easier to see why Adams believed that attacks on his friend Rush's book would be a good, and not a bad, thing. Controversy was "salutary" to the extent that it inspired one to do better and to be better. One strove to do the "greatest good" in pursuit of the "greatest honor." Franklin and Rush—the subjects of Adams's imaginary essay contest—agreed. In his educational writings, for example, Rush commented positively on "that spirit of competition which is so common among young people," and which he believed could be harnessed for the benefit of all, while Franklin proposed that "Emulation be excited among . . . Boys by giving, Weekly, little Prizes, and other small Encouragements" for the best school work.[27] While it is true that Adams, Rush, and Franklin all complained at times about the negative press they received, they all also understood the centrality of the fame they courted and the primacy of the emotions that drove it.[28]

Indeed, Adams was so convinced of the importance of routinely inspired and well-regulated emulation that he passed a resolution at the Continental Congress to encourage each colony to establish premium societies, while James Madison even proposed—albeit unsuccessfully—

that the Constitution include provisions for a variety of federally fund-
ed competitions to encourage emulation in the fields of agricultural and
technological innovation.[29] By the 1780s, it would be safe to say, competitions—or at least the idea of them—were a fixed part of the economic
and cultural scene, and they quickly became a key feature of the literary
world as well.

In fact, literary competitions in America from the 1780s on describe a
fairly clear trajectory. Through the first two decades of the early national
period, competitions were sporadic affairs, the province of the rare in-
novative theater manager or magazine editor and the occasional college;
the prizes were typically non-monetary, and, while sometimes expensive,
of strictly symbolic value. Emulation was almost always mentioned as
the motivating spirit of such events. In an important sense, competitions
of this kind persisted throughout the antebellum period. They were encouraged in the 1820s by the rising tide of literary nationalism and in the
1830s by reform organizations whose reliance on moral suasion led them
to embrace emulation. Yet while this sort of competition never really
went away, it did go out of fashion. By the 1830s, the competition world
was dominated by prize plays, rather than poems, prose, prologues, or
tracts. Introduced by Edwin Forrest (of *Metamora* fame), the prize drama took on a life of its own; within months, other playwrights and theater managers organized copycat competitions. Between 1828 and 1852,
there were no less than twenty playwriting contests organized in the city
of New York alone. By the late 1840s, the focus of the competition world
had shifted again, this time from playhouses to story papers: large sheets,
the size of newspapers, but filled with racy, serialized novellas and packed
full of feisty chest-thumping nationalism. The prizes offered by the papers were sometimes immense, always cash, frequently advertised, and
almost always the subject of (sometimes justified) rumors of corruption
and deceit. Although many of the external trappings and some of the
rhetoric remained the same over the course of this fifty- or sixty-year period, the tone and tendency of the competitions themselves changed almost beyond recognition. Completely gone, for example, was either the
rhetoric or the reality of sociability or embedding; competitions in this
sense differed from Crambo games in being utterly impersonal. Between
the games played by Robert Treat Paine, Jr. and the competitions he entered subsequently was an immense social and conceptual gulf. All that
remained constant was a belief—at least on paper—in the salutary, perhaps even the salvific, power of competition itself.

THE PARK STREET COMPETITION

I have explained the ideas behind the ideal of competition at great length, both because the ideas themselves are both important and complex, and, equally, because the actual competitions that claimed to draw on them were more complicated still. Many questions at this juncture require attention: How did an *actual* literary competition work? What were the mechanics of its operation? Its characteristic traits? Its cast of characters? What kind of trajectory did a competition follow? What principles were articulated and debated? And what interpretive methodologies best unlock such events? While every competition was unique unto itself, seven elements could be said to constitute any given event: the context, the call, the prize, the judges, the entrants, the judging, and the follow-up. In this section, I offer both a documentary account of an 1821 competition in which these elements came together and also a somewhat 'thicker' description of each. Such an analysis will put us in a better position to see how each functioned as a distinct variable, looming larger in some competitions, while receding to the background in others.

The Context. The immediate context of our competition was the 1821 reopening of the Park Theatre in New York. The Park, for some years New York's only theatrical establishment—and a decade later the scene of Edwin Forrest's triumphant premiere as Metamora—had been consumed by fire in May 1820 along with "almost everything it contained." Eventually, it was decided to rebuild, on an opulent plan.[30] Theaters seemed to burn down with depressing regularity in nineteenth-century America, a consequence of the flammable materials used in set design, together with the extensive use of candles, and those who had witnessed the Park conflagration might well have been reminded of the disastrous burning of Virginia's Richmond Theater on Christmas Eve, 1811, at which approximately seventy-one people died.[31] It is far more likely, however, that they came to identify the burning of the Park with an earlier and more remote event: the burning of the Drury Lane Theatre in London in 1808. This distant event was significant, because the Park Theatre modeled itself quite explicitly on Drury Lane; many of the actors at the Park had worked at Drury Lane before being drawn to America by manager Stephen Price, and, indeed, the Park was sometimes known as Old Drury. The burning of Drury Lane had been widely reported, and to celebrate its reopening in 1812, the managers decided to organize a competition, with a prize of 20 guineas offered for the best prologue.[32] These events were all widely reported in American magazines, and in June 1821, as the new Park Theatre was close to being completed, the proprietors announced that they, too, would run a competition for a prize prologue to be delivered at the reopening.[33] In an important sense, the organizers of the Park Theatre event sought not only to promote emulation *through* a competition but also to promote emulation *between* competitions, indeed between theaters; the participants, that is, would compete against one another but would also, collectively, seek to supersede the Drury Lane event and the theater itself. Later on, the echoes of Drury Lane would become quite explicit, but it is clear that the organizers and participants had this circumatlantic frame of reference in mind from the very outset, and it raised the stakes considerably higher than a superficial reading of the event would suggest.

The Call and The Prize. An advertisement placed in the *National Advocate* predictably justified the competition as a means of "exciting the attention and emulation of men of talents and genius." The poems, it said, were to be submitted to the scrutiny of a "committee of literary gentlemen" who would judge which was best, and the author of this address would win "if a resident of this city . . . the *freedom of the Theatre*; if a resident of any other part of the state or Union . . . a *Gold Medal* of the value of fifty dollars." Elaborate requirements were outlined: a poem of no less than fifty and no more than sixty lines; the author's name in a separate sealed envelope with a unique mark that corresponded to one on the poem; the requirement that the authors pay for the postage on their submissions; and the sincere promise that only the envelope of the winning entrant would be opened. (Unlike the other economies considered in *The Business of Letters*, the rules governing conduct in the competitive economy were explicit, even overstated.) A little less than three months was allowed, and the committee would meet to make their deliberations on 20 August.[34]

The Judges. So who were the committee? The panel of eleven judges (a large number for a competition) were described as "literary gentlemen." Among their number were six lawyers, two editors (one of whom served also as a sheriff), one physician, one state assemblyman, and one merchant who had previously served as a state assemblyman. Only one judge cannot be identified.[35] The preponderance of lawyers and legislators on this literary committee was, in fact, singularly appropriate, not only because—as Robert Ferguson has reminded us—the legal world was attractive to those with literary inclinations, but also inasmuch as literary criticism itself in the early republic evinced, in William Charvat's phrase, a strongly "judicial" tendency.[36] These representatives of the bench and bar were to judge poems in much the same way that in the course of their careers they judged defendants or mooted points of Constitutional ambiguity: fairly, freely, and impartially. Indeed, in discussing the work of the committee, one member said he believed their work of deliberation to be "as sacred as our Congress, or . . . our Legislature."[37] The image of elected, representative office conjured up by this description suggests that the axiology of the judges was strongly neoclassical. According to the tenets of neoclassical axiology (or philosophy of judgment), standards of literary excellence, like those of the law, were held to be objective and, indeed, rationally self-evident, but their self-evidence was apparent only to those who had sufficient taste, or, in legal terms, prudence. The neoclassical critic, as one scholar explains, could "formulate certain norms" in the act of judgment, but in so doing he was "merely citing standards that were already independently established as valid." The judges reflected an elitism defended in the name of universalism, or, to recall words of a seventeenth-century minister Samuel Stone, they were "a speaking *Aristocracy* in the face of a silent *Democracy*."[38] The universality of the judges' critical dicta was meant to assure the public of their capacity for fairness and objectivity.

The Entrants. As it turns out, the judges had more than adequate materials on which to exercise their objectivity. Around sixty poems were submitted for consideration, and because they were all subsequently printed, it is possible to offer at least an informal demographic analysis of the entrants. After discounting a handful of duplicate submissions, we find entrants from New York, New Jersey, Massachusetts, Illinois, Missouri, South Carolina, North Carolina, Virginia, Pennsylvania, Maine, Rhode Island, and "The Wilds of the West." In other words, competitions had broad national appeal, and while not all of them were as well advertised as this one was, it seems safe to assume that they drew significant attention. Gender is harder to determine, since most of the submissions remained anonymous, but in addition to several readily identifiable men, two entrants identified themselves as ladies, and one poem was "supposed to have been written by a lady." It was also conjectured, based on the handwriting of some of the poems, that several of the contenders were "little masters and misses."[39] That we know as much as we do of the identity of the entrants is largely a result of indiscretion since, according to the axiological ideals on which literary competitions were predicated, *who* one was was far less important than *what* one said. At least one white theatrical competition—and they were all *implicitly* white—was advertised in the pages of the African-American owned and operated *Freedom's Journal*, and at least one prize winner in another competition (apparently) was Native American. In theory, at least, literary competitions offered a completely level playing field.[40]

The Judging. The judges met on 22 August 1821 at the New York Historical Society to evaluate the submissions and, eventually, settled on an address written by Charles Sprague, a bank clerk from Boston. In selecting a winner, the judges provide an excellent example of what Bourdieu has called a 'ritual of consecration': a mystifying act of social alchemy, in which performance is magically turned into prestige in such a way as to render it completely inexplicable yet utterly credible.[41] Certainly, some alchemy was going on, for the judging of a literary competition was an elaborate act of capital conversion. The author presented a poem (cultural capital) and in winning, received a prize (economic capital) that actually, or also, served as a token of prestige (symbolic capital). This prestige, in turn, could be leveraged in order to obtain connections (social capital) that, in turn, translated into further success (in the form of yet more symbolic and economic capital). The cyclical nature of the consecration process is revealed in the fact that many competition winners—including Charles Sprague—ended up becoming competition judges themselves. It also suggests, however, that in the final instance the competitions were somewhat less than fair, inasmuch as the winners tended to be those who had been endowed with sufficient social and economic capital in their youth to have access to the sort of cultural capital that enabled one to win competitions in the first place. The act of consecration helped naturalize this socially marked form of expertise and turn it into something anyone *could* possess but that, in reality, only a few did.

The Follow-Up. Precisely because the rewards of consecration were so substantial over the long haul, the question of who won, and why, frequently became an issue of contention in the aftermath of a competition. After the Park Theatre event, for example, it soon became apparent that one of the judges—Mordecai M. Noah—had been unhappy with the decision to award the prize to Sprague. Noah subsequently damned Sprague with some extremely faint praise in the pages of his newspaper, for which he in turn was quite roundly criticized.[42] The sniping between editors in Boston (Sprague's hometown) and Noah in New York, with their mutual incriminations and charges of dishonesty, corruption, and bad faith, would appear to indicate a breakdown in the mechanics of the competition model, but as James English has astutely noted, post-competition scandals are almost de rigueur and serve an important role in suggesting that a wholly fair competition is hypothetically feasible. It was a debatable, and at least a debated, assumption, even in the nineteenth century.[43]

In debating the fairness of the Park Theatre competition, pundits again conjured up—and then quite explicitly invoked—memories of Drury Lane and especially of the scandal that had surrounded its competition of 1812. In that event, the judges had received more than one hundred submissions, and after some wrangling decided that *none* of them were good enough to receive the prize. Rather than make an award to the least bad poet, the committee instead commissioned Lord Byron to compose a prologue for the opening night, which, after some vacillation, he did. The competition entrants were absolutely outraged. One indignant young man forced his way onto the stage to try and read his father's effort before being hauled away by the police, and when his father read the prologue some nights later, a riot was only scarcely averted. In the wake of the affair, two local wits, Horace and James Smith, published a spoof volume, entitled *Rejected Addresses*, which featured fake submissions for the Drury Lane contest, written in the style of various famous poets (including Byron). Less than a month after that, an enterprising publisher named Buchanan McMillan issued a volume entitled *Genuine Rejected Addresses*, which printed all the poems that in reality had been entered in the contest, together with Byron's commissioned piece. While the Smith brothers were entirely in jest, however, McMillan was quite serious, and in his preface he lambasted Byron and the aristocratic competition judges for the disdain with which they treated the "plebian swarm of Candidates."[44] For McMillan, the outcome of the Drury Lane event raised important questions about not just this competition in particular but about competitions more generally, and especially about the nature and location of axiological authority. *Was* a cabal of gentlemen the most reliable and trustworthy medium through which to judge the excellence of a poem, or were the people at large a more authoritative voice? Perhaps public opinion was the soundest judge? McMillan believed so.

Given the shadowy presence of the Drury Lane competition haunting the Park Theatre events, it was perhaps inevitable that New York publisher Nathaniel Smith, with Drury Lane clearly in mind, would also publish a volume entitled *Rejected Addresses*. Indeed, for those who preferred their poetry explicitly circumatlantic, he even advertised a few copies of his text and the London *Rejected Addresses* "bound neatly in one volume." Like McMillan's English volume, Nathaniel Smith's included all the losing submissions from the Park Theatre event, together with Sprague's winning entry. And although Smith (unlike McMillan) clearly sided with the judges and believed that Sprague's poem was the best, he sided with McMillan in believing that members of the reading public should be given a chance to decide for themselves; his assumption, of course, was that the public would concur with the judges.[45] Inadvertently, though, his publication raised a crucial question, which was where, precisely, was one to locate the wellspring of axiological authority: with a select group of literary gentlemen who were 'disinterested' enough to judge fairly, or in the court of public opinion? And if they disagreed, then whose judgment was to be trusted?

In their own ways, McMillan and Smith both appealed to what social theorist Jürgen Habermas has called the public sphere: an ideal realm of judgment less official than any state institution but more representative of the common interest than any individual or family. The public sphere was understood as a conceptual space in which private individuals could come together in a public capacity and from which they were able to exercise their judgment on matters of collective interest. Predicated on an Enlightenment notion of rationality and a republican appreciation for civic duty, the integrity of the public sphere—or, if you like, public opinion—was a powerful ideal in the nineteenth century. It was also the very epitome of an impersonal and socially disembedded form of adjudication.[46] Several subsequent competitions would conclude in the publication of 'rejected address' volumes, and individual authors stung by the experience of rejection would also appeal from time to time to the judgment of the public. In a more general sense, every literary competition implicitly pit the authority of the public sphere against the authority of a group of judges, each side taking agreement as a sign of the reliability of taste and disagreement as an aberrant deficiency in the other.[47]

Of course, not everyone was happy with this appeal to the public. One anonymous entrant in the Park Theatre contest resented Nathaniel Smith's publication of the rejected addresses, asking "by what authority, and under whose direction" the publication was to appear. The volume, to this entrant, seemed nothing more than "the speculation of a bookseller." Certainly, Smith's publication seemed somewhat less disinterested than its prefatory rhetoric might suggest. In his initial advertisement for the volume, he reprinted in its entirety the copyright he had taken out on the text, indicating the somewhat unseemly intrusion of a proprietary mentality into the competition, as if the submitted poems were his to own and sell, and, several weeks later, when he had ceased to advertise the volume for sale, he continued to reprint the copyright notice.[48] Then, too, Smith sought to maximize profits by selling the volume in a variety of formats, ranging from a simple volume in boards for seventy-five cents, through "full bound" for a dollar, and "calf extra gilt" at a dollar and fifty cents, up to the opulent "morocco, calf and Russia, super extra rich" version for two dollars and fifty cents.[49] Smith's strategy was not wholly inconsistent with the goals of literary competitions, however, for as scholars have pointed out, the public sphere not only offered a model of impersonal competition between ideas, but also "served as a synecdoche for nascent theories of a rational, self-regulating economy." It was a short step, in other words, from the competition organizers' marketplace of ideas to the economic marketplace, plain and simple.[50]

The trends implicit in these advertisements were as troubling as they were clear: while pundits debated ineffectually as to whether authority emerged from a panel of judges or from the public sphere, the actions of Smith meant that unless care was exercised, authority ultimately come to rest in the marketplace; purchasers would exercise their pocketbooks rather than their critical judgment, and the best poet would be the one whose works sold the most. It was a concern that would not go away; indeed, the question of the relationship of money and markets to the world of competitions became one of the institution's fault lines, and in due time it would send tremors through the literary world. No one understood this better than Charles Sprague, to whom we now turn.

THE EXAMPLE OF CHARLES SPRAGUE

For Charles Sprague, the winner of the Park Theatre competition, the receipt of first prize was not the end of his literary adventure, but in fact just the beginning. Over the course of the next nine years, he would go on to win an unprecedented six literary competitions, all of them for theatrical prologues, three of them in a dizzying three-year period. Awards offered by the Park Theatre (1821); the New Philadelphia Theatre (1822); the Tremont Theatre (1824); the Salem Theatre (1828); the Arch Street Theatre (1828); and the Portsmouth Theatre (1830) all fell to Sprague's polished pen. Indeed, it was said that Sprague never entered a competition that he did not win. In the 1820s, when one thought of literary competitions, one inevitably thought of Sprague, and when one thought of Sprague, one inevitably thought of competitions. By 1829, when he was awarded an honorary degree from Harvard, Sprague was considered by many to be the best poet in America, and his poems had been reprinted from Canada to Calcutta. The controversy surrounding his first prize notwithstanding, his meteoric rise to fame exemplified everything that pundits found admirable about the literary competitions of the early national period.[51]

Of course, a great deal of what made Sprague so appealing, quite apart from the competitive context of his writing, was that he offered something for everyone. Bostonians looked upon him as a source of local pride; nationalists championed him as the Great American Poet; classicists enjoyed the purity of his diction, satirists his wit, and romantics his delicate sensibility; teachers pointed proudly to the fact that he had received only a common school education; and everyone admired what one editor called "the modesty with which he wears these repeated and well-deserved honours." But what was most striking in Sprague, however, was not his avocation but rather his vocation, for Sprague was not a lawyer, doctor, editor, or minister, like the "literary gentlemen" who so often judged his works. Sprague, rather, was a banker. He was, in other words, a member of an occupation considered the least poetic in the nation.[52]

When pundits commented on Sprague's profession—which they did often—they made allusion to two distinct concerns that might be entertained of a banker-poet, and especially a banker-poet who routinely entered literary competitions. The first was that, as a true poet, he would be too otherworldly to conduct his day job responsibly. As one critic wittily recalled: "Every man who owned a dollar in the bank in which he was employed, must have been in a cold sweat at the thought of the risk he had run in suffering any of his property to pass through the hands of a man of genius." ("Man of genius" here served, of course, as cultural shorthand for hopeless dreamer, impractical visionary.) The second concern was the exact opposite of the first: that as a true man of business, Sprague might be too materialistic, too ruthless even, to either write good poetry or be trusted in entering high-stakes competitions. Inasmuch as literary competitions sought to replicate the competitive structure of the capitalist marketplace without introducing the moral taint of capitalism itself, in other words, the questions was whether it was possible for a banker-poet to keep the two worlds separate. William Leggett, for example, who had himself won a competition, wondered whether Sprague might not be "emulous . . . of a business, rather than of a poetic reputation," while satirist William Joseph Snelling came out and said plainly what others merely insinuated when he wrote:

> My heart sweats blood, that he, so prized by all,
> Should only string his harp at Mammon's call.
> 'T is clear his bank accounts and studies clash:
> He counts his numbers as he counts his cash.[53]

He need hardly have worried. Sprague was noted, famous even, for his unflinching sense of probity as both a banker and a poet. While Sprague's ledgers contained whimsical drawings and geometrical doodles, the accounts themselves were impeccably kept. Indeed, he came for many people to represent the ideal union of business and letters, competition and contemplation, accumulation and imagination, and he was celebrated in prose and verse as the exemplary man of business as man of letters. Favorable comparisons with Samuel Rogers (1763–1855), the Banker Poet of England, were made; strangers wrote him poems on the back of his bank's notes, praising his dual occupations; he served, himself, as a judge in several competitions; and visitors sometimes made financial transactions at the Globe Bank simply in hopes of seeing the famous poet who "dares to acknowledge his homage to the Nine, in the very temple of the money changers."[54] An undated poem by F.J.H. published in the *New York Commercial Advertiser* seemed in particular to be a direct rebuttal of Snelling's insinuation that Sprague's "harp" was played only at the bidding of "Mammon":

> Thou makest thy harp, O Sprague, a holy thing!
> And from its strings thy visions genius let
> Go forth and make us prize what thou hast writ,
> And wish that thou wouldst oft thus nobly sing!
>
> Unbought, unsought for praise is given to thee,
> As men, will praise the beauty of a star,
> And joy within themselves that such things are,
> To charm with unobtrusive brilliancy![55]

Where Snelling accused Sprague, in essence, of being mercenary in his motivations, F.J.H. here argued the opposite: that Sprague sought neither praise nor prize, but was given these things effortlessly, naturally, inevitably. His or her invocation of the star analogy was wholly appropriate too, since by the 1820s the older resonances of the star as symbol of the divine will were fusing with newer theatrical connotations of star players and star-struck audiences to whom Sprague's prologues were addressed. Sprague's fame was as inevitable, F.J.H. implied, as it was beautiful and divine.[56] A still more effusive hymn to Sprague's capacity for balancing letters and business is found in R. C. Waterston's 1845 poem, in which he asked: "May not our land be termed enchanted ground, / Where, on Bank-bills, a Poet's name is found? / Where Poet's notes may pass for notes of hand, / And valued good long as the Globe shall stand?"[57] And Sprague, too, enjoyed the occasional playful comment on the intersections of business and letters, as when he wrote on the back of what we would now call a bounced check from fellow poet (and sometime competition judge) John Pierpont: "Behold a wonder seldom seen by men, / Lines *of no value*, from JOHN PIERPONT's pen."[58] Sprague, it was suggested, and as these lines themselves suggest, had a flair for financial responsibility as impressive as his flair for verse.

This was precisely F.J.H.'s point. When he conjured up the line "Unbought, unsought for praise is given to thee," the word "unbought" served double duty, suggesting both Sprague's integrity (he could not be bought) and the essentially symbolic nature of the prizes he received (which could not, themselves, be bought, sold, or used as currency). In order to appreciate the full significance of these lines, however, and to see why, precisely, Sprague's engagements with the world of competitions were so highly praised, we need to examine more closely the pivotal role of prizes in the economy of competitions, for—as we shall see—it was in the perfect balancing of prize, praise, and prose (or in this case poetry), as much as in what he actually wrote, that Sprague's achievement lay. Handling prizes was rarely easy, especially by 1830, when Sprague received his final award.

By 1830, in fact, when literary competitions in America had begun to reach their peak, George Pope Morris of the *New-York Mirror* claimed that his newspaper had "originated" the "system of offering premiums for well written literary essays in prose and poetry." We have already seen that there were earlier competitions; indeed, formally organized literary competitions in America can be traced back at least forty years to those arranged by Mathew Carey, the editor of the *American Museum*. The contrasts, as well as the continuities, between Carey's competitions and those of Morris are instructive, however, especially in the realm of prizes. In common with all competition organizers, Carey (writing in 1789) believed that offering premiums would encourage emulation and could "hardly fail to produce salutary effects." For the best essay "on the liberty of the press," therefore, Carey offered a gold medal; for the best essay on domestic manufacturing policy, a "complete set of the American Museum, neatly bound"; and for the best essay on "the influence of luxury upon morals," a copy of "Paley's moral philosophy—and Locke's essay on the human understanding." The many competitions organized by the *New-York Mirror* in the 1820s sounded the same note as Carey's, in seeking to "encourage laudable emulation among native writers by offering *prizes* to the successful competitors in different branches of composition," but the prizes offered by the *Mirror* to inspire emulation were strikingly different.[59] Where the *American Museum* in 1789 had offered a gold medal, periodicals, and books, the *New-York Mirror* offered cash: thirty dollars for the best short story and the best poem, and twenty dollars for the second best in each category.[60] The introduction of cash into the economy of competitions significantly complicated the model of emulation outlined by Adams and practiced by Carey in the 1790s and marked a break with tradition. Since the era of classical antiquity, prizes had remained free of the taint of money. The prizes awarded in the great competitions of ancient Greece and Rome, for example, had included palms, laurels, and ivy, and their conventionality had insinuated itself into the language in such phrases as "to bear the palm," or to be appointed "laureate."[61] Prizes offered by scientific and agricultural societies in the eighteenth century were likewise non-monetary in nature: medals, cups, trophies, silverware, ribbons, and certificates. It was in this tradition that a competition organizer like Carey positioned himself, as did the managers of the Park Theatre in their 1821 competition, when they offered free theater admission to the winner for life, or (for an out-of-towner) a gold medal worth fifty dollars.

That such prizes as the gold medal, the theater admission, and the volume of Locke had value is beyond question—indeed, as Johan Huizinga has pointed out, the root of the word prize is *pretium*, meaning price—but the value (the price) attached to prizes was meant to be strictly symbolic and non-fungible, even when a specifically monetary value could be attached to them (as in the Park Theatre medal) or when it was readily obvious.[62] Indeed, in Bourdieu's terms as we have seen, prizes functioned as symbolic capital or tokens of prestige, and particularly the type of prestige that accrued from the successful use of other forms of capital (here cultural). The differing forms of capital involved in a prize were neatly dissected by Laura Lyman, who won a set of expensive silverware in an 1860 agricultural fair competition. "They shine on the table as I write," she confided to her diary, "and much as I prize them for their intrinsic value, the honor of which they are a pledge, I rate of far more worth."[63] Although Lyman recognized that her silverware had a monetary value in the form of economic capital and even considered it "intrinsic," it was as a token of symbolic capital ("honor") that she valued it. She understood, that is, that honor did not inhere in the silverware, but that the silverware was an effective "pledge" for it. The economic value was almost beside the point, and for some competition organizers, in fact, it was wholly beside the point. Indeed, in competitions organized by cash-strapped schools, teachers started to offer cheap printed tickets in lieu of more substantial rewards such as medals and silverware. A small 'reward of merit,' in the form of a printed sheet of paper dated 1832 carried the following remarkable example of capital conversion: "This is considered equal to the Gold Medal, to obtain which requires excellence during four weeks." The prize was still a tangible object—albeit quite literally paper thin—but one that signified the intangible prestige that had been bestowed on its recipient. [64]

The same is true of the medal won by Charles Sprague in the 1821 contest organized by the Park Theatre in New York. Although the medal was advertised as being of fifty dollars' value, the money in itself was trifling and, more to the point, irrelevant. After all, the managers of the Park also offered fifty dollars to anyone who was able to provide information leading to the prosecution of audience members who threw food from the tiers down on the actors, but *that* fifty dollars was hardly redolent of emulative honor; if anything, it was 'dirty' money, gained through snitching.[65] The two sums of fifty dollars—identical in purely quantitative terms—were utterly different qualitatively, both in the economies through which they circulated and the meanings each suggested. The fifty dollars of cash offered to theater informants circulated within an 'intelligence economy,' while the fifty dollars spent on Sprague's medal, and, still more, the medal itself, were part of an economy of prestige. And again, the fifty dollars given to theater snitches was fungible and its uses unrestricted; it was, theoretically, exchangeable wherever legal tender was accepted. The medal of fifty dollars value, by contrast, was non-fungible and could not really be used or spent in the same way as fifty dollars cash, although it carried a freight of prestige that fifty dollars in coins or notes did not. In order to make this distinction clear (in order, in other words, to earmark the prize) the proprietors of the Park had Sprague's medal engraved: one side gave his name, the other bore the legend: "Palman Qui Meruit Ferat" ("Who takes the palm deserves the palm"). The invocation of the traditional award of a palm leaf makes clear here that the fifty dollars' value was merely symbolic. Moreover, the engraving of the name, to borrow a term from legal scholar Lee Anne Fennell, rendered the medal 'illiquid': it essentially took it out of the realm of fungible objects and into a private, even static, economy of prestige. It would not have been impossible for Sprague to sell his medal, that is, but to have done so would have been deeply socially inappropriate, both for Sprague and for his purchaser.[66]

A medal "worked" as an award, because it was traditionally and conventionally accepted as a token of esteem. Although an arbitrary signifier, consensus suggested that it had value in the economy of symbolic capital. The same was true, to a greater or lesser degree, of ribbons, diplomas, staffs of office, presentation books, and book plates. In 1824, award-winning poet Ann-Maria Wells received as first prize in a theatrical prologue competition "a *Grecian Cross*, composed of triple rows of pearls, set in pure gold, with a large diamond in the centre": a prize so utterly laden with gems and symbols as to be simultaneously priceless and worthless.[67]

Yet as even John Adams conceded, albeit grudgingly, in *Discourses on Davila*, money, too, could invoke prestige. "Riches," he explained, "attract the attention, consideration, and congratulations of mankind."[68] Over the course of the early nineteenth century, as traditional forms of prestige and personally embodied forms of authority began to erode, competition organizers increasingly found themselves introducing money into their practices as a new token of prestige. In the first instance, money appeared only virtually and only as a source of capital conversion, as when, for example, the Park Theatre explained that the gold medal was 'of fifty dollars' value.' The amount of money the medal cost was not meant to reflect directly on the recipient, but rather on the organizer, as if to suggest how much he or she was willing to spend or give away to encourage emulation and promote excellence. By the 1820s, competition organizers routinely listed the cumulative cost of the prizes to be won, as when the organizers of the Maryland Cattle Show announced in 1824 that there would be "premiums distributed consisting of various pieces of Silver Plate amounting to $1040."[69] It was a short step, however, from offering an equation of money to prestige, to offering money *as* a form of prestige.

It is hard to say exactly when money was first introduced as a form of prize for competitions, or why. The earliest American example of which I am aware is from 1789, when the Philadelphia Society for Promoting Agriculture (PSPA) decided that the winners of its agricultural essay contests could elect to receive their award in the form of either a gold medal or ten pounds, Philadelphia currency.[70] Perhaps the agriculturally oriented community to which the PSPA looked found money more *useful* than a medal. By the 1820s, however, many literary competition organizers were also offering their successful entrants a choice: either a medal worth fifty dollars *or* the fifty dollars itself. One conflicted theater offered a medal *and* cash, as if somehow this relieved the successful entrant of having to choose. Still other organizers dispensed with medals, cups, and silver services altogether and offered exclusively cash-based rewards. In a period of shifting forms of prize, lawyer and inventor John H. B. Latrobe was thrown into a quandary when he won first prize in an architectural competition and had to choose between fifty dollars in cash and a medal that was worth fifty dollars. His mother was poor and in ill health, and he "looked wistfully at the money," before doing what he believed to be the right thing in taking the medal. It was not an easy decision, but he felt that it was ultimately the right one to make from an ethical point of view.[71]

The problem with using money as a prize for competitions was that it was difficult, if not impossible, to earmark. Unlike the illiquid, non-fungible medals, cups, and certificates of earlier competitions, there was no way to control the meanings or uses of cash, and, of course, money meant things other than prestige in the nineteenth century. While it could be suggestive of charity toward one's mother, it also connoted, for example, worldliness, materialism, vice, and corruption. Then, too, using money seemed in some very literal sense to put a price on excellence. In essence, it introduced what economic anthropologist David Graeber calls an element of "proportionality" into the economy of competitions. This, according to Graeber, is "precisely what makes money unique—that it can indicate exactly how much more one [object] is worth than another."[72] The thousand dollar premiums offered by Edwin Forrest in the 1830s, that is, were worth precisely one hundred times more than the ten dollar premiums offered by the *Rural Repository*. Not only did this suggest, of course, that the Forrest premiums were one hundred times *better*, but, in a fluctuating literary market, it also meant that the going rate for a premium could inflate, leading to invidious comparisons that could distract authors from the goal of excellence to the goal of income. We see evidence of 'premium inflation' as early as 1832, when the *New-York Mirror* criticized a Southern theater manager for only offering a fifty dollar premium for his essay contest. "We do not think the sum mentioned . . . is sufficient for the occasion," they commented tartly. "The best writers will scarcely enter the lists, for the certainty of such a slender inducement; and, risk and all considered, we fear few will strive. A good essay should be well paid for. Literary labor is too *cheap*."[73] Likewise, the American Peace Society found itself compelled, between 1829 and 1831, to raise its premium from thirty dollars to fifty and then to five hundred after the two initial sums failed to elicit more than handful of entries in its essay contests. By 1833, when the Pennsylvania State Temperance Society organized an essay contest, it noted that its premium "should be at least five hundred dollars, and efforts will be made to raise it to one thousand dollars."[74] Such issues were never at stake when a medal or piece of plate was being competed for, because even when a price was attached to it, the prize itself remain illiquid and its value, ultimately, symbolic.

As early as 1804, in fact, a humorous sketch in a Hudson, New York, magazine indicated the corrosive moral effect that money had on literary emulation. The Provost of a Scottish University, the sketch ran, died and left in his will one guinea to whomever would pen his epitaph. A writer was appointed, but the Provost's "executors, thinking to defraud the poet, agreed to meet and share the guinea among them, each contributing a line." Their composition ran as follows:

> 1st. Here lies Dickson, provost of Dundee
> 2d. Here lies Dickson, here lies he.

The third was embarrassed for a long time, but unwilling to lose his share of the Guinea, vociferously bawled

> Hallalujah, hallaluje.[75]

The sketch is, of course, funny, but when one reads its title—"Prize Poetry"—it also becomes pointed and bitter, for what the Provost's friends were offering was, in essence, a tasteless post-mortem Crambo: one propelled not by mild-mannered sociability and wit-driven approbation, but by a rapacious greed driven by the desire for a guinea. Cash, the author of the sketch suggests, so perverts the spirit of emulation that it would lead a man to crow over the death of another. Put together with the title of the piece, the message is not hard to miss. Those who pursued literary approbation by way of literary emulation *solely* for the sake of money were morally bankrupt. Insofar as such claims were widely held to be true—and they were—cash prizes raised all sorts of difficult questions about the propriety of the organizers, the motives of the entrants, and the integrity of the judges. In introducing cash into an economy of prestige and using it as a form of symbolic capital, competition organizers opened a potential Pandora's box of economic interpretations.

It was precisely for the decorum with which he treated competition prizes, monetary and otherwise, that Charles Sprague was admired. As a banker as well as a man of letters, Sprague understood fully the dangers of mixing currencies, crossing economies, and misapplying funds, and in his career as a competition entrant, he walked a delicate tightrope in his attempts to make sure his receipt of prizes remained beyond reproach. His second prize was easy enough in this respect. It was an engraved silver cup received in 1822 for a prologue on the opening of the New Philadelphia Theater, built to replace the theater that had burned down. (Quipped one wag, "Should rogues continue to burn down Theatres, and Mr. Sprague to write them up, he will soon be in a fair way to have a full service of plate.")[76] His unprecedented third award, for an ode delivered at the Shakespeare Jubilee in Boston in 1824, earned him another gold medal. By this point, however, he had already become a subject of scrutiny and cynical examination and began to adopt an increasingly self-effacing persona: his pseudonym for the Prize Ode was "Airy Nothing."[77] The prize for the best prologue read at the opening of the Salem Theatre in 1828, which Sprague of course won, was the first in which a cash only award was offered ($50) and it also evidently made him uncomfortable. Although he accepted it, he retained his pseudonym "Naumkeke"; communicated with the awards committee only through pseudonymous letters published in the newspaper; and had the money delivered to him privately.[78] When he won his second prize of that year, for the prologue read at the opening of the Arch-Street Theatre in Philadelphia, and which he had submitted under the deliberately misleading pseudonym of "Penn" (to suggest a Philadelphian competitor), he again remained anonymous and this time actually declined his prize, an engraved silver cup, requesting instead that the money spent on it be given to a charity. When it became apparent that the cup had already been purchased and partially engraved, Sprague, still wrapped in the cloak of "Penn," requested by letter that it be forwarded to Josiah Quincy, the mayor of Boston and a friend of the author, who would then pass it on to the author himself.[79] Sprague entered one more competition: for the opening of the Portsmouth Theatre in 1830, with a fifty dollar premium. He won. But by this time it had become apparent that Sprague's skill in winning competitions was matched only by his embarrassment at having won so many. For some time now, commentators had been making unseemly suggestions concerning Sprague's interest in the prizes, and it is for this reason, it would seem, that he withdrew first from giving his name, then from receiving the prizes, and eventually from entering the competitions.[80] Although he continued to write wildly popular occasional odes and orations, and while he lived until 1875, a hale and active banker and man of affairs, he never again entered a competition. The implication seems clear: while Sprague valued emulation, he found its marriage to tangible, and especially, fungible rewards problematic. His withdrawal from competitions seems to suggest that, finally, he was unable to reconcile the two.

PRIZE INFLATION AND PRIZE CRITICISM

In 1829, Sprague was awarded an honorary degree from Harvard, in part a recognition (symbolic capital) of his skillful uses of money. Yet even as Sprague was receiving his degree in Massachusetts and was coming to the end of his competitive career, Edwin Forrest, reading over theatrical submissions, was beginning his with the discovery of John Augustus Stone's *Metamora*. Forrest came to acting, and to competitiveness, early. A pugnacious, driven, and slightly self-righteous young man, he managed through hard work and shrewd dealing to establish himself as a major player in the late 1820s. Forrest was inspired by the theatrical prologue competitions that had flourished earlier that decade, and he adopted, but also—crucially—adapted the common competition format to his own ends. So important were the competitions to Forrest, in fact, that between 1828 and 1847, he organized no less than nine of them.[81]

The competitions organized by Forrest in the 1830s and 1840s differed dramatically from those entered by Sprague in the 1820s in several important ways. To begin with, all of Forrest's competitions centered on cash prizes exclusively and at values five to ten times larger than the paltry fifty dollars spent on the medals that Sprague typically won. Too, the competitions were for far more substantial works of literature—plays— than the fifty- or sixty-line prologues written by Sprague and his fellow entrants. The nature of the genre meant, in turn, that the performance of the winning text would not be a one off, symbolic event—quite literally an occasional piece—but an instantly canonized and frequently repeated part of Forrest's repertoire. The stakes, in other words, were considerably higher than they had been for Sprague. Lastly, where the earlier contests shone a spotlight on the winning entrant, the contests now tended to reflect glory on the contest organizer. As the *New-York Mirror* put it on the eve of Forrest's first competition, "Patronage alone was wanting to encourage the sons of genius to write for the stage; and what the public refused or neglected to do, Forrest resolved to do himself."[82] The competitions organized by Forrest were, in other words, all about Forrest: he organized them; he assisted in judging them; he was the focus of them, inasmuch as the plays submitted were designed specifically to showcase his acting skills; and he paid personally for the immense prizes. When combined, these factors produced a radically different economy of competitions.

The reconfigured economics of Forrest's competitions are nowhere better captured than in his relations with playwright Robert Montgomery Bird, who entered (and won) four of Forrest's events between 1830 and 1834. The first thing to note is the substantial sums of money that were involved; each of the contests won by Bird carried a premium of $1,000. The second innovative factor was a shift away from emulation, in which the real award was based on the showcasing of the winner's work, and the corresponding bestowal of public approbation. Bird's first winning entry, *Pelopidas* (1830) was never even performed, because when Forrest read another of Bird's plays, *The Gladiator*, he decided that this would be a better vehicle for his skills. Forrest simply considered the first competition moot and gave Bird the award for the second year's competition too. (In 1833, Bird again won Forrest's competition, this time with *Oralloosa*, and the year after that, with *The Broker of Bogota*.) The third innovation in Forrest's competitions was that he came very quickly to think of the prize money as less an honorarium or symbolic gesture and more as a commercial transaction that resulted in the legal transfer of manuscript from the playwright to the player. In his first competition, it is true, he had offered, in addition to the five hundred dollar premium, half a night's takings from the box-office. As such, Forrest's first prize was Janus-faced, looking forward to the competitions of the next few decades, but looking back to the traditional charity economy of playwrighting in which the authors received the box office takings from a special benefit performance, often given on a play's third night. After his first competition, however, Forrest set his sights firmly on the future. The point at which the playwright received his premium, he decided, all obligations were met. Bird disagreed and felt that he had a right to a traditional 'third night' benefit, if not a cut of all the profits from the performance, which would net him at least an additional two thousand dollars per play. The conflict between Bird and Forrest reflected the final struggle between, respectively, an embedded (albeit weakly) and a disembedded understanding of prizes. For Forrest, playwrights were not competing to do, or be, their best; they were competing to have Forrest buy their plays.[83] By the late 1840s, it would appear, Forrest had more or less given up on even the pretense of running competitions in the traditional mold. Manuscripts were sent to him directly, rather than to a committee for evaluation; Forrest had become judge, jury, and executioner. Forrest, that is to say, had become a purchaser.[84]

The mid-1830s not only witnessed the consolidation of a new understanding of literary competitions, however; they also saw a profound backlash against the very idea of competitiveness in both its old and new guises. Much of this debate took place in schools and colleges, where teachers influenced by the so-called 'monitorial' system had introduced a highly monetized version of competitiveness. Established by Joseph Lancaster in England and then imported to America in the 1810s, the monitorial system was based first and last on emulative models of education. An important part of Lancaster's regime entailed issuing merit cards and (sometimes) money-like tickets for good behavior and scholarly achievement, confiscating them for bad conduct or poor work, and allowing students periodically to 'cash them in' for prizes, including books and toys. As Lancaster explained: "It is no unusual thing with me to deliver one or two hundred prizes at the same time."[85] The influence of Lancasterianism was still more clearly seen in the education efforts of Josiah Quincy, who became president of Harvard in 1829. Quincy's system assigned points for each student's work and deducted points for tardiness, disciplinary infractions, and weak scholarship. Students could, in fact, earn as many as 29,920 points, and based on their cumulative scores, they could receive both *deturs* (books with special presentation plates) and cash awards as well as exhibition parts.[86] In his first year at Harvard, for example, Henry David Thoreau won twenty-five dollars in "exhibition money"; in his second year another twenty-five dollars and—due to a mathematical miscalculation on Quincy's part—a detur and a part in a public exhibition; and in his final year, yet another twenty-five dollars together with a speaking part in a graduation 'conference.'[87] Yet even though he put in a creditable performance, Thoreau detested Quincy's system, and in his freshman year, he signed his name to a petition denouncing the College's use of emulation. "We have no doubt," wrote the authors of the petition, "that the original design of this system was good" but it "tends to produce envy and jealousy among those whose interests require that they should at least in some degree be united." The authors of the petition also advanced a proto-Romantic axiology in place of neoclassical standards in arguing "that the time has arrived when literary standing must depend on something more than mere college rank, when a nobler motive must prompt the student to action than the petty emulation of the school-boy, when he must have a higher standard of action than the mere marks of his instructor."[88] Although he continued to perform adequately, his role in the petition drive did not pass unnoticed, and in 1837 Quincy tartly informed Ralph Waldo Emerson that Thoreau had "imbibed some notions concerning emulation and college rank which had a natural tendency to diminish his zeal, if not his exertions."[89]

Thoreau was not the only person to question the efficacy of emulation specifically, and competitiveness more generally, in the 1830s. While all educational theorists agreed on emulation's centrality as a human motivation, few agreed on its implications. The problem, in the first instance, was definitional. Everyone understood that emulation meant "an Ambition to excel," but there was considerable debate over the relative weight of the words in the definition. Was emulation more likely to promote excellence or merely naked ambition for its own sake? Was this ambition inherently good (or bad), or was it a morally neutral phenomenon that could be turned to either good or bad ends? Other questions followed. Was emulation consistent with Christianity and with republicanism? Was it appropriate for children, and if so, was it appropriate for adults? Was it more fitting for men than women? And ought it to be encouraged, ignored, or actively suppressed? Throughout the 1830s, such questions were debated endlessly in educational journals and conferences: in four years, the *American Annals of Education and Instruction* published no less than twelve articles on emulation, and many other pamphlets and speeches were given on the subject. Overwhelmingly, the authors of these articles opposed emulation. They believed that it encouraged hubris in winners and shame in those who had not won, so that winners ended up developing a morbid addiction to praise, while those who did not win either came to think of themselves as losers and gave up trying or resorted to subterfuge to gain approbation. They claimed that emulation led to competitiveness for its own sake and encouraged competitors to think in terms of defeating their opponents rather than merely striving for the sake of aspiration. They argued that emulation overstimulated the senses and led people to try only when prizes were being offered, and that it caused selfishness, greed, and even ill-health. Perhaps no single author confirmed such worries more than Edgar Allan Poe. Eschewing even a veneer of respectability, or an interest in emulation, Poe, as we shall see in the next section, showed how literary competitions became simply attempts to enter the market by proxy.

EDGAR ALLAN POE AND THE WORLD
OF COMPETITIONS

In 1829, two down-at-heel poets met in a bookstore in Baltimore and traded insults. Their dispute might have ended in blows or a duel, but before it could do so, a different sort of challenge was issued. "I'll bet you five dollars," said one, "I can write more stanzas in one hour than you can in a day." The other picked up the gauntlet with a sneer. Pencils and paper were produced and so began one of the period's stranger "tournament[s] of rhymes." The challenger was the wretchedly obscure John Lofland, also known as the Milford Bard; his competitor was Edgar Allan Poe.[90] Familiar though we are with Poe's contentious personality, and even with his habit of competing with his peers, we have failed until now to appreciate the extent to which Poe was also engaged in the world of formal literary competitions. Over the course of his career, Poe acted as a competition entrant, organizer, and judge; he reviewed prize winning plays and poetry; he became involved in competition scandals, law suits, even fist fights; and, crucially, he wove the central themes of competition into his poetry and fiction, as well as into his non-fictional prose. Few figures, in fact, were involved so intimately in so many aspects of the com-

petitive world as Poe, and, importantly, perhaps none more fully dramatized the tensions inherent in literary competitions.

Poe's engagement with competitiveness began early. His classmates
at Joseph Clarke's academy in Richmond remembered the thirteen-year-
old Poe as being "eager for distinction" and "inclined to be imperious,"
while Clarke himself invoked the text-book definition of emulation in
describing his young charge as being "ambitious to excel." In 1821 or
1822, Poe won his first competition: a public elocution contest, or exhibition, held in Richmond. By the time he entered William Burke's academy in 1823, he had become an expert at the Crambo-like exercise of
"capping verses," and it was at this time, too, that he swam an alleged
six miles up the James River against the tide, in deliberate emulation of
Lord Byron's famous swim of the Hellespont. (Byron was, of course,
and would remain for some time, *the* figure whom Americans emulated.)
Even at the University of Virginia, Poe showed no let up in his competitive drive. He "grew noted as a debater," as one student recalled, and also
participated in boxing and jumping competitions.[91]

Poe's relentless drive to compete and succeed, according to Kenneth
Silverman, can be traced back directly to his status as an orphan and to
his need to be recognized and approved of by figures of authority. It was
a lifelong and, apparently, insatiable hunger. Years later, a friend recalled
of Poe that "no man living loved the praises of others better than he did
. . . whenever I happened to communicate to him anything touching his
abilities as a writer, his bosom would heave like a troubled sea."[92] What
the world of competitions gave him was a stage on which to act out these
deep-seated needs; what the concepts of emulation and approbation gave
others was a convenient language with which to explain his actions. So
far from seeming aberrant, then, Poe's emulative drive was seen as, in
fact, quite admirable, at least initially.

Unfortunately for Poe, his chief judge—at least in his own mind—
would always be his guardian, John Allan, a bitter man who was determined not to see him win. Poe's early letters to Allan are filled with anguished pleas, in which he asks to be judged, but flinches from the judgment: "you can judge for yourself," "I will give you the reason . . . then
judge," "suspend your judgement until you hear *of* me again," "I begged
that you would suspend any judgement," "If you conclude upon giving
me a *trial* please enclose me the letter," "I would beg you to judge me impartially," and, revealingly, "I have offended only in asking your approbation."[93] But Allan was unwilling to give his approbation. An orphan
himself, he bore an unresolved grudge at his own foster father's failure to
support his intellectual development, and he seemed determined to inflict

on Poe the neglect he had received himself. No matter what Poe achieved, it was rarely ever enough to merit his flinty foster father's approval, and as Poe entered his mid teens, their relationship grew increasingly tense. A man who could in private admit to his own "pride and ambition," Allan came to revile those same traits in his young charge, and he left Poe with a painfully skewed view of the world: one in which he felt it necessary to win the approval of those who judged him, but which at the same time left him convinced that he would never be judged fairly. Life, for Poe, was a rigged competition in which he nonetheless had no choice but to participate.[94]

Fittingly enough, Poe's first published poem, "Tamerlane," which appeared mere months after he had fled Allan's household, both denounced "the folly of even *risking* the best feelings of the heart at the shrine of Ambition" and at the same time vaunted that very impulse as a means of achieving greatness. It was, in fact, a text utterly characteristic of Poe's ambivalent feelings concerning competitiveness.[95]

Poe makes a fascinating case study, then, both because he felt such a powerful need to compete with others, and because he betrayed an equally powerful contempt for such competitions and, indeed, for competitiveness as a whole. His conflicted feelings, moreover, were only exacerbated by the fact that he tended to enter writing contests at moments of acute financial and emotional vulnerability, when the promise of winning prizes seemed to hold out redemption on several distinct levels: monetary, vocational, and emotional. Poe's complex motives and ambivalent reactions are valuable, in other words, because they allow one to see simultaneously the psychological *and* sociological dimensions of literary competitions under stress.

Poe's entry into the world of adult competitions came in May 1831, when he learned of a contest in the Philadelphia *Saturday Courier* offering a premium of one hundred dollars for the best American tale submitted.[96] Poe submitted five. That he was driven by something like emulation and approbation is apparent, but he was driven just as much if not more by poverty, for he was in desperate straits, living in a tiny Baltimore apartment with his impoverished aunt, Maria Clemm, and several others. Indeed, even as he was submitting his work to the *Courier* and awaiting the decision of the judges, he was writing, over and over, to John Allan, begging for relief from crushing debt. So far from having money, he had been arrested recently for one of his deceased brother Henry's outstanding debts. At a period in time when it was common for periodical authors to receive little more than two dollars a page, the opportunity to win one hundred dollars must have been hard to resist.[97]

Poe's decision to enter the competition, however, should not be taken as an indication that he approved of such events. Many dozens of contests were advertised over the twenty or so years Poe was writing to sustain himself, but he entered only three of which we are aware, and in every case he entered at a time of absolute financial desperation, treating the contests as a high stakes gamble. Indeed, there is reason to believe that he experienced a deep humiliation at having to hawk his wares in such a way. That Poe's feelings about competitive success were conflicted was apparent from the tales themselves, one of which, "A Decided Loss," featured a few well-placed swipes at Edwin Forrest, John Augustus Stone, and their prize-winning script, *Metamora*. Whatever he thought of Indian dramas—and the evidence is that he thought very little of them indeed—it is clear that he resented the pair's prize-driven celebrity. The approbation and money that came with being a star were precisely what Poe wanted, and lacked, and therefore despised. The fact that one of the *Courier's* judges—Richard Penn Smith—was a friend of Forrest's who had himself just won (and very likely fraudulently) a Forrest prize of one thousand dollars for his play *Caius Marius* would have galled Poe deeply, and simply reinforced his conviction that all competitions were rigged, had he been aware of it.[98] Poe, as it turns out, was neither as lucky, nor as well connected, as Penn Smith. He lost the competition and, with it, control over his five stories; while all of them were published in the *Courier* in 1832, he received no money from them and, besides, very little caché, for his name appeared over only the first, and none indicated that they had been competition entries. If, as I am arguing, Poe entered the world of competitions with a well-entrenched prejudice against them on the score of fairness, then his first experience simply reinforced such beliefs.

By 1833, Poe was in yet more desperate straits, writing to Allan in April of that year that he was "perishing—absolutely perishing for want of aid." Allan never replied. Starved for both attention and money, Poe could hardly have ignored the news that the *Baltimore Saturday Visiter* was also running a competition, this time with a fifty-dollar premium for the best short story and twenty-five for the best poem submitted. He had some reason, in fact, to be optimistic. The *Visiter* had until recently been edited by his friend, Lambert Wilmer, and he had already published several pieces in its pages. At the same time, however, he knew that the competition represented a serious gamble. If he won in both the prose and poetry divisions, he stood to make seventy-five urgently needed dollars—or, if he chose, two "Silver medals"—but if he lost, his submissions automatically became the "property of the Publishers." Risking much, Poe again employed a saturation technique, sending in six short stories and a poem entitled "The Coliseum."[99]

Ironically, the six tales Poe submitted to the *Visiter* formed the nucleus of his new and still unpublished story collection, *Tales of the Folio Club*, which evinced a deeply critical suspicion of the entire axiological process on which literary contests were predicated. The narrative that frames the collection describes the inner workings of the intensely competitive Folio Club. Each month, the narrator of the frame explains, the members of the Club convene over food and wine, read aloud their stories, critique one another, and then vote on the works read. "Much rivalry will ensue," he adds, for the members of the Club compete not merely to win, but also to avoid losing, since while the winner is made club president, the loser is compelled to pay for the food and wine at the club's next meeting. The organization of the Club's meetings seems a striking and pointed commentary on Poe's view of competitions. In the first place, it suggests that he saw the competitive world as an incestuous clique where authors wrote for, and judged, one another. More important still, it indicates that Poe saw contests less as noble and emulatory events in which, to the extent that one tried one's best, 'everyone won,' and more as zero sum games with losers as well as winners. Losing, indeed, seemed to be both costly and humiliating. When the narrator of the frame loses the contest, however, he does not submit to the decision of the members; rather, he grabs all of the manuscripts, "and, rushing from the house, determines to appeal, by printing the whole, from the decision of the Club, to that of the public." It is these stories, then, together with the Club's comments, that comprise Poe's volume, and from which he selected six for the *Visiter*.[100]

While scholars have seen the roots of Poe's projected volume in works as diverse as Plato's *Symposium*, Thomas Moore's *Lalla Rookh* (1817), and Washington Irving's *Tales of a Traveler* (1824), the parallels with the rejected address tradition are hard to miss. Like the aggrieved participants in that genre, the narrator of the Folio Club collection seeks to shift the center of axiological gravity from a small group, or club, of judges to the opinion of "the public." Poe's decision to frame his narrative in this way was anything but arbitrary; he was familiar with the works of Horace and James Smith and more generally with the history of British theater, so his reliance on this axiological maneuver, and especially in the context of his own entry into a literary contest, is telling indeed. If nothing else, it suggests his deep ambivalence about competitions and makes clear the irony of his engagement in a zero-sum authorial economy in whose fairness he reposed so little trust.[101]

In the instance, Poe ended up being both winner *and* loser. The committee of judges—whose meeting sounded remarkably like that of the Folio Club, complete with cigars, wine, and balloting—unanimously voted Poe's story collection the best, selecting one tale, 'MS. Found in a Bottle,' for the prize. The judges also admired Poe's poem and they came close to voting for it too, but in the end they settled on another, entitled "The Song of the Wind," written by one Henry Wilton.[102]

Poe, recalled *Visiter* editor John Hill Hewitt many years later, was "greedy for fame, as well as in need of money," and in winning this competition, he managed to gain a combination of both.[103] Desperately as he needed the money, however, he seemed to need fame, and the approval it suggested, still more. In 1835 he sent Thomas Willis White, the proprietor of the *Southern Literary Messenger*, a copy of the *Visiter* containing the judges' warm praise of his work and begged him to have it "copied into any of the Richmond papers." White immediately printed it in his own magazine. Indeed, Poe continued to harp on his competition successes long after others might have left them behind, and he milked them for all that they were worth. An 1843 biographical sketch ghost-written by Poe claimed that the author had received "first honours" at the University of Virginia, "headed every class" at West Point, jumped "the distance of twenty-one feet, six inches, on a dead level, with a run of twenty yards," swam the James in an effort that made "Byron's paddle across the Hellespont" look like "mere child's play in comparison," and, significantly, won "*both* premiums" in the *Visiter* contest. Almost every statement was a falsehood.[104]

In fact Poe might well have felt that he *had* won the poetry as well as the prose division, for shortly after the awards were announced, he discovered that the poetry winner "Henry Wilton" was none other than John Hill Hewitt, the editor of the very paper in which the competition had been run. He discovered, too, that the judges had initially favored his poem over Hewitt's but had felt uncomfortable awarding all the prizes to one entrant and so had given Hewitt's poem first place instead.[105] The fact that Hewitt had entered pseudonymously and that his pseudonym was not even known to the judges until after they had selected his poem seemed irrelevant to Poe. Attuned, as he was, to even the slightest taint of bias in the act of judgment and, moreover, predisposed to see competitions as zero-sum games, Poe felt that, in some ill-defined way, Hewitt had defrauded him of a prize that was rightly his.

Days later, Poe confronted the editor on the street and an ugly scene ensued. "You have used underhanded means, sir, to obtain that prize over me," said Poe. Hewitt vehemently denied the accusation. "Then why did you keep back your real name?" Poe persisted. Hewitt explained that he had had his "reasons," but Poe pushed on. "But you tampered with the committee, sir," he said. "The committee are gentlemen," retorted Hewitt, "and above being tampered with; and if you say that you insult them." This was too much for Poe. "I agree that the committee are gentlemen," he said, "but I cannot place *you* in that category." On hearing this, Hewitt turned and punched Poe in the face, and a fight was only averted by the interference of friends. It was hardly the most decorous conclusion to what was, in many respects, the most important moment in Poe's literary coming of age, but in some sense it is typical. The committee, for Poe, was both above reproach and yet also capable of being tampered with. Winning a prize was both priceless (to the extent that it validated Poe) and worthless (to the extent that it could also, for whatever reason, validate a scoundrel like Hewitt). When Poe's poem was reprinted in the *Southern Literary Messenger* two years later, Poe very pointedly retitled it, "The Coliseum, a Prize Poem."[106]

As the aftermath of the *Visiter* affair suggests, Poe evinced a curious double consciousness regarding competitions. When he won, he not only endorsed the justice of the judges, but he bragged endlessly of his attainments, magnified them, and at times simply fabricated 'facts' that were not true. When, by contrast, he lost, or when he was commenting on competitions in which he was not an entrant, he cast scorn on the proceedings in their entirety, vilifying the judges, belittling the entrants, and ridiculing the winner. At times, he offered up witheringly cynical and, the truth be told, devastatingly accurate critiques of the hypocrisy and deceit on which such competitions were based. The fact that he so often saw deceit where none was to be detected does not mean that his analyses of those situations that *were* fraudulent lacked bite. They did not.

In the case of the *Visiter* competition, for example, Poe was perhaps right in suspecting dishonesty but wrong in laying the charge at Hewitt's door. In submitting his poem pseudonymously, Hewitt had, in fact, been operating strictly within the conventions of the traditional competition; in choosing to spread the wealth among the entrants, however, the judges had not. That Poe did not criticize the judges was directly a result of their having awarded him first place in the story contest and, equally, of his continuing reliance on their largesse.

Of course, it is quite possible that both Hewitt *and* the judges colluded in rigging the competition, as Poe might have suspected deep down. If this was the case, it would have been neither the first nor the last time that such a fait accompli had taken place. Just six months after the announcement of the *Visiter* results, the *New Yorker* ran a similar contest, with a one hundred dollar premium for best short story and fifty dollars for the best poem and the best essay. Contest judge Lewis Gaylord Clark arranged for his friend, a Bowdoin College professor named Henry Wadsworth Longfellow to win the contest, but in the end, the panel (Clark, H. W. Herbert, and Samuel Woodworth) decided to give him only half the prize, the other being given out of pity to none other than Poe's recent publisher Eliza Leslie: a combination of deceit, then, and meddling.[107] Although it is highly unlikely that Poe ever learned of the machinations that took place in this event, he already had his eye on Clark and would very soon accuse him, and a small cadre of fellow writers, of orchestrating a generally corrupt clique that rigged everything from contests and contracts to puffs and plagiarism.[108]

But the problem went further, in fact, than even this isolated incident. While there were honest competition judges, there were just as many—and probably more—who bent, if they did not outright break, the rules, typically through nepotism. Although there were few cut and dried cases of cheating, many savored of dishonesty and collusion. Consider: Nathaniel P. Willis won several poetry competitions in a newspaper edited by his father; Harriet Beecher won a prize in the school contest run by her sister Catharine; Judge James Hall later begged Harriet to enter a story in his *Western Literary Magazine* contest after deciding that the submissions entered on time were inadequate and then promptly awarded her first prize; Ann Stephens won first prize in a contest run by *Snowden's Ladies' Companion*, a journal she co-edited; and Edwin Forrest, as we have seen, routinely awarded prizes to plays that had not yet been written, that had been written years earlier, or that had not been submitted formally to his contests.[109]

Such juxtapositions are highly suggestive of deceit or collusion but no more than that. Yet definitive evidence of competition rigging does exist. In 1847, Maine author Elizabeth Oakes Smith received a remarkable and remarkably frank letter from magazine editor Alice B. Neal. With little apology, Neal explained that her periodical, *The Gazette*, had organized a competition with a hefty $150 premium for the best tale on the American Revolution, and with only three weeks left before the deadline no submissions had been made that were worthy of the award. Completely unwilling to either cancel the contest or extend the deadline, Neal decided to commission a story from Smith. "Will you not be so good," asked Neal, "if previous engagements do not interfere—as to write one, for which we guarantee you shall receive the prize." Undaunted, Smith cranked out a story—"The Bald Eagle"—for which she was duly awarded first place.[110]

When Poe began to write for the *Southern Literary Messenger* in late 1834, he was propelled in part by a campaign designed to expose this kind of literary fraud in all its manifestations, and while he did not challenge the results of competitions specifically during his tenure in Richmond, he would perhaps never have begun his campaign had it not been for his own competition disappointments. Poe raged against puffing, plagiarism, and the power of ruthless literary cliques. Even his benign essays, such as "Maelzel's Chessplayer," were designed to unveil hidden machinations, or, to quote Willis himself, to reveal "who pulls the wire to all the literary puppets."[111] Upon firing Poe in 1836, *Messenger* owner Thomas W. White heaved a sigh of relief that he was now free of this self-appointed "Judge or Judge Advocate." Poe had, indeed, made it his mission to judge judges. All that remained now was for him to become, himself, a judge.[112]

Poe's conflicted feelings concerning competitions and their judging were merely reinforced by his experiences as an editorial assistant for *Burton's Gentleman's Magazine* between 1839 and 1840. In November 1839, the magazine announced its own competition with one thousand dollars in prizes, editor William Burton's novel twist on the literary competition being to dispense altogether with the typical committee of judges, who, he opined, "generally select, unread, the effusion of the most popular candidate as the easiest method of discharging their onerous duties." The submissions in this case, he said, would be read "by the Editors alone." Poe was horrified, not only because this scheme dispensed with even the semblance of objectivity held out by most competition organizers, but also because he had nothing but contempt for Burton's critical prowess. If Burton was to be judge, then everyone was in trouble. Poe suspected, too, that Burton intended not to make any awards, a suspicion that was simply reinforced when Burton decided to cancel the competition and sell his magazine. Several of the submissions were not returned and appeared later in *Graham's Magazine*, unpaid for. Poe's view from within the world of competitions was as disappointing as the view from without.[113]

Yet as we have seen, Poe was unable to walk away from the need to compete. Even as he was deploring the fraudulence of Burton's premium scheme in letters to friends, he was establishing his own informal and eccentric competition, which, much like Burton's, dispensed with a committee of judges in favor of a more singular form of adjudication. The venue for this contest was *Alexander's Weekly Messenger*, a newspaper at which Poe moonlighted between December 1839 and May 1840. (It was, fittingly enough, published by the same firm that issued *Burton's.*) In the issue for 18 December 1839, Poe claimed rather boldly that there was no cryptogram that he could not solve. "Let this be put to the test," he announced. "Let any one address us a letter in this way, and we pledge ourself to read it forthwith—however unusual or arbitrary may be the characters employed."[114] Poe's readers immediately leapt to the challenge, and his throwaway comment became a strange two-way competition: the readers challenging Poe to decode their ciphers, and Poe challenging his readers to figure out how he did it. Prizes, too, entered the equation, as Poe offered to reveal his secret in exchange for forty subscribers, and one reader promised him "ten subscribers and the cash" if he could solve his puzzle.[115]

Poe's 'competition' differed from the usual events in many ways. In the first place, rather than pitting a group of entrants against one another, Poe sought to compete against the entrants, taking on all comers; as such, Poe's contest had absolutely nothing to do with emulation, which was meant to be a collectively ennobling venture. In the second place, where a typical contest involved acts of creation, Poe's claim was that he could take apart any cryptogram presented him; it was not an act of encoding but an instance of decoding, less creative, on other words, than destructive. Third, and most significantly, Poe's contest was predicated on a deep-seated need to reveal precisely the kind pretense he saw going on in other competitions. For every cryptogram he solved, he showed several more to be based upon deceit or dishonesty: using inconsistent codes, foreign words, and so on. It was Poe's ideal competition: one in which he not only won (being the only competitor) but in which, in so doing, he managed to defeat everyone else and show how mendacious and deceitful most of the entrants were. He was also the judge, passing summary judgment on the coding abilities of the entrants.[116]

Poe's dual strategy of critique and engagement continued into the 1840s when he became an editorial assistant at *Graham's Magazine.* It was at this time that he issued perhaps his sternest criticism of the competitions by attacking the nation's best-known prize poet, Charles Sprague. In an 1841 review of Sprague's writings, Poe derided "Prize Odes for Festivals and Opening Nights of new theatres" as "a species of literature almost beneath contempt," noting only that inasmuch as "all prize articles are bad *ex officio,*" the most that could be said of Sprague's "Shakespeare Ode" was that it was "the best of them." Angrily criticized by pundits in Boston, Poe repeated the claims again in 1842, describing the "Shakespeare Ode" as "mawkish, *passé,* and absurd," and noting that it was "just such a one as would have obtained its author an Etonian prize some forty or fifty years ago," an ironic comment for a man who had still not finished trumpeting his teenaged achievements as a jumper and swimmer. In a review of Robert Walsh's *Sketches of Conspicuous Living Characters of France*, published in April 1841, Poe continued his attack on competitions, noting several anecdotes in that text recounting instances in which French competition judges had defrauded authors of their rightfully won prizes.[117]

Again, however, and even as he denounced competitions as corrupt and competition genres as beneath contempt, Poe was reviving his own cryptography competitions, issuing new challenges and even offering a year's free subscription to the reader who could decode a cryptogram that Poe himself had just succeeded in decoding. In December 1841, Poe printed a letter from a reader named W. B. Tyler, whom many critics believe to be Poe himself, dubbing the author "the king of 'secret-readers.'" If Tyler really was Poe's stand-in, then this was a remarkable act of self-consecration; if not, it was an even more compelling act of vindication.[118]

In March 1843, the *Dollar Newspaper* announced a short story competition with two hundred dollars in prizes: one hundred for the best story, sixty for the second best, and forty for the third. It was to be Poe's final competition, and everything about it seems familiar. He was, again, desperately poor; the panel of judges again included a recent Forrest prize winner; and again he made a rash gamble, buying back a story he had already sold to his former employer, George Graham. For Poe, the one hundred dollars he believed that he *might* win were more appealing than the fifty-two that Graham had already paid him and which he was compelled to pay back with other materials. Poe's gamble, however, paid off; in June, the *Dollar Newspaper* announced that Poe's short story, "The Gold Bug," had won first prize. There followed a giddying period of celebrity, in which Poe saw the paper containing his story sell out within one day, go into a second and then a third authorized printing, appear elsewhere in pirated form, and occasion enthusiastic reports and extensive summaries in publications around the nation. Poe had the immense satisfaction, too, of seeing the story reprinted in the Philadelphia *Saturday Courier*, scene of his impoverishing competition loss in 1831, while the *Baltimore Saturday Visiter* obligingly reprinted an abridgement of his ghost-written and exaggeration-filled biography, leaving uncorrected his assertion that he had won both poetry and prose divisions in their 1833 contest. The prize-winning tale was even adapted for the stage and performed twice in August 1843. In a letter to a friend written much later, Poe claimed that he had written his story "for the sole purpose of running," an allusion to his own childhood racing experiences perhaps; for a while, at least, "The Gold Bug" ran far and fast. Yet even this was not enough for Poe. In a revealing indication of his insatiable hunger for praise, he claimed in private that he had only submitted the tale to the *Dollar Newspaper* after it had been rejected by Graham, seeking thereby to amplify both his consecration and vindication still more by making it seem as if his achievement was a *success d'estime*.[119]

Yet Poe's satisfaction was hardly unalloyed. Less than a fortnight after the results of the contest had been announced, the *Daily Forum* published a letter from Francis Duffee claiming that the competition had been rigged and that the judges had arranged to offer Poe first prize if he was willing to accept fifteen dollars. It was a stunning and extraordinarily clever accusation, since it implied both the corruption of the judges and stinginess of Poe, who was willing to sell himself for so trifling a sum. Poe filed suit and Duffee retracted his claim but not before another pundit suggested that Poe had plagiarized his story from a thirteen-year-old girl, Ann Humphreys Sherburne, who had written a story entitled "Imogene; or the Pirate's Treasure" in 1839. The accusations were, again, retracted, but they cast a pall over Poe's achievement, depreciating the prestige he might otherwise have accumulated. Although Poe claimed a year after the contest that more than 30,000 copies of his story had been disseminated, the story was never completely free of the taint of scandal.[120]

In a sense, Poe brought this misery upon himself. His relentless criticism of the achievements of others and his carping accusations that the entrants and organizers of contests were in cahoots were being turned back upon him. While Poe was correct in assuming that many contests of the 1830s and 1840s were rigged, he could hardly make such accusations and not expect recriminations. His criticisms notwithstanding, it was becoming increasingly clear to his enemies how desperately Poe relied on competitions when at his most economically and emotionally vulnerable moments, and so it was with some satisfaction that they set about discrediting his own competitive achievements. Duffee's assault on the integrity of the *Dollar Newspaper* competition was only the first instance. Penning his infamous 'Ludwig Article' immediately after Poe's death, Rufus Griswold not only savaged Poe's character and morality but also claimed that his success in the *Saturday Visiter* competition was based solely on his handwriting, the judges having "unanimously decided that the prizes should be paid to the first of the geniuses who had written legibly," adding as a coup a grace: "Not another MS. was unfolded." When John Hill Hewitt, the winner of the *Visiter's* poetry section, recalled in his 1877 memoirs Poe's tipsy rhyming tournament with John Lofland, then, he was simply joining the company of those who were motivated to discredit every element of Poe's competitive endeavor.[121]

Perhaps the most striking example of how critical the antebellum literary establishment was of Poe's position on competitions is the fact that it took so long for him to be invited to judge one. While most prize winners were invited to serve as judges soon after having won their own competitions, it was a dozen years before Poe was extended that privilege. In 1845, finally, he received the call, but even here he was dogged by embarrassment. The competition in question was at the Rutgers Institute, a private girl's school in New York: hardly the prestigious venue for which he might have hoped. More frustrating still, the other judge, Rufus Griswold, who would later tarnish his reputation, backed out at the last moment, leaving one of Poe's many other enemies, Henry Tuckerman, take his place. The two "sat alone" together for most of the afternoon, reading the students' manuscripts. For Charles Fenno Hoffman, writing to Griswold, it was "a good joke," but for Poe, it must have been excruciatingly embarrassing. It was a fitting finale to his engagement with the competitive world. Poe would never again become involved with a competition.[122]

Poe's engagement with literary competitions in the 1830s and 1840s reflects an attitude completely at variance with the ideal expounded in the 1820s and exemplified by an author like Charles Sprague. Where Sprague competed for honor, Poe dueled for money. The premium from the 'MS found in a Bottle' represented something like three months' room and board in Baltimore at the time he lived there. At the same time, Poe understood that no matter what the dollar amount of the premium, the prestige it accrued offered both status, social connection, and further potential earnings. For these rewards, too, Poe fought vigorously, fuelled by his insatiable need for approbation, yet he fell afoul of the social networks that reproduced and protected social and cultural distinction. Poe was simply too belligerent and too poorly connected to capitalize effectively on the dynamic potentialities of the competitions. His goodwill, that is, ran out almost as fast as the cash he received. It is little wonder that Poe was as much repelled by as drawn to contests. No honors could appease this brilliantly talented author, because he was dueling as much with the dead as with the living, and the dead, as his stories showed time after time, could never be beaten.

In the final year of his life, Edgar Allan Poe began to contribute poems and stories to a Boston paper entitled *The Flag of Our Union*. (We encountered it already in Chapter Four, since it was a leader in the 'cash system' of pay-and-go purchases.) A big, brash publication that looked like a huge newspaper but that contained, instead, poems, stories, squibs, and much nationalist rhetoric, *The Flag* represented a new wave in publishing. It was audacious and sensational, and much of its sensationalism was fuelled by the competitions that it organized.[123] A competition announcement from an issue of 1847 is both so typical of the paper and yet so strikingly different from the competition calls we have seen already that it is worth quoting in its entirety:

$5000!!
To Be Awarded in Prizes!!!

We have resolved to show the readers of the Flag what enterprise will do; and therefore have laid by Five Thousand Dollars to be awarded to the successful competitors among our writers, $100 each! This liberal sum will command the first talent in the country; and the readers of the Flag will get all the benefit without any extra charge.

To Authors,

then, we say, send us your manuscripts. None but experienced writers need apply; and such tales as are well written will be carefully and honestly considered. We do not offer prizes like some of our contemporaries, retaining the liberty of keeping *all* manuscripts and stories, awarding pay *only* to the premium one. We do not wish to publish anything in the Flag that we are not willing to pay for, and that liberally.

Look Out for the Prize Tales

We shall continue them through the entire volume of the Flag, and commence again next year with renewed vigor.

Many things strike one as significant in this announcement, especially when contrasted with earlier contests. In the first place, there is no stated topic to shape or define each author's efforts, and as a result the competition seems less than emulative. Then, too, no mention is made of judges or panels, and in fact there were none. Moreover, the language of the announcement is markedly capitalistic. Rather than being called a competition, the event is characterized as a form of "enterprise," a word that, by the mid-nineteenth century had become clearly and positively associated with commercial investment and the monetary rewards it could offer. Indeed, the emphasis seems to be on the total sum of money "laid aside" and the way this reflects on the largesse of the proprietors, rather than on the skill of the authors. The awards, likewise, are described as "pay" rather than as something symbolic like an honor, or a palm. And lastly, the emphasis is on the readers, who will "get the benefit," rather than on the emulative benefits accruing to the authors.[124]

Subsequent competition announcements published by *The Flag* reflected yet further alterations in the nature of the institution; the editor noted, for example, that entries not winning the prize would still be published (at the authors' discretion) and paid between one and two hundred dollars. Competition entries were continuously solicited.[125]

Offering five thousand dollars of prizes a year in units of one hundred dollars per person, the competition ceased to be an event and became an ongoing condition. (Indeed, the sums of money offered to non-winning manuscripts were never less than those awarded to winners and could be up to twice as much.) What we see in the competitions of *The Flag*, then, is the absorption of literary competitions into the more generally competitive marketplace. The two had become more or less indistinguishable.

The influence of a commodified marketplace on the organization of the story papers' competitions was also revealed in the tendency of *The Flag* to describe its winning entries in terms not of their content, nor even in terms of their 'winningness,' but rather in terms of how much they had won. Henry P. Cheever's story, "The Witch of the Wave" was preceded by a banner announcing "100 Dollar Prize Tale" in bold font, while readers of the 4 December 1847 issue were informed that they could find in its pages another "hundred dollar prize tale."[126] Nor was this form of locution peculiar to *The Flag* alone. In reporting such events, the *Boston Herald*, announced, for example, that a *The Flag* "contains a $100 tale written for it by Ned Buntline." In this case, the very subsumation of the story in its monetary value and the implication that it has been commissioned—it was, in fact, a prize story—makes this competitive piece, and the competition into which it was entered, wholly indistinguishable from the wider competitive market.[127] Nathaniel P. Willis *may* have been in jest when he called his poems "five dollar inspirations," and Louis Godey *may* have been in jest when he asked Robert Montgomery Bird to "hammer me out . . . one of your solid pieces about twenty-five dollars' worth of Literature," but what the story papers were describing was too consistent and its adoption too widespread to be anything other than the indication of a profound transformation in the nature of this authorial economy. Here, surely, we see an example of Polanyi's wholly disembedded economy, in which social and cultural relations are subordinated to, and defined by, commercial values.[128]

Yet even as literary competitions were being absorbed into the literary marketplace, the literary marketplace was starting to ape the rhetoric, if not the reality, of the competitions in turn. Thus when *The New-York Courier and Enquirer* dismissed Fanny Fern's widely touted 1854 novel, *Ruth Hall*, by claiming that "Almost any well educated girl of fair abilities, and the command of her tongue . . . could make such stories, if not better," Fern's publishers, Mason Brothers, shot back, publishing a front page advertisement in the *New York Tribune*, offering "Ten Thousand Dollars each to any and every 'well educated girl' (or other person for that matter) who will furnish us for publication the manuscript of a Tale equal to Ruth Hall." Here was the language of competition, even of emulation, but pressed into the service of commerce. The money offered by Mason Brothers was not a symbolic amount designed to provoke competition, but an indication of what they felt Fern's—and any comparable work's—market value might be. Indeed, given that they claimed Fern was uniquely gifted and their money would, therefore, be safe, it is clear that the firm's pronouncement was not intended to encourage, but rather to discourage, creativity.[129]

Competitions—indeed even the prize theatrical prologues so popular in the 1820s—continued to be organized through the 1860s. In 1863, Henry Timrod won first prize for his "Address Delivered at the Opening of the New Theatre in Richmond." In 1867, likewise, Paul Hamilton Hayne won a hundred dollar premium from *Southern Opinion*, for the best poem concerning the Civil War. On reading it, Timrod wrote him: "It is a very noble production indeed—quite worthy of the crown—but may I be so frank as to tell you that its excellence seems to me rather rhetorical than poetical. This fault, however, belongs to all prize poems,—to mine, I think, in far greater degree than your own. The poet cannot draw his purest and subtlest strains except from his unremunerated heart."[130] In contrasting the works produced by the remunerated poet and those that came from his unremunerated heart, and by placing more value on the works for which one was *not* paid, and for which one did *not* win prizes, Timrod revealed the emergence of a new attitude toward competitions best summarized in Pierre Bourdieu's elegant phrase, the "loser wins." As Bourdieu explains, the later nineteenth century saw a reaction against the dominance of the marketplace and a rejection—indeed an inversion—of its values.[131] Literary competitions had been established in order to create a venue parallel to, yet free from the corruptions of, the marketplace, and as such they were embraced by writers; when competitions became indistinguishable from the market itself, winning the prizes ceased to be a token of prestige and became, as Timrod suggested, a form of selling out. To make little or no money—indeed, to lose money—became a sign of cultural distinction. It was the very triumph of the marketplace, ironically, that gave rise to the ideology of amateurism upon which narratives of professionalization were built. In these narratives, professionalism grew out of, and displaced, amateurism. Amateurism, however, did not precede professionalism and the dominance of the marketplace; it was invented by them. My goal in writing this book has been to restore the complexity to authorial history that such narratives have suppressed and put amateurism back where it belongs, in the later nineteenth century.

Epilogue

From the Business of Letters to the
Profession of Authorship

≈

Throughout this book, I have been arguing that authors in antebellum America participated in a world of multiple and deeply embedded economies, and that over the course of this period, those economies progressively, although unevenly, disembedded. This is not to say, of course, that there are not still multiple economies available to authors (there are), nor that they are not, to a greater or lesser degree embedded (this is true also), only that the extent, variety, and significance of these multiple embedded economies has diminished. One of the places where multiple embedded authorial economies persist, however, is within the world of modern academic research and scholarly publishing, a subject I have been obliged to research, so to speak, even as I researched the worlds of nineteenth-century authorial economies. The economics of academic publishing is a phenomenon that has recently garnered a great deal of attention, from both a practical and scholarly perspective, but that still sometimes engenders misapprehension. James J. O'Donnell, for example, has talked of the "unbudgeted or underbudgeted costs" of publishing in the modern academic world, where "the university pays a faculty member to do research and write an article . . . then allows the faculty member to give the article away . . . to a commercial publisher who then sells it back to the university in a journal."[1]

While the irony observed by O'Donnell is, from a strictly financial point of view, irrefutable, his account neglects to mention the remarkable alchemy by which this ostensibly irrational series of economic transactions converts financial capital into cultural capital—in the form of books and other research materials for the scholar—and then into symbolic capital, in the form of prestige for the author, as well as for the school that provided the funds in the first place. It misses, too, especially if the scholar is in the humanities, the fact that in passing through and engaging in these various economic transactions, he or she very likely accumulates social capital that creates and sustains a number of reciprocal indebtednesses and other connections. The act of publishing a book or journal article will entail gratitude to a departmental chair or dean for research funds, for example; it entails patronage for graduate students and research assistants who assist directly or otherwise in the project and who will require letters of recommendation; it begins with overtures to editors of journals or acquisitions editors for university presses who, having published a piece, might ask the author to review manuscripts for the journal or press in the future; and it demands kudos for one's colleagues and those who have assisted in the research, and who expect offprints or presentation copies of books as acknowledgment. Whatever else it is, and whatever else it costs or pays, the act of academic authorship is markedly socially embedded and embedding.

Although little formal scholarship has, to my knowledge, been undertaken on the phenomenon of embedded economies deployed by modern academics, such practices are clearly advocated in handbooks for young scholars. One author suggests that neophyte academics purchase 100 offprints of each article they publish to facilitate networking, a strategy that recalls the acts of Thomas Willis White, of the *Southern Literary Messenger*, while another, using an explicitly economic analogy, counsels recent PhDs to write to those who assisted them in completing their dissertations, noting that "Thank-you notes are one of the major currencies of networking." She also makes it quite clear that gifting one's work-in-progress facilitates embedding, suggesting: "If you have an article draft, try it out on some new colleagues to build network connections." The language of networks may not be Polanyian, but the sentiment surely is.[2]

Such embedded and embedding practices are not simply advocated by scholars, however, but are practiced widely, if unselfconsciously, by most in the academy, as a glance at almost any academic memoir makes clear. In *Beyond the Tenure Track* (1991), for example, a memoir that covers fifteen busy months of his long teaching career, English professor James Phelan records several instances of his participation in a patronage economy, noting his gratification at receiving "a very nice gift—a well-preserved old copy of *Pride and Prejudice*—along with a gracious note" from one of his favorite graduate students, as well as his disappointment at not receiving a bound copy of an MA thesis from a student whose work he had directed. He also switches roles from patron to client, when one of his former graduate school professors at the University of Chicago offers to pass his recently completed manuscript on to the University of Chicago Press for consideration. And he observes the perpetuation of patron-client relationships among others in ways that remind one of the advice books cited above, when he recalls an assistant professor in his department being advised to "share his work more widely among his colleagues" if he wishes to secure tenure. Other economies also appear in his account. The competition economy with its multiple fungible and non-fungible prizes also shows up, for example, when his favorite graduate student enters a university-sponsored competition and "wins the $500 prize, the respect of the outside judges, and publication in a volume of proceedings." And while Phelan is happy to dispense and receive the fruits of patronage, and observe competitions, he also notes his discomfort at receiving a gift from the students in one of his graduate classes ("a token of their gratitude for the course and their esteem for my teaching") and struggles to pen an appropriate thank you note with which to neutralize the debt the embarrassing gift entails. Even his terms for academic conversation, "give-and-take" and "mutual exchange," reflect his tacit appreciation for the protocols of balanced reciprocity that one associates with barter and gift-giving. Although Phelan never analyzes any of these transactions qua transaction—his self-conscious reflections on the economics of being a professor, although astute, are strictly limited to discussions of salaries and course-loads—the existence of multiple embedded economies is apparent throughout his narrative.[3]

Although almost any modern academic memoir offers similar examples, I draw from Phelan's because he has spent his career teaching at Ohio State University, arriving in 1977, just a little more than a decade after William Charvat's untimely death there in 1966. A comparison of Phelan's experiences and Charvat's is instructive, for when we examine Charvat's personal papers it becomes apparent that he, like Phelan, participated in, yet failed to analyze formally, a variety of authorial economies. While these multiple economies may not have informed the *content* of his writings on antebellum authorship, that is to say, they certainly shaped the way those writings were undertaken. Indeed, the great irony is that Charvat, who offered such a flattened and desocialized model of authorship, understood the social dimensions and the multiple economies of authorial practice intimately.

Charvat had a keen appreciation for the protocols of balanced reciprocity, for example, and since so much of his research was based on manuscript materials that were still being recovered from private collections, he was drawn into a wide circle of scholars who shared their archival findings with one another in a tit-for-tat fashion akin to gift exchange, or perhaps bartering. Sending a collection of his handwritten and typed notes on Melville to John H. Birss, he explained: "I have swapped material with practically all of the scholars who are doing biographies, letters, and bibliographies for the nineteenth century." That such trading created a sense of community is suggested by his use, in the subsequent sentence, of the first person plural: "We all feel that since our jobs are pretty well-defined it doesn't matter very much who prints or uses a particular document first." Charvat also went on to note that only one major scholar of antebellum literature refused to share his notes and transcriptions with others prior to publication, and that such a policy was "indefensible." Birss concurred, offering a firm denunciation of negative, and a clear defense of balanced, reciprocity. "If a chap is cooperative and not all 'gimme,'" he wrote, "I like to exchange and keep my eyes peeled for leads that may help him." Others felt the same way. "You have been most helpful to me," one scholar told Charvat, in the characteristically parallel syntax that so often accompanied balanced reciprocity, "and I hope you may find these remarks of service to you." Participating in such reciprocal exchanges, Charvat was drawn into an embedded knowledge economy that generated collegiality even as it facilitated scholarship.[4]

It was also something that he advocated to other scholars. Writing to Gay Wilson Allen, who was working on a biography of Walt Whitman, Charvat offered, with a revealing economic metaphor, to "contribute my mite to your heroic enterprise," and he went on to suggest that, "if it would not be too expensive you might unearth a lot of Whitman letters by circulating a mimeographed checklist such as Ostrom got out on Poe." Charvat's point was that if Allen was willing to make a gift of his checklist to scholars, they would be happy to reciprocate by sharing their own findings, making his list yet more useful and yet more worth circulating.[5]

If research notes and transcriptions of primary documents were the currency exchanged by authors of work in progress, then offprints were coin of the realm for settling one's scholarly debts once that work was completed. Over the course of his career, Charvat received and sent innumerable offprints, the bestowal and receipt of which honored debts incurred and, at the same time, solidified relationships.[6] Presentation copies were likewise exchanged. Writing to Charvat after the first two volumes of his edition of James Fenimore Cooper's letters had been published, James Beard wondered if Harvard University Press had sent him "a complimentary set, as I requested."[7]

Bestowing presentation copies did not always operate within a horizontal, gift-like economy, however. When he published his *Literary Publishing in America, 1790–1850* in 1959, for example, Charvat engaged in a number of other embedded and embedding transactions. He enacted a very traditional ritual of authorial clientage, for example, in dedicating his work to his dissertation director, Arthur Hobson Quinn, to whom he sent an inscribed copy. In a similar vein, he also sent a copy to the Guggenheim Foundation, which had served as an institutional patron by providing him with a prestigious Fellowship in 1943. The copy sent to a younger Ohio State colleague—Roy Harvey Pearce—was, by way of contrast, taken by the recipient in the spirit of an act of patronage. ("I've tried to learn from you," wrote Pearce. "But the test will come fifteen or so years from now, when I am in your position.") Many other copies of his own book—he gave away more than twenty, gratis—were part of the more pervasive gift economy that circulated offprints and research notes. Charvat not only saved all the thank you notes (and reviews) he received but also kept a checklist indicating who had, and who had not, responded. Indeed, copies of Charvat's books even came to generate bridging social capital, with one colleague requesting "2 or 3 to use nefariously," presumably as gifts for yet other academics with whom he wished to put Charvat in contact.[8]

Charvat's practice of participating in vertical as well as horizontal exchanges within his institution was by no means unique; indeed, it was the norm at Ohio State. Charvat's colleague, Richard Altick, describing the departmental culture of the 1940s and 1950s, recalled hearing that at "some universities . . . interaction between young and veteran faculty mostly took the limited form of inscribed copies of journal articles or first books, judiciously distributed. We did this too . . . But we also read one another's manuscripts and frankly critiqued them." It was such authorial exchanges, Altick believed, that promoted his colleagues' "easy sociability" and "contributed to our outside reputation as an exceptionally harmonious department."[9]

Charvat clearly appreciated the harmony such exchanges facilitated, but he was also mindful of the sometimes problematic consequences they entailed. When Jay Hubbell, as a "slight token of appreciation," dedicated an anthology to him, it was, Charvat told him, "one of the nicest things that has happened to me in a long time." Yet he also felt distinctly awkward about the sorts of obligations this sort of patron-client relationship engendered. While he promised to suggest to his colleagues that they adopt the anthology for their classes, he hoped "no one will notice the dedication, lest they see some connection between it & my evaluation of the book!" Indeed, Charvat was subsequently responsible for "a departmental rule that faculty could not require students to buy texts they had written."[10]

Charvat, in fact, was the co-author of several college textbooks and anthologies himself and also edited at least one edition of Hawthorne's *The Scarlet Letter* for a trade press, yet even when dealing with commercial publishers, he sometimes evinced an appreciation for the sort of embedded and embedding economies that recalled antebellum practice. Thus, just as antebellum historian William Hickling Prescott (about whom Charvat wrote extensively) confessed that he felt "bound in honor and disposed to give . . . preference" to publishers Little & Brown, because he had a prior relationship with them, so Charvat in discussing his history of professional authorship with an editor at Houghton Mifflin, told her that he had "felt, almost from the beginning of my project, that I owed a special debt to your company, and that I was almost honor-bound to give you the refusal of it first." The editors with whom Charvat communicated sought to draw him into yet another authorial economy with antebellum antecedents, sending him brochures and fliers for book competitions, such as that co-organized by publishers Macmillan, together with the Modern Language Association, which offered a "five hundred dollar cash prize in addition to all the royalties payable under the Company's usual contract."[11]

Given the number of authorial economies in which Charvat participated, and on which he commented, one wonders why he did not draw connections between what he practiced and what he studied. How, for example, could Charvat have echoed Prescott almost word for word, in his dealings with a publisher, yet never have recognized the role played by economies of obligation when he himself wrote about Prescott? How could he have participated in authorial patronage relationships and not seen that Hawthorne had also? How was it that he engaged in authorial gift exchange yet ignored it as an operating principle in his seminal discussion of puffing and book promotion? How could he have been invited to submit a book manuscript to compete for a cash prize and never have noticed that so many of the authors about whom he wrote had entered such competitions also? Why, in a nutshell, was Charvat so exclusively and admiringly concerned with professionalism?

The answer, I believe, lies in the circumstances of Charvat's own life and career. The son of Czechoslovakian immigrants, Charvat (b. 1905) endured a childhood of considerable privation. After his father left his mother in 1909, Charvat was placed in an orphanage for two years, before his mother, who worked first as a live-in maid in Manhattan and then in a thread mill, was able to reclaim him. The separation from his mother, and the poverty that caused it, traumatized Charvat deeply; indeed, his daughter Cathy explains that he "struggled with that experience the rest of his life." Precarious finances would also continue to dog Charvat throughout his career, and his daughter Judy recalled that her parents were "generally anxious about money." While the family were never straitened, they were, according to Cathy, "quite frugal without making a big deal of it."[12]

For Charvat's close contemporary, Richard Altick, "the crucial test of a scholar's devotion" was "his indifference to the rewards, in rank and salary, that his publications bring him," but this was a luxury that Charvat could not afford. In a family in which "talk of the Depression still colored everything," Charvat came to associate success—and by implication professionalism—with a steady, substantial income. Charvat's own writings were, for him, a crucial source of income. Indeed, the income from a single textbook put his children through college.[13] Even his never-completed study of professional authorship was conceived of as a "semi-popular scholarly work" for a more profitable trade press, "with perhaps separate publication, by a University Press, of important documents—contracts, sales, records, etc." For Charvat, in fact, financial concerns often drove his academic and scholarly practices. Writing to an editor at Houghton Mifflin for whom he had edited a trade paperback of *The Scarlet Letter* in 1962, he asked to "receive the advance as soon as you can send it without stretching company policy," explaining that while a forthcoming visiting professorship at the University of Madrid would give him "plenty of pesetas . . . for the next few months the strain on my dollar commitments at home will be pretty rough." A decade earlier, while negotiating for a visiting professorship at the University of Copenhagen, he had apologized to a State Department official for seeming "importunate about money," explaining "I have just bought a house and I feel the burden of having to pay for it."[14]

Charvat's concern to meet his mortgage payments and enjoy the stability of suburban life in Columbus not only shaped such professional activities as his pursuit of visiting academic appointments and his own authorship of various books; it also very directly shaped his conception of what antebellum professional authors wanted too. Indeed, it is here that I believe we see the roots of both his admiration for authorial professionalization, and his dislike of both amateurs and hacks alike. The for-profit, cash-based, market-located economy—*the* economy—seemed eminently real and eminently consequential to Charvat personally. The various non-monetary economies of gift exchange, patronage, and competition, while no less real, doubtless struck him as less consequential and less—indeed, not at all—economic. The need for money and the security it afforded doubtless struck him as irreducibly real and unproblematically transhistorical in ways that confounded present and past, personal and academic, professorial and professional. The projection of his own personal ambitions for house and home onto his historical subjects, and perhaps a veiled reference to his impoverished childhood, is seen most clearly in an unpublished portion of his book, where he wrote that "in a democracy the writing of belles lettres cannot be called a profession . . . until writers are able to support themselves by writing—not occasionally, but year in and year out; not in the traditional garret of Grub Street, complete with rats and cockroaches, but in urban or suburban respectability, complete with family and mortgage." It is difficult, when reading this formula not to believe that Charvat was writing as much about his own memories and aspirations as he was of those in the nineteenth century.[15]

The greatest irony, however, is not how anachronistic Charvat was being in defining authorial aspirations in such a manner, but that one is able to find an antebellum antecedent who defined his authorial ambitions in almost the same way, wishing for money in order to secure "suburban respectability, complete with family and mortgage." Thus my study ends, as it began, by invoking that most cynical and disembedded of all antebellum authors, Nathaniel P. Willis, who wrote to Moses Brown Ives of Rhode Island in 1844 that he had just written a "Lecture on Fashion" that he wished to deliver in Providence, and preferably to a capacity audience. "Frankly speaking," said Willis, "I wish to transform this lecture into mahogany & upholstery, as I have lately gone to housekeeping & require the *Extra* to make up the gap of furnishing."[16] Charvat, doubtless, would have approved.

It is sobering to consider that the most influential academic formulation of American authorial history in the twentieth century might have been a result of Charvat's mortgage payment anxieties, rather than a reflection of antebellum reality, but academic research is never conducted in a vacuum. If there is anything to take away from the example of Charvat, with his curious juxtaposition of blindness and insight, it is that our attempts to understand the past—its aspirations, its economies—will always, to a greater or less extent, be a product of the present and its needs. Mindful as I have tried to be of my own historical situatedness, and my own embedded subjectivity, it is doubtless true of this book too. About the business of letters, a great deal can be said; about the business of *The Business of Letters* much still remains to be discovered.

Notes

Notes

Introduction

1. Henry James, *The Art of the Novel: Critical Prefaces* (N.Y.: Charles Scribner's Sons, 1934), 5.

2. See Phillip H. Round, *By Nature and by Custom Cursed: Transatlantic Civil Discourse and New England Cultural Production, 1620–1660* (Hanover: Univ. Press of New England, 1999), 153–204; Michael Anesko, *"Friction with the Market": Henry James and the Profession of Authorship* (Oxford: Oxford Univ. Press, 1986); Stuart M. Blumin, *The Emergence of the Middle Class: Social Experience in the American City, 1760–1900* (Cambridge: Cambridge Univ. Press, 1989), 316 n 42.

3. Leah Price, "Introduction: Reading Matter," *PMLA* 121 (2006): 10. Price is summarizing a question posed by Peter D. McDonald, "Implicit Structures and Explicit Interactions: Pierre Bourdieu and the History of the Book," *Library* 6th Ser. 19 (1997): 105–121.

4. See Robert Scholes, *Textual Power: Literary Theory and the Teaching of English* (New Haven: Yale Univ. Press, 1985), 33.

5. The anthropology-history-criticism nexus emerges from Clifford Geertz, *The Interpretation of Cultures* (N.Y.: Basic, 1973); Geertz, *Local Knowledge: Further Essays in Interpretive Anthropology* (N.Y.: Basic, 1983), esp. 19–35; Robert Darnton, *The Great Cat Massacre and Other Episodes in French Cultural History* (Harmondsworth: Penguin, 1985); Roger Chartier, "Text, Symbols, and Frenchness," *Journal of Modern History* 57 (1985): 682–695; and Darnton, "The Symbolic Element in History," *Journal of Modern History* 58 (1986): 218–234. The phenomenon of a discipline reappropriating—sometimes inadvertently—its own already appropriated methodology is anatomized by David A. Hollinger, "T. S. Kuhn's Theory of Science and Its Implications for History," in *In the American Province: Studies in the History and Historiography of Ideas* (Bloomington: Indiana Univ. Press, 1985), 105–129.

6. The objections to commodity histories as written have been laid out convincingly by Bruce Robbins, "Commodity Histories," *PMLA* 120 (2005): 454–463.

7. Gregory H. Nobles, "Commerce and Community: A Case Study of the Rural Broommaking Business in Antebellum Massachusetts," *Journal of the Early*

Republic 4 (1984): 287–308; Laurel Thatcher Ulrich, *The Age of Homespun: Objects and Stories in the Creation of an American Myth* (N.Y.: Vintage, 2001), 340–373.

8. [Samuel Kettell], "Biography of a Broomstick," in *Yankee Notions: A Medley* 2d. edn. (Boston: Otis, Broaders, 1838), 34–65, viii (quotation).

9. For newspaper linings, see *A Key into the Language of Woodsplint Baskets*, ed. Ann McMullen and Russell G. Handsman (Washington, Conn.: American Indian Archaeological Institute, 1987), 30, 88–89, 94, 100, 110–111, 116; and Ulrich, *Age of Homespun*, 341–342, 352–353.

10. For the ways in which readers invested printed materials with emotional significance, see Ronald J. Zboray and Mary Saracino Zboray, "Books, Reading, and the World of Goods in Antebellum New England," *American Quarterly* 48 (1996): 587–622.

11. On the Market Revolution, see, inter alia, Charles Sellers, *The Market Revolution: Jacksonian America, 1815–1846* (Oxford: Oxford Univ. Press, 1991); *The Market Revolution in America: Social, Political, and Religious Expressions, 1800–1880*, ed. Melvyn Stokes and Stephen Conway (Charlottesville: Univ. Press of Virginia, 1996); and *Cultural Change and the Market Revolution in America, 1789–1860*, ed. Scott C. Martin (Lanham: Rowman and Littlefield, 2005).

12. Brook Thomas, *The New Historicism and Other Old-Fashioned Topics* (Princeton: Princeton Univ. Press, 1991), 20.

Chapter One

1. K.K., "The Profession of Authorship," *American Monthly Magazine* 1 (December 1829): 589–598 (quotations 589, 591, 592).

2. Nathaniel P. Willis to Sarah Josepha Hale, 14 December [1829], Letters to Sarah Josepha Hale, HM 6867, The Huntington Library, San Marino, Calif.

3. Nathaniel P. Willis to George James Pumpelly, 4 February 1829, quoted in Stewart Desmond, "The Widow's Trials: The Life of Fanny Fern" (PhD diss., New York University, 1988), 41.

4. John Neal to John Greenleaf Whittier, 4 September 1829, John Greenleaf Whittier Papers, used by permission of the Phillips Library of the Peabody Essex Museum, Salem.

5. Charvat was undoubtedly familiar with K.K.'s essay, since the *American Monthly Magazine*, in which it appeared, was one of the periodicals he explored thoroughly in his doctoral dissertation, later revised and published as *The Origins of American Critical Thought, 1810–1835* (Philadelphia: Univ. of Pennsylvania Press, 1936), esp. 28, 195–196.

6. William Charvat, *Literary Publishing in America, 1790–1850* (Philadelphia: Univ. of Pennsylvania Press, 1959); *The Profession of Authorship in America, 1800–1870: The Papers of William Charvat*, ed. Matthew J. Bruccoli (Columbus: Ohio State Univ. Press, 1968), esp. 3–48 (quotation 48); "Literature as Business," in *Literary History of the United States* ed. Robert E. Spiller, et al. (N.Y.: Macmillan, 1948), 2:953–968 (quotations 966, 967–968).

7. For Charvat's late disavowal of his socioeconomic approach to authorship, see *Literary Publishing in America*, 7–8.

8. Lawrence Buell, "Transcendentalist Literary Legacies," in *Transient and Permanent: The Transcendentalist Movement and Its Contexts*, ed. Charles Capper and Conrad Edick Wright (Boston: Massachusetts Historical Society, 1999), 616 n 3; Cathy N. Davidson, "Toward a History of Books and Readers," in *Reading in America: Literature and Social History*, ed. Davidson (Baltimore: Johns Hopkins Univ. Press, 1989), 20; David Leverenz, *Manhood and the American Renaissance* (Ithaca: Cornell Univ. Press, 1989), 14; Michele Moylan and Lane Stiles, "Introduction" in *Reading Books: Essays on the Material Text and Literature in America*, ed. Moylan and Stiles (Amherst: Univ. of Massachusetts Press, 1996), 3, 4; Michael Newbury, *Figuring Authorship in Antebellum America* (Stanford: Stanford Univ. Press, 1997), 5; R. Jackson Wilson, *Figures of Speech: American Writers and the Literary Marketplace, from Benjamin Franklin to Emily Dickinson* (N.Y.: Alfred A. Knopf, 1989), xiii; and Richard F. Teichgraeber III, *Sublime Thoughts / Penny Wisdom: Situating Emerson and Thoreau in the American Market* (Baltimore: Johns Hopkins Univ. Press, 1995), 157 n 4. The papers from the Ohio State University conference were published as *Reciprocal Influences: Literary Production, Distribution, and Consumption in America*, ed. Steven Fink and Susan S. Williams (Columbus: Ohio State Univ. Press, 1999).

9. For recurrent emphases on the professionalization of authorship in this important work, see Michael T. Gilmore, "The Literature of the Revolutionary and Early National Periods," in *The Cambridge History of American Literature: 1590–1820*, ed. Sacvan Bercovitch (Cambridge: Cambridge Univ. Press, 1994), 544–547, 552–554, 560, 583–584, 600–602, 611, 615, 625, 659, 661, 668, 684, 690; and Michael Davit Bell, "Conditions of Literary Vocation," in *The Cambridge History of American Literature: 1820–1865*, ed. Sacvan Bercovitch (Cambridge: Cambridge Univ. Press, 1995), 11–123, passim. Each author's work is, in all other respects, outstanding.

10. Leverenz, *Manhood and the American Renaissance*, 89.

11. Works that adopt and refine Charvat's narrative to accommodate for women authors but leave his focus on professionalism essentially uncontested include Mary Kelley, *Private Women, Public Stage: Literary Domesticity in Nineteenth-Century America* (Oxford: Oxford Univ. Press, 1984); Geraldine Moyle, "The Tenth Muse Lately Sprung Up in the Marketplace: Women and Professional Authorship in Nineteenth-Century America" (PhD diss., University of California, Los Angeles, 1985); Susan Coultrap-McQuin, *Doing Literary Business: American Women Writers in the Nineteenth Century* (Chapel Hill: Univ. of North Carolina Press, 1990); and Wendy Ripley, "Women Working at Writing: Achieving Professional Status in Nineteenth-Century America" (PhD diss., George Washington University, 1996). All of them are, nonetheless, excellent. Notes in the William Charvat Papers at Ohio State University suggest that he had planned to discuss Catharine Sedgwick and E. D. E. N. Southworth in his never-completed book.

12. I quote here, with many thanks, from Paul C. Gutjahr to Leon Jackson,

20 June 2002. Two recent exceptions to his observation are Meredith L. McGill, *American Literature and the Culture of Reprinting, 1834–1853* (Philadelphia: Univ. of Pennsylvania Press, 2003); Ronald J. Zboray and Mary Saracino Zboray, *Literary Dollars and Social Sense: A People's History of the Mass Market Book* (London: Routledge, 2005). By focusing not on the creative acts of authors and their subsequent commercialization but on the commercial re-creation of texts beyond their authorized contexts, McGill is able to reconceive of literary economics in a wholly new light. McGill dispenses with Charvat's "professionalization of authorship" paradigm, that is, because she dispenses with authorship altogether. Zboray and Zboray's account of authorial practices in the antebellum period challenges quite categorically the orthodoxies of Charvat's account, although its focus is less on authorial economies per se and more on the career trajectories of those on "the borderline between amateurism and professionalism" (44).

13. Brigitte Bailey, "Hawthorne and the Author Question," *College English* 57 (1995): 87.

14. On Charvat's flirtation with Marxism, see Michael T. Gilmore, "Politics and the Writer's Career: Two Cases," in *Reciprocal Influences*, 200–201, 207–211.

15. On Progressive historiography, see Richard Hofstadter, *The Progressive Historians: Turner, Beard, Parrington* (N.Y.: Alfred A. Knopf, 1968); and Gene Wise, *American Historical Explanations: A Strategy for Grounded Inquiry* (Minneapolis: Univ. of Minnesota Press, 1980), 82–107, 179–288.

16. For examples of Charvat's published but uncollected work in the Parringtonian/Progressive vein—tinged with class-based terminology but without ever being specifically Marxist in interpretation—see William Charvat, 'Professor Charvat Replies,' *Science and Society: A Marxian Quarterly* 2 (1938): 259; "Let Us Then Be Up and Doing," *English Journal* 28 (1939): 374–383; "A Course in the History of American Society," *Journal of Higher Education* 11 (1940): 247–251; and review of *The Movement for International Copyright in Nineteenth Century America*, by Aubert J. Clark, *Mississippi Valley Historical Review* 48 (1961): 308–309. In addition to assigning Parrington's *Main Currents* at New York University, Charvat indicated his familiarity with Parrington's work on the Connecticut Wits in *Origins of American Critical Thought*, 4. For a later and slightly more dismissive allusion, see Charvat, *Profession of Authorship*, 132.

17. Charvat, *Profession of Authorship*, 3.

18. See *From Max Weber: Essays in Sociology*, ed. H. H. Gerth and C. Wright Mills (Oxford: Oxford Univ. Press, 1946), 77–128; and, for a valuable exposition, George Ritzer, "Professionalization, Bureaucratization and Rationalization: The Views of Max Weber," *Social Forces* 53 (1975): 627–634. One hears an echo of Weber's conceptual distinction in Charvat's contention that "Civilized society . . . lives off poetry but it rarely allows poets to do so." *Profession of Authorship*, 100.

19. Charvat, *Profession of Authorship*, 68–69.

20. *National Gazette and Literary Register*, 17 January 1829, quoted in David Kaser, *Messrs. Carey & Lea of Philadelphia: A Study in the History of the*

Book Trade (Philadelphia: Univ. of Pennsylvania Press, 1957), 70–71; [George Pope Morris], "Compensation to Authors and Editors," *New-York Mirror*, 30 November 1833. Charvat refers vaguely to a "rumor that in 1836 they paid $30,000 to native writers," but never sought to corroborate or investigate the claim. See *Profession of Authorship*, 79.

21. For monies paid to Cooper and Dewees, see *Cost Book of Carey & Lea, 1825–1838*, ed. David Kaser (Philadelphia: Univ. of Pennsylvania Press, 1963); Kaser, *Messrs. Carey & Lea*, 120.

22. Alexis de Tocqueville, *Democracy in America*, ed. Phillips Bradley (N.Y.: Vintage Books, 1945), 2:64.

23. James Hardie, *An Impartial Account of the Trial of Levi Weeks, for the Supposed Murder of Miss Julianna Elmore Sands* (N.Y.: Printed for M. M'Farland, 1800), v. On Hardie, see Lawrence B. Romaine, "Talk of the Town: New York City, January 1825," *Bulletin of the New York Public Library* 63 (1959): 173–188 (quotation 178); and Rollo G. Silver, "Grub Street in Philadelphia, 1794–1795: More about James Hardie," *Bulletin of the New York Public Library* 64 (1960): 130–142.

24. See Evert A. Duyckinck and George L. Duyckinck, *Cyclopaedia of American Literature* (N.Y.: Charles Scribner, 1856).

25. Charvat, *Profession of Authorship*, 108. See also Charvat, *Literary Publishing in America*, 7–8. For a brief history of American hack writers who lived "off" but not "for" literature, and that is positioned in explicit contrast to Charvat's paradigm, see Ronald Weber, *Hired Pens: Professional Writers in America's Golden Age of Print* (Athens: Ohio Univ. Press, 1997).

26. "Passages in the Lives of Poets," *American Monthly Magazine* 2 (1830): 403. For Hillhouse's complex vocational experiments, see Karen Sue Kauffman, "In the Society of Our Friends: Two Generations of the Hillhouse Family, 1770–1840" (PhD diss., University of Connecticut, 1996), 142–182.

27. See Rhoda Halperin, *The Livelihood of Kin: Making Ends Meet "The Kentucky Way"* (Austin: Univ. of Texas Press, 1990), esp. 19–20. Engaging in multiple livelihood strategies entails more than simply having a main job and several subordinate ones; it involves, rather, an ability to work in several distinct economies simultaneously, whereby no one activity is seen as centrally defining.

28. Jonathan Plummer, *A Sketch of the History of the Life and Adventures of Jonathan Plummer, Junr. Written by Himself* (Newburyport: Printed by Blunt and March, 1796), 132–133. Plummer's will is quoted in John J. Currier, *History of Newburyport, Mass., 1764–1909* (Newburyport: Printed for the Author, 1909), 438. See also Daniel E. Williams, "Reckoned to Be Almost a Natural Fool: Textual Self-Construction in the Writings of Jonathan Plummer—No Hermaphrodite," *Early American Literature* 33 (1998): 149–164. For another striking endorsement of the composite occupational lifestyle, see John Neal, *Wandering Recollections of a Somewhat Busy Life* (Boston: Roberts Brothers, 1869), 392–393.

29. Julius H. Ward, *The Life and Letters of James Gates Percival* (Boston: Ticknor and Fields, 1866), 19. For Percival's "fickleness," see Nathaniel P. Wil-

lis to George James Pumpelly, [ca. 1828], quoted in Thomas N. Baker, *Sentiment and Celebrity: Nathaniel Parker Willis and the Trials of Literary Fame* (Oxford: Oxford Univ. Press, 1999), 202 n 15.

30. Percival to James Lawrence Yvonnet, 11 June 1822, in Ward, *Life and Letters of James Gates Percival*, 95–96.

31. On fallacies of false dichotomy, see David Hackett Fischer, *Historians' Fallacies: Toward a Logic of Historical Thought* (N.Y.: Harper and Row, 1970), 9–12. Geoffrey Turnovsky reveals a similar dichotomy in scholarship on French literary authorship in this period in his important essay: "The Enlightenment Literary Market: Rousseau, Authorship, and the Book Trade," *Eighteenth-Century Studies* 26 (2003): 387–410.

32. Robert A. Stebbins, *Amateurs: On the Margin Between Work and Leisure* (Beverly Hills: Sage, 1979), 19–44. While Stebbins points out that professionalism tends to define amateurism, he fails to follow his observation to the conclusion that the two are necessarily mutually constitutive; throughout his study he refers to amateurs having existed before the advent of professionalism.

33. Noah Webster, *American Dictionary of the English Language* (N.Y.: S. Converse, 1828), s.v. amateur, profession. For an outstanding publishing history of Webster's *American Spelling Book*, see E. Jennifer Monaghan, *A Common Heritage: Noah Webster's Blue-Back Speller* (Hamden: Archon Books, 1983). The integrity and consistency of Webster's ideological vision is underscored by Joseph J. Ellis, *After the Revolution: Profiles of Early American Culture* (N.Y.: W. W. Norton, 1979), 161–212.

34. *Massachusetts Journal and Tribune*, 25 December 1830, 3; "The Amateur," *The Amateur: A Semi-Monthly Journal of Literature and the Arts* 1 (1 January 1831): 168.

35. Nathaniel P. Willis to Sarah Eldredge Farrington, n.d., quoted in Joyce W. Warren, *Fanny Fern: An Independent Woman* (New Brunswick: Rutgers Univ. Press, 1992), 93. Fern went by Sarah as well as Sara.

36. "Amateur Authors and Small Critics," *United States Magazine and Democratic Review* 17 (July 1845): 62. In 1843, Edgar Allan Poe had published a series of disparaging reviews in *Graham's Magazine* under the title "Our Amateur Poets." The earliest instance of amateur authorship being defined in strictly economic terms that I have found is in Park Benjamin to John Neal, 3 December 1838, John Neal Papers, Houghton Library, Harvard University.

37. Augustine J. H. Duganne, *Parnassus in Pillory* (Port Washington, N.Y.: Kennikat Press, 1971), 8. Some, of course, embraced the new concept of amateurism readily. Even though he had earned one thousand dollars just for editing the works of Byron in 1832 and was offered—and presumably took—five hundred to write a new canto for his own popular poem, *Fanny*, in 1821, Fitz-Greene Halleck declared in 1859 that he had "ever been but an amateur in the literary orchestra, playing only upon a pocket flute, and never aspiring, even in a dream, to the dignity of the bâton, the double bass, or oboe." Nelson Frederick Adkins, *Fitz-Greene Halleck: An Early Knickerbocker Wit and Poet* (New Haven: Yale Univ. Press, 1930), 248 n 126, 123, 217 (quotation).

38. See Russell Jacoby, *The Last Intellectuals: American Culture in the Age*

of Academe (N.Y.: Farrar, Strauss, and Giroux, 1987), 225–226 (quotation 225). The study was published by Paul William Kingston and Jonathan R. Cole, *The Wages of Writing: Per Word, Per Piece, or Perhaps* (N.Y.: Columbia Univ. Press, 1986).

39. *Baltimore Literary Monument* 2 (August 1839): 154, quoted in Joseph Lawrence Yeatman, "Baltimore Literary Culture, 1815–1840" (PhD diss., University of Maryland, 1983), 189.

40. For ". . . and the marketplace" scholarship, see Michael T. Gilmore, *American Romanticism and the Marketplace* (Chicago: Univ. of Chicago Press, 1985); William G. Rowland, Jr., *Literature and the Marketplace: Romantic Writers and their Audiences in Great Britain and the United States* (Lincoln: Univ. of Nebraska Press, 1996); Wilson, *Figures of Speech: American Writers and the Marketplace from Benjamin Franklin to Emily Dickinson*; Sheila Post-Lauria, *Correspondent Colorings: Melville in the Marketplace* (Amherst: Univ. of Massachusetts Press, 1996); Steven Fink, *Prophet in the Marketplace: Thoreau's Development as a Professional Writer* (Princeton: Princeton Univ. Press, 1992); Teichgraeber, *Sublime Thoughts / Penny Wisdom: Situating Emerson and Thoreau in the American Market*; and Terence Whalen, *Edgar Allan Poe and the Masses: The Political Economy of Literature in Antebellum America* (Princeton: Princeton Univ. Press, 1999). For a trenchant assessment of this type of scholarship and its shortcomings, see C. Deirdre Phelps, "Market Studies and Book History in American Literature," *Review* 12 (1990): 273–301.

41. The most recent work to use the amateur author label, Zboray and Zboray's *Literary Dollars and Social Sense*, defines an amateur as, variously, someone who publishes "sporadically"; someone "unable or unwilling" to live by their pen; or someone "eluding canonization." While the Zborays' work offers an extraordinarily acute and penetrating account of authorial practice in the antebellum period, I find their composite definition of "amateur" authorship problematic, inasmuch as it is made to mean too many distinct things, thereby troubling the already muddy waters of economic taxonomy. See *Literary Dollars and Social Sense*, 233 n 14.

42. Robert Darnton, "What is the History of Books?" in *Reading in America*, 30. Other overviews of the field of book history and print culture that I have found useful include Thomas R. Adams and Nicolas Barker, "A New Model for the Study of the Book," in *A Potencie of Life: Books in Society*, ed. Barker (London: British Library, 1993), 5–43; C. Deirdre Phelps, "Where's the Book? The Text in the Development of Literary Sociology," *Text* 9 (1996): 63–92; and Ronald J. Zboray and Mary Saracino Zboray, *A Handbook for the Study of Book History in the United States* (Washington, D.C.: Library of Congress, 2000).

43. Richard H. Brodhead, *Cultures of Letters: Scenes of Reading and Writing in Nineteenth-Century America* (Chicago: Univ. of Chicago Press, 1993); Robert A. Ferguson, *Law and Letters in American Culture* (Cambridge, Mass.: Harvard Univ. Press, 1984); and Ann Fabian, *The Unvarnished Truth: Personal Narratives in Nineteenth-Century America* (Berkeley: Univ. of California Press, 2000); Lawrence Buell, *New England Literary Culture: From Revolution through Renaissance* (Cambridge: Cambridge Univ. Press, 1986), esp. 375–397. Buell's work

should be supplemented by Paul Joseph Erickson's detailed prosopography of antebellum city-mysteries authors: "Welcome to Sodom: The Cultural Work of City-Mysteries Fiction in Antebellum America" (PhD diss., University of Texas at Austin, 2005), esp. 159–218.

44. For an exceptionally well documented introduction, see Mark Osteen and Martha Woodmansee, "Taking Account of the New Economic Criticism: An Historical Introduction," in *The New Economic Criticism: Studies at the Intersection of Literature and Economics*, ed. Woodmansee and Osteen (London: Routledge, 1999), 3–50.

45. "Pay in Boards," *Freedom's Journal*, 8 August 1828. Since few scholars today will laugh quite as loudly as I did on reading this, a point of clarification is perhaps in order: when publishers advertised a book "in boards," they meant one bound in cheap but durable cardboard covers that could either be left intact or removed and replaced with a more expensive binding. The raftsman's boards, by contrast, are simply lumber planks. See Joseph W. Rogers, "The Rise of American Edition Binding," in *Bookbinding in America: Three Essays*, ed. Hellmut Lehmann-Haupt (N.Y.: R. R. Bowker, 1967), 140–141; and Charvat, *Literary Publishing in America*, 88–89. For a similar sketch on books costing "twenty five dollars in sheep," see "Technical Phrase," *Star Spangled Banner*, 27 July 1850.

46. Buell, *New England Literary Culture*, 335–350.

47. On Russwurm and *Freedom's Journal*, see Jacqueline Bacon, *"Freedom's Journal": The First African American Newspaper* (Lanham: Lexington, 2007). The "bookishness" of the urban African-American elite in this era is underscored by Elizabeth McHenry, *Forgotten Readers: Recovering the Lost History of African American Reading Societies* (Durham: Duke Univ. Press, 2002), 23–140.

48. See Caroline Howard to Anna Maria White, 10 April 1815, quoted in *A Balcony in Charleston*, ed. Mary Scott Saint-Armand (Richmond: Garret and Massie, 1941), 11. For an example of an African-American being handed a forged note to cash, see "Naivete," *Gloucester Telegraph*, 28 June 1828.

49. John Bard McNulty, *Older than the Nation: The Story of the Hartford Courant* (Stonington: Pequot Press, 1964), 30; M. M. Noah, *Marion; Or, The Hero of the Lake* (N.Y.: E. Murden, 1822), 4; John Scott, receipt for the *Burlington Gazette*, 25 May 1847–25 May 1850, Newspaper and Periodical Receipts Collection, 1760–1890, Box 3, Folder 1, American Antiquarian Society. See, for similar examples of bartering for literary wares, Philip F. Gura, "Early Nineteenth-Century Printing in Rural Massachusetts: John Howe of Greenwich and Enfield, c. 1803–1845," in *The Crossroads of American History and Literature* (University Park: Pennsylvania State Univ. Press, 1996), 137–138; and Jack Larkin, "The Merriams of Brookfield: Printing in the Economy of Rural Massachusetts in the Early Nineteenth Century," *Proceedings of the American Antiquarian Society* 96 (1986): 39–73.

50. Nell Irvin Painter, "Thinking about the Languages of Money and Race: A Response to Michael O'Malley, 'Specie and Species,'" *American Historical Review* 99 (1994): 398. In fact, and to pursue the wood motif just a little further, it should be noted that slaves were sometimes even referred to as "*live lumber.*" See "American Slavery," *Genius of Universal Emancipation*, 6 September 1828.

51. For an excellent overview of the variety of currencies in circulation in the

early national and antebellum periods, see Arthur Nussbaum, *A History of the Dollar* (N.Y.: Columbia Univ. Press, 1957), esp. 34–99 (church currencies 42); also George Rogers Taylor, *The Transportation Revolution, 1815–1860* (N.Y.: Harper & Row, 1951), 324–330 (library currencies 327); and, for the antebellum period in particular, William H. Dillistin, *Bank Note Reporters and Counterfeit Detectors, 1826–1866* (N.Y.: American Numismatic Society, 1949), 1–40. On abolitionist coins, see Herbert Aptheker, "Antislavery Medallions in the Martin Jacobowitz Collection," *Negro History Bulletin* 33 (1970): 115–121. The idea that currency circulated "promiscuously" is borrowed from David M. Henkin's fine discussion of paper money in *City Reading: Written Words and Public Spaces in Antebellum New York* (N.Y.: Columbia Univ. Press, 1998), 137–165.

52. See, for example, Daniel Vickers, "Competency and Competition: Economic Culture in Early America," *William and Mary Quarterly* 3d Ser. 47 (1990): 3–29.

53. Careful accountings of authorial income which tend, nonetheless, to focus on cash, include Patricia G. Holland, "Lydia Maria Child as a Nineteenth-Century Professional Author," *Studies in the American Renaissance 1981*, ed. Joel Myerson (Boston: Twayne, 1981), 157–167; J. Albert Robbins, "Mrs. Emma C. Embury's Account Book: A Study of Some Periodical Contributions," *Bulletin of the New York Public Library* 51 (1947): 479–485; Joel Myerson, "Ralph Waldo Emerson's Income from His Books," in *Professions of Authorship: Essays in Honor of Matthew J. Bruccoli*, ed. Richard Layman and Joel Myerson (Columbia: Univ. of South Carolina Press, 1996), 135–149; Wayne Allen Jones, "The Hawthorne-Goodrich Relationship and a New Estimate of Hawthorne's Income from 'The Token,'" *Nathaniel Hawthorne Journal 1975*, ed. C. E. Frazer Clark (Englewood: Microcard Editions Books, 1975), 91–140; G. Thomas Tanselle, "The Sales of Melville's Books," *Harvard Library Bulletin* 17 (1969): 195–215; Ralph M. Aderman, "James Kirke Paulding's Literary Income," *Bulletin of the New York Public Library* 64 (1960): 117–129; John Ward Ostrom, "Edgar Allan Poe: His Income as Literary Entrepreneur," *Poe Studies* 15 (1982): 1–7; Susan Geary, "Mrs. Stowe's Income from the Serial Version of 'Uncle Tom's Cabin,'" *Studies in Bibliography* 29 (1976): 380–382; Earl L. Bradsher, "The Financial Rewards of American Authors," *Sewanee Review* 28 (1920): 186–202; and J. Albert Robbins, "Fees Paid to Authors by Certain Periodicals," *Studies in Bibliography* (1949–50): 94–104.

54. See Viviana Zelizer, *The Social Meaning of Money: Pin Money, Pay Checks, Poor Relief, and Other Currencies* (Princeton: Princeton Univ. Press, 1997), esp. 1–35 (quotation 29); Zelizer, "Payments and Social Ties," *Sociological Forum* 11 (1996): 481–495; and Zelizer, "The Many Enchantments of Money," in *Sociological Visions*, ed. Kai Erikson (Lanham: Rowman and Littlefield, 1997), 83–93.

55. David Everett to Joseph Dennie, 9 May 1797, Joseph Dennie Papers, bMS Am 715 (85), by permission of the Houghton Library, Harvard University. During the economic depression of 1838, at least one hair dresser, Edward Phalon, actually issued his own coins, each good for one hair cut. See Russell Rulau, *The Standard Catalog of Hard Times Tokens: The Most Complete Catalog Ever Assembled of the Coin Substitutes, Merchant Counterstamps, and Satirical Scrip of the Jacksonian Period, 1832–1844* (Iola: Krause Publications, 2001), 86.

56. Playwright Mordecai Noah was not only paid in wood, as we saw above,

but also in books from his publisher's store, while essayist Benjamin Browne Foster received a free subscription to paper in which his writings appeared. See Jonathan D. Sarna, *Jacksonian Jew: The Two Worlds of Mordecai Noah* (N.Y.: Holmes and Meier, 1981), 7; Joseph F. Kett, *The Pursuit of Knowledge Under Difficulties: From Self-Improvement to Adult Education in America, 1750–1990* (Stanford: Stanford Univ. Press, 1994), 48.

57. Frederick Douglass, *My Bondage and My Freedom* (N.Y.: Miller, Orton, and Mulligan, 1855), 424. In a later autobiographical work, Douglass recalled the precise form of payment: "*two silver half dollars.*" Frederick Douglass, *The Life and Times of Frederick Douglass, Written by Himself* (Hartford: Park Publishing, 1881), 210. Augusta Rohrbach has explored the "dynamic use of money as a potent signifier in the slave narrative genre," arguing that references to money—in specific amounts—indicate an emerging realist aesthetic. See *Truth Stranger than Fiction: Race, Realism, and the U.S. Literary Marketplace* (N.Y.: Palgrave, 2002), 35–46 (quotation 44).

58. Merton L. Dillon, *Benjamin Lundy and the Struggle for Negro Freedom* (Urbana: Univ. of Illinois Press, 1966), 118–120 (quotation 118). Other authors who received a dollar from the judicial system include Edgar Allan Poe and Nathaniel P. Willis. Courts sometimes issued awards of a single penny with the same goal of rebuking the plaintiff. See Daniel A. Cohen, "Alvah Kelley's Cow: Household Feuds, Proprietary Rights, and the Charlestown Convent Riot," *New England Quarterly* 74 (2001): 551 and n 30

59. Maurice Bloch and Jonathan Parry, "Introduction: Money and the Morality of Exchange," in *Money and the Morality of Exchange*, ed. Parry and Bloch (Cambridge: Cambridge Univ. Press, 1989), 22.

60. John Davis, *Exchange* (Minneapolis: Univ. of Minnesota Press, 1992), 11, 29.

61. James Raven, "Print for Free: Unsolicited Literature in Comparative Perspective," in *Free Print and Non-Commercial Publishing Since 1700*, ed. Raven (Aldershot: Ashgate, 2000), 9.

62. For ransom: Kathryn Zabelle Derounian-Stodola and James Arthur Levernier, *The Indian Captivity Narrative, 1550–1900* (N.Y.: Twayne, 1993), 16. For bail: George G. Foster to Rufus W. Griswold, 12 March 1835, Rufus W. Griswold Papers, Courtesy of the Trustees of the Boston Public Library. For legacies: Fabian, *Unvarnished Truth*, 56–60, 202 n 24. Although Charvat denied the existence of a patronage system in America, B. R. Brubaker identified at least forty-five authors in the nineteenth century who benefited from government appointments under the so-called "spoils system." See Brubaker, "Spoils Appointments of American Writers," *New England Quarterly* 48 (1975): 556–564.

63. In 1825 and 1826, North Carolina granted Archibald D. Murphey the right to conduct two lotteries to help him fund the writing of a history of the state. See John Samuel Ezell, *Fortune's Merry Wheel: The Lottery in America* (Cambridge, Mass.: Harvard Univ. Press, 1960), 171.

64. Adkins, *Fitz-Greene Halleck*, 248 (Byron), 184 (Sedgwick), 302 (Poe), 243 (Clarke).

65. *Dover Times and Enquirer*, 21 July 1829; Olaudah Equiano, *The 'Inter-*

esting Narrative' and Other Writings, ed. Vincent Caretta (N.Y.: Penguin, 2003), 116–130. On the economic practices of eighteenth-century sailors, see Marcus Rediker, *Between the Devil and the Deep Blue Sea: Merchant Seamen, Pirates, and the Anglo-American Maritime World, 1700–1750* (Cambridge: Cambridge Univ. Press, 1987), 116–152; and, especially, W. Jeffrey Bolster, *Black Jacks: African American Seamen in the Age of Sail* (Cambridge, Mass.: Harvard Univ. Press, 1977), 86–88, 160–161.

66. See Vincent Caretta, " 'Property of Author': Oluadah Equiano's Place in the History of the Book," in *Genius in Bondage: Literature of the Early Black Atlantic*, ed. Vincent Caretta and Philip Gould (Lexington: Univ. Press of Kentucky, 2001), 132–133; and James Green, "The Publishing History of Olaudah Equiano's *Interesting Narrative*," *Slavery and Abolition* 16 (1995): 362–375.

67. See Bruce H. Mann, *Republic of Debtors: Bankruptcy in the Age of American Independence* (Cambridge, Mass.: Harvard Univ. Press, 2002).

68. Robert W. Weathersby, II, *J. H. Ingraham* (Boston: Twayne, 1980), 24. For the four-part typology, see Michael Merrill, "Gifts, Barter, and Commerce in Early America: An Ethnography of Exchange," paper presented at the annual Organization of American Historians conference, April 1985.

69. The now-classic discussion of this Marxist dichotomy is Raymond Williams, "Base and Superstructure in Marxist Cultural Theory," *New Left Review* 82 (1973): 3–16. For two excellent overviews of Bourdieu's work, see David Swartz, *Power and Culture: The Sociology of Pierre Bourdieu* (Chicago: Univ. of Chicago Press, 1997); and Paul DiMaggio, "On Pierre Bourdieu," *American Journal of Sociology* 84 (1979): 1460–1474.

70. Pierre Bourdieu, *Outline of a Theory of Practice*, trans. Richard Nice (Cambridge: Cambridge Univ. Press, 1977), 178.

71. See, especially, Pierre Bourdieu, "The Forms of Capital," in *Handbook of Theory and Research for the Sociology of Education*, ed. J. G. Richardson (N.Y.: Greenwood, 1986): 241–258; and Pierre Bourdieu, "The Purpose of Reflexive Sociology (The Chicago Workshop)," in Pierre Bourdieu and Loïc J. D. Wacquant, *An Invitation to Reflexive Sociology* (Chicago: Univ. of Chicago Press, 1992), 118–119. On cultural and social capital more generally, see Michèle Lamont and Annette Lareau, "Cultural Capital: Allusions, Gaps, and Glissandos in Recent Theoretical Developments," *Sociological Theory* 6 (1988): 153–168; and Michael Woolcock, "Social Capital and Economic Development: Toward a Theoretical Synthesis and Policy Framework," *Theory and Society* 27 (1998): 151–208.

72. [William Leggett], "Eminent Living American Poets," *New-York Mirror*, 26 January 1828.

73. William Tudor, *Letters on the Eastern States* (Boston: Wells and Lilly, 1821), 152–153. On Tudor's connections with the business community see Lewis Simpson, "Boston Ice and Boston Letters," in *The Man of Letters in New England and the South: Essays on the History of the Literary Vocation in America* (Baton Rouge: Louisiana State Univ. Press, 1973), 32–61.

74. "A Comparitive [sic] View of the Utility of Different Branches of Education," *Universal Asylum and Columbian Magazine* 6 (May 1791): 293–294.

75. [William Crafts], "Literary Sparring, No. IV," *Charleston Courier*, re-

printed in Joseph T. Buckingham, *Miscellanies Selected from the Public Journals* (Boston: Joseph T. Buckingham, 1822), 1:109. This authorial attribution is made in a contemporary hand in the copy owned by the Thomas Cooper Library, University of South Carolina.

76. For a learned discussion of the ways in which discourses about language and money have intersected since the Ancient Greeks, see Marc Shell, *The Economy of Literature* (Baltimore: Johns Hopkins Univ. Press, 1978). Shell, however, is decidedly interested in intersection rather than in interconversion.

77. Philip Pendleton Cooke to Rufus W. Griswold, 1 February 1847, Griswold Papers. On Longfellow's education, see Lawrance Thompson, *Young Longfellow (1807–1843)* (N.Y.: Macmillan, 1938). Ronald Story has emphasized more generally the ways in which a degree from Harvard in the nineteenth century provided access to wealth. See *Harvard and the Boston Upper Class: The Forging of an Aristocracy, 1800–1870* (Middletown: Wesleyan Univ. Press, 1980).

78. Swartz, *Power and Culture*, 80.

79. On the publication of Trumbull's poems, see S[amuel] G[riswold] Goodrich, *Recollections of a Lifetime, or Men and Things I Have Seen* (N.Y.: Miller, Orton, and Mulligan, 1857), 2:111–112; J. C. Derby, *Fifty Years among Authors, Books and Publishers* (N.Y.: G. W. Carleton, 1886), 110–111; and Alexander Cowie, *John Trumbull: Connecticut Wit* (Chapel Hill: Univ. of North Carolina Press, 1936), 190–191. Goodrich's loss is discussed by Charvat, *Profession of Authorship*, 9.

80. Pierre Bourdieu, *The Logic of Practice*, trans. Richard Nice (Stanford: Stanford Univ. Press, 1990), 119; Goodrich, *Recollections of a Lifetime*, 2:112. My point is not that Goodrich *set out* to lose money, so much as that his willing and extravagant investment of economic capital in cultural capital accrued him symbolic capital, his financial losses notwithstanding. For Goodrich's increasing prestige in the early 1820s, see the testimonials and letters by John Quincy Adams, Oliver Wolcott, David Hosack, and DeWitt Clinton in the Samuel G. Goodrich Collection, Archives and Special Collections, Amherst College Library.

81. Monaghan, *A Common Heritage*, 95–96 (quotation 96). On charitable donation as capital conversion, see Bourdieu, *Logic of Practice*, 133.

82. Thomas Willis White to Lucian Minor, 15 February 1838, David K. Jackson, "Some Unpublished Letters of T. W. White to Lucian Minor," *Tyler's Quarterly Historical and Genealogical Magazine* 18 (1936): 34. Minor's rare request for payment was a consequence, apparently, of his own pressing debts. See James Norman McKean, "Lucian Minor: Cosmopolitan Virginia Gentleman of the Old School" (MA thesis, College of William and Mary, 1948), 98–99.

83. On pin money, see Zelizer, *The Social Meaning of Money*, 61–66 (quotation 65); and, more generally, Susan Staves, "Pin Money," *Studies in Eighteenth-Century Culture* 14 (1985): 47–77.

84. Two essays examining economic misrepresentation that I have found enormously helpful are Daniel Hack, "Literary Paupers and Professional Authors: The Guild of Literature and Art," *Studies in English Literature, 1500–1900* 39 (1999): 691–713; and Scott A. Sandage, "The Gaze of Success: Failed

Men and the Sentimental Marketplace, 1873–1893," in *Sentimental Men: Masculinity and the Politics of Affect in American Culture*, ed. Mary Chapman and Glenn Hendler (Berkeley: Univ. of California Press, 1999), 181–201.

85. See C. Harvey Gardiner, "Prescott's Most Indispensable Aide: Pascual de Gayangos," *Hispanic American Historical Review* 39 (1959): 81–115.

86. See Ann Fabian, "Speculation on Distress: The Popular Discourse of the Panics of 1837 and 1857," *Yale Journal of Criticism* 3 (1989): 127–142; and Joseph Fichtelberg, *Critical Fictions: Sentiment and the American Market, 1780–1870* (Athens: Univ. of Georgia Press, 2003).

87. Charvat, *Literary Publishing in America*, 7.

88. Regenia Gagnier, *The Insatiability of Human Wants: Economics and Aesthetics in Market Society* (Chicago: Univ. of Chicago Press, 2000), 10.

89. For major statements on Formalist economic anthropology, see Raymond Firth, *Primitive Polynesian Economy* (London: Routledge, 1939); Melville J. Herskovits, *Economic Anthropology: A Study of Comparative Economics* (N.Y.: Knopf, 1952); Robins Burling, "Maximization Theories and the Study of Economic Anthropology," *American Anthropologist* 64 (1962): 802–821; E. Edward LeClair, "Economic Theory and Economic Anthropology," *American Anthropologist* 64 (1962): 1179–1203; and Scott Cook, "The Obsolete 'Anti-Market' Mentality: A Critique of the Substantivist Approach to Economic Anthropology," *American Anthropologist* 68 (1966): 323–345.

90. The key Substantivist manifesto is Karl Polanyi, "The Economy as Instituted Process," in *Primitive, Archaic, and Modern Economies: Essays of Karl Polanyi*, ed. George Dalton (Garden City: Doubleday and Company, 1968), 139–174. I have also found useful Polanyi, *The Great Transformation: The Political and Economic Origins of Our Time* (Boston: Beacon Press, 1957); Polanyi, *The Livelihood of Man*, ed. Harry W. Pearson (N.Y.: Academic Press, 1977), esp. 5–74; George Dalton, "Economic Theory and Primitive Society," *American Anthropologist* 63 (1961): 1–25; and Marshall Sahlins, *Stone Age Economics* (N.Y.: Aldine de Gruyter, 1972), 4 (quotation).

91. Using parallel methodologies and a distinct archive, Zboray and Zboray arrive at essentially the same conclusions, although what I call embedded authorial economies, they, following Margaret J. M. Ezell, refer to as "social authorship." See *Literary Dollars and Social Sense*; and Ezell, *Social Authorship and the Advent of Print* (Baltimore: Johns Hopkins Univ. Press, 1999).

92. Indeed, one of the criticisms sometimes leveled at Bourdieu is that his theories leave little room for change, especially as it is effected by individuals. See, for example, Scott Lash, "Pierre Bourdieu: Cultural Economy and Social Change," in *Bourdieu: Critical Perspectives*, ed. Craig Calhoun, Edward LiPuma, and Moishe Postone (Chicago: Univ. of Chicago Press, 1993), 193–211.

93. For the ways in which the household has functioned in social fact, political theory, and cultural fantasy, see Vincent P. Pecora, *Households of the Soul* (Baltimore: Johns Hopkins Univ. Press, 1997). For the "invisibility" of domestic work, I am indebted to Jeanne Boydston, although it should be noted that her argument is that women's labor became *increasingly* invisible over the course of

the nineteenth century as men's became less so. See Boydston, *Home and Work: Household, Wages, and the Ideology of Labor in the Early Republic* (Oxford: Oxford Univ. Press, 1990), 18–21, 26–29, 142–163.

94. Marcel Mauss, *The Gift: Forms and Functions of Exchange in Archaic Societies*, trans. Ian Cunnison (N.Y.: W. W. Norton, 1967), 1.

95. Polanyi, *Great Transformation*, 57. It is almost de rigueur, unfortunately, for scholars to equate embeddedness with situatedness, even though this is categorically *not* what Polanyi meant by the term. See, for noted misappropriations, Mark Granovetter, "Economic Action and Social Structure: The Problem of Embeddedness," *American Journal of Sociology* 91 (1985): 481–510; Granovetter, "The Old and the New Economic Sociology: A History and an Agenda," in *Beyond the Marketplace: Rethinking Economy and Society*, ed. Roger Friedland and A. F. Robertson (N.Y.: Aldine de Gruyter, 1990), 89–112; Alberto Martinelli, "The Economy as an Institutional Process," *Telos* 73 (1987): 131–146; John Lie, "Embedding Polanyi's Market Society," *Social Perspectives* 34 (1991): 219–235; João Rodrigues, "Endogenous Preferences and Embeddedness: A Reappraisal of Karl Polanyi," *Journal of Economic Issues* 38 (2004): 189–200; and Bernard Barber, "All Economics Are 'Embedded': The Career of a Concept, and Beyond," *Social Research* 62 (1995): 388–413. For an excellent discussion of the ways in which scholars have distorted Polanyi's meaning in their treatment of embeddedness, see Greta R. Krippner, "The Elusive Market: Embeddedness and the Paradigm of Economic Sociology," *Theory and Society* 30 (2001): 775–810.

96. The signature essays on this world are: Michael Merrill, "Cash Is Good to Eat: Self-Sufficiency and Exchange in the Rural Economy of the United States," *Radical History Review* 3 (1977): 42–71; James A. Henretta, "Families and Farms: *Mentalité* in Pre-Industrial America," *William and Mary Quarterly* 3d Ser. 35 (1978): 3–32; and Christopher Clark, "Household Economy, Market Exchange, and the Rise of Capitalism in the Connecticut Valley, 1800–1860," *Journal of Social History* 13 (1979): 169–189. For an explicitly Polanyian account, see James A. Henretta, "The 'Market' in the Early Republic," *Journal of the Early Republic* 18 (1998): 289–304.

97. Scholarship on the "transition to capitalism debate" is voluminous. The key arguments are staked out in Winifred B. Rothenberg, "The Market and Massachusetts Farmers, 1750–1855," *Journal of Economic History* 41 (1981): 283–314; Allan Kulikoff, "The Transition to Capitalism in Rural America," *William and Mary Quarterly* 3d Ser. (1989): 120–144; Christopher Clark, "Economics and Culture: Opening Up the Rural History of the Early American Northeast," *American Quarterly* 43 (1991): 279–301; Michael Merrill, "Putting 'Capitalism' in Its Place: A Review of Recent Literature," *William and Mary Quarterly* 3d Ser. 52 (1995): 315–326; Paul A. Gilje, "The Rise of Capitalism in the Early Republic," *Journal of the Early Republic* 16 (1996): 159–181; and Naomi R. Lamoreaux, "Rethinking the Transition to Capitalism in the Early American Northeast," *Journal of American History* 90 (2003): 437–461. Two outstanding syntheses on which I have drawn are Christopher Clark, *The Roots of Rural Capitalism: Western Massachusetts, 1780–1860* (Ithaca: Cornell Univ. Press, 1990); and Catherine E. Kelly, *In the New England Fashion: Reshaping Women's Lives in the Nineteenth Century* (Ithaca: Cornell Univ. Press, 1999).

98. To be fair, literary historian Michael Gilmore refers to the works of Michael Merrill, Christopher Clark, James Henretta, and Karl Polanyi in his discussion of antebellum literature and economics, but for him they constitute only a 'background' against which texts can be read, and not the conditions that actually constitute the production and exchange of that literature. See Gilmore, *American Romanticism and the Marketplace*, 1–17, 155 n 2, 156 n 12.

99. Fairfield's wife, who remembered with bitterness every penny her husband did or did not earn, recalled raising forty dollars worth of subscriptions in Clark's home town of Philadelphia at this time. See Jane Frazee Fairfield, *The Autobiography of Jane Fairfield* (Boston: Bazin and Ellsworth, 1860), 97. For the review of Clark's volume, *The Spirit of Life*, see *North American Magazine* 3 (March 1834): 364.

100. Willis Gaylord Clark to Morton McMichael, [June 1834], *Letters of Willis Gaylord Clark and Lewis Gaylord Clark*, ed. Leslie W. Dunlap (N.Y.: New York Public Library, 1940), 66. A "personality" was an ad hominem insult.

101. Sahlins, *Stone Age Economics*, 186.

102. See Fairfield, *Autobiography of Jane Fairfield*, 61; and Willis Gaylord Clark to Sumner Lincoln Fairfield, 7 December 1829, in *Letters of Willis Gaylord Clark*, 26. Clark had also sought to review Fairfield's work. See Willis Gaylord Clark to John Greenleaf Whittier, 12 August 1829, quoted in John Hepler, "Two Editors and John G. Whittier (Willis G. and Lewis G. Clark)," *Bulletin of the New York Public Library* 70 (1966): 609. For evidence that Clark and Fairfield soon reestablished their friendship, see Willis Gaylord Clark to Willis Gaylord, 26 January 1835, William Jarvis Papers, Vermont Historical Society.

103. On embeddedness through subordination, see Yair Levi and Marie Louise Pellegrin-Rescia, "A New Look at the Embeddedness / Disembeddedness Issue: Cooperatives as Terms of Reference," *Journal of Socio-Economics* 26 (1997): 159–179. The concept of variable "marketness" is developed by Fred Block, *Postindustrial Possibilities: A Critique of Economic Discourse* (Berkeley: Univ. of California Press, 1990), 51–59.

104. See William J. Novak, "Public Economy and the Well-Ordered Market: Law and Economic Regulation in 19th-Century America," *Law and Social Inquiry: Journal of the American Bar Foundation* 18 (1993): 1–32; Helen Tangires, *Public Markets and Civic Culture in Nineteenth-Century America* (Baltimore: Johns Hopkins Univ. Press, 2003), xv–xix, 3–25, 61–63, 65–68, 71–94; and, more generally, Barbara Clark Smith, "Markets, Streets, and Stores: Contested Terrain in Pre-Industrial Boston," in *Autre Temps, Autre Espace / An Other Time, An Other Space: Etudes sur l'Amérique pré-industrielle*, ed. Elise Marienstras and Barbara Karsky (Nancy: Presses Universitaires de Nancy, 1986), 181–197. On the conceptual shift of the market from place to process, see Jean-Christophe Agnew, *Worlds Apart: The Market and the Theater in Anglo-American Thought, 1550–1750* (Cambridge: Cambridge Univ. Press, 1986), 17–56. On the moral economy, see E. P. Thompson, *Customs in Common: Studies in Traditional Popular Culture* (N.Y.: The New Press, 1993), 185–351.

105. David Paul Nord, *Faith in Reading: Religious Publishing and the Birth of Mass Media in America* (Oxford: Oxford Univ. Press, 2005), 50.

106. Ann Douglas, *The Feminization of American Culture* (N.Y.: Anchor

Press, 1988), 83; Nina Baym, "Reinventing Lydia Sigourney," in *Feminism and American Literature: Essays* (New Brunswick: Rutgers Univ. Press, 1992), 152. See also Melissa Ladd Teed, "A Passion for Distinction: Lydia Huntley Sigourney and the Creation of a Literary Reputation," *New England Quarterly* 77 (2004); 51–69.

107. Lydia Huntley Sigourney to Theodore Dwight, Jr., 26 September 1830, quoted in Betty Harris Day, "'This Comes of Writing Poetry': The Public and Private Voice of Lydia H. Sigourney" (PhD diss., University of Maryland, 1992), 92; Sigourney to G. & C. Merriam, 22 December 1832, quoted in Melissa Ladd Teed, "Work, Domesticity, and Localism: Women's Public Identity in Nineteenth-Century Hartford, Connecticut" (PhD diss., University of Connecticut, 1999), 136.

108. Charles Sigourney to Lydia Huntley Sigourney, October 1827; [Lydia Huntley Sigourney], '1860 Memoranda of Employments,' Lydia Huntley Sigourney Papers, Library of the Connecticut Historical Society Museum, Hartford, Conn.

109. Ronald J. Zboray and Mary Saracino Zboray, "Cannonballs and Books: Reading and the Disruption of Social Ties on the New England Home Front," in *The War was You and Me: Civilians in the American Civil War*, ed. Joan E. Cashin (Princeton: Princeton Univ. Press, 2002), 237–261.

110. Nathaniel P. Willis to George James Pumpelly, 26 November 1827, Nathaniel P. Willis Papers, Beinecke Library, Yale University; Louis A. Godey to Robert Montgomery Bird, n.d., quoted in Clement E. Foust, *The Life and Dramatic Works of Robert Montgomery Bird* (N.Y.: Burt Franklin, 1971), 99; Catharine Maria Sedgwick to Kate Sedgwick, 24 April 1837, Catharine Maria Sedgwick Papers, Courtesy of the Massachusetts Historical Society; Willis to Pumpelly, 24 May 1828, Letters, 1825–1830, Rare Book and Manuscript Library, Columbia University.

111. A much earlier instance might be cited in Joseph Dennie and Royall Tyler's newspaper series "From the Shop of Messrs. Colon & Spondee," which debuted in 1794 with the offer of "Anagrams, Acrostics, Anacreontics . . . Charades, Puns and Conundrums, by the *gross*, or *single dozen*." Dennie and Tyler, however, seemed to have been satirizing the consumption rather than the production and dissemination of authorial products; they foreground quantification but not price. See G. Thomas Tanselle, *Royall Tyler* (Cambridge, Mass.: Harvard Univ. Press, 1967), 112.

112. "Specimen of Composition by Steam," *New-York Mirror*, 8 September 1832. See also "Machine Poetry," *Yankee Nation*, 21 May 1842. On the human machine as a potent symbol of literary alienation at mid-century, see Ronald J. Zboray, "Technology and the Character of Community Life in Antebellum America: The Role of Story Papers," in *Communication and Change in American Religious History*, ed. Leonard I. Sweet (Grand Rapids: William B. Eerdmans, 1993), 185–215.

113. Samuel Griswold Goodrich to Nathaniel Hawthorne, 23 September 1836, quoted in Julian Hawthorne, *Nathaniel Hawthorne and His Wife: A Biog-*

raphy (Boston: James R. Osgood, 1884), 1: 138. See B. Bernard Cohen, "Hawthorne and 'Parley's Universal History,'" *Papers of the Bibliographical Society of America* 58 (1954): 77–90.

114. For Goodrich's account of the Solomon Bell affair, see his *Recollections of a Lifetime*, 2:276. Reviews that attribute Snelling's texts to Goodrich include *Massachusetts Journal & Transcript*, 20 November 1830; and *Ladies' Magazine and Literary Gazette* 4 (January 1831): 48. Snelling was revealed as the author in *Massachusetts Journal & Transcript*, 25 December 1830.

115. "Parley's Magazine," *New England Galaxy*, 27 July 1833.

116. On the "Spurious Parleys," see Daniel Roselle, *Samuel Griswold Goodrich, Creator of Peter Parley: A Study of His Life and Work* (Albany: State Univ. of New York, 1968), 85–98; and Goodrich, *Recollections of a Lifetime*, 2:543–554.

117. See Lillian B. Gilkes, "Hawthorne, Park Benjamin, and S. G. Goodrich: A Three-Cornered Imbroglio," *Nathaniel Hawthorne Journal 1971*, ed. C. E. Frazer Clarke, Jr. (Dayton: NCR Microcard Editions, 1971), 83–112; and Merle M. Hoover, *Park Benjamin: Poet and Editor* (N.Y.: Columbia Univ. Press, 1948).

118. "Agency for Authors," *New World*, 24 July 1841. See also Lillian B. Gilkes, "Park Benjamin: Literary Agent, Et Cetera," *Proof* 1 (1971): 36, 68–77, 80–82, 87–88.

119. For "commodity frontier," see Arlie Russell Hochschild, *The Commercialization of Intimate Life: Notes from Home and Work* (Berkeley: Univ. of California Press, 2003), 30–44.

120. Indeed, Zboray and Zboray concede this point repeatedly in their recent work, describing postbellum literary sociability as, variously, a "residual effect," a "substantial countervailing force," and as possibly "unerasable." See *Literary Dollars and Social Sense*, 202, 205, 203.

121. For a small sampling of scholarship revealing the ways in which acts of authorship and the dissemination of literature are still deeply embedded and embedding, see Micaela Di Leonardo, "The Female World of Cards and Holidays: Women, Families, and the Work of Kinship," *Signs* 12 (1987): 440–453; Mitchell Duneier, *Sidewalk* (N.Y.: Farrar, Strauss, and Giroux, 1999), esp. 17–111; and Janice A. Radway, *Reading the Romance: Women, Patriarchy, and Popular Literature* (London: Verso, 1987), 46–85.

122. See Stephen Gudeman, *The Anthropology of Economy* (Oxford: Blackwell, 2001).

123. See Thomas L. Haskell, "Capitalism and the Origins of the Humanitarian Sensibility, Part 2," in *The Antislavery Debate: Capitalism and Abolitionism as a Problem in Historical Interpretation*, ed. Thomas Bender (Berkeley: Univ. of California Press, 1992), esp. 138–156. A similar irony is explored in Ronald J. Zboray, *A Fictive People: Antebellum Economic Development and the American Reading Public* (Oxford: Oxford Univ. Press, 1993).

124. See F. G. Bailey, "Gifts and Poison," in *Gifts and Poison: The Politics of Reputation*, ed. Bailey (Oxford: Basil Blackwell, 1971), 1–25.

Chapter Two

1. The two most sustained discussions of Horton's life and work are Richard Walser, *The Black Poet, Being the Remarkable Story (Partly Told by My* [sic] *Himself) of George Moses Horton, a North Carolina Slave* (New York: Philosophical Library, 1966); and M. A. Richmond, *Bid the Vassal Soar: Interpretive Essays on the Life and Poetry of Phillis Wheatley (ca. 1753–1784) and George Moses Horton (ca. 1797–1883)* (Washington, D.C.: Howard Univ. Press, 1974), 81–198. Both are marred by innumerable misleading conjectures and occasional factual errors. Other biographical studies that I have found useful, although they sometimes replicate the errors of Walser and Richmond, include W. Edward Farrison, "George Moses Horton: Poet for Freedom," *CLA Journal* 14 (1971): 227–241; William Carroll, "Naked Genius: The Poetry of George Moses Horton, Slave Bard of North Carolina, 1797?–1883?" (PhD diss., University of North Carolina, 1977), esp. ix–lxii; Carroll, "George Moses Horton," in *Dictionary of Literary Biography*, Vol. 50, *Afro-American Writers before the Harlem Renaissance*, ed. Trudier Harris and Thadious M. Davis (Detroit: Gale Research, 1986), 190–201; and Joan R. Sherman, "Introduction," in *The Black Bard of North Carolina: George Moses Horton and His Poetry*, ed. Sherman (Chapel Hill: Univ. of North Carolina Press, 1997), 1–46. Where necessary, I have sought to corroborate or correct details offered in these studies through my own inspection of the primary sources. Basic information on Horton's life is drawn from his "Life of George M. Horton, The Colored Bard of North-Carolina," in *The Poetical Works of George M. Horton, the Colored Bard of North Carolina, to which is Prefixed the Life of the Author, Written by Himself* (Hillsborough: Printed by D. Heartt, 1845), iv, v. All references to this sketch hereafter cited parenthetically in the text.

2. Horton's ability to read but not write was typical of literate slaves in this era. As E. Jennifer Monaghan explains, whites associated slaves' ability to read with perusing the Bible and so considered it a benign skill, while they associated the ability to write with self-assertion and authority, and so considered it dangerous. See Monaghan, "Reading for the Enslaved, Writing for the Free: Reflections on Liberty and Literacy," *Proceedings of the American Antiquarian Society* 108 (1998): 309–341.

3. On slave singing and improvisation, see Lawrence W. Levine, *Black Culture and Black Consciousness: Afro-American Folk Thought from Slavery to Freedom* (Oxford: Oxford Univ. Press, 1978), 25–30.

4. On Chapel Hill's slaves and their services, see Kemp P. Battle, *History of the University of North Carolina* (Raleigh: Edwards and Broughton, 1907), 1:602, 606. Eliza Richards has argued that Horton remained estranged from his lyric voice and in many of his poems linked this estrangement to the utterances of animals. See "Intelligibility in George Moses Horton's Animal Poems," paper presented at the Third Biennial George Moses Horton Society Conference, University of North Carolina, Chapel Hill, 6 April 2002.

5. See Thomas Gibbons, *Memoirs of the Rev. Isaac Watts, D.D.* (London: Printed for James Buckland, 1780), 5. My thinking on the hybridity of acrostics is

indebted to Walter J. Ong, *Orality and Literacy: The Technologizing of the Word* (London: Methuen, 1982), esp. 33–36, 128–129.

6. [George Moses Horton], "An Acrostic on the Pleasures of Beauty," [ca. 1835], Pettigrew Family Papers, Southern Historical Collection, Wilson Library, The University of North Carolina at Chapel Hill. This is, I believe, the first complete and accurate transcription of the poem, which is typically sanitized with punctuation and printed without the final two stanzas.

7. On Horton's weekly output, see Richard Benbury Creecy, *Grandfather's Tales of North Carolina History* (Raleigh: Edwards and Broughton, 1901), 212; *Greensborough Patriot*, 13 August 1839, quoted in Walser, *Black Poet*, 58.

8. Battle, *History of the University of North Carolina*, 1:329, 274.

9. Artisanal, post-artisanal, market professional, and corporate professional modes of literary production are the elements of a four-stage typology outlined by Raymond Williams, *The Sociology of Culture* (Chicago: Univ. of Chicago Press, 1995), 44–51. Williams's typology is taken up briefly but instructively by Lawrence Buell, *New England Literary Culture: From Revolution through Renaissance* (Cambridge: Cambridge Univ. Press, 1986), 57–58; Steven Fink, "Margaret Fuller: The Evolution of a Woman of Letters," in *Reciprocal Influences: Literary Production, Distribution, and Consumption in America*, ed. Steven Fink and Susan S. Williams (Columbus: Ohio State Univ. Press, 1999), 55–74; and Christopher Grasso, *A Speaking Aristocracy: Transforming Public Discourse in Eighteenth-Century Connecticut* (Chapel Hill: Univ. of North Carolina Press, 1999), 322–323.

10. For legal injunctions on slaves' independent economic activities in 1820s North Carolina, see Guion Griffis Johnson, *Ante-Bellum North Carolina: A Social History* (Chapel Hill: Univ. of North Carolina Press, 1937), 533–534; and Ernest James Clark, Jr., "Aspects of the North Carolina Slave Code," *North Carolina Historical Review* 39 (1962): 154–156.

11. On the informal economy as a conceptual category, I have found especially useful Stuart Henry, "The Political Economy of Informal Economies," *Annals of the American Academy of Political and Social Science* 493 (1987): 137–153; and Gerald Mars, *Cheats at Work: An Anthropology of Workplace Crime* (Aldershot: Dartmouth, 1994), esp. 6–17, 23–39.

12. In his 1845 autobiographical sketch, Horton implies his professional status in referring to Caroline Lee Hentz as "a professional poetess herself," suggesting that he believed they shared this trait in common (xvii). For modern invocations of Horton's professional status, see, for example, Blyden Jackson, "George Moses Horton, North Carolinian," *North Carolina Historical Review* 53 (1976): 142; Carroll, "George Moses Horton," 190; *Black Writers of America: A Comprehensive Anthology*, ed. Richard Barksdale and Keneth Kinnamon (N.Y.: Macmillan, 1972), 219; and *The Norton Anthology of African American Literature*, ed. Henry Louis Gates, Jr., and Nellie Y. McKay (N.Y.: W. W. Norton, 1997), 190.

13. On reciprocation practices, see Joan E. Cashin, "The Structure of Antebellum Planter Families: 'The Ties that Bound us was Strong,'" *Journal of Southern History* 56 (1990): 55–70. For courtship rituals mediated by the writ-

ten word, see Ronald J. Zboray and Mary Saracino Zboray, *Everyday Ideas: Socioliterary Experience among Antebellum New Englanders* (Knoxville: Univ. of Tennessee Press, 2006), 61–63, 91–99. On courtship more generally, I have relied on Steven M. Stowe, *Intimacy and Power in the Old South: Ritual in the Lives of the Planters* (Baltimore: Johns Hopkins Univ. Press, 1987), 50–121; Guion Griffis Johnson, "Courtship and Marriage Customs in Ante-Bellum North Carolina," *North Carolina Historical Review* 8 (1931): 384–402; Ellen K. Rothman, *Hands and Hearts: A History of Courtship in America* (Cambridge, Mass.: Harvard Univ. Press, 1984), 9–13; and Karen Lystra, *Searching the Heart: Women, Men, and Romantic Love in Nineteenth-Century America* (Oxford: Oxford Univ. Press, 1989), 12–27.

14. Winifred Gales to Jared Sparks, 25 March 1825, Jared Sparks Collection of American Manuscripts, Sparks MS (153), by permission of the Houghton Library, Harvard University; Sarah (Redwood) Fisher to Hannah Redwood, [1778?], quoted in Konstanin Dierks, "Letter Writing, Gender, and Class in America, 1750–1800" (PhD diss., Brown University, 1999), 415; *Charleston Courier*, 9 July 1806, quoted in Len Travers, *Celebrating the Fourth: Independence Day and the Rites of Nationalism in the Early Republic* (Amherst: Univ. of Massachusetts Press, 1997), 145; William Wirt to Elizabeth Gamble, 3 August 1802, quoted in Anya Jabour, "'No Fetters But Such as Love Shall Forge': Elizabeth and William Wirt and Marriage in the Early Republic," *Virginia Magazine of History and Biography* 104 (1996): 216–217; *The Letters of William Lloyd* Garrison, ed. Walter M. Merrill (Cambridge, Mass.: Harvard Univ. Press, 1971), 1:81 n 6.

15. Works on literary patronage that I have found especially useful include Paul J. Korshin, "Types of Eighteenth-Century Literary Patronage," *Eighteenth-Century Studies* 7 (1974): 453–473; Linda Zionkowski, "Strategies of Containment: Stephen Duck, Ann Yearsley, and the Problem of Polite Culture," *Eighteenth-Century Life* 13 (1989): 91–108; Betty J. Rizzo, "The Patron as Poet Maker: The Politics of Benefaction," *Studies in Eighteenth-Century Culture* 20 (1990): 43–79; and, especially, Dustin Griffin, *Literary Patronage in England, 1650–1800* (Cambridge: Cambridge Univ. Press, 1996), (quotation 14). For Charvat's comments on the absence of patronage in America, see *The Profession of Authorship in America, 1800–1870: The Papers of William Charvat*, ed. Matthew J. Bruccoli (Columbus: Ohio State Univ. Press, 1968), 6–13, 298–316 (quotation 7).

16. On Southern paternalism I have relied on Eugene D. Genovese, *Roll, Jordan, Roll: The World the Slaves Made* (N.Y.: Vintage, 1976); and Philip D. Morgan, *Slave Counterpoint: Black Culture in the Eighteenth-Century Chesapeake and Lowcountry* (Chapel Hill: Omohundro Institute of Early American History and Culture, 1998), esp. 273–300. On gifts on the plantation, see Stephen Nissenbaum, *The Battle for Christmas* (N.Y.: Vintage, 1997), 264–273. Scholarship on paternalism—Genovese's in particular—has been criticized to the extent that it has been used to buttress two other rather controversial historical arguments: that the South sustained a precapitalist regional economy, and that slaves' resistance was hampered by their acceptance of paternalist ideology. The hegemony and sincerity of paternalist ideology is almost certainly less profound than Geno-

vese might at times have implied, but few, I think, would question that many whites and at least some African-Americans invoked the *language* of paternalism in their daily interactions and it is this, largely, that concerns me here. On the distinction between language and conviction in this context, see Sydel Silverman, "Patronage as Myth," in *Patrons and Clients in Mediterranean Societies*, ed. Ernest Gellner and John Waterbury (London: Duckworth, 1977), 7–19.

17. Creecy, *Grandfather's Tales of North Carolina History*, 212.

18. On the bestowal of clothes as a paternalist ritual, see Morgan, *Slave Counterpoint*, 281, 282–283, 385, 470; Genovese, *Roll, Jordan, Roll*, 556–557.

19. See Alpheus Jones to Peter W. Hairston, 23 October 1837, Wilson and Hairston Family Papers, Southern Historical Collection, Wilson Library, The University of North Carolina at Chapel Hill; William H. Thomson to Ruffin Thomson, 21 October 1859, quoted in Richmond, *Bid the Vassal Soar*, 149. This sort of nostalgic longing for absent slaves seems absolutely characteristic of the paternalist ethos. See Morgan, *Slave Counterpoint*, 270.

20. Caroline Lee Hentz, *Lovell's Folly. A Novel* (Cincinnati: Hubbard and Edmands, 1833), 256 (Burns); *Microcosm*, 6 July 1839 (Dryden).

21. For the centrality of vassalage to the Southern defense of paternalism, see George Fitzhugh, *Sociology for the South, or the Failure of Free Society* (Richmond: A. Morris, 1854), 9, 34, 88–89, 233, 265, 275–276, 292, 300. Horton might well have picked up the idea from his patron, Caroline Lee Hentz, who was to invoke the image repeatedly herself in the 1850s. See *The Planter's Northern Bride* (Philadelphia: T. B. Peterson and Brothers, 1854), 231, 239, 241, 297–298, 371, 474.

22. *Southern Literary Messenger* 9 (April 1843): 237; Creecy, *Grandfather's Tales of North Carolina History*, 212. On alcohol bestowal as paternalist ritual, see Nissenbaum, *Battle for Christmas*, 266–269.

23. My argument here draws heavily on Lawrence T. McDonnell, "Money Knows No Master: Market Relations and the American Slave Community," in *Developing Dixie: Modernization in a Traditional Society*, ed. Winfred B. Moore, Jr., Joseph F. Tripp, and Lyon G. Tyler, Jr. (N.Y.: Greenwood, 1988), 31–44; and Betty Wood, *Women's Work, Men's Work: The Informal Slave Economies of Lowcountry Georgia* (Athens: Univ. of Georgia Press, 1995). Of course, the choices of which Horton could avail himself, such as the purchase and consumption of alcohol, were socially determined, and determined in ways that still subordinated the slave. Horton could buy alcohol but he could not buy himself, a point I owe to Eliza Richards. On regulation of alcohol purchase, see Clark, "Aspects of the North Carolina Slave Code," 155–156.

24. Quoted in *Slave Testimony: Two Centuries of Letters, Speeches, Interviews, and Autobiographies*, ed. John W. Blassingame (Baton Rouge: Louisiana State Univ. Press, 1977), 643. For examples of covert or semi-covert reading and writing by slaves, see Janet Duitsman Cornelius, *When I Can Read My Title Clear: Literacy, Slavery, and Religion in the Antebellum South* (Columbia: Univ. of South Carolina Press, 1991), 59–84.

25. See Francis Jennings, *The Invasion of America: Indians, Colonialism, and the Cant of Conquest* (N.Y.: W. W. Norton, 1976), 118–119.

26. Elisha Mitchell to the Board of Trustees, quoted in Battle, *History of the University of North Carolina*, 1:304. On Nicholas Marcellus Hentz, see E. D. Lloyd-Kimbrel, "Nicholas Marcellus Hentz," in *Dictionary of American Biography* (N.Y.: Scribners, 1928–1936), 8:624–626; Edward Burgess, "Preface," in *The Spiders of the United States: A Collection of the Arachnological Writings of Nicholas Marcellus Hentz, M.D.*, ed. Burgess (Boston: Boston Society of Natural History, 1875), v–xi; Collier Cobb, "Nicholas Marcellus Hentz," *Journal of the Elisha Mitchell Scientific Society* 47 (1932): 47–51; and Arnold Mallis, *American Entomologists* (New Brunswick: Rutgers Univ. Press, 1971), 405–408.

27. Easily the most thorough and reliable study of Hentz's life is Iman Lababidi, "A Study in Domesticity: The Life and Literary Works of Caroline Lee Hentz, 1800–1856" (PhD diss., University of Nottingham, 1989), esp. 11–160. An excellent and readily accessible overview may be found in Jamie Stanesa, "Legacy Profile: Caroline Lee Whiting Hentz (1800–1856)," *Legacy* 13 (1996): 130–139.

28. Caroline Lee Hentz to Maria Whiting, 5 November 1826, Hentz Family Papers, Southern Historical Collection, Wilson Library, The University of North Carolina at Chapel Hill. For the argument that patronage helped establish the sponsor's status or identity, see Rizzo, "Patron as Poet Maker," 242, 244.

29. For Hentz's move to a proslavery position, see Elizabeth Moss, *Domestic Novelists in the Old South: Defenders of Southern Culture* (Baton Rouge: Louisiana State Univ. Press, 1992), 76–77.

30. Hentz's payment for Horton's elegy would seem to belie Mary Louise Kete's assertion that the work of literary mourning operated strictly within the parameters of a gift economy. See her *Sentimental Collaborations: Mourning and Middle-Class in Nineteenth-Century America* (Durham: Duke Univ. Press, 1999), 1–82.

31. "For the Lancaster Gazette," *Lancaster Gazette*, 8 April 1828. On the disputed question of African-Americans' capacity to feel pain, see Elizabeth B. Clark, "'The Sacred Rights of the Weak': Pain, Sympathy, and the Culture of Individual Rights in Antebellum America," *Journal of American History* 82 (1995): 463–493.

32. Slavery and suicide were closely linked in early abolitionist rhetoric. See Richard J. Bell, "Do Not Despair: The Cultural Significance of Suicide in America, 1780–1840" (PhD diss., Harvard University, 2006), 250–312.

33. *Bower of Taste* 1 (12 April 1828): 240; "Slavery. By a Carolinian Slave Named Geo. Horton," *Village Record, or Chester and Delaware Federalist*, 7 May 1828; "Slavery," *Genius of Universal Emancipation*, 14 June 1828; "Slavery," *Freedom's Journal*, 18 July 1828.

34. *Lancaster Gazette*, 24 June 1828. A lengthy editorial headnote accompanied the poem.

35. "George M. Horton," *Raleigh Register*, 18 July 1828; "Lines on the Evening and the Morning," *Raleigh Register*, 18 July 1828. For the members of the Committee of Visitation, see "University of North Carolina," *Raleigh Register*, 6 May 1828. It has not been possible to identify Horton's benefactor.

36. "To the Gad-Fly," *Raleigh Register*, 22 July 1828; "On the Poetic Muse,"

Raleigh Register, 1 August 1828; "The Loss of Female Character," *Raleigh Register,* 5 August 1828; "On the Consequences of Happy Marriage," *Raleigh Register,* 8 August 1828. For reprints of "George M. Horton": *Lancaster Gazette,* 29 July 1828; "George Horton," *Bunker Hill Aurora: and Farmers' and Mechanics Journal,* 2 August 1828; *Freedom's Journal* 2 (8 August 1828): 153; "Negro Intellect," *Genius of Universal Emancipation,* 9 August 1828; "George M. Horton," *Village Register, or Chester and Delaware Federalist,* 17 September 1828; *The Friend: A Religious and Literary Magazine* 1 (20 September 1828): 384. For reprints of "Lines on the Evening and the Morning,": "Poetry," *Freedom's Journal* 2 (15 August 1828): 166; "Lines on the Evening and the Morning," *Village Record, or Chester and Delaware Federalist,* 17 September 1828; "Lines on the Evening and the Morning: By George M. Horton, a colored man (slave) in Carolina," *Genius of Universal Emancipation,* 13 December 1828.

37. For poems in response to Horton, see "To George M. Horton, the Sable Poet of Chatham, N.C.," *Free Press,* 29 August 1828; "On the Evening," *Genius of Universal Emancipation,* 18 October 1828.

38. I am using the concept of interpellation here to suggest something akin to Althusser's description of how an "individual" is transformed, ineluctably, into a "subject." See Louis Althusser, "Ideology and Ideological State Apparatuses (Notes towards an Investigation)," in *Lenin and Philosophy and Other Essays,* trans. Ben Brewster (London: NLB, 1971), esp. 162–165.

39. The distinction between sentimental and anti-sentimental charity is offered by Susan M. Ryan, *The Grammar of Good Intentions: Race and the Antebellum Culture of Benevolence* (Ithaca: Cornell Univ. Press, 2003), esp. 16–21. On suffering and immediate emotional connection, see Karen Halttunen, "Humanitarianism and the Pornography of Pain in Anglo-America," *American Historical Review* 100 (1995): 303–334; Norman S. Fiering, "Irresistible Compassion: An Aspect of Eighteenth-Century Sympathy and Humanitarianism," *Journal of the History of Ideas* 38 (1976): 195–218; and Clark, "Sacred Rights of the Weak." For the more suspicious and calculating view of the needy, see David J. Rothman, *The Discovery of the Asylum: Social Order and Disorder in the New Republic* (Boston: Little, Brown, 1971).

40. On the distance that sympathy necessarily engendered, see Julie Ellison, *Cato's Tears and the Making of Anglo-American Emotion* (Chicago: Univ. of Chicago Press, 1999), 18, 122. For charity as rewarding for donors, see John Saillant, "Black, White, and 'The Charitable Blessed': Race and Philanthropy in the American Early Republic," *Essays in Philanthropy* no. 8 (Indianapolis: Indiana University Center on Philanthropy, 1993). On fugitive and former slaves' sale of stories in person, see Ann Fabian, *The Unvarnished Truth: Personal Narratives in Nineteenth-Century America* (Berkeley: Univ. of California Press, 2000), 102–107.

41. On Horton's desire to be bought by the Manumission Society, see "For the Register," *Raleigh Register,* 7 October 1828. No mention of Horton is to be found in the Society's annual minutes. See *Minutes of the N.C. Manumission Society, 1816–1834,* ed. H. M. Wagstaff (Chapel Hill: Univ. of North Carolina Press, 1934). On the scope of the Society, see P. M. Sherrill, "The Quakers and

the North Carolina Manumission Society," *Trinity College Historical Society Papers* 10 (1914): 32–51 (number of branches 39); and Patrick Sowle, "The North Carolina Manumission Society," *North Carolina Historical Review* 42 (1965): 47–69.

42. On pleas for funding in *Freedom's Journal*, see "Extract," *Freedom's Journal*, 29 August 1828; "George M. Horton," *Freedom's Journal*, 12 September 1828; and "George M. Horton," *Freedom's Journal*, 3 October 1828. No subsequent references have been found.

43. The language here is Horton's. See George Moses Horton, An Address to the Collegiates of the University of N.C. By George M. Horton (the Black Bard), [1859], 8, North Carolina Collection, Wilson Library, The University of North Carolina at Chapel Hill.

44. "Extract," *Freedom's Journal*, 29 August 1828.

45. Kenneth S. Greenberg, *Honor and Slavery: Lies, Duels, Noses, Masks, Dressing as a Woman, Gifts, Strangers, Humanitarianism, Death, Slave Rebellions, the Proslavery Argument, Baseball, Hunting, and Gambling in the Old South* (Princeton: Princeton Univ. Press, 1996), 51–86 (quotation 66).

46. One possible reason for the decline in activity was the birth, on 11 October 1828, of Caroline Lee Hentz's daughter, Julia.

47. Henry Louis Gates, Jr., *Figures in Black: Words, Signs, and the "Racial" Self* (Oxford: Oxford Univ. Press, 1987), 13; Gates, Jr., "Editor's Introduction: Writing 'Race' and the Difference it Makes," *Critical Inquiry* 12 (1985): 9; Gates, Jr., "From Wheatley to Douglass: The Politics of Displacement," in *Frederick Douglass: New Literary and Historical Essays*, ed. Eric J. Sundquist (Cambridge: Cambridge Univ. Press, 1990), 56.

48. My singling out of Gates here is not intended as a slight on his exemplary scholarly career but is simply a reflection of the fact that his work is both critically acclaimed and extraordinarily widely disseminated, which means, as a result, that his flawed and poorly documented accounts of Horton have been accepted without question. The *Critical Inquiry* essay mentioning the full page ads, for example, has been reprinted in both anthologies and textbooks. See *"Race," Writing, and Difference*, ed. Henry Louis Gates, Jr. (Chicago: Univ. of Chicago Press, 1986), 1–20; and *Social Theory: The Multicultural and Classic Readings*, ed. Charles C. Lemert (Boulder: Westview Press, 1998), 532–538. True full-page advertisements appeared first in the 1880s; earlier examples, in which a smaller advertisement was reiterated to fill a page, date from the mid-1850s. See Frank Presbrey, *The History and Development of Advertising* (Garden City: Doubleday, 1929), 244–248; and Augusta Rohrbach, "'Truth Stronger and Stranger than Fiction': Reexamining William Lloyd Garrison's *Liberator*," *American Literature* 73 (2001): 727–755.

49. Samuel Gilman to Caroline Gilman, 16 April 1821, Samuel and Caroline Gilman Papers, American Antiquarian Society. Overviews of Gales's life can be found in Willis G. Briggs, "Joseph Gales, Editor of Raleigh's First Newspaper," *North Carolina Booklet* 7 (1907): 105–130; Clement Eaton, "Winifred and Joseph Gales, Liberals in the Old South," *Journal of Southern History* 10 (1944):

461–474; Margaret J. Boeringer, "Joseph Gales, North Carolina Printer" (MLS thesis, University of North Carolina, 1989); and William E. Ames, *A History of the National Intelligencer* (Chapel Hill: Univ. of North Carolina Press, 1972), 69–80. For Gales's radical activities in England, I have relied on W. H. G. Armytage, "The Editorial Experience of Joseph Gales, 1786–1794," *North Carolina Historical Review* 28 (1951): 332–361; E. P. Thompson, *The Making of the English Working Class* (Harmondsworth: Penguin, 1980), 144–145; and Albert Goodwin, *The Friends of Liberty: The English Democratic Movement in the Age of the French Revolution* (Cambridge, Mass.: Harvard Univ. Press, 1979), 222–223, 325–326 (quotation 325).

50. Joseph and Winifred Gales, Recollections, 141, Gales Family Papers, Southern Historical Collection, Wilson Library, University of North Carolina at Chapel Hill (Gales quotes 2 Kings 3:13); *Raleigh Register*, 23 September 1825, quoted in R. H. Taylor, "Humanizing the Slave Code of North Carolina," *North Carolina Historical Review* 2 (1925): 330; Edgar W. Knight, "Notes on John Chavis," *North Carolina Historical Review* 7 (1930): 339–340, 343; Jeffrey L. Pasley, *"The Tyranny of Printers": Newspaper Politics in the Early American Republic* (Charlottesville: Univ. Press of Virginia, 2001), 158–159; *Stealing a Little Freedom: Advertisements for Slave Runaways in North Carolina, 1791–1840*, ed. Freddie L. Parker (N.Y.: Garland, 1994), 197–332; Eaton, "Winifred and Joseph Gales," 464 (quotation). Michael Durey considers Gales's slide toward conservatism as typical of radical émigrés who settled in the South. See his *Transatlantic Radicals and the Early American Republic* (Lawrence: Univ. of Kansas Press, 1997), 283–288.

51. See Early Lee Fox, *The American Colonization Society, 1817–1840* (Baltimore: Johns Hopkins Univ. Press, 1919); P. J. Staudenraus, *The African Colonization Movement, 1816–1865* (N.Y.: Columbia Univ. Press, 1961); Lawrence J. Friedman, "Purifying the White Man's Country: The American Colonization Society Reconsidered, 1816–40," *Societas* 6 (1976): 1–24; David M. Streifford, "The American Colonization Society: An Application of Republican Ideology to Early Antebellum Reform," *Journal of Southern History* 45 (1979): 201–220; Hugh Davies, "Northern Colonizationists and Free Blacks, 1823–1837: A Case Study of Leonard Bacon," *Journal of the Early Republic* 17 (1997), 651–675; and, especially, Eric Burin, *Slavery and the Peculiar Solution: A History of the American Colonization Society* (Gainesville: Univ. Press of Florida, 2005).

52. For the members of the Committee of Visitation, see *Raleigh Register*, 6 May 1828. On the activities of the ACS in North Carolina, see John Michael Shay, "The Antislavery Movement in North Carolina" (PhD diss., Princeton University, 1971), 317–364; and Claude A. Clegg III, *The Price of Liberty: African Americans and the Making of Liberia* (Chapel Hill: Univ. of North Carolina Press, 2004).

53. See Dickson D. Bruce, Jr., *The Origins of African American Literature, 1680–1865* (Charlottesville: Univ. Press of Virginia, 2001), 135–174. The strongest argument in favor of Horton's colonizationist sentiment is the recent revelation that he did eventually move to Liberia in 1866. On the other hand, he never

once mentioned Liberia in either his published or unpublished works prior to the year of his departure, while he did publish at least one letter that expressed a clear American literary nationalist sentiment.

54. "Explanation," in George M. Horton, *The Hope of Liberty. Containing a Number of Poetical Pieces* (Raleigh: J. Gales & Son, 1829), [3]–4.

55. For "uncorrected," see *Hope of Liberty*, 4. Compare "Liberty and Slavery," *Lancaster Gazette*, 8 April 1828 with *Hope of Liberty*, 8–9; "Slavery," *Lancaster Gazette*, 8 April 1828 with *Hope of Liberty*, 4. Although Richard Walser observed the roar/soar distinction as he transcribed "Liberty and Slavery" while taking notes for his book on Horton, he did not consider the change significant, and in the book as published he refers only to a "few alterations" without specifying what they were. See Richard Gaither Walser Papers, Series 1, Folder 302, Southern Historical Collection, Wilson Library, The University of Carolina at Chapel Hill; Walser, *Black Poet*, 111. Even abolitionists could—and did—minimize or deny the extent to which their editorial revisions altered the meaning of African-American texts, a fact that is brought home with striking clarity by Robanna Sumrell Knott in her important study of Lydia Maria Child's editing of Harriet Jacobs. See "Harriet Jacobs: The Edenton Biography" (PhD diss., University of North Carolina, 1994).

56. On the various modes of, and motivations for, subscription publication, Donald Farren, "Subscription: A Study of the Eighteenth-Century American Book Trade" (DLS diss., Columbia University, 1982); and Walter Sutton, *The Western Book Trade: Cincinnati as a Nineteenth-Century Publishing and Book-Trade Center* (Columbus: Ohio State Univ. Press, 1961), 215–233. For a focused study, see William S. Powell, "Patrons of the Press: Subscription Book Purchases in North Carolina, 1733–1850," *North Carolina Historical Review* 39 (1962): 423–499.

57. The on-line databases I searched were: American Periodical Series Online, 1740–1900; Early American Newspapers, Series 1, 1690–1876; African American Newspapers: The 19th Century; The Making of America; Documenting the American South; and The Library of Congress: American Memory. There is no reference to subscription sheets or advertisements, either, in the checklist of Gales's publications in Boeringer, "Joseph Gales," or in the list of subscription books published in North Carolina in Powell, "Patrons of the Press," 440–449.

58. Noah Webster, *American Dictionary of the English Language* (N.Y.: S. Converse, 1828), s.v. subscription.

59. "Colonization Society," *Raleigh Register*, 2 July 1829. For "colonization box," see "Intelligence," *African Repository and Colonial Journal* 7 (August 1831): 182.

60. *The Hope of Liberty* has a duodecimo format, meaning that it was printed on a single sheet of paper folded twice along its length and then three times along its breadth to create a pamphlet of twelve leaves, or twenty-four pages. The "Explanation" states that more poems might have been included but that expense was an issue; the selection of poems included was thus almost certainly determined by the need to fit them, and the explanation, onto a single sheet making twenty-two pages (the other two being occupied by the title page and back

wrapper) rather than by any aesthetic concerns. See "Explanation," *Hope of Liberty*, [3]; Philip Gaskell, *A New Introduction to Bibliography* (New Castle: Oak Knoll Press, 1995), 81. The expeditious production of the pamphlet might well have been a Gales family effort, for they often pitched in; in 1818, Winifred Gales told her daughter "We are all engaged every evening in folding Almanacks until a certain hour." See Winifred Gales to Winifred M. Johnson, 30 December 1818, Robert E. Johnson Papers, Rare Book, Manuscript, and Special Collections Library, Duke University. It is just as likely however—and more fittingly ironic—that Gales's printing shop slaves did the work.

61. On front-end prospecting, see Robert D. Putnam, *Bowling Alone: The Collapse and Renewal of American Community* (N.Y.: Touchstone, 2000), 53. For Gales's use, see Robert Neal Elliott, Jr., *The Raleigh Register, 1799–1863* (Chapel Hill: Univ. of North Carolina Press, 1955), 3. For another antebellum example of a free first issue, see Benjamin Quarles, "Sources of Abolitionist Income," *Mississippi Valley Historical Review* 32 (1945): 67.

62. "Explanation," in Horton, *The Hope of Liberty*, [3]–4.

63. *Raleigh Register*, 16 July 1829; Thomas P. Hunt to Ralph R. Gurley, 4 August 1829, 3 September 1829, Records of the American Colonization Society, Series 1, Volume 10, Library of Congress. Total North Carolina donations to the ACS in 1829 were $468.31. See John Hope Franklin, *The Free Negro in North Carolina, 1790–1860* (Chapel Hill: Univ. of North Carolina Press, 1943), 204, 239.

64. On transportation costs, see "Transportation Subscriptions," *African Repository and Colonial Journal* 5 (May 1829): 95.

65. For North Carolina's exemplary contributions to the colonization cause, see Clegg, *Price of Liberty*, 5.

66. John Moody to Richard Smith, 28 July 1829, Thomas P. Hunt to Ralph R. Gurley 4 August 1829, 3 September 1829, Records of the American Colonization Society; *Thirteenth Annual Report of the American Society for Colonizing the Free People of Colour of the United States* (Washington [D.C.]: James C. Dunn, 1830), 14.

67. "Expedition for Africa," *African Repository and Colonial Journal* 5 (December 1829): 317.

68. Ann Royall, *Mrs. Royall's Southern Tour, or Second Series of the Black Book* (Washington [D.C.]: Printed for the Author, 1830–1831), 1:136. For the date of Royall's visit to Raleigh, see Bessie Rowland James, *Anne Royall's U.S.A.* (New Brunswick: Rutgers Univ. Press, 1972), 273.

69. See Peter P. Hinks, *To Awaken My Afflicted Brethren: David Walker and the Problem of Antebellum Slave Resistance* (University Park: Pennsylvania State Univ. Press, 1997), 137–145; Clement Eaton, "A Dangerous Pamphlet in the Old South," *Journal of Southern History* 2 (1936): 331–332 (quotation).

70. Winifred Gales to Jared Sparks, 6 June 1831, Sparks Collection; Herbert Aptheker, *American Negro Slave Revolts* (N.Y.: International Publishers, 1963), 293–324; Charles Edward Morris, "Panic and Reprisal: Reaction in North Carolina to the Nat Turner Insurrection," *North Carolina Historical* Review 62 (1985): 40–41, 48–50.

71. See "Poems by a Slave," *National Enquirer and Constitutional Advocate of Universal Liberty*, 28 September 1837. Gales sold his Almanacs on a comparable scale, ranging from ten cents each and seventy-five cents per dozen up to twenty-three dollars for five hundred and forty dollars per thousand. See *Gales and Seaton's North Carolina Almanack, for the Year: 1813* (Raleigh: Printed by J. Gales, [1812]), front wrapper.

72. *Poems by a Slave* [Philadelphia: Merrihew and Gunn, 1837], 2. Coffin's friend had almost certainly received the text from Caroline Lee Hentz, who was living in Cincinnati between 1832 and 1834.

73. Joshua Coffin to [Merrihew and Gunn], 12 September 1837, *Poems by a Slave*, sheet tipped between 2–3. For reactions to this edition, see "George Horton," *National Enquirer and Constitutional Advocate of Universal Liberty*, 26 October 1837; *Human Rights* 3 (October 1837): 3; "Letter to the Minister of the Gospel," *The Anti-Slavery Record* 3 (October 1837): 110–111.

74. Vernon Loggins, *The Negro Author: His Development in America to 1900* (1931; Port Washington: Kennikat, 1964), 109. The "hint" claim is repeated by Richmond, *Bid the Vassal Soar*, 113–114.

75. J. Saunders Redding, *To Make a Poet Black*, ed. Henry Louis Gates, Jr. (1939; Ithaca: Cornell Univ. Press, 1988), 15.

76. Blyden Jackson, "George Moses Horton, North Carolinian," *North Carolina Historical Review* 2 (1976): 146.

77. Hentz, *Lovell's Folly*, 256. Word of Hentz's novel, if not the novel itself, came to Horton's attention, for he alluded to "Lovel's fine folly" in a poem included in his 1845 collection: "The Musical Chamber," *Poetical Works*, 24.

78. See "Let Us Go," *African Repository* 43 (January 1867): 28–29; Reginald H. Pitts, "'Let Us Desert This Friendless Place': George Moses Horton in Philadelphia—1866," *Journal of Negro History* 80 (1995): 145–156.

79. Richard H. Brodhead, *Cultures of Letters: Scenes of Reading and Writing in Nineteenth-Century America* (Chicago: Univ. of Chicago Press, 1993), 109, 5.

80. See Stephen Nissenbaum, "The Firing of Nathaniel Hawthorne," *Essex Institute Historical Collections* 114 (1978): 57–86 (quotation 65). It is also important to be reminded that some authors sought political appointments in order to *avoid* having to write. "If nothing is to be obtained from government," fretted author John Howard Payne to a potential benefactor, "I am necessarily thrown back upon literary labor." John Howard Payne to William L. Mary, 24 September 1847, Yale Collection of American Literature, Beinecke Library, Yale University. For a documentarily extensive but conceptually thin discussion of government patronage of antebellum authors, see Bill R. Brubaker, "The Political Appointment of American Writers" (PhD diss., Ohio State University, 1967).

81. John Pendleton Kennedy, *Swallow Barn; or, A Sojourn in the Old South*, ed. Lucinda H. MacKenthun (Baton Rouge: Louisiana State Univ. Press, 1986), [xxxv–xxxvi]; George Lippard to James Fenimore Cooper, 21 May 1844, George Lippard Papers, American Antiquarian Society; Caroline Lee Hentz to Jared Sparks, 7 November 1830, 10 August 1833, Sparks Collection. For an explicitly

Bourdieuvian interpretation of dedications as a patronage strategy, see Deborah C. Payne, "The Restoration Dramatic Dedication as Symbolic Capital," *Studies in Eighteenth-Century Culture* 20 (1990): 27–42.

82. "To Citizen Dexter," *Impartial Herald*, 5 May 1795; "To Sir Timothy Dexter, on His Returning to Newburyport," *Impartial Herald*, 17 March 1797.

83. See Jonathan Plummer, *A Sketch of the History of the Life and Adventures of Jonathan Plummer, Junr. Written by Himself* [Newburyport: Printed by Blunt and March, 1795–1798], 139, 170–174 (clothes), 133–134 (books and thanks by name). For "humorous": "To Sir Timothy Dexter, On His Returning to Newburyport."

84. Jonathan Plummer, *Dying Confession of Pomp, a Negro Man*, Broadside, [1795]; Jonathan Plummer, *The Portsmouth Harbour Tragedy*, Broadside, [1809]. A yet further striking parallel with Horton is that Plummer served as an amanuensis and editor for an African-American unable to write. For a brief discussion, see William L. Andrews, *To Tell a Free Story: The First Century of Afro-American Autobiography, 1760–1865* (Urbana: Univ. of Illinois Press, 1988), 33, 49–50.

85. On the unwaged nature of the printers' apprenticeship, see W. J. Rorabaugh, *The Craft Apprentice from Franklin to the Machine Age in America* (Oxford: Oxford Univ. Press, 1986).

86. [Samuel Woodworth], "Memoirs of a Sensitive Man About Town," *New-York Mirror*, 5 April 1834.

87. [Robert Stevenson Coffin], *The Life of the Boston Bard* (Mount Pleasant: Stephen Marshall, 1825), 92.

88. William W. Smithers, *The Life of John Lofland, "The Milford Bard"* (Philadelphia: Wallace M. Leonard, 1894), 127–128, 101. For an African-American contemporary of Horton who also offered a letter-writing service, see the brief mention in Dorothy B. Porter, "David Ruggles, an Apostle of Human Rights," *Journal of Negro History* 28 (1943): 28.

89. John H. Hewitt, *Shadows on the Wall, Or, Glimpses of the Past* (Baltimore: Turnbull Brothers, 1877), 51; "Pop Emmons," Portland *Daily Advertiser*, 14 November 1851.

90. My argument here diverges from that of Daniel E. Williams, who sees Plummer's engagement with the world of printed materials and the public sphere as singularly enabling. See Williams, "Reckoned to Be Almost a Natural Fool: Textual Self-Construction in the Writings of Jonathan Plummer—No Hermaphrodite," *Early American Literature* 33 (1998): 149–172.

91. Currier, *History of Newburyport, Mass., 1764–1909*, 431.

92. See John Benson, *The Penny Capitalists: A Study of Nineteenth-Century Working-Class Entrepreneurs* (Dublin: Gill and Macmillan, 1983).

93. George Thompson, *My Life: Or the Adventures of Geo. Thompson. Being the Auto-Biography of an Author* [1854], in Thompson, *Venus in Boston and Other Tales of Nineteenth-Century City Life*, ed. David S. Reynolds and Kimberly R. Gladman (Amherst: Univ. of Massachusetts Press, 2002), 327.

94. Joel Munsell, "The Singularly Interesting Life and Adventures of a Print-

er!!" [1828], 27 (BV Munsell, Joel), courtesy of the New York Historical Society; Helen Lefkowitz Horowitz, *Rereading Sex: Battles over Sexual Knowledge and Suppression in Nineteenth-Century America* (N.Y.: Vintage, 2002), 34.

95. For a sensitive meditation on the historical specificities of the shadow economy, see Jason Ditton, "Perks, Pilferage, and the Fiddle: The Historical Structure of Invisible Wages," *Theory and Society* 4 (1977): 39–71.

96. The study of shadow literary economies has tended to attract scholars of oppressive regimes practicing systematic surveillance, since such regimes both engendered and documented illegal activities. See, for example, Robert Darnton, "A Police Inspector Sorts His Files: The Anatomy of the Republic of Letters," in *The Great Cat Massacre and Other Episodes in French Cultural History* (Harmondsworth: Penguin, 1985), 141–183; Darnton, *The Literary Underground of the Old Regime* (Cambridge, Mass.: Harvard Univ. Press, 1982); Darnton, "Literary Surveillance in the British Raj: The Contradictions of Liberal Imperialism," *Book History* 4 (2001): 133–176; and Iain McCalman, *Radical Underworld: Prophets, Revolutionaries, and Pornographers in London, 1795–1840* (Cambridge: Cambridge Univ. Press, 1988).

97. "Editorial Notices," in S. H. DeKroyft, *A Place in Thy Memory* (N.Y.: John F. Trow, 1851), n.p. See also James Emmett Ryan, "The Blind Authoress of New York: Helen De Kroyft and the Uses of Disability in Antebellum America," *American Quarterly* 51 (1999): 385–418. Although DeKroyft relied often on amanuenses, she came also in time to use a stencil that allowed her to write unassisted.

98. DeKroyft, *A Place in Thy Memory*, n.p. (quotation 1). For an example of her promotional tours, see "A Blind Lady," *Christian Register*, 28 September 1850.

Chapter Three

1. Daniel Pierce Thompson to John Neal, [1835], John Neal Papers, bMS Am 1949 (307), by permission of the Houghton Library, Harvard University. I date this letter based on the publication date of the novel itself, although one announcement suggests that it might not have gone on sale until early the following year. See D. P. Thompson, *May Martin: Or The Money Diggers. A Green Mountain Tale* (Montpelier: E. P. Walton and Son, 1835); "May Martin, or The Money Diggers," *State Journal*, 23 February 1836.

2. Social status, as we saw in Chapter Two, is the key variable in this equation: to give a thing of value to a social superior is to make a tribute, while to bestow it upon an inferior is a form of charity. See Viviana A. Zelizer, *The Social Meaning of Money: Pin Money, Pay Checks, Poor Relief, and Other Currencies* (Princeton: Princeton Univ. Press, 1997), 78.

3. Thompson's novel won first prize in a competition sponsored by Neal's newspaper, the *New England Galaxy*, but Neal was not himself a judge for the competition and seems to have had no prior contact with the author. See "Prize Articles," *New England Galaxy*, 14 March 1835; "Award," *New England Galaxy*, 13 June 1835; Daniel Pierce Thompson to Mr. B., [1835], Charles Follen

Papers, Massachusetts Historical Society. Thompson also sent his work to other editors and badgered them in much the same way he would Neal. See "To Correspondents," *Boston Pearl, and Literary Gazette* 4 (18 July 1835): 363; "May Martin, & c. & c.," *Boston Pearl, and Literary Gazette* 4 (8 August 1835): 387. For Thompson's admiration for Neal, see Daniel Pierce Thompson to Josiah Pierce, 2 July 1829, 26 December 1829, Montpelier Letters, Vermont Historical Society.

4. Emily Chubbuck to Urania Nott, November 1843, quoted in A. C. Kendrick, *The Life and Letters of Mrs. Emily C. Judson* (N.Y.: Sheldon & Co., 1860), 88–89.

5. Lewis Hyde, *The Gift: Imagination and the Erotic Life of Property* (N.Y.: Vintage Books, 1979).

6. Lydia Huntley Sigourney to James Abraham Hillhouse, 21 January 1837, Letters, 1835–1845, John Hay Library, Brown University. Cf. 1 Cor. 12:31. Hillhouse appears not to have contributed. See *Indices to American Literary Annuals and Gift Books, 1825–1865*, ed. E. Bruce Kirkham and John W. Fink (New Haven: Research Publications, 1975), 312–314. Almost identical language was used by the editor of an abolitionist gift book who wrote "earnestly to solicit a contribution" from the "gifted pen" of E. D. E. N. Southworth. See Mrs. Charles H. Webb to E. D. E. N. Southworth, 14 May 1853, Emma Dorothy Eliza Nevitte Southworth Papers, Rare Book, Manuscript, and Special Collections Library, Duke University.

7. For "anarchist property," see Hyde, *The Gift*, 84. Works that draw approvingly on Hyde's distinction include Ronald A. Sharp, "Keats and the Spiritual Economies of Gift Exchange," *Keats-Shelley Journal* 38 (1989): 66–81; Sharp, "Gift Exchange and the Economies of Spirit in 'The Merchant of Venice,'" *Modern Philology* 83 (1986): 250–265; Jane Donawerth, "Women's Poetry and the Tudor-Stewart System of Gift Exchange," in *Women, Writing, and the Reproduction of Culture in Tudor and Stuart Britain*, ed. Mary E. Burke, Jane Donawerth, Linda L. Dove, and Karen Nelson (Syracuse: Syracuse Univ. Press, 2000), 3–18; Reggie Allen, "The Sonnets of William Hayley and Gift Exchange," *European Romantic Review* 13 (2002): 383–392; Cathy N. Davidson, *Revolution and the Word: The Rise of the Novel in America* (Oxford: Oxford Univ. Press, 1986), 14; and Lori Merish, *Sentimental Materialism: Gender, Commodity Culture, and Nineteenth-Century American Literature* (Durham: Duke Univ. Press, 2000), 71. For a measured assessment of Hyde's appeal and a forceful critique of his work, see Blake Leland, "Voodoo Economics: Sticking Pins in Eros," *Diacritics* 18 (1988): 38–46.

8. See Marcel Mauss, *The Gift: Forms and Functions of Exchange in Archaic Societies*, trans. Ian Cunnison (N.Y.: W. W. Norton, 1967).

9. Jacques Derrida, *Given Time: 1. Counterfeit Money*, trans. Peggy Kamuf (Chicago: Univ. of Chicago Press, 1992), 7–33.

10. See Barry Schwartz, "The Social Psychology of the Gift," *American Journal of Psychology* 73 (1967): 1–11; and for an excellent study that emphasizes the hostile potential of gift-giving in the antebellum period, on which I have drawn extensively, Kenneth S. Greenberg, *Honor and Slavery: Lies, Duels, Noses, Masks, Dressing as a Woman, Gifts, Strangers, Humanitarianism, Death,*

Slave Rebellions, the Proslavery Argument, Baseball, Hunting, and Gambling in the Old South (Princeton: Princeton Univ. Press, 1996), 51–86.

11. Hyde, *The Gift*, xvi. Such phenomena, he argues, are a "misuse" of gifts. For two excellent surveys that seek to move beyond the gift-commodity distinction posited by Hyde, see John Frow, "Gift and Commodity," in *Time and Commodity Culture: Essays in Cultural Theory and Postmodernity* (Oxford: Oxford Univ. Press, 1997), 102–217; and Mark Osteen, "Introduction: Questions of the Gift," in *The Question of the Gift: Essays Across Disciplines*, ed. Osteen (London: Routledge, 2002), 1–41.

12. *The Letters of William Gilmore Simms*, ed. Mary C. Oliphant, et al. (Columbia: Univ. of South Carolina Press, 1952), 1:xcix; Pierre Bourdieu, *Outline of a Theory of Practice*, trans. Richard Nice (Cambridge: Cambridge Univ. Press, 1977), 4–6, 171–173 (quotations 5); Bourdieu, "Marginalia—Some Additional Notes on the Gift," in *The Logic of the Gift: Toward an Ethic of Generosity*, ed. Alan D. Schrift (N.Y.: Routledge, 1997), 231–241 (quotation 232). For "alternating disequilibrium," see C. A. Gregory, *Gifts and Commodities* (London: Academic Press, 1982), 53.

13. Daniel Pierce Thompson to Henry Wadsworth Longfellow, 16 October 1839, Letters to Henry Wadsworth Longfellow, bMS Am 1340.2 (5507), by permission of the Houghton Library, Harvard University.

14. On Thompson's distant familial connection to Longfellow, see Frederic Beech Pierce, *Pierce Genealogy, Being the Record of the Posterity of Thomas Pierce*, ed. Frederick Clifton Pierce (Worcester: Chas. Hamilton, 1882), 133–141. For Thompson more generally, see John E. Flitcroft, *The Novelist of Vermont: A Biographical and Critical Study of Daniel Pierce Thompson* (Cambridge, Mass.: Harvard Univ. Press, 1929). In writing to Longfellow, Thompson acknowledged that they were "personally unacquainted." Thompson to Longfellow, 16 October 1839, Longfellow Papers. For Thompson's preemptive plan to send Longfellow a copy of his novel, see Daniel Pierce Thompson to Josiah Pierce, 30 October 1838, Montpelier Letters.

15. Henry Wadsworth Longfellow to Daniel Pierce Thompson, 12 November 1839, *The Letters of Henry Wadsworth Longfellow*, ed. Andrew Hilen (Cambridge, Mass.: Belknap Press of Harvard Univ. Press, 1966–1982), 2:185–186.

16. [Daniel Pierce Thompson], Review of *Green Mountain Boys*, December 1840, North American Review Papers, 1831–1843, Houghton Library, Harvard University. Although the manuscript is signed only with the letter C, the handwriting is unmistakably Thompson's. Thompson and Longfellow met for the first time in 1844; in 1851 he sent Longfellow *another* new novel with a request for a feedback. Longfellow again praised the book, declined to review it, and was therefore mortified later to see his private words printed on advertising sheets covering the novel. See Daniel Pierce Thompson to Josiah Pierce, 21 December 1844, Montpelier Letters; Longfellow to Jared Sparks, 25 December 1851, *The Letters of Henry Wadsworth Longfellow*, 3:324–325.

17. See, for example, John Neal to Henry Wadsworth Longfellow, 6 August 1833, Longfellow Papers; Henry Wadsworth Longfellow to John Neal, 10 October 1839, *Letters of Henry Wadsworth Longfellow*, 2: 180–181.

18. For work on coteries and literary networks, see *Only for the Eye of a Friend: The Poems of Annis Boudinot Stockton*, ed. Carla Mulford (Charlottesville: Univ. Press of Virginia, 1995), 1–68; *Milcah Martha Moore's Book: A Commonplace Book from Revolutionary America*, ed. Catherine La Courreye Blecki and Karin A. Wulf (University Park: Pennsylvania State Univ. Press, 1997), 1–106; David S. Shields, *Civil Tongues and Polite Letters in British America* (Chapel Hill: Institute of Early American History and Culture, 1997); Caleb Crain, *American Sympathy: Men, Friendship, and Literature in the New Nation* (New Haven: Yale Univ. Press, 2001); and Susan M. Stabile, *Memory's Daughters: The Material Culture of Remembrance in Eighteenth-Century America* (Ithaca: Cornell Univ. Press, 2004).

19. Edgar Allan Poe, "Alone," *Complete Poems*, ed. Thomas Ollive Mabbott (Urbana: Univ. of Illinois Press, 2000), 146. For context, see I. B. Cauthen, Jr., "Poe's 'Alone': Its Background, Source, and Manuscript," *Studies in Bibliography* 3 (1950–1951), 284–291; and Kevin J. Hayes, *Poe and the Printed Word* (Cambridge: Cambridge Univ. Press, 2000), 20–24.

20. On the origins of the album, see Charles Francis Potter, "Autograph Album Rimes," *Funk and Wagnall's Standard Dictionary of Folklore, Mythology, and Legend*, ed. Maria Leach (N.Y.: Funk & Wagnalls, 1949–1950), 1:94–96; and Tatsuhiko Itoh, "Music and Musicians in German *Stammbücher* from circa 1750 to circa 1815" (PhD diss., Duke University, 1992), 31–40.

21. The earliest American album I have seen dates to 1817, although apparently albums were kept at least a year earlier. See Ann M. Edmond, Album [1817–1841], Library of the Connecticut Historical Society Museum, Hartford, Conn.; Caroline Howard, "For Miss Clay's Album / 1816 Savannah," Samuel and Caroline Gilman Papers, American Antiquarian Society.

22. These observations are based on an examination of approximately one hundred and forty albums kept between the 1810s and the 1860s. The heterogeneity of albums is underscored by Starr Ockenga, *On Women and Friendship: A Collection of Victorian Keepsakes and Traditions* (N.Y.: Stewart, Tabori & Chang, 1993), 8–45; and, especially, Todd Gernes, "Recasting the Culture of Ephemera: Young Women's Literary Culture in Nineteenth-Century America" (PhD diss., Brown University, 1992), 57–109.

23. Dalinda Ann Roby, Album, [1836–1846], Beinecke Library, Yale University. This was not an original poem. See "Acrostic. Written in a Young Lady's Album," *New England Magazine* 2 (May 1832): 367. Others versions of this acrostic were less flattering. One reads: "A thing of beauty, gleam and gold, / Loose thoughts, loose words, unmeaning, old, / Big words, that sound a thousand fold; / Unfinished scraps, conceit and cant, / Mad stanzas and a world of rant." Charlotte Gardner, Album [1838–1840], Bindings Coll. D. No. 031, American Antiquarian Society.

24. I am indebted here to Hyde's discussion of "threshold gifts" and "gifts of passage." See Hyde, *The Gift*, 40–45.

25. Elizabeth Turnbull, Album [1823–1824], Bindings Coll. D. No. 016, American Antiquarian Society. This poem was not original either. For printed versions, some with slightly less religious concluding remarks, see *Weekly Muse-*

um, 4 November 1797; *Philadelphia Minerva* 4 (14 April 1798): 43; *New-York Weekly Museum*, 7 July 1810. On the ways in which arithmetical ability was gendered in early national America, see Patricia Cline Cohen, *A Calculating People: The Spread of Numeracy in Early America* (N.Y.: Routledge, 1999), 139–148.

26. Marshall Sahlins, *Stone Age Economics* (N.Y.: Aldine de Gruyter, 1972), 194–195.

27. Henry Lease, "To Elisabeth," Elisabeth B. Packard, Album [1841–1868], Bindings Coll. D. No. 034, American Antiquarian Society.

28. Sahlins, *Stone Age Economics*, 195. For a charming poetic treatment of this theme, see Frances S. Osgood, "The Suitor's Reply to the Maiden Who Wished to Return His Gift," *Poems* (N.Y.: Clarke & Austin, 1845), 140. Here the suitor asks the maiden not to return his ring but rather his love.

29. For razored pages, see Hannah Weyman, Album [1824], Bindings Coll. D. No. 039; Caroline Turnbull, Album [1824–1830] Bindings Coll. D No. 14. For glued down pages, see Sarah E. Webb, Album [1841–1842], Bindings Coll. D. No. 026, all at the American Antiquarian Society. Courting poems do exist, however, in albums whose owners seem not to have married the authors. For other courting poems, see "Is Love a Crime," Mary Wentworth, Album [1833–1883] Ms. SBd-87, Massachusetts Historical Society; and "The Accepted," Lucina Campbell, Album [1832–1843], Wigglesworth Family Papers II, Massachusetts Historical Society.

30. Harriet, Album [1830–1855], Bindings Coll. D. No. 071, American Antiquarian Society. For Hood's actual verses, see Emily Clark, Album, [1827–1828], Bindings Coll. D. No. 19, American Antiquarian Society.

31. I draw the idea of courtship as conversation from Steven M. Stowe, *Intimacy and Power in the Old South: Ritual in the Lives of the Planters* (Baltimore: Johns Hopkins Univ. Press, 1987), 89.

32. Sara Willis, Album [1828–1831], Fanny Fern and Ethel Parton Papers, Sophia Smith Collection, Smith College, Northampton, Mass. For Willis's confession of coquetry, see Stewart Desmond, "The Widow's Trials: The Life of Fanny Fern" (PhD diss., New York University, 1988), 30; and for her experiences at Hartford Female Seminary more generally, Joyce C. Warren, *Fanny Fern: An Independent Woman* (New Brunswick: Rutgers Univ. Press, 1992), 26–42.

33. Ann Eliza Mitchell, Album [1839–1849], Bindings Coll. D. No. 042, American Antiquarian Society; Susan L. Gowdie, Album [1840s], Bindings Coll. D. No. 046, American Antiquarian Society; Julia H. Perry, Album [1860], South Caroliniana Library, University of South Carolina; Julia Ann Goodwin Stillman, Album [1833–1835], Library of the Connecticut Historical Society Museum.

34. On intense bonding among female academy students, see Carol Lasser, "'Let Us Be Sisters Forever': The Sororal Model of Nineteenth-Century Female Friendship," *Signs: Journal of Women in Culture and Society* 14 (1988): 158–181; and Steven M. Stowe, "The Not-So-Cloistered Academy: Elite Women's Education and Family Feeling in the Old South," in *The Web of Southern Social Relations: Women, Family, and Education*, ed. Walter J. Fraser, Jr., R. Frank Saunders, Jr., and Jon L. Wakelyn (Athens: Univ. of Georgia Press, 1985), 90–106. For an album poem that addresses a friend as "sister," see Minerva A. Gardner, "To

Sister Jane," Elizabeth Jane Deming, Album [1834–1835], Rare Book, Manuscript, and Special Collections Library, Duke University.

35. Anya Jabour, "Albums of Affection: Female Friendship and Coming of Age in Antebellum Virginia," *Virginia Magazine of History and Biography* 107 (1999): 125–158. Jabour's argument is problematic not only because she looks at only fifteen albums, all of them owned by women, but because she very deliberately chooses not to discuss inscriptions in them written by men. For the essentialist model of antebellum women's homosociality on which Jabour's argument is built, see Carroll Smith-Rosenberg, "The Female World of Love and Ritual: Relations Between Women in Nineteenth-Century America," in *Disorderly Conduct: Visions of Gender in Victorian America* (Oxford: Oxford Univ. Press, 1985), 53–76.

36. J. Cowen, Album [1827], Bindings Coll. D. No. 044, American Antiquarian Society. For "loving brother," see Samuel Chandler to Joseph Dennie 11 March 1790, Joseph Dennie Papers, Houghton Library, Harvard University. On male student bonding in the early republic, see Leon Jackson, "The Rights of Man and the Rites of Youth: Fraternity and Riot at Eighteenth Century Harvard," *History of Higher Education Annual* 15 (1995): 5–49. For nineteenth-century male homosociality more generally, see Karen V. Hansen, " 'Our Eyes Behold Each Other': Masculinity and Intimate Friendship in Antebellum New England," in *Men's Friendships*, ed. Peter M. Nardi (Newbury Park: Sage Publications, 1992), 35–58; and Donald Yacovone, "Abolitionists and the 'Language of Fraternal Love,' " in *Meanings for Manhood: Constructions of Masculinity in Victorian America*, ed. Mark C. Carnes and Clyde Griffen (Chicago: Univ. of Chicago Press, 1990), 85–95. The Friends' School, also known as New England Yearly Meeting Boarding School, and Moses Brown's School, was coeducational, and while it is impossible to determine Cowen's gender, every name signed to a poem was male. See Rayner Wickersham Kelsey, *Centennial History of Moses Brown School, 1819–1919* (Providence: Moses Brown School, 1919).

37. *Annual Catalogue of the Hartford Female Seminary* (Hartford: George F. Olmstead, 1831), 7. For the increasingly dispersed geographical origins of the Seminary's students, see Kathryn Kish Sklar, *Catharine Beecher: A Study in American Domesticity* (N.Y.: W. W. Norton, 1976), 79. Catherine E. Kelly has argued that the challenge of sustaining academy friendships after graduation was especially daunting for poorer, provincial women. I find her class-based analysis more convincing than Jabour's gender-oriented claim. See *In the New England Fashion: Reshaping Women's Lives in the Nineteenth Century* (Ithaca: Cornell Univ. Press, 1999), 64–92.

38. Catharine Emerson, Album [1845–1864], Bindings Coll. D. No. 023, American Antiquarian Society; Helen M. Everest, Album [1836], Bindings Coll. D. No. 059, American Antiquarian Society. The sentiment comes from Heb. 13:3.

39. Sahlins, *Stone Age Economics*, 195. See also Sally Price, "Reciprocity and Social Distance: A Reconsideration," *Ethnology* 17 (1978): 339–350.

40. HWR, "Emeline," Emeline Camp, Album [1830–1835], Library of the Connecticut Historical Society Museum. For this attitude toward life and death,

see Lewis O. Saum, "Death in the Popular Mind of Pre-Civil War America," in *Death in America*, ed. David E. Stannard (Philadelphia: Univ. of Pennsylvania Press, 1975), 30–48. On the contemptus mundi tradition, see David E. Stannard, *The Puritan Way of Death: A Study in Religion, Culture, and Social Change* (Oxford: Oxford Univ. Press, 1977), 21–28. More generally, I have found useful James J. Farrell, *Inventing the American Way of Death, 1830–1920* (Philadelphia: Temple Univ. Press, 1980), 16–43.

41. Weltha Ann Beckley, Album [1832–1880], Bindings Coll. D. No. 02, American Antiquarian Society.

42. See James Wood, Album [1828–1829], Bindings Coll. D. No. 012, American Antiquarian Society; Jane R. Warner, Album [1833–1834], Bindings Coll. D. No. 072, American Antiquarian Society; Elizabeth Calkins, Album [1833–1838], Library of the Connecticut Historical Society Museum.

43. For an extended discussion of one Vermont album that emphasizes the ways in which the gift of poetry helped turn solitary grief into collective, even collaborative, mourning, see Mary Louise Kete, *Sentimental Collaborations: Mourning and Middle-Class Identity in Nineteenth-Century America* (Durham: Duke Univ. Press, 1999), esp. 19–82. While I am quite sympathetic to Kete's approach, I feel that her emphasis on this single and rather singular album leads her to overstate the significance of both mourning verse and generalized reciprocity for, specifically, album keepers. Although mourning poems were quite commonly given as gifts, few of them appear in the pages of albums, and, indeed, several of those discussed by Kete are on loose sheets tucked in the back of her album. The only example of a mourning album I have found is Alfred B. Connell, Album [1835], South Caroliniana Library, University of South Carolina. Connell prepared the album for his bereaved cousin, Louise Adeline Muldrow. A comparable but not identical instance (because it used letters rather than poems) is discussed by Alan Taylor, *William Cooper's Town: Power and Persuasion on the Frontier of the Early American Republic* (N.Y.: Vintage, 1995), 310–311. For rare individual mourning verses in albums, see J. A. Albro, "On the Death of E. S. Trowbridge," Louisa Trowbridge, Album [1821–1828], Library of the Connecticut Historical Society Museum; and "Thoughts on the Death of Miss Mead," Margaret Maria Neal, Album [1845–1855], Phillips Library, Peabody Essex Museum, Salem.

44. [Lydia Huntley Sigourney], "Extempore on seeing Miss E. D. Tracy, Knitting a Cap, at the Montague Circle," Elizabeth Dorr Tracy Williams, Album [1820–1842], Library of the Connecticut Historical Society Museum.

45. Sahlins, *Stone Age Economics*, 194.

46. "Old Things New Vamped," *American Advocate*, 30 November 1822.

47. "Albums and Album Writing," *Yale Literary Magazine* 13 (July 1848): 363.

48. "Albums," *Cincinnati Mirror, and Chronicle* 4 (30 May 1835): 246; "Albums," *New-York Mirror* (10 August 1833): 47.

49. See, for example, "The Trials of a Poet," *New-Hampshire Gazette*, 6 December 1831; Eliza Leslie, "The Album," in *Pencil Sketches; or, Outlines of Character and Manners. Second Series* (Philadelphia: Carey, Lea, & Blanchard,

1835), 35–65; and "The Omnibus," *Yale Literary Magazine* 1 (August 1836): 216–227.

50. Willis G. Clark, "Ollapodiana Number Seventeen, March, 1837," in *The Literary Remains of the Late Willis Gaylord Clark*, ed. Lewis Gaylord Clark (N.Y.: Burgess, Stringer, and Co., 1844), 184–185.

51. Clark also made such 'stages of life' comments in private. "Deceit and cap-setting, occupy half the time of all Ladies after they are 17 . . . Oh a young Quaker of 15—and I know scores of such—is the most perfect being on the face of the Earth." Willis Gaylord Clark to Willis Gaylord, 3 August 1830, William Jarvis Papers, Vermont Historical Society.

52. Although Clark's scenario is fictional, the unidentified owner of a 1797 diary/account book wrote or had written for her several poems that ran across vertical account-keeping columns. These poems are not courting gifts, however, and do not integrate the columns of the accounting grid into the poem itself. See *The American Ladies Pocket Book for MDCCXCVII* (Philadelphia: W. Y. Birch, [1796]), American Antiquarian Society; and Molly McCarthy, "A Page, A Day: A History of the Daily Diary in America" (PhD diss., Brandeis University, 2004), 107.

53. James Kirke Paulding to James Madison, 28 February 1827, *The Letters of James Kirke Paulding*, ed. Ralph M. Aderman (Madison: Univ. of Wisconsin Press, 1962), 88; [Paulding], *Letter on the Use and Abuse of Incorporations* (N.Y.: G. & C. Carvill, 1827), 5.

54. For a suggestive application of gift theory to the world of learned letter writing in early modern Europe, see Ann Goldgar, *Impolite Learning: Conduct and Community in the Republic of Letters, 1680–1750* (New Haven: Yale Univ. Press, 1995), 12–30. For courtiers' letters as gifts, see Donawerth, "Women's Poetry," 9.

55. F. E. F., "Answer to 'Write to Me,'" *Pebbles of Poetry* (Boston: Foster and Co., 1858), 32. I follow the *National Union Catalog* in attributing this poem to Foster.

56. See M. H. Abrams, "The Correspondent Breeze: A Romantic Metaphor," in *The Correspondent Breeze: Essays on English Romanticism* (N.Y.: W. W. Norton, 1984), 25–43. For the ideal of perfectly unmediated epistolary communion, see William Merrill Decker, *Epistolary Practices: Letter Writing in America before Telecommunications* (Chapel Hill: Univ. of North Carolina Press, 1998), 5, 37–38, 45–46.

57. On letter manuals, I have found useful Janet Gurkin Altman, "The Letter Book as a Literary Institution, 1539–1789: Toward a Cultural History of Published Correspondence in France," *Yale French Studies* 71 (1986): 17–62; Altman, "Political Ideology in the Letter Manual (France, England, New England)," *Studies in Eighteenth Century Culture* 18 (1988): 105–122; Altman, "Teaching the 'People' to Write: The Formation of a Popular Civic Identity in the French Letter Manual," *Studies in Eighteenth Century Culture* 22 (1992): 147–180; Harry B. Weiss, "American Letter-Writers, 1698–1943," *Bulletin of the New York Public Library* 48 (1944): 959–982; and Konstantin Dierks, "Letter Manuals, Liter-

ary Innovation, and the Problem of Defining Genre in Anglo-American Epistolary Instruction, 1568–1800," *Papers of the Bibliographical Society of America* 94 (2000): 541–550. Elsewhere, Dierks points to the profound divergence between prescriptive literature on letter writing and actual epistolary practice in the eighteenth century. See Konstantin Dierks, "Letter Writing, Gender, and Class in America, 1750–1800" (PhD diss., Brown University, 1999).

58. *New and Complete Letter Writer* (Pittsburgh: Cramer & Spear, 1829), [4]; *Lowell Letter Writer* (Lowell: N. L. Dayton, 1845), [xiv]; *The Useful Letter Writer* (N.Y.: Appleton & Co., 1844), [ix].

59. The manuals I consulted were: *The New Complete Letter Writer* (Worcester: Isaiah Thomas, 1791); *The American Letter Writer* (Philadelphia: John M'Culloch, 1793); The *Complete Letter-Writer* (Hartford: Oliver D. and I. Cooke, 1976); *New Universal Letter-Writer* (Philadelphia: D. Hogan, 1800); *A New Academy of Compliments: Or, Complete Secretary* (New York: John Low, 1802); *The Complete Letter-Writer* (Salem: William Hunt, 1802); *The Complete American Letter-Writer* (Otsego: H. & H. Phinney, 1808); *The Fashionable Letter Writer* (N.Y.: George Long, 1818); *The Expert Letter Writer* (Philadelphia: Franklin Scott, 1826); *New and Complete Letter Writer* (Pittsburgh: Cramer & Spear, 1829); *The Fashionable American Letter Writer: Or, The Art of Polite Correspondence* (Brookfield: E. P. Merriam, 1830); *The Letter Writer and Its Accompaniments* (Watertown: Knowlton & Rice, 1833); *The Letter Writer, Containing a Great Variety of Letters* (Boston: Charles Gaylord, 1835); *The Pocket Letter Writer* (Providence: B. Cranston, 1836); *The New Universal Letter-Writer* (Philadelphia: Hogan & Thompson, 1839); *Young Man's Book of Classical Letters* (Philadelphia: Thomas, Copperthwait & Co., 1839); *The Letter Writer's Own Book: Or, The Art of Polite Correspondence* (Philadelphia: John B. Perry, 1843); *The Useful Letter Writer* (N.Y.: Appleton & Co., 1844); *American Fashionable Letter Writer, Original and Selected* (Troy: W. & H. Merriam, 1845); *Lowell Letter Writer* (Lowell: N. L. Dayton, 1845); *The Model Letter Writer; Or Polite Manual* (Boston: Star Spangled Banner Office, 1848); and *American Fashionable Letter Writer* (Boston: G. W. Cottrell, [1859]). The one text that discussed issues of epistolary economy and materiality at length was an etiquette book not a letter-writing manual: Eliza Leslie, *The Behaviour Book* (Philadelphia: Willis P. Hazard, 1853), 150–173.

60. Emily Chubbuck to Maria Bates, 23 June 1841, *Life and Letters of Mrs. Emily C. Judson*, 62.

61. Sarah Margaret Fuller to Timothy Fuller, 25 December 1818; Sarah Margaret Fuller to Timothy Fuller, 16 January 1820; Sarah Margaret Fuller to Timothy Fuller, 4 December 1820; Sarah Margaret Fuller to Timothy Fuller, 15 January 1821; Sarah Margaret Fuller to Timothy Fuller, 30 December 1822; Sarah Margaret Fuller to Timothy Fuller, 20 December 1824, *The Letters of Margaret Fuller*, ed. Robert N. Hudspeth (Ithaca: Cornell Univ. Press, 1983), 1:90, 1:93, 1:105, 1:109, 1:123, 1:144. On Timothy Fuller's challenging program for educating his daughter, see Charles Capper, *Margaret Fuller, An American Romantic: The Private Years* (Oxford: Oxford Univ. Press, 1992), 29–37.

62. Timothy Fuller to Sarah Margaret Fuller, 22 February 1820, 13 April

1820, 3 December 1820, 23 July 1824, 23 June 1824, Margaret Fuller Family Papers, bMS Am 1086 (5:5, 5:6, 5:7, 5:28, 5:24), by permission of the Houghton Library, Harvard University.

63. On prompt responses, see *The New Universal Letter-Writer*, 24–25; *The Letter Writer's Own Book*, xxiii.

64. See Dierks, "Letter Writing, Gender, and Class," 168–169.

65. Sarah Margaret Fuller to Timothy Fuller, 5 January 1821, *Letters of Margaret Fuller*, 1:107.

66. Robert Montgomery Bird to James Lawson, 14 November 1832, James Lawson Papers, South Caroliniana Library, University of South Carolina.

67. Caroline Howard to Harriet Fay, 19 March 1819, Samuel and Caroline Gilman Papers.

68. Lydia Huntley Sigourney to Mrs. Porter, 14 May 1849, L. H. Sigourney Papers, Mount Holyoke College Archives and Special Collections.

69. Henry Wadsworth Longfellow to Zilpah Longfellow, 29 June 1823, *Letters of Henry Wadsworth Longfellow*, 1:48. Longfellow's mother in fact worried endlessly over how often to write to her family. See Zilpah Longfellow to Stephen Longfellow, 18 January 1824, 4 April 1824, Wadsworth-Longfellow Family Papers, Longfellow National Historical Site.

70. Martha C. Derby to Henry Wadsworth Longfellow, 10 October 1829; Parker Cleaveland to Henry Wadsworth Longfellow, 15 June 1844, Letters to Longfellow, bMS Am 1340.2 (1545, 1182).

71. George Bailey Loring to James Russell Lowell, 7 May 1839; James Russell Lowell to Charles Briggs, 13 November 1847, James Russell Lowell Papers, bMS Am 765 (502, 8), by permission of the Houghton Library, Harvard University.

72. James Gates Percival to James Lawrence Yvonnet, 11 June 1822; Percival to Yvonnet, 26 June 1822; Percival to Yvonnet, 17 April 1823; Percival to Yvonnet, 23 September 1823, Julius H. Ward, *The Life and Letters of James Gates Percival* (Boston: Ticknor and Fields, 1866), 95, 102, 153, 176.

73. Mary Moody Emerson to Ralph Waldo Emerson, 19 July [1822]; Mary Moody Emerson to Sarah Alden Bradford, 1 January 1817; Mary Moody Emerson to Ellen Tucker Emerson and Ralph Waldo Emerson, 14–30 January [1831]; Mary Moody Emerson to Ralph Waldo Emerson and Charles Chauncy Emerson, 22 January [1831], *Selected Letters of Mary Moody Emerson*, ed. Nancy Craig Simmons (Athens: Univ. of Georgia Press, 1993), 161, 98, 300, 304.

74. Caroline Howard to Louisa Gilman, 25 October 1813, Samuel and Caroline Gilman Papers.

75. Decker, *Epistolary Practices*, 14.

76. See *The Post-Office Law, with Instructions, Forms and Tables of Distances* (Philadelphia: Charles Cist, 1798), 13–14; *Post-Office Law, Instructions and Forms, Published for the Regulation of the Post-Office* (City of Washington: Way & Gideon, 1825), 8. For a tabular overview, see *United States Domestic Postal Rates, 1789–1956* (Washington, D.C.: Post Office Department, 1956).

77. See Konstantin Dierks, "'Let Me Chat a Little': Letter Writing in Rhode Island before the Revolution," *Rhode Island History* 53 (1995): 121–133; Rich-

ard R. John, *Spreading the News: The American Postal System from Franklin to Morse* (Cambridge, Mass.: Harvard Univ. Press, 1995); and Michael S. Foley, "A Mission Unfulfilled: The Post Office and the Distribution of Information in Rural New England, 1821–1835," *Journal of the Early Republic* 17 (1997): 611–641. Dierks and John see an increasingly broad use of the postal service, while Foley suggests that—at least in rural New Hampshire—that broadening was far less decisive.

78. Robert Montgomery Bird to James Lawson, 6 April 1832; Bird to Lawson, 4 June 1835, Lawson Papers; Charles Fenno Hoffman to Rufus Griswold, 24 January 1844, *Passages from the Correspondence and Other Papers of Rufus W. Griswold* (Cambridge, Mass.: W. M. Griswold, 1898), 149.

79. James Gates Percival to Elizabeth Porter, 17 July 1823, *Uncollected Letters of James Gates Percival: Poet and Geologist, 1795–1856*, ed. Harry R. Warfel (Gainesville: Univ. of Florida Press, 1959), 11–12.

80. Benjamin Rodman to E. Mollineaux, Jr., 6 November 1839; E. Mollineaux, Jr., to Benjamin Rodman, 13 November 1839; Benjamin Rodman to S. N. Douglas, 25 November 1839, all in New Bedford *Mercury*, 29 January 1840. The circumstances surrounding the exchange are explored in Earl Mulderink, III, "'The Whole Town Is Ringing with It': Slave Kidnapping Charges against Nathan Johnson of New Bedford, Massachusetts, 1839," *New England Quarterly* 61 (1988): 341–357.

81. "Letter to the Editor," *Emancipator* 1 (September 1820); "Poindexter's Letter," *Emancipator* 1 (October 1820), both reprinted in *The Emancipator (Complete) Published by Elihu Embree, Jonesborough, Tennessee, 1820*, ed. B. H. Murphy (Nashville: B. H. Murphy, 1932), 91 (quotation), 111. Embree's magazine was sometimes mutilated or misdelivered by postal workers opposed to his anti-slavery politics. See Lawrence B. Goodheart, "Tennessee's Antislavery Movement Reconsidered: The Example of Elihu Embree," *Tennessee Historical Quarterly* 41 (1982): 236.

82. William Lloyd Garrison to Stephen Foster, 30 March 1829, *The Letters of William Lloyd Garrison*, ed. Walter M. Merrill (Cambridge, Mass.: Belknap Press of Harvard Univ. Press, 1971–1981), 1:78.

83. Emily Chubbuck to Catharine [Chubbuck], 16 June 1841, *Life and Letters of Mrs. Emily C. Judson*, 60.

84. Mary Moody Emerson to Charles Chauncy Emerson, 4 February 1826; Mary Moody Emerson to Charles Chauncy Emerson and Edward Bliss Emerson, 1 January 1827, *Selected Letters of Mary Moody Emerson*, 204, 225.

85. Thomas Holley Chivers to Edgar Allan Poe, 15 May 1844, Rufus Griswold Papers, Courtesy of the Trustees of the Boston Public Library.

86. "Dictionaria," *Burlington Sentinel*, 17 March 1837; [John Neal] to Grenville Mellen, 8 December 1819, quoted in [John Neal], "The Unforgotten Dead," *Brother Jonathan* 1 (19 February 1842): 206; [John Neal] to Grenville Mellen, [December 1819], quoted in [John Neal], "Old Letters," *Brother Jonathan* 5 (5 August 1843): 409.

87. John, *Spreading the News*, 4, 38. See also Richard B. Kielbowicz, *News*

in the Mail: The Press, Post Office, and Public Information, 1700–1860s (Westport: Greenwood Press, 1989).

88. Richard Gabriel Stone, *Hezekiah Niles as an Economist*, Johns Hopkins University Studies in Historical and Political Science 51, no. 5 (Baltimore: Johns Hopkins Univ. Press, 1933), 51.

89. Willis T. Hanson, *The Early Life of John Howard Payne* (Boston: The Bibliophile Society, 1913), 34 n 1; Alonzo Lewis and James R. Newhall, *History of Lynn* (Lynn: G. C. Herbert, 1890), 1:517.

90. See David J. Russo, "The Origins of Local News in the U.S. Country Press, 1840s–1870s," *Journalism Monographs* 65 (February 1980): 1–43. For *Godey's* and *Graham's* exchange lists see, respectively, Frank Luther Mott, *A History of American Magazines, 1741–1850* (Cambridge, Mass.: Harvard Univ. Press, 1939), 515; and "Graham's Small-Talk," *Graham's Magazine* 43 (November 1853): 554.

91. "To Editors of Newspapers," *Niles' Weekly Register*, 25 May 1821. See also "Exchange of Newspapers," *Niles' Weekly Register*, 13 July 1822.

92. "Acknowledgement," *African Repository and Colonial Journal* 18 (September 1841): 277; "Exchange Papers," *Reformer* 12 (August 1831): 80. For the language of favors, courtesies, and friends, see "Our Exchange Table," *Cincinnati Mirror* 2 (May 1833): 136; "To Our Exchanges," *Olive Branch*, 4 August 1849; *Rose Bud* 1 (26 December 1832): 67. For newspapers as gifts, see Thomas C. Leonard, *News for All: America's Coming-of-Age with the Press* (N.Y.: Oxford Univ. Press, 1995), 118–124; Ronald J. Zboray and Mary Saracino Zboray, *Everyday Ideas: Socioliterary Experience among Antebellum New Englanders* (Knoxville: Univ. of Tennessee Press, 2006), 79–85.

93. "Exchange," *The National Advocate*, 14 September 1821; "Exchange Papers," *Boston Cultivator* 1 (16 March 1839): 2.

94. *Burlington Sentinel*, 6 October 1837, 14 July 1837.

95. [William Joseph Snelling], "Hints to Editors of Newspapers," *The New-England Magazine* 2 (May 1832): 365.

96. See, for example, Robert K. Stewart, "The Exchange System and the Development of American Politics in the 1820s," *American Journalism* 4 (1987): 30–42; and Jeffrey L. Pasley, *"The Tyranny of Printers": Newspaper Politics in the Early American Republic* (Charlottesville: Univ. Press of Virginia, 2001), 96, 173, 330.

97. "Readers of the Era in the South," *National Era* 8 (19 January 1854): 12. On Bailey's hope of converting hostile Southern readers, see Stanley Harold, *Gamaliel Bailey and the Antislavery Union* (Kent: Kent State Univ. Press, 1986), 85–91.

98. "Rather Saucy," *The Man* (NY), 25 June 1835; Lewis and Newhall, *History of Lynn*, 1:513.

99. The entire fracas, including the *Intelligencer's* summary, is described in the *Saturday Evening Post*, 10 January 1824.

100. Mauss, *The Gift*, 35.

101. "The Bower of Taste," *The Ariel* 1 (8 March 1828): 179.

102. "Proscription," *Olive Branch*, 7 July 1849. The *Olive Branch* insisted that its papers must have been lost in the mail and reassured the *Lynn News* that it was still on its exchange list.

103. John Neal to John Greenleaf Whittier, 4 September 1829, John Greenleaf Whittier Papers, Phillips Library, Peabody Essex Museum, Salem.

104. *Burlington Sentinel*, 14 July 1837, American Antiquarian Society.

105. On bridging and bonding, or more accurately, to my mind, 'bridged' and 'bonded,' forms of social capital, see Robert D. Putnam, *Bowling Alone: The Collapse and Revival of American Community* (N.Y.: Touchstone, 2001), 22–24.

106. See John Earle Uhler, "The Delphian Club: A Contribution to the Literary History of Baltimore in the Early Nineteenth Century," *Maryland Historical Magazine* 20 (1925): 305–346; Joan D. Hedrick, "Parlor Literature: Harriet Beecher Stowe and the Question of 'Great Women Artists,'" *Signs* 17 (1992): 293–300; Lewis P. Simpson, "A Literary Adventure of the Early Republic: The Anthology Society and the Monthly Anthology," *New England Quarterly* 27 (1954): 168–190; Bryan Waterman, *Republic of Intellect: The Friendly Club of New York and the Making of American Literature* (Baltimore: Johns Hopkins Univ. Press, 2007); S[amuel] G[riswold] Goodrich, *Recollections of a Lifetime, or Men and Things I Have Seen* (N.Y.: Miller, Orton, and Mulligan, 1857), 2:109–110.

107. See Catherine Kaplan, "'He Summons Genius . . . To His Aid': Letters, Partisanship, and the Making of the Farmer's Weekly Museum, 1795–1800," *Journal of the Early Republic* 23 (2003): 545–571. For other examples, see Ronald J. Zboray and Mary Saracino Zboray, *Literary Dollars and Social Sense: A People's History of the Mass Market Book* (London: Routledge, 2005), 16–20, 53. Lack of bridging social capital, by contrast, could doom even so geographically well-positioned a periodical as Mathew Carey's Philadelphia *American Museum*. See Ric Northrup Caric, "Speculation and Competence: Case Studies in Capitalist Expansion, 1785–1815" (unpublished essay, 1985).

108. Mott, *A History of American Magazines, 1741–1850*, 21, 199, 511; Michael T. Gilmore, "The Literature of the Revolutionary and Early National Periods," in *The Cambridge History of American Literature: 1590–1820*, ed. Sacvan Bercovitch (Cambridge: Cambridge Univ. Press, 1994), 560; and Michael Davit Bell, "Conditions of Literary Vocation," in *The Cambridge History of American Literature: 1820–1865*, ed. Sacvan Bercovitch (Cambridge: Cambridge Univ. Press, 1995), 52, 53. For similar arguments, see John Tebbel, *The Media in America* (N.Y.: Mentor, 1976), 110.

109. Ellery Sedgwick, "Magazines and the Profession of Authorship in the United States, 1840–1900," *Papers of the Bibliographical Society of America* 94 (2000): 399–425 (quotation 403).

110. For histories of *The Southern Literary Messenger* under White, see Benjamin Blake Minor, *"The Southern Literary Messenger," 1834–1864* (N.Y.: Neale, 1905), 13–80; David K. Jackson, *Poe and "The Southern Literary Messenger"* (Richmond: Dietz, 1934); Jackson, *The Contributors and Contributions to "The Southern Literary Messenger," 1834–1864* (Charlottesville: Historical Publish-

ing Co., 1936), 1–67; and Mott, *A History of American Magazines, 1741–1850*, 629–645. For White's self-deprecation, see Thomas Willis White to George Shattuck, 15 October 1835, Shattuck Family Papers, Courtesy of the Massachusetts Historical Society; Thomas Willis White to Beverley Tucker, 19 February 1835, Letters of Thomas Willis White to Nathaniel Beverley Tucker, MSS 258, Special Collections, University of Virginia Library, hereafter cited as Tucker Letters; and Thomas Willis White to Lucian Minor, 9 April 1835, 14 December 1835, 19 June 1838, David K. Jackson, "Some Unpublished Letters of T. W. White to Lucian Minor," *Tyler's Quarterly Historical and Genealogical Magazine* 18 (1936): 229, 240, 42.

111. Poe's claims to have substantially raised the *Messenger*'s circulation figures have been effectively debunked by Terence Whalen, *Edgar Allan Poe and the Masses: The Political Economy of Literature in Antebellum America* (Princeton: Princeton Univ. Press, 1999), 58–75.

112. Robert D. Jacobs, "Campaign for a Southern Literature: 'The Southern Literary Messenger,'" *Southern Literary Journal* 11 (1969): 83, 71, 70, 81. See also Robert D. Jacobs, *Poe: Journalist and Critic* (Baton Rouge: Louisiana State Univ. Press, 1969), 61–72.

113. The ideological tenor of White's inner circle is usefully described by David A. Rawson, "The Publishing World of Poe's Richmond, or Thomas Willis White and the Southern Periodical Trade," paper presented at the International Edgar Allan Poe Conference, Richmond, October 2002.

114. Thomas Willis White to Nathaniel Beverley Tucker, 4 November 1834, Tucker Letters.

115. Thomas Willis White to Nathaniel Beverley Tucker, 29 January 1835, Tucker Letters; White to Tucker, 5 February 1835, quoted in *The Poe Log: A Documentary Life of Edgar Allan Poe, 1809–1849*, comp. Dwight Thomas and David K. Jackson (N.Y.: G. K. Hall, 1987), 146.

116. Thomas Willis White to Nathaniel Beverley Tucker, 12 March 1835, 19 March 1835, Tucker Letters.

117. For Tucker's genuine interest in the *Messenger*, see Philip Pendleton Cooke to Nathaniel Beverley Tucker, 25 October 1835, quoted in John D. Allen, *Philip Pendleton Cooke* (Chapel Hill: Univ. of North Carolina Press, 1942), 25.

118. White to Minor, 9 November 1835, Jackson, "Unpublished Letters," 235 (quotation); White to Minor, 23 November 1835, Jackson, *Poe and "The Southern Literary Messenger,"* 105; White to Minor, 10 November 1835, Jackson, "Unpublished Letters," 235; White to Minor, 30 October 1835, Jackson, "Unpublished Letters," 233 (quotation).

119. White to Minor, 18 August 1835; White to Minor, 18 April 1835; White to Minor, 8 September 1835; White to Minor, 21 September 1835; Minor to White, 20 October 1835; White to Minor, 23 November 1835, Jackson, *Poe and "The Southern Literary Messenger,"* 97, 97, 99, 100, 103, 105.

120. Joseph Hopkinson to Thomas Willis White, 11 September 1836, Griswold Papers.

121. Philip Pendleton Cooke to Edgar Allan Poe, 16 September 1839, Griswold Papers.

122. Thomas Willis White to James Lawson, 27 November 1837, Lawson Papers.

123. Thomas Willis White to Barber Badger, 27 May 1836, 30 July 1836, Papers of James Southall Wilson, MSS 12708, Special Collections, University of Virginia Library.

124. Thomas Willis White to William Scott, 5 August, 24 November 1836, Wilson Papers. White's placing Scott on his published list of paying subscribers, even though he was receiving the magazine without charge, suggests that Terence Whalen's calculations of the *Messenger*'s income are not wholly accurate, although the degree to which such gifts materially impact his calculations is probably negligible.

125. Edgar Allan Poe to Thomas Willis White, 12 June 1835, *The Letters of Edgar Allan Poe* (N.Y.: Gordian Press, 1966), 61–62. See also David K. Jackson, "Four of Poe's Critiques in the Baltimore Newspapers," *Modern Language Notes* 50 (1935): 251–256.

126. Thomas Willis White to Charles Campbell, 20 July 1839, quoted in Michael O'Brien, *Conjectures of Order: Intellectual Life and the American South, 1810–1860* (Chapel Hill: Univ. of North Carolina Press, 2004), 540.

127. Thomas Willis White to James Lawson, 3 December 1839, Lawson Papers.

128. Thomas Willis White to James Lawson, 27 November 1839, Lawson Papers; Thomas Willis White to Lucian Minor, 31 April 1838, Jackson, "Some Unpublished Letters," 40.

129. Thomas Willis White to Nathaniel Beverley Tucker, 24 January 1837, Jackson, *Poe and "The Southern Literary Messenger,"* 113.

130. Thomas Willis White to Rufus Griswold, 4 August 1841, Griswold Papers.

131. Thomas Willis White to Charles Campbell, 13 February 1840, quoted in O'Brien, *Conjectures of Order*, 537.

132. James Russell Lowell to George Bailey Loring, 26 March 1840 (quotation), 29 March 1840; George Bailey Loring to James Russell Lowell, 25 May 1840, Lowell Papers, bMS Am 765 (58).

133. James Russell Lowell to George Bailey Loring, 22 April 1840, Lowell Papers, bMS Am 765 (58). White's letter, which Lowell transcribes, is dated 13 April 1840.

134. James Russell Lowell to George Bailey Loring, 13 June 1840, Lowell Papers, bMS Am 765 (59). See also Lowell to Nathan Hale, Jr., 15 June 1840, quoted in Philip Graham, "Some Lowell Letters," *Texas Studies in Literature and Language* 3 (1962): 571.

135. James Russell Lowell to George Bailey Loring, [18 August 1840], Lowell Papers, bMS Am 765 (59); Martin Duberman, *James Russell Lowell* (Boston: Beacon Press, 1966), 405 n 51, 57–58 (quotation 58).

136. See Leon Howard, *Victorian Knight Errant: A Study of the Early Literary Career of James Russell Lowell* (Berkeley: Univ. of California Press, 1952), 100–101.

137. James Russell Lowell to Ralph Waldo Emerson, 27 November 1841, *New Letters of James Russell Lowell*, ed. M. A. DeWolfe Howe (N.Y.: Harper

and Brothers, 1932), 7. Ironically, neither Emerson, nor Margaret Fuller cared much for Lowell's sonnets, and Fuller published one only because she did not wish to "discourage these volunteers who are much wanted." See Ralph Waldo Emerson to Margaret Fuller, 1 December 1840; Margaret Fuller to Ralph Waldo Emerson, 6 December 1840; and Ralph Waldo Emerson to James Russell Lowell, 10 December 1840, *Letters of Ralph Waldo Emerson*, ed. Ralph L. Rusk (N.Y.: Columbia Univ. Press, 1939), 2:362–363, 363 n 475 (quotation), 367. Lowell's relations with the *Dial* are documented in Joel Myerson, *The New England Transcendentalists and "The Dial": A History of the Magazine and Its Contributors* (Rutherford: Fairleigh Dickinson Univ. Press, 1980), 177–178.

138. James Russell Lowell to Charles F. Briggs, 16 January 1845, *Letters of James Russell Lowell*, ed. Charles Eliot Norton (N.Y.: Harper & Brothers, 1894), 1:83–84. Lowell's generosity was especially poignant, since he and Briggs were at this point feuding over Lowell's insistence that the *Journal* take a more stridently abolitionist stance than Briggs wished; indeed, it was his abolitionist pieces that he wished to give Briggs gratuitously. See Bette S. Weidman, "The Broadway Journal (2): A Casualty of Abolition Politics," *Bulletin of the New York Public Library* 73 (1969): 94–113; and on Briggs's shaky finances more generally, Heyward Ehrlich, "The Broadway Journal (1): Briggs's Dilemma and Poe's Strategy," *Bulletin of the New York Public Library* 73 (1969): 74–93.

139. James Russell Lowell to Robert Carter, 14 January 1845, Edward L. Tucker, "James Russell Lowell and Robert Carter: The Pioneer and Fifty Letters from Lowell to Carter," *Studies in the American Renaissance: 1987*, ed. Joel Myerson (Charlottesville: Univ. Press of Virginia, 1987), 219; James Russell Lowell to Charles F. Briggs, 26 March 1848, *Letters*, 1:125.

140. James Russell Lowell to Robert Carter, [December 1844], Tucker, "James Russell Lowell and Robert Carter," 217.

141. For examples of Lowell's evasiveness concerning pay for contributors, see Lowell to John Neal, 18 November 1842, John Neal Collection, Maine Historical Society; James R. Mellow, *Nathaniel Hawthorne in His Times* (Baltimore: Johns Hopkins Univ. Press, 1980), 220–222.

142. Lydia Huntley Sigourney to E. Perry, 30 September 1835, reprinted in Gary E. Wait, Elizabeth Pratt Fox, and Everett C. Wilkie, Jr., " 'Good Thoughts in Good Dress': Lydia Sigourney, Hartford Poet," *Connecticut Historical Society Bulletin* 57 (1992): 70; Sigourney to Edgar Allan Poe, 23 April 1836, Griswold Papers.

143. Philip Pendleton Cooke to John E. Cooke, 8 January 1844, John Esten Cooke Papers, Rare Book, Manuscript, and Special Collections Library, Duke University. On the search for an editor, see Stephen Earl Meats, "The Letters of Henry William Herbert, 'Frank Forester,' 1815–1858" (PhD diss., University of South Carolina, 1972), 120, 124–125, 129, 131. For the loss of subscribers and revenue, see O'Brien, *Conjectures of Order*, 535; and Whalen, *Edgar Allan Poe and the Masses*, 288 n 19. For Thompson's gifts to contributors, see, for example, John R. Thompson to Augustin L. Taveau, 5 July 1848, David K. Jackson, "Some Unpublished Letters of John R. Thompson and Augustin L. Taveau," *William and Mary College Quarterly Historical Magazine* 2d ser. (1936): 209.

144. See Tamara Plakins Thornton, *Handwriting in America: A Cultural His-*

tory (New Haven: Yale Univ. Press, 1996), 86–88 (quotation 87); Nathaniel P. Willis to Unidentified Recipient, January 1861, Nathaniel P. Willis Papers, Beinecke Library, Yale University; Alexander R. Whitehill, quoted in Alexander P. Clark, " 'Princeton Memories with a Golden Sheen': Student Autograph Albums of the Nineteenth Century," *Princeton University Library Chronicle* 47 (1986): 306; Zboray and Zboray, *Literary Dollars and Social Sense*, 191.

145. On the rise of albums and gift books, see Ralph Thompson, *American Literary Annuals and Gift Books, 1825–1865* (N.Y.: Archon, 1967); Cindy Dickinson, "Creating a World of Books, Friends, and Flowers: Gift Books and Inscriptions, 1825–1860," *Winterthur Portfolio* 31 (1996): 53–66; Stephen Nissenbaum, *The Battle for Christmas* (N.Y.: Vintage, 1996), 140–150; and Isabelle Lehuu, *Carnival on the Page: Popular Print Media in Antebellum America* (Chapel Hill: Univ. of North Carolina Press, 2000), 76–101. On gift book presentation pages as vestiges of an affective gift economy, see Meredith L. McGill, *American Literature and the Culture of Reprinting, 1834–1853* (Pennsylvania: Univ. of Pennsylvania Press, 2003), 34–36. For the shift from production to consumption, see Zboray and Zboray, *Literary Dollars and Social Sense*, 193.

146. See Richard A. Schwarzlose, *The Nation's Newsbrokers*, vol. 1, *The Formative Years, from Pretelegraph to 1865* (Evanston: Northwestern Univ. Press, 1989), 203; Menahem Blondheim, *News over the Wires: The Telegraphic Flow of Public Information in America, 1844–1897* (Cambridge, Mass.: Harvard Univ. Press, 1994); and Charles Johanningsmeier, *Fiction and the American Literary Marketplace: The Role of Newspaper Syndicates, 1860–1900* (Cambridge: Cambridge Univ. Press, 1997).

147. Jonathan Parry, "*The Gift*, the Indian Gift, and the 'Indian Gift,' " *Man* 21 (1986): 453–473 (quotation 458). The tension between commercial and noncommercial visions of Christmas is the key theme of Nissenbaum's *The Battle for Christmas*.

Chapter Four

1. *Times and Dover Enquirer* receipt, 28 June 1829, Newspaper and Periodical Receipts Collection, 1760–1890, Box 2, Folder 40, American Antiquarian Society; Nathaniel Marsh account with James Hervey Pierrepont, 1829; Bartlett and Brewer to Pierrepont, 26 February 1829; James F. Shores to Pierrepont [1819], all in James Hervey Pierrepont, Booksellers' Accounts, 1812–1838, American Antiquarian Society; *Portsmouth Journal and Rockingham Gazette* receipt, 1 July 1833, Newspaper and Periodical Receipts Collection, Box 2, Folder 46; Brown, Shattuck, and Company, account with Pierrepont, 16 January 1834, Booksellers' Accounts. All newspaper receipts unless otherwise noted are a part of the Newspaper and Periodical Receipts Collection and will simply be cited by box and folder numbers.

2. For Pierrepont's "high standing . . . at Portsmouth" at this time, see Timothy Lindall Jennison to James Hervey Pierrepont, 15 February 1830, Autograph File, by permission of the Houghton Library, Harvard University. On his life and activities more generally, I have relied on Charles Burroughs, *Eulogy Delivered*

in St. John's Church, Portsmouth, N.H. at the Interment of James Hervey Pierrepont, M.D. (Portsmouth: J. W. Foster, 1839), esp. 13–44; "James Hervey Pierrepont," *Boston Medical and Surgical Journal* 20 (June 1839): 319–320; J. Worth Estes and David M. Goodman, *The Changing Humors of Portsmouth: The Medical Biography of an American Town, 1623–1983* (Boston: The Francis A. Countway Library of Medicine, 1986), 42–46; and James Hervey Pierrepont to John Ball, 3 September 1833, Miscellaneous Manuscripts, Massachusetts Historical Society. My depiction of Pierrepont's wealth is based on the Portsmouth Municipal Tax Assessments, Special Collections, Portsmouth Public Library. I am very grateful to Michael A. Baenen for providing me with a transcription of the assessments and helping to contextualize them.

3. James Kirke Paulding to New York Evening Post, 20 December 1827, *The Letters of James Kirke Paulding*, ed. Ralph M. Aderman (Madison: Univ. of Wisconsin Press, 1962), 92; *Massachusetts Ploughman* receipt, 1846, Box 1, Folder 38; Portland *Weekly Advertiser* receipt, 1 January 1829, Box 1, Folder 5; *Saturday Courier* receipt, 29 January 1847, Box 3, Folder 21; *Rhode Island Republican*, MSS 670, Subscription Book, 1809–1822, Rhode Island Historical Society; Berkshire County, Massachusetts, Subscription Account Book, 1828–1833, American Antiquarian Society.

4. See Waldemar H. Fries, *The Double Elephant Folio: The Story of Audubon's Birds of America* (Chicago: American Library Association, 1973), 139–140, 226–227, 250, 294; Richard W. Morin, "Statesman and Artist," *Dartmouth College Library Bulletin* 10 (1969): 2–9; "Pay in Boards," *Freedom's Journal*, 8 August 1828.

5. "To Our Delinquent Subscribers," *Western Monthly Review* 3 (April 1830): 559; Milton W. Hamilton, *The Country Printer: New York State, 1785–1830* (N.Y.: Columbia Univ. Press, 1936), 60; Jeffrey L. Pasley, *"The Tyranny of Printers": Newspaper Politics in the Early American Republic* (Charlottesville: Univ. Press of Virginia, 2001), 129–130 (quotation 130).

6. *The Liberator*, 1 January 1831; William Lloyd Garrison to Samuel J. May, 26 December 1835, *The Letters of William Lloyd Garrison*, ed. William M. Merrill (Cambridge, Mass.: Belknap Press of Harvard Univ. Press, 1971), 1:586–587 (quotation 586); Black List [1839], Liberator Account Books, Anti-Slavery Collection, Courtesy of the Trustees of the Boston Public Library; *The Liberator*, 29 December 1865. For philanthropic support for the *Liberator*, see Julie Winch, *A Gentleman of Color: The Life of James Forten* (Oxford: Oxford Univ. Press, 2002), 241, 246.

7. See Joel Myerson, *The New England Transcendentalists and "The Dial": A History of the Magazine and Its Contributors* (Rutherford: Fairleigh Dickinson Press, 1980), 76; Charles E. Blackburn, "Some New Light on the 'Western Messenger,'" *American Literature* 26 (1954): 320–336.

8. Hamilton, *The Country Printer*, 65–66; Don C. Seitz, *Horace Greeley: Founder of the New York Tribune* (Indianapolis: Bobbs-Merrill, 1926), 56–57; Pasley, *"Tyranny of Printers,"* 57, 115.

9. Thomas C. Leonard, *News for All: America's Coming-of-Age with the Press* (Oxford: Oxford Univ. Press, 1995), 36, 42, 40, 40, 45, 45, 44, 45, 45. The locus

classicus of transactional analysis is Eric Berne, *Games People Play: The Psychology of Human Relationships* (N.Y.: Grove Press, 1967), 13–34 (general theory), 80–83 (debt). For Leonard's indebtedness to Berne, see *News for All*, 243 n 21.

10. Agent's List of Subscribers in Various Towns, 1803–1813, Book Trades Collection, American Antiquarian Society; Spencer Merrill to Elijah Lovejoy, 22 April 1837, quoted in Merton L. Dillon, *Elijah P. Lovejoy: Abolitionist Editor* (Urbana: Univ. of Illinois Press, 1961), 105; Sylvester Judd to [*National Anti-Slavery Standard*], 29 September 1851, quoted in Richard D. Hathaway, *Sylvester Judd's New England* (University Park: Pennsylvania State Univ. Press, 1981), 318–319.

11. Failure to pay butchers: "Importunate Dun," *Lancaster Gazette*, 26 August 1828. Failure to pay tailors: Michael Zakim, *Ready-Made Democracy: A History of Men's Dress in the American Republic, 1760–1860* (Chicago: Univ. of Chicago Press, 2003), 74–75. Failure to pay doctors: George Rosen, *Fees and Fee Bills: Some Economic Aspects of Medical Practice in Nineteenth Century America* (Baltimore: Johns Hopkins Univ. Press, 1946), 17, 33–35.

12. Sympathetic though I am to the basic ideas of transactional analysis, I find its mass historical application here to be largely unsupported and probably unsupportable by the available evidence. For an elaboration of the exchange element in Berne's theory at least structurally congruent with my own approach, however, and especially applicable to gift exchange, see Claude M. Steiner, "The Stroke Economy," *Transactional Analysis Journal* 1 (July 1971): 9–15.

13. Charles G. Steffen, "Newspapers for Free: The Economies of Newspaper Circulation in the Early Republic," *Journal of the Early Republic* 23 (2003): 381–419 (quotations 390, 384, 399). Steffen's argument quite explicitly builds on Leonard's. For the moral economy, see E. P. Thompson, *Customs in Common: Studies in Traditional Popular Culture* (N.Y.: The New Press, 1993), 185–351; and for American applications, Ruth Bogin, "Petitioning and the New Moral Economy in Post-Revolutionary America," *William and Mary Quarterly* 3d Ser. 45 (1988): 391–425; Alex Lichtenstein, "'That Disposition to Theft, With Which They Have Been Branded': Moral Economy, Slave Management, and the Law," *Journal of Social History* 22 (1988): 413–440; and Barbara Clark Smith, "Food Rioters and the American Revolution," *William and Mary Quarterly* 3d Ser. 51 (1994): 3–38.

14. Alden Spooner to Benjamin F. Thompson, 13 October 1817, Book Trades Collection; Calvin Spaulding, Account Books, 1829–1830, American Antiquarian Society. The remaining 25.5 percent of Spaulding's revenue consisted of promissory notes; even assuming that every one of these was for advertising (a wildly implausible supposition) the total would still amount to less than half the paper's revenue. For the *Gazette*, see Fred F. Endres, "'We Want Money and Must Have It': Profile of an Ohio Weekly, 1841–1847," *Journalism History* 7 (1980): 68–71, esp. Table B.

15. Spaulding, Account Books, 1829–1830; Carolyn Stewart Dyer, "The Business History of the Antebellum Wisconsin Newspaper, 1833–1860: A Study of Concentration of Ownership and Diversity of Views" (PhD diss., University of Wisconsin–Madison, 1978), 354 n 105.

16. On the social and cultural history of debt, see Lendol Calder, *Financing the American Dream: A Cultural History of Consumer Credit* (Princeton: Princeton Univ. Press, 1999); Rosa-Maria Gelpi and François Julien-Labruyère, *The*

History of Consumer Credit: Doctrines and Practices, trans. Mn Liam Gavin (N.Y.: St. Martin's, 2000); Philip T. Hoffman, Gilles Postel-Vinay, and Jean-Laurent Rosenthal, *Priceless Markets: The Political Economy of Credit in Paris, 1660–1870* (Chicago: Univ. of Chicago Press, 2000); Craig Muldrew, *The Economy of Obligation: The Culture of Credit and Social Relations in Early Modern England* (N.Y.: St. Martin's Press, 1998); and Bruce H. Mann, *Republic of Debtors: Bankruptcy in the Age of American Independence* (Cambridge, Mass.: Harvard Univ. Press, 2002).

17. My invocation here is indebted to David Hackett Fischer, who describes folkways as "the normative structure of values, customs and meanings that exist in any culture." His own massive study excavates dozens of folkways, including work ways, time ways, and wealth ways; debt ways, it might be said, exist at the intersection of these three. See *Albion's Seed: Four British Folkways in America* (Oxford: Oxford Univ. Press, 1989), 7.

18. Burroughs, *Euology*, 13; Carole Shammas, "How Self-Sufficient Was Early America?" *Journal of Interdisciplinary History* 13 (1982): 247–272; Bettye Hobbs Pruitt, "Self-Sufficiency and the Agricultural Economy of Eighteenth-Century Massachusetts," *William and Mary Quarterly* 3d Ser. 41 (1984): 333–364. For the antebellum romanticization of rural life, see Laurel Thatcher Ulrich, *The Age of Homespun: Objects and Stories in the Creation of an American Myth* (N.Y.: Vintage, 2001), 12–40.

19. The scholarship on rural mutuality is immense. I have found especially useful Christopher Clark, *The Roots of Rural Capitalism: Western Massachusetts, 1780–1860* (Ithaca: Cornell Univ. Press, 1990), 23–27; John Mack Faragher, *Sugar Creek: Life on the Illinois Prairie* (New Haven: Yale Univ. Press, 1986), 130–142; Steven Hahn, *The Roots of Southern Populism: Yeoman Farmers and the Transformation of the Georgia Upcountry, 1850–1890* (Oxford: Oxford Univ. Press, 1983), 50–85; Karen V. Hansen, *A Very Social Time: Crafting Community in Antebellum New England* (Berkeley: Univ. of California Press, 1994); and Susan Geib, " 'Changing Works': Agriculture and Society in Brookfield, Massachusetts, 1785–1820" (PhD diss., Boston University, 1981). On sitting with the sick and dying, see Jack Larkin, *The Reshaping of Everyday Life, 1790–1840* (N.Y.: Harper & Row, 1988), 93–94. For gatherings at childbirth, see Laurel Thatcher Ulrich, *A Midwife's Tale: The Life of Martha Ballard, Based on Her Diary, 1785–1812* (N.Y.: Vintage, 1990), 65–66.

20. On rural conflict, see Clark, *Roots of Rural Capitalism*, 55–58. On warning out, see Ruth Wallis Herndon, *Unwelcome Americans: Living on the Margin in Early New England* (Philadelphia: Univ. of Pennsylvania Press, 2001), esp. 1–22; and Gordon S. Wood, *The Radicalism of the American Revolution* (N.Y.: Vintage, 1991), 130. For exchange as "neighboring," see Barbara Clark Smith, *After the Revolution: The Smithsonian History of Everyday Life in the Eighteenth Century* (N.Y.: Pantheon, 1985), 76; and Hahn, *Roots of Southern Populism*, 55.

21. Tobias Walker, Diary, 27 November 1852, quoted in Thomas C. Hubka, "Farm Family Mutuality: The Mid-Nineteenth-Century Maine Farm Neighborhood," in *The Farm: The Dublin Seminar for New England Folklife Annual Proceedings 1986*, ed. Peter Benes (Boston: Boston University, 1988), 17.

22. Alvin Gouldner, "The Norm of Reciprocity: A Preliminary Statement," *American Sociological Review* 25 (1960): 172.

23. Smith, *After the Revolution*, 74–76.

24. On reputation as social currency, see Hansen, *A Very Social Time*, 114–136.

25. On thick and thin trust, see Robert D. Putnam, *Bowling Alone: The Collapse and Revival of American Community* (N.Y.: Touchstone, 2001), 136–137, 466 n 12; and Russell Hardin, *Trust and Trustworthiness* (N.Y.: Russell Sage Foundation, 2002), 21–23. Scholars sometimes refer to thin trust as social trust, which sidesteps the pejorative equation of thinness and weakness.

26. On double-entry accounting, see B. S. Yamey, "Scientific Bookkeeping and the Rise of Capitalism," *Economic History Review* 1 (1949): 99–113; and Mary Poovey, *A History of the Modern Fact: Problems of Knowledge in the Sciences of Wealth and Society* (Chicago: Univ. of Chicago Press, 1998), 43, 54, 55–57, 62. On hybrid diary-account books, see Marcie Cohen, "The Journals of Joshua Whitman, Turner, Maine, 1809–1846," in *The Farm*, 52; and Molly McCarthy, "A Page, A Day: A History of the Daily Diary in America" (PhD diss., Brandeis University, 2004), 58–115.

27. On rural account books, see Jack Larkin, "Accounting for Change: Exchange in the Rural Economy of Central New England" (unpublished essay, 1988); Michael Merrill, "How to Read an Account Book: Money, Trade and Barter in Preindustrial America" (unpublished essay, 1997); and Winifred Barr Rothenberg, *From Market-Places to a Market Economy: The Transformation of Rural Massachusetts, 1750–1850* (Chicago: Univ. of Chicago Press, 1992), 56–78. On the relatively weak promissory force of book debt, see Bruce H. Mann, *Neighbors and Strangers: Law and Community in Early Connecticut* (Chapel Hill: Univ. of North Carolina Press, 1987), 11–46; and Cornelia Hughes Dayton, *Women before the Bar: Gender, Law, and Society in Connecticut, 1639–1789* (Chapel Hill: Institute of Early American History and Culture, 1995), 77–78.

28. On the variety of credit instruments available to early national Americans, see Mann, *Republic of Debtors*, 7–18. For the different "ethics of exchange," see Clark, *Roots of Rural Capitalism*, 27–38 (quotation 37).

29. *The New Universal Letter-Writer* (Philadelphia: D. Hogan, 1800), 32. It should in fairness be noted that the tradesman in this exchange appears to be dunning a social superior to whom deference and courtesy would have been due, but the point, I think, more generally stands that dunning letters were courteous and apologetic, a contention borne out by the letters I cite below.

30. Population figures are taken from Stephen Hahn and Jonathan Prude, "Introduction," in *The Countryside in the Age of Capitalist Transformation: Essays in the Social History of Rural America*, ed. Hahn and Prude (Chapel Hill: Univ. of North Carolina Press, 1985), 3; Gary Kulik, "Dams, Fish, and Farmers: Defense of Public Rights in Eighteenth-Century Rhode Island," in *Countryside in the Age of Capitalist Transformation*, 25–50.

31. *Bunker-Hill Aurora and Farmers' and Mechanics' Journal*, 12 July 1827 (reprinted, with additions, from the *Missouri Gazette*). For other, and sometimes slightly different, versions, see *Universalist Magazine* 8 (May 1827): 196 (reprint-

ed from the *Vermont Aurora*); *New-York Mirror*, 14 April 1827; *The Ariel*, 19 May 1827; *Album and Ladies' Literary Gazette* 1 (May 1827): 5; and *Carolina Centinel*, 3 June 1820.

32. "Black-List," *New-York Mirror*, 15 June 1833; *Otsego Herald*, 5 November 1808; *Western Monthly Magazine* 5 (January 1836): inside front wrapper. I used a copy at the American Antiquarian Society. On the background of Phinney's avowals, see Alan Taylor, *William Cooper's Town: Power and Persuasion on the Frontier of the Early American Republic* (N.Y.: Vintage Books, 1995), 351–355.

33. *Massachusetts Spy*, 4 May 1780; *Salem Register*, 1809, quoted in Harriet Silver Tapley, *Salem Imprints, 1768–1825* (Salem: Essex Institute, 1927), 149; *Weekly Tribune*, 17 December 1847, quoted in William H. Lyon, *The Pioneer Editor of Missouri, 1808–1860* (Columbia: Univ. of Missouri Press, 1965), 90.

34. *Rhode Island Republican*, MSS 670, Subscription Book; Hezekiah Kimball to William Simons, 5 September 1820, tipped into the same volume; Solomon Clark, Account Book, 1820–1826, American Antiquarian Society.

35. Calvin Spaulding, Account Books; *New Hampshire Statesman & Concord Register* receipt, 14 May 1831, Box 2, Folder 43; Estate of Edward S. Vose to C. Harris, 2 August 1831, Book Trades Collection.

36. *Boston Morning Post*, 1835, quoted in James Hannan Butler, "Indiana Newspapers, 1829–1860," *Indiana Magazine of History* 22 (1926): 306.

37. Horace Greeley, *Recollections of a Busy Life* (N.Y.: Chelsea House, 1983), 141. Greeley would later come to endorse up-front cash subscriptions, as I discuss below.

38. Isaac C. Pray to John Greenleaf Whittier, 27 February 1838; J. L. O'Sullivan to Whittier, 5 April 1843, John Greenleaf Whittier Papers, used by permission of the Phillips Library of the Peabody Essex Museum; Henry William Herbert to George Roberts, 24 April 1841, quoted in Stephen Earl Meats, "The Letters of Henry William Herbert, 'Frank Forester,' 1815–1858" (PhD diss., University of South Carolina, 1972), 76.

39. James F. Shores to James Hervey Pierrepont, 17 November 1828; Monroe and Brown to Pierrepont, 2 July 1832; Carter and Hendee to 29 January 1830; Cummings and Hilliard to Pierrepont, 13 April 1825, all in Booksellers' Accounts, 1812–1838.

40. William Wells, Jr., to John Hervey Pierrepont, 16 August 1816, Booksellers' Accounts, 1812–1838.

41. My account is based on Thomas Jordan to Carey and Lea, 30 April 1822; Jordan to Carey and Lea, 5 May 1822 ("any jury"); Wells and Lilly to Carey and Lea, 25 July 1822, Lea and Febiger Records, Collection #227B, Historical Society of Pennsylvania; and Thomas Jordan v. William Wells et al. [May 1822]; William Wells et al. v. Thomas Jordan [May 1822]; and Civil Docket Book, October 1822 Term, Suffolk County Court of Common Pleas, Judicial Archives, Massachusetts Archives, Boston. On the background of Wells and Lilly's dispute with Jordan, see David Kaser, *Messrs. Carey & Lea of Philadelphia: A Study in the History of the Book Trade* (Philadelphia: Univ. of Pennsylvania Press, 1957), 146–148. Massachusetts' laws, which allowed creditors to imprison debtors or attach their

property (but not both) are discussed by Peter J. Coleman, *Debtors and Creditors in America: Insolvency, Imprisonment for Debt, and Bankruptcy, 1607–1900* (Madison: State Historical Society of Wisconsin, 1974), 3–5, 39–52.

42. Thomas Jordan to Carey and Son, 30 April 1822; Jordan to Carey and Lea, 5 May 1822, Lea and Febiger Records. On the ways in which credit, social standing, and manhood were associated in early national discourse, see Sarah Kidd, "'To be harassed by my Creditors is worse than Death': Cultural Implications of the Panic of 1819," *Maryland Historical Magazine* 95 (2000): 161–189; and Toby L. Ditz, "Shipwrecked; or Masculinity Imperiled: Mercantile Representations of Failure and the Gendered Self in Eighteenth-Century Philadelphia," *Journal of American History* 81 (1994): 51–80.

43. Jordan to Carey and Lea, 5 May 1822, Lea and Febiger Records; *New-Hampshire Gazette*, 5 October 1821.

44. "Terms of the Mirror," *Literary Mirror*, 23 April 1808.

45. George B. Allen to Henry Wadsworth Longfellow, 17 June 1855, Letters to Henry Wadsworth Longfellow, bMS Am 1340.2 (93), by permission of the Houghton Library, Harvard University; Timothy Flint to Lydia Huntley Sigourney, 3 March 1834, Lydia Huntley Sigourney Papers, Library of the Connecticut Historical Society Museum, Hartford, Conn.; Henry I. Bowditch to John Greenleaf Whittier, [11 November 1843], Whittier Papers; Lewis Gaylord Clark to John Pendleton Kennedy, 3 August 1835, John Pendleton Kennedy Papers, Peabody Library, Baltimore.

46. On the power of seriality to create intimacy, see Linda K. Hughes and Michael Lund, *The Victorian Serial* (Charlottesville: Univ. Press of Virginia, 1991), 8, 10–11.

47. [N. P. Willis], "The Editor's Table," *American Monthly Magazine* 1 (July 1829): 275–289; "Editor's Table," *American Monthly Magazine* 1 (August 1829): 354–364; "Editor's Table," *American Monthly Magazine* 1 (September 1829): 428–438 (quotation 428). For reaction to Willis's editorial persona, see Thomas N. Baker, *Sentiment and Celebrity: Nathaniel Parker and the Trials of Literary Fame* (Oxford: Oxford Univ. Press, 1999), 43–45. For Graham, see Estelle Lewis to George R. Graham, 12 June 1843, Rufus W. Griswold Papers, courtesy of the Trustees of the Boston Public Library. For a sensitive meditation on the blurring of boundaries between author Ik Marvel and his readers, see Lisa Spiro, "Reading with a Tender Rapture: 'Reveries of a Bachelor' and the Rhetoric of Detached Intimacy," *Book History* 6 (2003): 57–93. On gifts to editors and their intimacy with readers, see Albert Lowther Demaree, *The American Agricultural Press, 1819–1860* (N.Y.: Columbia Univ. Press, 1941), 91–92.

48. Fred M. Nelson to Gales & Seaton, 4 July 1823, Gales & Seaton Records, Rare Book, Manuscript, and Special Collections Library, Duke University. See, more generally, Michael Warner, *The Letters of the Republic: Publication and the Public Sphere in Eighteenth-Century America* (Cambridge, Mass.: Harvard Univ. Press, 1990).

49. *Salem Register*, 1808, quoted in Tapley, *Salem Imprints, 1768–1825*, 149.

50. For a suggestive account of dunning strategies employed by *Godey's Lady's Book*, which habitually described its readers as friends, see Elizabeth White

Nelson, *Market Sentiments: Middle-Class Market Culture in 19th-Century America* (Washington, D.C.: Smithsonian Books, 2004), 36, 63–69.

51. "Pay the Printer," *A Collection of Songs of the American Press and Other Poems Relating to the Art of Printing*, comp. Charles Munsell (Albany: Munsell, 1868), 88–89.

52. "The Editor's Message," *Western Monthly Magazine* 3 (February 1835): 93.

53. *Songs of the American Press*, 42. For other "living on air" quips, see "The Printer's Soliloquy," *Independent Chronicle*, 12 May 1812; "The Editor's Table," *Godey's Lady's Book* 11 (1835): 285.

54. *Schenectady Cabinet*, 23 October 1816, quoted in Hamilton, *New York Country Printer*, 210. Also printed in *New Hampshire Gazette*, 5 May 1829. The bear's paw image seems to have been well known to printers. See Elisha Waldo to Isaiah Thomas, 14 February 1795, Isaiah Thomas Papers, Box 3, Folder 1, American Antiquarian Society.

55. "Depravity of Delinquents," *Philadelphia Commercial Herald*, 1838, quoted in *Songs of the American Press*, 70; William W. Smithers, *The Life of John Lofland, "The Milford Bard"* (Philadelphia: Wallace M. Leonard, 1894), 62; *Western Press* quoted in "A Printer in Extremities," *Portsmouth Journal and Rockingham Gazette*, 22 December 1827; *Political Repository: or, Farmer's Journal*, quoted in Jack Larkin, "The Merriams of Brookfield: Printing in the Economy and Culture of Rural Massachusetts in the Early Nineteenth Century," *Proceedings of the American Antiquarian Society* 96 (1986): 40. See also "Pay the Printer," *Maine Farmer*, 12 December 1837.

56. "Two Thousand Hints," *Freedom's Journal* 2 (31 January 1829): 345. Reprinted from the *Gloucester Telegraph*. For another version, see "Pay the Printer," *Greensborough Patriot*, 25 July 1829.

57. "Remember the Printer!" *State Journal*, 5 January 1836.

58. *Western Carolinian*, 15 December 1829.

59. When a Louisiana printer's apprentice dunned a physician and the physician retorted by calling the printer a "puppy," the apprentice shot him dead on the spot. See *New-Hampshire Gazette*, 29 January 1828. Still more fittingly, in 1841 an author of several texts on double-entry bookkeeping murdered his printer after a disagreement over a small debt. See Andie Tucher, *Froth and Scum: Truth, Beauty, Goodness, and the Ax Murder in America's First Mass Medium* (Chapel Hill: Univ. of North Carolina Press, 1994), 99–102.

60. Sigmund Freud, *Jokes and Their Relation to the Unconscious*, trans. James Strachey (Harmondsworth: Penguin, 1976), 144. James F. English has made a strong claim for the socially (as opposed to the psychologically) mediatory function of jokes, while still endorsing Freud's analytical techniques. See English, *Comic Transactions: Literature, Humor, and the Politics of Community in Twentieth-Century Britain* (Ithaca: Cornell Univ. Press, 1994), esp. 5–19.

61. "The New Year," *Western Monthly Magazine* 2 (January 1834): 47; "A Dead Subscriber," *Flag of Our Union*, 23 October 1847. In a later example, a dead subscriber sends the message to "pay the printer" to the participants in a séance: "Editor's Drawer," *Harper's New Monthly Magazine* 7 (July 1853): 277.

62. "A Touch of the Sublime," *Burlington Sentinel*, 5 May 1837.

63. "A Word to All Concerned," *The Knickerbocker* 17 (April 1841): 358. The list of delinquents appeared on the wrapper of the June 1841 issue, copy at the American Antiquarian Society. For the earliest and friendliest dun, see "A Word from the Proprietors," *The Knickerbocker* 8 (September 1836): 376. For circulation figures, Frank Luther Mott, *A History of American Magazines, 1850–1865* (Cambridge, Mass.: Harvard Univ. Press, 1938), 607.

64. "Advertisement," *Port Folio* 16 (1823): 4. For another example, see "Black List," *Paul Pry*, 4 April 1835. For a threat, see "To Our Delinquent Subscribers," *Western Monthly Review* 3 (April 1830): 560.

65. "To Subscribers," *Ladies' Companion* 11 (May 1839): 50. For circulation figures: "Editor's Table," *Ladies' Companion* 12 (November 1839): 50. Blacklists appear on the paper wrappers of the magazine: 12 (December 1839); 12 (January 1840); 12 (February 1840); 12 (April 1840); 13 (July 1840). The copies I consulted are owned by the American Antiquarian Society. For the later plea: "Our New Series," *Ladies' Companion* ns 1 (May 1844). Several months later, the magazine folded.

66. On colored wrappers, see "Leaf and Stem Basket" *Southern Rose* 5 (27 May 1837): 159. For the broad diffusion of knowledge about serials arriving at the Post Office, see Leonard, *News for All*, 13–19.

67. Caroline Gilman to Harriet Fay [1832], quoted in Janice Joan Thompson, "Caroline Howard Gilman: Her Mind and Art" (PhD diss., University of North Carolina, 1975), 29.

68. On Charleston's declining white population in the 1830s, see William H. Pease and Jane H. Pease, *The Web of Progress: Private Values and Public Styles in Boston and Charleston, 1828–1843* (Oxford: Oxford Univ. Press, 1984), 45, 217–218.

69. My account of the Mercantile Agency relies on Bertram Wyatt-Brown, "God and Dun & Bradstreet, 1841–1851," *Business History Review* 40 (1966): 432–450; James H. Madison, "The Evolution of Commercial Credit Reporting Agencies in Nineteenth-Century America," *Business History Review* 48 (1974): 164–186; Scott A. Sandage, *Born Losers: A History of Failure in America* (Cambridge, Mass.: Harvard Univ. Press, 2005), 99–128; and, especially, Sandage, "Deadbeats, Drunkards, and Dreamers: A Cultural History of Failure in America, 1819–1893" (PhD diss., Rutgers University, 1995), 268–294 (quotation 289).

70. For references to Mercantile Agency reports on publishers, see Joseph Fichtelberg, *Critical Fictions: Sentiment and the American Market, 1780–1870* (Athens: Univ. of Georgia Press, 2003), 206–207; and Michael Winship, "'The Greatest Book of Its Kind': A Publishing History of 'Uncle Tom's Cabin,'" *Proceedings of the American Antiquarian Society* 109 (1999): 316 n 20. For an antebellum publishing firm that developed its own reports on creditors, see Thomas Augst, *The Clerk's Tale: Young Men and Moral Life in Nineteenth-Century America* (Chicago: Univ. of Chicago Press, 2003), 224–225.

71. See, for example, "Agent for the Rose Bud," *Rose Bud* 1 (8 December 1832): 59; "Depositories for the Rose Bud," *Rose Bud* 1 (9 March 1833): 111.

72. Park Benjamin to John Neal, 3 December, 1838, John Neal Papers, bMS

Am 1949 (12), Houghton Library, Harvard University; Caroline Gilman to Harriet Fay, 27 October 1835, quoted in *A Balcony in Charleston*, ed. Mary Scott Saint-Armand (Richmond: Garret and Massie, 1941), 33. For an excellent discussion of women as business agents, including for various publication ventures, see Lori D. Ginzberg, *Women and the Work of Benevolence: Morality, Politics, and Class in the Nineteenth-Century United States* (New Haven: Yale Univ. Press, 1990), 36–66.

73. Hezekiah Niles to D. B. Stockholm, 14 October 1817, Book Trades Collection; Sarah Griffin to John Neal, 3 August 1842, Neal Papers, bMS Am 1949 (124); Amelia Bloomer to Lydia Huntley Sigourney, 9 May 1849, Sigourney Papers.

74. *Ladies' Companion* 12 (December 1839): inside back wrapper.

75. For Gilman's reaching out to strangers as agents, see, for example, Caroline Gilman to Hilliard and Gray [c. 1833], Caroline Gilman Papers, South Caroliniana Library, University of South Carolina. For brief but helpful discussions of fraudulent subscription agents, Nelson, *Market Sentiments*, 69–72; and Ronald J. Zboray and Mary Saracino Zboray, *Literary Dollars and Social Sense: A People's History of the Mass Market Book* (London: Routledge, 2005), 130–139. On the growth of the sincere hypocrite in antebellum America more generally, see Karen Halttunen, *Confidence Men and Painted Women: A Study of Middle-Class Culture in America, 1830–1870* (New Haven: Yale Univ. Press, 1982), esp. 33–55.

76. Quoted in Cindy Ann Stiles, "Windows into Antebellum Charleston: Caroline Gilman and the *Southern Rose* Magazine" (PhD diss., University of South Carolina, 1994), 41.

77. While, doubtless, there were scores of legal actions taken by newspaper and magazine proprietors against delinquent subscribers, such evidence is buried in county-level court records, and digging it up would be an immense effort. We do have collateral evidence, however. In 1834, for example, the New York *Daily Sentinel* successfully sued a subscriber who had taken the paper without ever paying for it, and it became a topic of discussion in print. See the report in the (Nova Scotia) *Yarmouth Herald*, 12 December 1834. This report also mentions "similar cases decided in the same way in this Province." An 1849 piece also alludes to court rulings on subscription payments made in favor of proprietors. See "The Law of Periodicals," *The Ladies' Wreath* 4 (May 1849), inside front wrapper, copy in the American Antiquarian Society. I am grateful to Lyndsay Campbell for bringing the former item to my attention.

78. On *Harper's*, see Mott, *History of American Magazines, 1850–1865*, 383–405; Eugene Exman, *The Brothers Harper: A Unique Publishing Partnership and Its Impact upon the Cultural Life of America from 1817–1853* (N.Y.: Harper & Row, 1965), 303–322; and John Gray Laird Dowgray, "A History of 'Harper's New Monthly Magazine,' 1850–1900" (PhD diss., University of Wisconsin–Madison, 1956). For the 1855 sales figures, see Jacob Abbott, *The Harper Establishment: How the Story Books are Made* (N.Y.: Harper & Brothers, 1855), 158.

79. "A Letter to the Proprietors of Harper's Magazine," *American Whig Review* 16 (July 1852): 12–20.

80. Almost all scholars ascribe the success of the magazine to its contents and the (nationalistic) cultural work they performed rather than looking to the social or economic conditions that governed its production, dissemination, and purchase, which I mention above. See, for recent examples, Jennifer Phegley, "Literary Piracy, Nationalism, and Women Readers in 'Harper's New Monthly Magazine,' 1850–1855," *American Periodicals* 14 (2004): 63–90; and Thomas Lilly, "The National Archive: 'Harper's New Monthly Magazine' and the Civic Responsibilities of a Commercial Literary Periodical, 1850–1853," *American Periodicals* 15 (2005): 142–162.

81. "A Letter to the Proprietors of Harper's Magazine," 12.

82. Herman Melville, "The Paradise of Bachelors and the Tartarus of Maids," *The Piazza Tales and Other Prose Pieces, 1839–1860*, ed. Harrison Hayford et al. (Evanston and Chicago: Northwestern Univ. Press and the Newberry Library, 1987), 324. Subsequent page references cited parenthetically in the text. For Melville's periodical work for Harper and Brothers, see Sheila Post-Lauria, *Correspondent Colorings: Melville in the Marketplace* (Amherst: Univ. of Massachusetts Press, 1996), 165–209.

83. See Judith A. McGaw, *Most Wonderful Machine: Mechanization and Social Change in Berkshire Paper Making, 1801–1885* (Princeton: Princeton Univ. Press, 1987), 334–336 n 1. My account of the technologies and economics of paper making is greatly indebted to McGaw's work. On Melville's actual visit to the Dalton mill, see Jay Leyda, *The Melville Log: A Documentary Life of Herman Melville, 1819–1891* (N.Y.: Gordian Press, 1969), 1:403–404.

84. On the sense of insecurity in the papermaking trade in the 1820s, see John Bidwell, "American Papermakers and the Panic of 1819," in *A Potencie of Life: Books in Society*, ed. Nicolas Barker (London: British Library, 1993), 89–112; Larkin, "The Merriams of Brookfield," 42–58 (quotation 57). The Merriams were by no means unique in shifting to cash payments for printing and paper; see Philip F. Gura, "Early Nineteenth-Century Printing in Rural Massachusetts: John Howe of Greenwich and Enfield, c. 1803–1845," in *The Crossroads of American History and Literature* (University Park: Pennsylvania State Univ. Press, 1996), esp. 137–138.

85. "To Our Delinquent Subscribers," *Western Monthly Review* 3 (April 1830): 560.

86. McGaw, *Most Wonderful Machine*, 67. Paper makers were also on the cutting edge of accounting and bookkeeping practices, which reflected this new economic ethos. See Judith A. McGaw, "Accounting for Innovation: Technological Change and Business Practice in the Berkshire County Paper Industry," *Technology and Culture* 26 (1985): 703–725. The facts about mummy paper are carefully teased apart from the myths by S. J. Wolfe and Robert Singerman, " 'Better than Stealing Pennies from the Eyes of Dead Men': Commercial Exploitation of Mummies in Victorian America" (unpublished essay, 2003).

87. On newsboys and their street sales, see Vincent Richard DiGirolamo, "Crying the News: Children, Street Work, and the American Press, 1830s–1920s" (PhD diss., Princeton University, 1997), 25–26, 45, 48–51, 172–173, 177 (quotation). John Nerone points out that street sales accounted for only a small portion of penny press sales; what was significant, he argues, was the rise of cash-in-hand

payments. See John C. Nerone, "The Mythology of the Penny Press," in *Media Voices*, ed. Jean Folkerts (N.Y.: Macmillan, 1992), esp. 158–159, 164. For Milwaukee's street sales, see Dyer, "The Business History of the Antebellum Wisconsin Newspaper," 312.

88. "The Cash System," *Arkansas State Gazette*, 20 January 1841; *Arkansas State Gazette*, 27 January 1841. See also Cathleen Ann Baker, "The Press that Cotton Built: Printing in Mobile, Alabama, 1850–1865" (PhD diss., University of Alabama, 2004), 39–40.

89. *Barre Gazette*, 29 November 1839.

90. "New Yorker," *New Hampshire Sentinel*, 25 March 1840; "The Cash System," *Arkansas State Gazette*, 20 January 1841.

91. *Pittsfield Sun*, 30 July 1840.

92. Phil C. Bing, *The Country Weekly: A Manual for the Rural Journalist and for Students of the Country Field* (N.Y.: D. Appleton, 1917), 233–236. On residual and emergent practices, see Raymond Williams, *Marxism and Literature* (Oxford: Oxford Univ. Press, 1986), 121–127.

93. "Harper's New Monthly Magazine," *The Literary World* 7 (November 1850): 364. For an astute and suggestive study of the Harpers' immense periodical advertising campaigns in the 1850s, see Ronald J. Zboray, *A Fictive People: Antebellum Economic Development and the American Reading Public* (Oxford: Oxford Univ. Press, 1993), 59–66. On charges for agents' specimen copies, see Weeks, Jordan, and Company to Cyrus Farnham, [1840], Hooker Collection, Schlesinger Library, Radcliffe Institute, Harvard University.

94. [George Foster], *New York in Slices: By an Experienced Carver* (N.Y.: W. F. Burgess, 1849), 104.

95. Junius Henri Browne, *The Great Metropolis: A Mirror of New York* (Hartford: American Publishing Company, 1869), 94.

96. George D. Strong, quoted in Digirolamo, "Crying the News," 36. On the criminal activities of newsboys, see Timothy J. Gilfoyle, "Street-Rats and Gutter-Snipes: Child Pickpockets and Street Culture in New York City, 1850–1900," *Journal of Social History* 37 (2004): 853–882.

97. *New York Herald*, 21 November 1837, quoted in Michael Schudson, *Discovering the News: A Social History of American Newspapers* (N.Y.: Basic Books, 1978), 21. Street sales, of course, needn't *necessarily* be disembedded. In his study of African-American book and magazine vendors working the streets of contemporary New York City sociologist Mitchell Duneier, has discovered a world of loyalty and complex sociability between vendors and customers, which he describes as a 'sustaining habitat.' Vendors of 'homeless newspapers,' likewise, often rely upon an affective, albeit brief, relationship with their prospective and actual customers. My point is simply that while credit-based subscriptions have historically tended to presuppose and generate trust, street sales have not. See Mitchell Duneier, *Sidewalk* (N.Y.: Farrar, Strauss, and Giroux, 1999); and Norma Fay Green, "Chicago's 'Street Wise' at the Crossroads: A Case Study of a Newspaper to Empower the Homeless in the 1990s,' in *Print Culture in a Diverse America*, ed. James P. Danky and Wayne Wiegand (Urbana: Univ. of Illinois Press, 1998), 34–55.

98. "The Cash Principle," *Flag of Our Union*, 16 October 1847.

99. Peter Benson, "Gleason's Publishing Hall," in *Publishers for Mass Entertainment in Nineteenth Century America*, ed. Madeleine B. Stern (Boston: G. K. Hall, 1980), 137–145 (quotation 142). Gleason was able to retire at the age of 35.

100. "What We Call Duties," *True Flag*, 13 March 1852. For an almost identical imperative, see "Duties," *Saturday Evening Post*, 28 April 1860.

101. *The Dew Chalice* 1 (11 January 1854), Amateur Newspaper Collection, American Antiquarian Society.

102. For a good overview of Melville's relations with Harper and Brothers, see Exman, *The Brothers Harper*, 282–302. On Melville's purchase of, and subscriptions to, *Harper's New Monthly Magazine*, see Merton M. Sealts, Jr., *Melville's Reading: Revised and Enlarged Edition* (Columbia: Univ. of South Carolina Press, 1988), 87–88, 181.

103. For Melville's accounts with Harper's, see Exman, *The Brothers Harper*, 285, 288, 290, 291, 295, 298, 299, 300; Herman Melville to Lemuel Shaw, 22 May 1856 (interest on advances); Harper & Brothers to Herman Melville, 30 April 1851 (declining advance), *Correspondence*, ed. Lynn Horth, vol. 14, *The Writings of Herman Melville*, ed. Harrison Hayford (Evanston and Chicago: Northwestern Univ. Press and The Newberry Library, 1993), 295, 613.

104. "Cock-A-Doodle-Doo! Or, the Crowing of the Noble Cock Beneventano," *Harper's New Monthly Magazine* 8 (December 1853): 78.

105. See Helen P. Trimpi, "Three of Melville's Confidence Men: William Cullen Bryant, Theodore Parker, and Horace Greeley," *Texas Studies in Literature and Language* 21 (1979): 368–395; Herman Melville, *The Confidence-Man: His Masquerade*, ed. Harrison Hayford, vol. 10, *The Writings of Herman Melville*, ed. Harrison Hayford (Evanston and Chicago: Northwestern Univ. Press and The Newberry Library, 1984), 4.

106. "Northern and Southern Patronage," *Charleston Mercury*, 26 October 1860. On antebellum Southern views of the extension of credit as a matter of honor, see Kenneth S. Greenberg, *Honor and Slavery: Lies, Duels, Noses, Masks, Dressing as a Woman, Gifts, Strangers, Humanitarianism, Death, Slave Rebellions, the Proslavery Argument, Baseball, Hunting, and Gambling in the Old South* (Princeton: Princeton Univ. Press, 1996), 78–80.

107. My understanding of *The New Yorker*'s economic organization and culture is greatly indebted to Trysh Travis, "What We Talk About When We Talk about 'The New Yorker,'" *Book History* 3 (2000): 253–285 (quotation 271).

108. See Ben Yagoda, *About Town: "The New Yorker" and the World It Made* (N.Y.: Scribner, 2000), 181–182 (Armed Service edition), 95–96 (advertising versus editorial departments), 325–326 (writers in debt to magazine), 331–332; Travis, "What We Talk About," 272 (quotation).

109. Travis, "What We Talk About," 253.

110. On the introduction of the "bill me later" option, see Gigi Mahon, *The Last Days of "The New Yorker"* (N.Y.: McGraw-Hill 1988), 314. Mahon deplores this innovation, which she associates with the purchase of *The New Yorker* by S. I. Newhouse, the owner of media conglomerate, Advance Communications, in 1985. My own sense is that it was a very deliberate attempt to shore up pre-

cisely the sort of trust and amity that Mahon believes was lost when the magazine was purchased.

111. Letter to Leon Jackson, 18 November 2004.

112. On modern debt collection practices, see Paul Rock, *Making People Pay* (London: Routledge & Kegan Paul, 1973); and Arlie Russell Hochschild, *The Managed Heart: The Commercialization of Human Feeling* (Berkeley: Univ. of California Press, 2003), 138–147.

Chapter Five

1. On the build-up to the premiere of *Metamora*, see "Varieties," *The Critic: A Weekly Review of Literature, Fine Arts, and the Drama*, 22 November 1828 (quotation); "The Prize Tragedy," *New-York Mirror*, 31 October 1829; and "Metamora," *New-York Mirror*, 12 December 1829. For the premiere itself, see "The Park Theatre," *New-York Mirror*, 19 December 1829 (quotation).

2. John Augustus Stone, *Metamora; or, The Last of the Wampanoags*, in *Metamora and Other Plays*, ed. Eugene R. Page (Princeton: Princeton Univ. Press, 1941), 40. On the political context of Stone's play, see Scott C. Martin, "Interpreting 'Metamora': Nationalism, Theater, and Jacksonian Indian Policy," *Journal of the Early Republic* 19 (1999): 73–101.

3. The lasting popularity of *Metamora* as played by Forrest is anatomized by Sally L. Jones, "The First but not the Last of the 'Vanishing Indians': Edwin Forrest and the Mythic Re-Creations of the Native Population," in *Dressing in Feathers: The Constructions of the Indian in American Popular Culture*, ed. S. Elizabeth Bird (Boulder: Westview Press, 1996), 13–27; Jill Lepore, *The Name of War: King Philip's War and the Origins of American Identity* (N.Y.: Alfred A. Knopf, 1998), 191–226; and Theresa Strouth Gaul, "'The Genuine Indian Who Was Brought Upon the Stage': Edwin Forrest's 'Metamora' and White Audiences," *Arizona Quarterly* 56 (2000): 1–27.

4. On Forrest's income, see *Metamora and Other Plays*, 4; Lepore, *Name of War*, 316 n 11; "Receipts on the Nights of Edwin Forrest's Performances at the Park Theatre, N.Y, 1821–1841," Edwin Forrest Papers, Harvard Theater Collection. The estimate of 200 performances is offered by Eugene H. Jones, *Native Americans as Shown on the Stage, 1753–1916* (Metuchen: Scarecrow Press, 1988), 66.

5. The one exception, more documentary in nature than analytic, is Eric Ray Marshall, "Playwriting Contests and Jacksonian Democracy, 1829–1841" (PhD diss., University of Southern California, 1983).

6. [William Cox], "Prize Tragedies," in *Crayon Sketches*, ed. Theodore S. Fay (New York: Conner and Cooke, 1833), 1:159.

7. "More Premiums," *New-York Mirror*, 8 April 1826.

8. The most thorough and penetrating work on antebellum competitions to date has been produced by agricultural historians, and as distinct as parsnips are from poems, I have drawn on this body of scholarship extensively. Works I have found especially useful include Linda J. Borish, "'A Fair, Without *the* Fair, Is No Fair at All': Women at the New England Agricultural Fair in the Mid-Nineteenth

Century," *Journal of Sports History* 24 (1997): 155–176; Donald B. Marti, "Early Agricultural Societies in New York: The Foundations of Improvement," *New York History* 48 (1967): 313–331; Mark A. Mastromarino, "'Cattle Aplenty and Other Things in Proportion': The Agricultural Society and Fair in Franklin County, Massachusetts, 1810–1860," *UCLA Historical Journal* 5 (1984): 50–75; Graeme Wynn, "Exciting a Spirit of Emulation Among the 'Plodholes': Agricultural Reform in Pre-Confederation Nova Scotia," *Acadiensis* 20 (1990): 5–51; and Tamara Plakins Thornton, *Cultivating Gentlemen: The Meaning of Country Life among the Boston Elite, 1785–1860* (New Haven: Yale Univ. Press, 1989), 61–63, 92–102, 159. See also, Elliott J. Gorn, *The Manly Art: Bare-Knuckle Prize Fighting in America* (Ithaca: Cornell Univ. Press, 1986); Charles L. Nichols, "The Literary Fair in the United States," in *Bibliographical Essays: A Tribute to Wilberforce Eames* (Freeport: Books for Libraries Press, 1967), 88–89; and Walker Rumble, "A Time of Giants: Speed Composition in Nineteenth-Century America," *Printing History* 28 (1992): 14–21.

    9. "Premium for a Tract," *The Christian Watchman*, 2 June 1826. The inability or unwillingness of antebellum pundits to see any connection between gambling and more respectable economic activities such as speculation, or for that matter entering literary competitions, is penetratingly discussed by Ann Fabian, *Card Sharps, Dream Books, and Bucket Shops: Gambling in 19th-Century America* (Ithaca: Cornell Univ. Press, 1990), 4–7, 13, 42.

    10. See Daniel T. McColgan, *Joseph Tuckerman: Pioneer in American Social Work* (Washington, D.C.: Catholic Univ. of America Press, 1940), 165–170 (quotation 165).

    11. See, especially, Kenneth G. Dennis, *'Competition' in the History of Economic Thought* (N.Y.: Arno, 1977), 1–130.

    12. Benjamin Rush to John Adams, 4 November 1812, *Letters of Benjamin Rush*, ed. L. H. Butterfield (Princeton: American Philosophical Society, 1951), 1164; John Adams to Benjamin Rush, 29 November 1812, in *The Spur of Fame: Dialogues of John Adams and Benjamin Rush, 1805–1813*, ed. John A. Schutz and Douglass Adair (San Marino: The Huntington Library, 1966), 254.

    13. John Adams, *Discourses on Davila*, in *The Political Writings of John Adams*, ed. George W. Carey (Washington, D.C.: Regnery, 2000), 347. Hereafter cited parenthetically. See also Bruce Miroff, "John Adams: Merit, Fame, and Political Leadership," *Journal of Politics* 48 (1986): 116–132; James M. Farrell, "John Adams's 'Autobiography': The Ciceronian Paradigm and the Quest for Fame," *New England Quarterly* 62 (1989): 505–528.

    14. Harold Bloom, *A Map of Misreading* (Oxford: Oxford Univ. Press, 1975), 3. Although Bloom frames the discussion of 'influence' in terms of Nietzsche, Freud, and Gnosticism, what he calls influence is very clearly allied to eighteenth-century notions of emulation, an absent referent that suggests his own creative swerve. See, especially, Bloom, *The Anxiety of Influence: A Theory of Poetry* (Oxford: Oxford Univ. Press, 1973), esp. 27–29.

    15. On emulation, see Arthur O. Lovejoy, *Reflections on Human Nature* (Baltimore: Johns Hopkins Univ. Press, 1961); G. W. Pigman III, "Versions of Imitation in the Renaissance," *Renaissance Quarterly* 33 (1980): 1–32; Howard

D. Weinbrot, "'An Ambition to Excell': The Aesthetics of Emulation in the Seventeenth and Eighteenth Centuries," *Huntington Library Quarterly* 48 (1985): 121–139; Dena Goodman, *The Republic of Letters: A Cultural History of the French Enlightenment* (Ithaca: Cornell Univ. Press, 1994), 90–94; "Forum: Emulation in France, 1750–1800," *Eighteenth-Century Studies* 36 (2003): 217–248; and William Huntting Howell, "'A More Perfect Copy than Heretofore': Imitation, Emulation, and Early American Literary Culture" (PhD diss., Northwestern University, 2005).

16. The mediatory functions of emulation in eighteenth-century America are underscored by Jay Fliegelman, *Declaring Independence: Jefferson, Natural Language, & the Culture of Performance* (Stanford: Stanford Univ. Press, 1993), 180–187. A similar point is made with respect to Renaissance humanists' uses of emulation by David Lowenthal, *The Past Is a Foreign Country* (Cambridge: Cambridge Univ. Press, 1985), 80–84. For "resistance-deference," see Lawrence Buell, "American Literary Emergence as a Postcolonial Phenomenon," *American Literary History* 4 (1992): 411–442 (quotation 421). On emulation and the emergence of liberal selfhood, see Stephen Carl Arch, *After Franklin: The Emergence of Autobiography in Post-Revolutionary America, 1780–1830* (Hanover: Univ. Press of New England, 2001), 43–52.

17. David S. Shields, *Civil Tongues and Polite Letters in British America* (Chapel Hill: Institute of Early American History and Culture, 1997), 165–169; Joseph Strutt, *The Sports and Pastimes of the People of England* (London: Thomas Tegg, 1831), 398–399.

18. On the Sketch Club and their Crambos, see James T. Callow, *Kindred Spirits: Knickerbocker Writers and American Artists, 1807–1855* (Chapel Hill: Univ. of North Carolina Press, 1967), 12–29 (quotation 20).

19. [William Cullen Bryant,] "Thanatopsis," *North American Review* 5 (September 1817): 338–340 (quotation 339).

20. Callow, *Kindred Spirits*, 24; Shields, *Civil Tongues and Polite Letters*, 165.

21. For Paine: James Spear Loring, *The Hundred Boston Orators* (Boston: John P. Jewett, 1852), 284–285; Shields, *Civil Tongues and Polite Letters*, 165, 261; William Dunlap, *History of the American Theatre* (N.Y.: Burt Franklin, 1963), 1:252–256. On Harvard's honor culture of the 1790s and its capacity for intense reprisal: Leon Jackson, "The Rights of Man and the Rites of Youth: Fraternity and Riot at Eighteenth Century Harvard," *History of Higher Education Annual* 15 (1995): 5–49. For Bryant: Tremaine McDowell, "The Juvenile Verse of William Cullen Bryant," *Studies in Philology* 26 (1929): 99–101. In 1825 Bryant claimed that he never entered formal competitions, but he appears to have entered (and placed first) in at least one after this date. See William Cullen Bryant to Sarah L. Howe, 10 January 1825, *The Letters of William Cullen Bryant*, ed. William Cullen Bryant II and Thomas G. Voss (N.Y.: Fordham Univ. Press, 1975), 1:168–169; "Prize Poem," *New-Hampshire Gazette*, 30 September 1828.

22. Susan Fenimore Cooper, *Pages and Pictures from the Writings of James Fenimore Cooper* (N.Y.: W. A. Townsend and Company, 1861), 17, 19. Cooper, according to Nina Baym, persisted in this competitive literary mentality, writing

The Last of the Mohicans (1826) as a way of challenging Lydia Maria Child's *Hobomok* (1824). See Baym, "How Men and Women Wrote Indian Stories," in *New Essays on "The Last of the Mohicans,"* ed. H. Daniel Peck (Cambridge: Cambridge Univ. Press, 1992), 67–86.

23. For other references to Crambo, see John Earle Uhler, "The Delphian Club: A Contribution to the Literary History of Baltimore in the Early Nineteenth Century," *Maryland Historical Magazine* 20 (1925): 305–346; "A Dab at Rhymes," *Bunker-Hill Aurora: and Farmers' and Mechanics Journal*, 25 October 1827; and "Passages from the Life of a Medical Eclectic, No. IV," *American Review* (September 1846): 275. In a related vein, see Frances Elizabeth Browne, "The Wager, In Answer to a Challenge from a Young Gentleman, in which each was to Write Twenty Lines of Poetry, which was to be Submitted to the Judgment of Friends," *Poems* (Cambridge, Mass.: Metcalf and Co., 1846), 51–52.

24. On the Sensus Communis and its roots in agonistic club culture, see David S. Shields, "Anglo-American Clubs: Their Wit, Their Heterodoxy, Their Sedition," *William and Mary Quarterly*, 3d Ser. 51 (1994): 293–304.

25. Bernard Bailyn, *The Ideological Origins of the American Revolution* (Cambridge, Mass.: Harvard Univ. Press, 1967), 56; Laura Auricchio, "The Laws of *Bienséance* and the Gendering of Emulation in Eighteenth-Century French Art Education," *Eighteenth-Century Studies* 36 (2003): 231.

26. See Albert O. Hirschman, *The Passions and the Interests: Political Arguments for Capitalism before Its Triumph* (Princeton: Princeton Univ. Press, 1977), 20–66; Richard Striner, "Political Newtonianism: The Cosmic Model of Politics in Europe and America," *William and Mary Quarterly* 3d ser. 52 (1995): 583–608.

27. Benjamin Rush, "Thoughts Upon the Amusements and Punishments Which Are Proper for Schools, Addressed to George Clymer, Esq.," in *Essays: Literary, Moral and Philosophical* (1798; rpt. Schenectady: Union College Press, 1988), 35; Benjamin Franklin, "Idea of the English School," in *Writings*, ed. J. A. Leo Lemay (N.Y.: Library of America, 1987), 351.

28. For a suggestive discussion of the Revolutionary generation's obsession with reputation and preeminence, see Douglass Adair, "Fame and the Founding Fathers," in *Fame and the Founding Fathers: Essays by Douglass Adair*, ed. Trevor Colbourn (N.Y.: Institute of Early American History and Culture, 1974), 4–26.

29. On Federal-level moves toward emulation, see Brooke Hindle, *Emulation and Invention* (N.Y.: New York Univ. Press, 1981), 16–18.

30. On the Park Theatre conflagration and its aftermath, see "Fire," *New-York Evening Post*, 25 May 1820; "Public Meeting," *New-York Evening Post*, 26 May 1820; "The Theatre," *New-York Evening Post*, 29 May 1820; *New-York Evening Post*, 30 May 1820; "Theatrical Communication," *New-York Evening Post*, 1 June 1820; "Theatre," *New-York Evening Post*, 12 June 1820; "Communication," *New-York Evening Post*, 10 July 1820, and "Proposed New Theatre," *New-York Evening Post*, 4 September 1820.

31. On the Richmond Theater fire, see James H. Dormon, Jr., *Theater in the Ante Bellum South, 1815–1861* (Chapel Hill: Univ. of North Carolina Press, 1967), 28–29.

32. On the history of Drury Lane Theatre, see Raymond Mander and Joe Mitchenson, *The Theatres of London* (London: Rupert Hart-Davis, 1961), 64–71. On the Park Theatre-Drury Lane equation, see "Things Theatrical," *The Knickerbocker* 17 (April 1841): 346; "Theatricals," *Ladies' Companion* 18 (February 1843): 208; and Barnard Hewitt, "'King Stephen' of the Park and Drury Lane," in *The Theatrical Manager in England and America: Player of a Perilous Game*, ed. Joseph W. Donohue, Jr. (Princeton: Princeton Univ. Press, 1971), 87–141.

33. On American reporting of Drury Lane's destruction, see "Drury-Lane Theatre," *Evangelical Intelligencer* 3 (1809): 538–541; on the opening, "New Drury-Lane Theatre," *The Olio* 1 (20 March 1813): 60–61; and on the competition, "The Drama," *Analectic Magazine* 1 (February 1813): 169–171; and "Rejected Addresses; or, The New Theatrum Poetarum," *Analectic Magazine* 1 (March 1813): 209–219.

34. "Theatre," *National Advocate*, 1 June 1821. This advertisement was also printed in the *New York American*, 31 May 1821 and quickly spread to other newspapers outside of New York.

35. The judges were: R. Bonner, James Hamilton, Richard Hatfield, Francis Johnson, Charles King, Hugh Maxwell, Mordecai M. Noah, William Price, William Van Hook, Gulian C. Verplanck, Johnston Verplanck, and Henry Wheaton. Occupations were determined using *Longworth's American Almanac, New-York Register, and City Directory* (N.Y.: Thomas Longworth, 1821). Only Bonner remains unidentified; he is not the famous editor of the *New York Ledger*.

36. Robert A. Ferguson, *Law and Letters in American Culture* (Cambridge, Mass.: Harvard Univ. Press, 1984), 5–10, 24–33, 66–84; William Charvat, *The Origins of American Critical Thought, 1810–1835* (Philadelphia: Univ. of Pennsylvania Press, 1936), 5.

37. [Johnston Verplanck], *The American (for the Country)*, 29 August 1821.

38. See Peter Uwe Hohendahl, *The Institution of Criticism* (Ithaca: Cornell Univ. Press, 1982), 47–49 (quotation 48). For Stone, see Christopher Grasso, *A Speaking Aristocracy: Transforming Public Discourse in Eighteenth Century Connecticut* (Chapel Hill: Omohundro Institute for Early American History and Culture, 1999), 1. My point is not that anyone in New York remembered Samuel Stone, merely that his sentiment reflected the argument for authority claimed by judges such as these.

39. Information on entrants was compiled from *The Rejected Addresses; Together with the Prize Address, Presented for the Prize Medal, Offered for the Best Address, on the Opening of the New Park Theatre, in the City of New-York* (N.Y.: Nathaniel Smith, 1821), viii–ix (quotation).

40. "Prize Poem," *Freedom's Journal*, 7 December 1827; "Aboriginal Poetry," *Freedom's Journal*, 15 February 1828. When William Brown opened his African Theatre a few weeks after the reopening of the Park Theatre, it was Mordecai Noah, one of the Park Theatre competition judges, who spearheaded the print campaign against his establishment. Indeed, as if to discount the possibility that African-Americans could be emulative, Noah describes them repeatedly as "very imitative," as prone to "ape their masters and mistresses," and as "imita-

tive inmates of the kitchen." Other commentators disagreed, and one reported that "Several black gentlemen in this City, actuated, no doubt, with a laudable emulation, recently resolved to open a theatre." See Michael Warner with Natasha Hurley, Luis Iglesias, Sonia Di Loreto, Jeffrey Scraba, and Sandra Young, "A Soliloquy 'Lately Spoken at the African Theatre': Race and the Public Sphere in New York City, 1821," *American Literature* 73 (2001): 1–46 (quotations 13, 14, 18, 25); and Marvin McAllister, *White People Do Not Know How to Behave at Entertainments Designed for Ladies and Gentlemen of Colour: William Brown's African and American Theater* (Chapel Hill: Univ. of North Carolina Press, 2003).

41. "Park Theatre," *National Advocate*, 21 August 1821. On consecration, or, as he sometimes calls it, institution, see Pierre Bourdieu, *Language and Symbolic Power*, trans. Gino Raymond and Matthew Adamson (Cambridge, Mass.: Harvard Univ. Press, 1991), 117–126; and Bourdieu, *The State Nobility*, trans. Lauretta C. Clough (Stanford: Stanford Univ. Press, 1996), esp. 102–115.

42. [Mordecai M. Noah], "Addresses," *National Advocate*, 23 August 1821; *National Advocate*, 4 September 1821; *National Advocate*, 13 September 1821. On "damn with faint praise," see "Prize Medal," unidentified clipping, Charles Sprague Writings and Notices Scrap Book, American Antiquarian Society, hereafter cited as Sprague Scrap Book.

43. James F. English, "Winning the Culture Game: Prizes, Awards, and the Rules of Art," *New Literary History* 33 (2002): 109–135.

44. See [Horace Smith and James Smith], *Rejected Addresses: Or, the New Theatrum Poetarum* (Boston: William D. Ticknor, 1841), esp. vii–xxx; Dennis Hall Sigmon, Jr., "Rejected Addresses and the Art of Poetic Parody" (PhD diss., Purdue University, 1976), 1–23 (quotation 12); and, especially, Michael Simpson, "Re-Opening after the Old Price Riots: War and Peace at Drury Lane," *Texas Studies in Literature and Language* 41 (1999): 378–402. See also Lord Byron, "Address, Spoken at the Opening of Drury-lane Theatre Saturday, October 10th, 1812," *The Complete Poetical Works*, ed. Jerome J. McGann (Oxford: Clarendon Press, 1981), 3:17–21. On McMillan, who also went by Millan, see Ian Maxted, *The London Book Trades, 1775–1800: A Preliminary Checklist of Members* (Folkestone: Dawson, 1977), 153.

45. For the omnibus edition of *Rejected Addresses*, see *Ladies' Literary Cabinet* 5 (27 October 1821): 200. Precisely how Smith—who edited the *Ladies' Literary Cabinet*—laid hands on the competition entries is unclear, although he apparently had a relationship with one or more of the committee of judges and might even have seen the submissions as they came in. See the suggestive hints in "Literary Premiums," *Ladies' Literary Cabinet* 4 (21 July 1821): 88. For Smith's defense of the "strict justice" of the judges, see *Ladies' Literary Cabinet* 4 (25 August 1821): 128; and for the appearance of Sprague's address in his magazine, "Opening of the Theatre," *Ladies' Literary Cabinet* 4 (8 September 1821): 142.

46. See Jürgen Habermas, *The Structural Transformation of the Public Sphere: An Inquiry into a Category of Bourgeois Society*, trans. Thomas Burger with Frederick Lawrence (Cambridge, Mass.: MIT Press, 1989).

47. For other rejected address volumes, see *Rejected Addresses, Presented for*

the Cup offered for the Best Address, on the Opening of the New Theatre, Phila-delphia. To Which Is Prefixed, The Prize Address (Philadelphia: H. C. Carey and I. Lea, 1823); *Boston Prize Poems, and Other Specimens of Dramatic Poetry* (Boston: Published by Joseph T. Buckingham, 1824); and [Jacob Bigelow], *Eo-lopoesis. American Rejected Addresses* (N.Y.: J. C. Derby, 1855). For single re-jected addresses, see "To Correspondents," *Bower of Taste* 1 (1828): 143; [John Neal], "High Court of Appeal," *Yankee and Boston Literary Gazette* 2 (12 Feb-ruary 1829): 54–55; Richard Emmons, "An Address Written for the Walnut-st. Theatre, Philadelphia, 1828 (Rejected)," *The National Jubilee and Other Miscel-laneous Poems* (Washington: F. S. Myer, 1830), 34–36; and "Rejected Address," *Southern Literary Messenger* 5 (December 1839): 833. The tendency of critics to naturalize critical assent and stigmatize critical dissent has been carefully anato-mized by Barbara Herrnstein Smith, *Contingencies of Value: Alternative Perspec-tives for Critical Theory* (Cambridge, Mass.: Harvard Univ. Press, 1988), esp. 36–41.

48. *The American (for the Country)*, 29 August 1821. Smith announced his *Rejected Addresses* in a two-column advertisement that included his copyright: *Ladies' Literary Cabinet* 4 (1 September 1821): 136. For the stand-alone copy-right notice, see *Ladies' Literary Cabinet* 4 (15 September 1821): 152.

49. See *Ladies' Literary Cabinet* 4 (1 September 1821): 136; *Ladies' Literary Cabinet* 4 (13 October 1821): 184.

50. Grantland Rice, *The Transformation of Authorship in America* (Chicago: Univ. of Chicago Press, 1997), 49.

51. The major sources for Sprague's life are Loring, *Hundred Boston Ora-tors*, 409–418; R. C. Waterston, *Remarks Upon the Life and Writings of Charles Sprague* (Boston: John Wilson and Son, 1875); and, especially, the various obit-uaries in the Sprague Scrap Book. By 1824, he had appeared in the *Montreal Herald* and the *Canadian Times*, by 1829 in the *Calcutta Literary Gazette*, and by 1830 in *Bengal Hurkaru and Chronicle*. See, again, clippings in the Sprague Scrap Book.

52. For prejudices against merchants as philistines and the ways in which the merchants themselves staked a cultural claim, see, respectively, "Taste for Poetry in Businessmen," *New-York Mirror*, 23 February 1833; and "Poets Men of Busi-ness!" *New-York Mirror*, 7 August 1830. For a learned discussion, see Thomas Augst, "The Commerce of Thought: Professional Authority and Business Ethics in 19th-Century America," *Prospects: An Annual of American Cultural Studies* 27 (2002): 49–76. For a modest defense by another banker-author, see J. F. Wat-son to Lydia Huntley Sigourney, 1 February 1833, Lydia Huntley Sigourney Pa-pers, Library of the Connecticut Historical Society Museum, Hartford, Conn.

53. "Literary Portraits. No. IV. Charles Sprague," *New-England Magazine* 3 (August 1832): 90; [William Leggett], "Eminent Living American Poets," *New-York Mirror*, 26 January 1828; [William Joseph Snelling], *Truth; A New Year's Gift for Scribblers* (Boston: Printed by Stephen Foster, 1831), 24.

54. Loring, *Hundred Boston Orators*, 413. For comparisons with Samuel Rogers, see [Leggett], "Eminent Living American Poets," 229. On Sprague-spot-ting expeditions: "A Poet," *United States Gazette*, 5 May 1832. On poems writ-

ten on bank notes: [Boston] *Evening Transcript*, 2 February 1875. On Sprague as judge, see "Prize Poem," *Boston Recorder and Telegraph*, 19 January 1827. Sprague's bank books are not available, but the ledgers he kept as co-partner in a dry goods company show him to be a scrupulous accountant. Doodles and designs are on neatly folded pieces of paper tucked into various pages. See Callender and Sprague, Account Book, 1810–1813, Massachusetts Historical Society.

55. F.J.H., "To Sprague," *New York Commercial Advertiser*, Sprague Scrap Book. Indeed, Sprague had taken a swipe at mercenary authors himself in his prologue for the Park Theatre competition, when he described playwrights who need "with servile pen to wait / On private friendship, or on private hate; / To flatter fools." Charles Sprague, *The Poetical and Prose Writings* (Boston: Ticknor, Reed, and Fields, 1850), 86.

56. On antebellum critics' use of celestial imagery to suggest the natural, inevitable, and unchangeable nature of literary value, see Leon Jackson, "Rising Stars and Raging Diseases: The Rhetoric and Reality of Antebellum Canonization," *Prospects: An Annual of American Cultural Studies* 25 (2000): 159–176.

57. R. C. Waterston, "Charles Sprague," Sprague Scrap Book.

58. "Curious Autographs," Sprague Scrap Book.

59. "To the Public," *The New-York Mirror*, 3 June 1826; *American Museum* 6 (July 1789): n.p.

60. "The Prizes," *The New-York Mirror*, 25 February 1826.

61. On prizes for ancient poetry competitions, see A. E. Haigh, *The Attic Theatre: A Description of the Stage and Theatre of the Athenians, and of the Dramatic Performances at Athens* (Oxford: Clarendon Press, 1889), 52–55, 90.

62. J. Huizinga, *Homo Ludens: A Study of the Play-Element in Culture* (Boston: Beacon Press, 1955), 51.

63. Quoted in Borish, "A Fair, Without *the* Fair, Is No Fair at All," 164.

64. Patricia Fenn and Alfred P. Malpa, *Rewards of Merit: Tokens of a Child's Progress and a Teacher's Esteem as an Enduring Aspect of American Religious and Secular Entertainment* (Charlottesville: Ephemera Society of America, 1994), 141–142.

65. Edwin G. Burrows and Mike Wallace, *Gotham: A History of New York City to 1898* (Oxford: Oxford Univ. Press, 1999), 404. On 'dirty' money, see Viviana Zelizer, *The Social Meaning of Money: Pin Money, Paychecks, Poor Relief, and Other Currencies* (Princeton: Princeton Univ. Press, 1997), 3–4.

66. On Sprague's medal, see "Reward of Merit," Sprague Scrap Book. I am grateful to Tom Knoles for the translation. On illiquidity, see Lee Anne Fennell, "Unpacking the Gift: Illiquid Goods and Empathetic Dialogue," in *The Question of the Gift: Essays Across Disciplines*, ed. Mark Osteen (London: Routledge, 2002), 85–101. Fennell argues that removing price tags from, inscribing, and wrapping up commodities renders them illiquid and "effectively removes" them "from the stream of commerce" (89); inscribing a medal would seem to serve the same function.

67. On Mrs. Wells's cross, see "Prize Address," *New-England Galaxy*, 14 May 1824. According to one observer, the cross was worth $100. See Caroline

Doane to Henry Wadsworth Longfellow, [March] 1824, Letters to Henry Wadsworth Longfellow, Houghton Library, Harvard University.

68. Quoted in Joseph J. Ellis, *Passionate Sage: The Character and Legacy of John Adams* (N.Y.: W. W. Norton, 2001), 167.

69. Quoted in Lucretia Ramsey Bishko, "Lafayette and the Maryland Agricultural Society: 1824–1832," *Maryland Historical Magazine* 70 (1975): 48.

70. E. P. Richardson, "A Rare Gold Medal of the Philadelphia Society for Promoting Agriculture," *American Art Journal* 14 (1982): 60.

71. John E. Semmes, *John H. B. Latrobe and His Times, 1803–1891* (Baltimore: Norman, Remington Co., [1917]), 126–127 (quotation 127). The competition took place in 1825. On the cash *and* medal award, see "Another Tragedy Wanted," *New-York Mirror*, 27 February 1830.

72. David Graeber, *Toward an Anthropological Theory of Value: The False Coin of Our Own Dreams* (N.Y.: Palgrave, 2001), 263 n 10, 15.

73. "Literary Prize," *New-York Mirror*, 23 June 1832. For the idea of premium inflation, I draw on Ronald J. Zboray, "Technology and the Character of Community Life in Antebellum America: The Role of Story Papers," in *Communication and Change in American Religious History*, ed. Leonard I. Sweet (Grand Rapids: William B. Eerdmans, 1993), 207.

74. "Advertisement," [William Ladd], *A Dissertation on a Congress of Nations*, Second Edition ([Boston]: Press of James Loring, 1832), [2]; "Preface," *Temperance Prize Essays* (Washington: Duff Green, 1835), 5.

75. "Prize Poetry," *The Balance and Columbian Repository* 3 (3 April 1804): 112.

76. On the silver cup, see "Reward of Merit"; the quip on burning theaters is from an undated clipping, both in the Sprague Scrap Book.

77. On the gold medal, see "Notice," *New-England Galaxy*, 19 September 1823. Sprague's self-effacing nom de plume is mentioned in Waterston, *Remarks on the Life and Writings of Charles Sprague*, 5.

78. "Salem Theatre"; "The Prize Address"; and several untitled clippings in the Sprague Scrap Book tell the story.

79. On the Arch-Street Theatre competition, see "Prize Address"; "The Prize Cup," *The Theatrical Censor*; "Prize Poem," all in Sprague Scrap Book.

80. In 1827, Sprague had been dragged into an ugly and protracted controversy, when he was accused of being the pseudonymous winner of an allegedly rigged competition organized by his friend Joseph T. Buckingham. The identity of the winner remains unclear. See Buckingham, *Personal Memoirs and Recollections of Editorial Life* (Boston: Ticknor, Reed, and Fields, 1852): 1:184–201.

81. In 1828 Forrest had performed a prize prologue by William Leggett. See "The Prize Address," *Bower of Taste* 1 (30 August 1828): 558. Mere months later, Forrest would choose Leggett's journal, *The Critic*, as the venue through which to announce his own first competition.

82. "Mr. Forrest," *New-York Mirror*, 24 October 1829. For other comments on Forrest's largesse, see "The Prize Tragedy," *New-York Mirror*, 31 October 1829; and "Liberality," *New-York Mirror*, 14 November 1829.

83. On Bird's competitive writing for Forrest, see Clement E. Foust, *The Life and Dramatic Works of Robert Montgomery Bird* (N.Y.: Burt Franklin, 1971), 28–75. On the tradition of the author's benefit night, see David Grimstead, *Melodrama Unveiled: American Theater and Culture, 1800–1850* (Berkeley: Univ. of California Press, 1987), 145–147.

84. For manuscripts being sent directly to Forrest, see M. Reid to James Lawson, 7 December 1847, James Lawson Papers, South Caroliniana Library, University of South Carolina.

85. See John Franklin Reigart, *The Lancasterian System of Instruction in the Schools of New York City* (N.Y.: Teachers College-Columbia University, 1916), 12 (quotation), 83–88; Carl F. Kaestle, "Introduction," in *Joseph Lancaster and the Monitorial School Movement: A Documentary History*, ed. Kaestle (N.Y.: Teachers College Press, 1973), 1–49. My comments on school competition prizes, Lancasterian and otherwise, are based on an examination of several hundred printed tokens in the Rewards of Merit Collection, American Antiquarian Society. Some of those printed by Henry Bowen of Boston in the 1810s and 1820s, for example, came in one-, three-, and five-dollar denominations (Box 1, Folder 2); those by Dorr and Howland of Worcester in two- and five-dollar denominations (Box 1, Folder 7).

86. See Robert A. McCaughey, *Josiah Quincy, 1772–1864: The Last Federalist* (Cambridge, Mass.: Harvard Univ. Press, 1974), 148–149.

87. Walter Harding, *The Days of Henry Thoreau: A Biography* (Princeton: Princeton Univ. Press, 1982), 35–37; Kenneth Walter Cameron, "Chronology of Thoreau's Harvard Years," *Emerson Society Quarterly* 15 (1959): 14, 15.

88. All four classes protested Quincy's use of emulation. For the text of their petitions, see Harvard University College Papers, Second Series, Volume VI (1833–1838): 109–119 (quotation 111), UAI 5.131.10, courtesy of the Harvard University Archives. The Freshman petition has been reproduced in Kenneth Walter Cameron, "Freshman Thoreau Opposes Harvard's Marking System," *Emerson Society Quarterly* 8 (1957): 17–18.

89. Josiah Quincy to Ralph Waldo Emerson, 25 June 1837, quoted in Cameron, "Chronology of Thoreau's Harvard Years," 19.

90. William F. Gill, *The Life of Edgar Allan Poe* (N.Y.: D. Appleton, 1877), 49. There is another version of this story in which the setting is a tavern, Poe rather than Lofland throws down the challenge, and the wager—significantly, in light of the Folio Club narrative—is for the loser to pay for everyone's drinks. See William W. Smithers, *The Life of John Lofland, "The Milford Bard"* (Philadelphia: Wallace M. Leonard, 1894), 108. In both versions, Poe loses.

91. Eugene Didier, *The Life and Poems of Edgar Allan Poe* (N.Y.: A. C. Armstrong, 1882), 32; J. T. L. Preston, "Some Reminiscences of Edgar A. Poe as a Schoolboy," in Sara Sigourney Rice, *Edgar Allan Poe: A Memorial Volume* (Baltimore: Turnbull Brothers, 1877), 40; Didier, *Life and Poems*, 30. See also Kenneth Silverman, *Edgar A. Poe: Mournful and Never-ending Remembrance* (N.Y.: HarperCollins, 1991), 23–24, 29–30, 41; and Arthur Hobson Quinn, *Edgar Allan Poe: A Critical Biography* (Baltimore: Johns Hopkins Univ. Press, 1998), 84–

85. On capping verses: Preston, "Some Reminiscences," 39–40. For Poe's very deliberate *emulation* of Byron's feat, see "Swimming," *Southern Literary Messenger* 1 (May 1835): 468.

92. See Silverman, *Edgar A. Poe*, 25, 458 (on competition); 155 (quotation).

93. See Poe to Allan, 21 September 1826; 19 March 1827; 1 December 1828; 28 December 1828; 29 May 1829; 25 June 1829; 26 July 1829, *The Letters of Edgar Allan Poe*, ed. John Ward Ostrom (N.Y.: Gordian Press, 1966), 1:6, 7, 10, 12, 20, 22, 26. All italics are in the originals.

94. Silverman, *Edgar A. Poe*, 11–14 (Allan's adoption); 22 (quotation). A slightly more nuanced argument along the same lines has been made by J. Gerald Kennedy, "The Violence of Melancholy: Poe against Himself," *American Literary History* 8 (1996): 533–551.

95. Edgar Allan Poe, "Tamerlane," *Complete Poems*, ed. Thomas Ollive Mabbott (Urbana: Univ. of Illinois Press, 2000), 22.

96. The announcement, rules, and results are reproduced in John Grier Varner, *Edgar Allan Poe and the Philadelphia Saturday Courier* (Charlottesville: Univ. of Virginia, 1933).

97. See Poe to Allan, 16 October 1831; Poe to Allan, 18 November 1831; Poe to Allan, 15 December 1831; Poe to Allan, 29 December 1831, *Letters of Edgar Allan Poe*, 1:46–49. On typical per page rates, see John Ward Ostrom, "Edgar Allan Poe: His Income as Literary Entrepreneur," *Poe Studies* 15 (1982): 1–7.

98. Smith had written his play in the 1820s; when he sent it to Forrest for feedback, the actor promptly awarded it first prize in his contest. See Marshall, "Playwriting Contests," 105; Richard Moody, *Edwin Forrest: First Star of the American Stage* (N.Y.: Alfred A. Knopf, 1960), 100.

99. Poe to Allan, 12 April 1833, *Letters*, 1:49–50; "Premiums," *Baltimore Saturday Visiter*, 15 June 1833. For a brief discussion of the competition, see John C. French, "Poe and 'The Baltimore Saturday Visiter,'" *Modern Language Notes* 33 (1918): 257–267.

100. For the frame of the collection, which was never published, see Edgar Allan Poe, "The Folio Club," *Tales and Sketches*, ed. Thomas Ollive Mabbott (Urbana: Univ. of Illinois Press, 2000), 1:200–207 (quotation 204). Poe developed the frame narrative further in Poe to Joseph T. and Edwin Buckingham, 4 May 1833; and Poe to Harrison Hall, 2 September 1836, *Letters of Edgar Allan Poe*, 1:54, 103–104 (quotation 104), and I have used these descriptions too. It is clear, however, that the basic idea was established by the time Poe entered the *Visiter* contest.

101. On the origin, organization, and final disposition of the collection, see Alexander Hammond, "A Reconstruction of Poe's 1833 'Tales of the Folio Club': Preliminary Notes" *Poe Studies* 5 (1972): 25–32; Hammond, "Further Notes on Poe's Folio Club Tales," *Poe Studies* 8 (1975): 38–42; Hammond, "Edgar Allan Poe's 'Tales of the Folio Club': The Evolution of a Lost Book," in *Poe at Work: Seven Textual Studies*, ed. Benjamin Franklin Fisher IV (Baltimore: Edgar Allan Poe Society, 1978), 13–43; and Kenneth Alan Hovey, "'These Many Pieces Are Yet One Book': The Book-Unity of Poe's Tale Collections," *Poe Studies* 31 (1998):

3–5. Poe's familiarity with Horace and James Smith is established by Burton R. Pollin, "Figs, Bells, Poe, and Horace Smith," *Poe Newsletter* 3 (1970): 8–10.

102. "The Premiums," *Baltimore Saturday Visiter*, 12 October 1833. The details of the judging emerge from two accounts of judge John H. B. Latrobe. See his "Reminiscences of Poe" [1875], in *Edgar Allan Poe: A Memorial Volume*, 57–62; and Latrobe to Burr, 7 December 1852, reprinted in Jay B. Hubbell, "Charles Chauncey Burr: Friend of Poe," *PMLA* 69 (1954): 837–839.

103. Hewitt, quoted in Vincent Starrett, "One Who Knew Poe," *Bookman* 66 (1927): 200.

104. Poe to White, 20 July 1835, *Letters of Edgar Allan Poe*, 1:65; "The Poets and Poetry of Philadelphia. Number II. Edgar Allan Poe," *Philadelphia Saturday Museum*, 4 March 1843.

105. The decision to award the prize to Hewitt was explained by Latrobe in "Reminiscences of Poe," 59–60.

106. John Hill Hewitt, *Recollections of Poe*, ed. Richard Barksdale Harwell (Atlanta: The Library, Emory University, 1949), 19. For a briefer account of the affair, see Hewitt, *Shadows on the Wall, Or, Glimpses of the Past* (Baltimore: Turnbull Brothers, 1877), 40–43, 154–159. For the reprinting of 'The Coliseum,' see *Southern Literary Messenger* 1 (August 1835): 706. Within the world of competitions, to call a piece a 'prize poem' was to imply, quite unambiguously, that it had *won* a prize.

107. See "Literary Notice," *New Yorker*, 22 March 1834; Lewis Gaylord Clark to Henry Wadsworth Longfellow, 2 November 1834, quoted in Lawrence Thompson, *Young Longfellow (1807–1843)* (N.Y.: Macmillan, 1938), 201.

108. For Poe's feud with Clark, and his circle, see Sidney P. Moss, *Poe's Literary Battles: The Critic in the Context of His Literary Milieu* (Carbondale: Southern Illinois Univ. Press, 1963).

109. On Willis: Thomas N. Baker, *Sentiment and Celebrity: Nathaniel Parker Willis and the Trials of Literary Fame* (Oxford: Oxford Univ. Press, 1999), 21–22. On Catharine Beecher: Catharine E. Beecher, *Truth Stranger than Fiction* (Boston: Phillips, Sampson, 1850), 18–20; Vivian C. Hopkins, *Prodigal Puritan: A Life of Delia Bacon* (Cambridge, Mass.: Belknap Press of Harvard Univ. Press, 1959), 24. On Harriet Beecher: "The Proprietors of the Western Monthly Magazine Offer a Premium of Fifty Dollars," *Western Monthly Magazine* 1 (September 1833): 429; "To Readers and Correspondents," *Western Monthly Magazine* 1 (December 1833): 592; Forrest Wilson, *Crusader in Crinoline: The Life of Harriet Beecher Stowe* (Philadelphia: J. B. Lippincott, 1941), 125–126. On Stephens: Madeleine B. Stern, "Ann S. Stephens: Author of the First Beadle Dime Novel, 1860," *Bulletin of the New York Public Library* 64 (1960): 306–307.

110. Alice C. Neal to Elizabeth Oakes Smith, 16 December 1847, John Neal Correspondence, Coll. S-1919, Maine Historical Society.

111. Nathaniel P. Willis, "Editor's Table," *American Monthly Magazine* 1 (November 1829), quoted in Baker, *Sentiment and Celebrity*, 44.

112. Thomas Willis White to Nathaniel Beverley Tucker, 24 January 1837, quoted in *The Poe Log: A Documentary Life of Edgar Allan Poe, 1809–1849*, comp. Dwight Thomas and David K. Jackson (N.Y.: G. K. Hall, 1987), 214.

113. See Dwight Thomas, "William E. Burton and his Premium Scheme: New Light on Poe Biography," *University of Mississippi Studies in English* ns 3 (1982): 68–80; Thomas S. Marvin, "'These Days of Double Dealing': Edgar Allan Poe and the Business of Magazine Publishing," *American Periodicals* 11 (2001): 81–94.

114. "Enigmatical and Conundrum-ical," *Alexander's Weekly Messenger*, 18 December 1839, reprinted in Clarence S. Brigham, "Edgar Allan Poe's Contributions to 'Alexander's Weekly Messenger,'" *Proceedings of the American Antiquarian Society* 52 (1942): 58.

115. "Another Poser," *Alexander's Weekly Messenger*, 22 January 1840; "Our Puzzles Once More," *Alexander's Weekly Messenger*, 26 February 1840, both reprinted in Brigham, "Edgar Allan Poe's Contributions," 66, 92 (quotation).

116. William K. Wimsatt, Jr., points out that Poe only grudgingly acknowledged when other readers were able to decode the ciphers he presented, a practice consistent with his habit of embellishing his own competitive successes even as he deplored the practice in others. See "What Poe Knew About Cryptography," *PMLA* 58 (1943): 757–759.

117. "Writings of Charles Sprague," *Graham's Magazine* (May 1841), *Complete Works of Edgar Allan Poe*, ed. James A. Harrison (N.Y.: AMS Press, 1965), 10: 140; "An Appendix on Autographs," *Graham's Magazine* (January 1842), *Complete Works*, 15: 248–249; "Sketches of Conspicuous Living Characters of France," *Graham's Magazine* (April 1841), *Complete Works*, 10:133–139. For retorts to Poe's Sprague bashing, see [Rufus W. Griswold], *Boston Notion*, 22 May 1841, quoted in B. Bernard Cohen and Lucian A. Cohen, "Poe and Griswold Once More," *American Literature* 34 (1962): 98–99; and Cornelia Wells Walter, *Boston Evening Transcript*, 5 March 1845, quoted in Moss, *Poe's Literary Battles*, 176 n 80.

118. "Secret Writing," *Graham's Magazine* (August 1841), *Complete Works*, 14:134; "Secret Writing," *Graham's Magazine* (December 1841), *Complete Works*, 14:141. For the suggestion that Tyler was Poe, see Louis A. Renza, "Poe's Secret Autobiography," in *The American Renaissance Reconsidered: Selected Papers from the English Institute, 1982–83*, ed. Walter Benn Michaels and Donald E. Pease (Baltimore: Johns Hopkins Univ. Press, 1985), 86–87 n 14; and Shawn Rosenheim, "The King of 'Secret Readers': Edgar Poe, Cryptography, and the Origins of the Detective Story," *English Literary History* 56 (1989): 393–395. I am less certain than other critics that Tyler was Poe, a scepticism I share with John A. Hodgson and that is additionally supported by Stephen Rachman's recent discovery of several possible Tyler pieces in both *Graham's Magazine* and *Alexander's Weekly Messenger*. See Hodgson, "Decoding Poe? Poe, W. B. Tyler, and Cryptography," *Journal of English and Germanic Philology* 92 (1993): 523–534; and Rachman, "Poe, Secret Writing, and Magazine Culture: In Search of W. B. Tyler" (unpublished essay, 2003).

119. Poe to Frederick W. Thomas, 4 May 1845, *Letters of Edgar Allan Poe*, 1:287. For a concise account of the publication and controversies surrounding "The Gold-Bug," see *Tales and Sketches*, 1:799–806.

120. Poe to James Russell Lowell, 28 May 1844, *Letters of Edgar Allan Poe,* 1:253; W. T. Bandy, "Poe, Duane, and Duffee," *University of Mississippi Studies in English* ns 3 (1982): 87–89.

121. "Death of Edgar A. Poe," *New York Daily Tribune,* 9 October 1849.

122. Hoffman to Griswold, 11 July 1845, quoted in *Poe Log,* 549.

123. On *The Flag of Our Union* and its publisher, Frederick Gleason, see Peter Benson, "Gleason's Publishing Hall," in *Publishers for Mass Entertainment in Nineteenth Century America,* ed. Madeleine B. Stern (Boston: G. K. Hall, 1980), 137–145. For an account of the story papers more generally that pays significant attention to their competitions, see Mary Noel, *Villains Galore . . . The Heyday of the Popular Story Weekly* (N.Y.: Macmillan, 1954).

124. "A Great Scheme," *Flag of Our Union,* 31 July 1847. On the evolving meanings of enterprise in antebellum America, see Leonard N. Neufeldt "Thoreau's Enterprise of Self-Culture in a Culture of Enterprise," *American Quarterly* 39 (1987): 231–251.

125. "Our Offer," *Flag of Our Union,* 11 March 1848; "Unprecedented Announcement!" *Flag of Our Union,* 7 October 1848; "Just as We Supposed," *Flag of Our Union,* 28 October 1848 (payment for all entries).

126. "The Witch of the Wave," *Flag of Our Union,* 15 May 1847; "The New Volume," *Flag of Our Union,* 4 December 1847.

127. "The Flag of Our Union," *Boston Herald,* 19 February 1847. See also *Boston Herald,* 10 April 1847.

128. Nathaniel P. Willis to George James Pumpelly, 24 May 1828, Letters, 1825–1830, Butler Library, Columbia University; Louis A. Godey to Robert Montgomery Bird, n.d., quoted in Clement E. Foust, *The Life and Dramatic Works of Robert Montgomery Bird* (N.Y.: Burt Franklin, 1971), 99.

129. "An Unfavorable Review of Ruth Hall," *New York Tribune,* 25 December 1854.

130. Henry Timrod to Paul Hamilton Hayne, 11 July 1867, in *The Last Years of Henry Timrod, 1864–1867,* ed. Jay B. Hubbell (Durham: Duke Univ. Press, 1941), 88. Timrod's prologue can be found in *Poems of Henry Timrod* (Richmond: B. F. Johnson, 1901), 69–73.

131. Pierre Bourdieu, *The Field of Cultural Production,* ed. Randal Johnson (N.Y.: Columbia Univ. Press, 1999), 39.

Epilogue

1. James J. O'Donnell, *Avatars of the Word: From Papyrus to Cyberspace* (Cambridge, Mass.: Harvard Univ. Press, 1998), 169. O'Donnell, to be fair, is discussing scientific journals, the prices of which are considerably more inflated than those in the humanities, but he concedes that the same circular arrangement applies to the latter field. O'Donnell to Leon Jackson, 11 January 2007. See also Theodore C. Bergstrom, "Free Labor for Costly Journals?" *Journal of Economic Perspectives* 15 (Autumn 2001): 183–198.

2. Gregory M. Colón Semenza, *Graduate Study for the Twenty-First Century: How to Build an Academic Career in the Humanities* (N.Y.: Palgrave Macmillan,

2005), 215; Kathryn Hume, *Surviving Your Academic Job Hunt: Advice for Humanities PhDs* (N.Y.: Palgrave Macmillan, 2005), 105, 106.

3. James Phelan, *Beyond the Tenure Track: Fifteen Months in the Life of an English Professor* (Columbus: Ohio State Univ. Press, 1991), 105, 89, 78, 183, 115, 11. Phelan has been taken to task by several critics for what is perceived to be his limited understanding of academic economics. See Terry Caesar, "Frameworks and Free Agents," *Minnesota Review* 44–45 (1996): 275–283; Jeffrey Williams, "The Life of the Mind and the Academic Situation," *College Literature* 23 (1996): 128–146.

4. William Charvat to John H. Birss, 18 February 1945; Birss to Charvat, 9 March 1945; Irving T. Richards to William Charvat, 21 February 1948, all in the William Charvat Papers, The Rare Books and Manuscripts Library of the Ohio State University Libraries. Because an act of bartering fulfills the wants of both parties to the transaction simultaneously, it is significantly less embedded a phenomenon than the giving of gifts. It is true, of course, that each party might wish to barter further items, but the relations developed by barter transactions are what Caroline Humphrey and Stephen Hugh-Jones call "discontinuous and unstable." While some acts of scholarly exchange took the form of bartering, what Charvat called swapping more nearly resembles gift-giving. See Caroline Humphrey and Stephen Hugh-Jones, "Introduction: Barter, Exchange, and Value," in *Barter, Exchange, and Value: An Anthropological Approach*, ed. Humphrey and Hugh-Jones (Cambridge: Cambridge Univ. Press, 1992), 8–11 (quotation 8).

5. William Charvat to Gay Wilson Allen, 5 January 1949, Gay Wilson Allen Papers, Box 1, Rare Book, Manuscript, and Special Collections Library, Duke University. John Ward Ostrom was the editor of Poe's correspondence.

6. See, inter alia, the inscriptions on J. Albert Robbins, "Mrs. Emma C. Embury's Account Book: A Study of Some Periodical Contributions," *Bulletin of the New York Public Library* 51 (1947): 479–485; Alexander C. Kern, "Emerson and Economics," *New England Quarterly* 13 (1940): 678–696; and Percy Adams, "Humor as Structure and Theme in Faulkner's Trilogy," *Wisconsin Studies in Contemporary Literature* 5 (1964): 205–212, Charvat Papers.

7. James Beard to William Charvat, 26 March 1960, Charvat Papers.

8. Arthur Hobson Quinn to William Charvat, 3 January 1960; Roy Harvey Pearce to William Charvat, 31 December 1959; William Charvat, Memorandum; Robert Estrich to William Charvat [1960], all in the possession of Charvat's daughter, Judy Watkins.

9. Richard D. Altick, *A Little Bit of Luck: The Making of an Adventurous Scholar* ([Philadelphia]: Xlibris, 2002), 104.

10. Jay B. Hubbell to William Charvat, 4 December 1947, Charvat to Hubbell, 29 September 1949, Jay B. Hubbell Papers, Rare Book, Manuscript, and Special Collections Library, Duke University; Judy Watkins to Leon Jackson, 12 March 2007.

11. C. Harvey Gardiner, *Prescott and His Publishers* (Carbondale: Southern Illinois Univ. Press, 1959), 61; William Charvat to Dorothy Hillyer, 25 February 1946; "Important Announcement of the Third Annual MLA-Macmillan Awards in English and American Literature" [n.d.], Charvat Papers.

12. Catherine Charvat Fitch to Leon Jackson, 12 March 2007; Watkins to Jackson.

13. Richard D. Altick, *The Art of Literary Research* rev. edn. (N.Y.: W. W. Norton 1963), 10; Watkins to Jackson.

14. William Charvat, untitled prospectus [1944]; William Charvat to Robert W. Hillegas, 10 July 1962; William Charvat to Gilbert Anderson, 15 January 1952, Charvat Papers.

15. William Charvat, Some Reflections on the Economics of Authorship, 1850–1870, n.d., Charvat Papers.

16. Nathaniel P. Willis to Moses Brown Ives, 12 June [1844], Letters, 1844–1857, John Hay Library, Brown University.

Index

The authorized representative in the EU for product safety and compliance is:
Mare Nostrum Group
B.V Doelen 72
4831 GR Breda
The Netherlands

www.ingramcontent.com/pod-product-compliance
Lightning Source LLC
Chambersburg PA
CBHW020406100426
42812CB00001B/216